The Classics in South America

Bloomsbury Studies in Classical Reception

Bloomsbury Studies in Classical Reception presents scholarly monographs offering new and innovative research and debate to students and scholars in the reception of Classical Studies. Each volume will explore the appropriation, reconceptualization and recontextualization of various aspects of the Graeco-Roman world and its culture, looking at the impact of the ancient world on modernity. Research will also cover reception within antiquity, the theory and practice of translation, and reception theory.

Also available in the Series:

Alexander the Great in the Early Christian Tradition: Classical Reception and Patristic Literature, Christian Thrue Djurslev

Ancient Greek Myth in World Fiction since 1989, edited by Justine McConnell and Edith Hall

Ancient Magic and the Supernatural in the Modern Visual and Performing Arts, edited by Filippo Carlà and Irene Berti

Antipodean Antiquities, edited by Marguerite Johnson

Classics in Extremis, edited by Edmund Richardson

Faulkner's Reception of Apuleius' The Golden Ass in The Reivers, Vernon L. Provencal

Frankenstein and its Classics, edited by Jesse Weiner, Benjamin Eldon Stevens and Brett M. Rogers

Greek and Roman Classics in the British Struggle for Social Reform, edited by Henry Stead and Edith Hall

Greeks and Romans on the Latin American Stage, edited by Rosa Andújar and Konstantinos P. Nikoloutsos

Homer's Iliad *and the Trojan War: Dialogues on Tradition*, Jan Haywood and Naoíse Mac Sweeney

Imagining Xerxes, Emma Bridges

Julius Caesar's Self-Created Image and Its Dramatic Afterlife, Miryana Dimitrova

Kinaesthesia and Classical Antiquity 1750–1820: Moved by Stone, Helen Slaney

Once and Future Antiquities in Science Fiction and Fantasy, edited by Brett M. Rogers and Benjamin Eldon Stevens

Ovid's Myth of Pygmalion on Screen, Paula James

Reading Poetry, Writing Genre, edited by Silvio Bär and Emily Hauser

Sex, Symbolists and the Greek Body, Richard Warren

The Classics in Modernist Translation, edited by Miranda Hickman and Lynn Kozak
The Codex Fori Mussolini, Han Lamers and Bettina Reitz-Joosse
The Gentle, Jealous God, Simon Perris
The Thucydidean Turn: (Re)Interpreting Thucydides' Political Thought Before, During and After the Great War, Benjamin Earley
Translations of Greek Tragedy in the Work of Ezra Pound, Peter Liebregts
Victorian Classical Burlesques, Laura Monrós-Gaspar
Victorian Epic Burlesques, Rachel Bryant Davies
Virgil's Map: Geography, Empire, and the Georgics, Charlie Kerrigan

The Classics in South America

Five Case Studies

Germán Campos Muñoz

BLOOMSBURY ACADEMIC
LONDON • NEW YORK • OXFORD • NEW DELHI • SYDNEY

BLOOMSBURY ACADEMIC
Bloomsbury Publishing Plc
50 Bedford Square, London, WC1B 3DP, UK
1385 Broadway, New York, NY 10018, USA
29 Earlsfort Terrace, Dublin 2, Ireland

BLOOMSBURY, BLOOMSBURY ACADEMIC and the Diana logo are
trademarks of Bloomsbury Publishing Plc

First published in Great Britain 2021
This paperback edition published 2023

Copyright © Germán Campos Muñoz 2021

Germán Campos Muñoz has asserted his right under the Copyright, Designs and
Patents Act, 1988, to be identified as Author of this work.

For legal purposes the Acknowledgments on pp. x–xi constitute an extension
of this copyright page.

Cover design: Terry Woodley
Cover image © Eight Real coin of King Charles III of Spain.
Robert Kawka / Alamy Stock Photo.

All rights reserved. No part of this publication may be reproduced or transmitted
in any form or by any means, electronic or mechanical, including photocopying,
recording, or any information storage or retrieval system, without prior
permission in writing from the publishers.

Bloomsbury Publishing Plc does not have any control over, or responsibility for,
any third-party websites referred to or in this book. All internet addresses given in
this book were correct at the time of going to press. The author and publisher regret
any inconvenience caused if addresses have changed or sites have ceased to exist,
but can accept no responsibility for any such changes.

A catalogue record for this book is available from the British Library.

A catalog record for this book is available from the Library of Congress.

ISBN: HB: 978-1-3501-7025-4
PB: 978-1-3501-9504-2
ePDF: 978-1-3501-7026-1
eBook: 978-1-3501-7027-8

Series: Bloomsbury Studies in Classical Reception

Typeset by RefineCatch Limited, Bungay, Suffolk

To find out more about our authors and books visit www.bloomsbury.com
and sign up for our newsletters.

Contents

List of Illustrations		ix
Acknowledgments		x
	Introduction: *Plus Ultra*	1
	Prospective Classicisms on Latin America	10
	The Class of the Classics	16
	Greek and Latin America? A Summary of the Chapters	23
	Note on the Translations	28
1	Avatars	31
	Preliminaries	31
	Acosta, the Elder	36
	The Antarctic Ovid	50
	The Austral Muse	62
	Conclusions: Culling, Cultivation, and Culture	68
2	Chorographers	73
	Preliminaries	73
	The Borders of the New World: Pedro Nolasco Mere's Maps of the Walls of Lima	85
	The Language of the New World: Rodrigo de Valdés's *Fundación y Grandezas*	98
	Conclusions	121
3	Personae	127
	Preliminaries	127
	Hypermetric History: José Joaquín de Olmedo's *Victoria de Junín*	134
	An Ides of March in September: The 1828 Conspiracy Against Bolívar	150
	Conclusions: History, Impersonation, Prosopopoeia	169
4	Mythographers	175
	Preliminaries	175
	The Other Asterion	178
	The Creation of a Carioca Orpheus	186

	Orpheus in Color	192
	Confirmations, Rebuttals, and Antitheses	200
	Conclusions	206
5	Coda: Pedagogues	209
	Preliminaries	209
	Monuments to the Origin	213
	Back to Erice	219

Bibliography	229
Index	247

Illustrations

0.1	Civdad. La villa rica Enpereal de Potocchi	4
2.1	Pedro Nolasco Mere, *Plano de Lima* (1685)	89
2.2	Pedro Nolasco Mere, *Plano de Lima* (1687)	90
3.1	*Bolívar*, by Pietro Tenerani, Plaza Bolívar, Bogotá, Colombia (1846)	128

Acknowledgments

I would like to express my gratitude to the many people who, in one way or another, had an impact on this book. My interest in the Classics began a long time ago, when I did not suspect that my native city would eventually find a place in my academic work, and I was surrounded by many dear friends and relatives. To Kazu, Lorena, Mario, Angelo, Johann, Verónica, Hans, María Fernanda, Jano, Nadia, Miguel, Mariana, Johnny, Leticia, César, and Vanessa—thank you all for your friendship. I thank my parents, Elma and Pedro, for their love, unwavering support, and all the books; my siblings Angel, Cynthia, and Sandra, for their great patience and humor; and Tarcila, for her sustaining care. From my time as a young student in Lima, I feel especially obliged to Carlos Gatti, Jorge Wiesse, and the great companions of the *Lectura Dantis*, who have been meeting for decades in a rare and beautiful exercise of close reading. I like to think that in those sessions I learned how to read for a second time.

I am deeply thankful to the brilliant and versatile Sophia McClennen, who encouraged me to begin my graduate studies in the US, mentored me through the process, taught me how to read films critically (the substance of Chapter 4 originated in her class), and has continued to support me to this day. While at Penn State, I also had the immense fortune of becoming a student of Djelal Kadir, who is not only one of the great comparatists of our time, but also a role model of the highest ethical and intellectual standard. The world is a constant lesson with him, and I feel that in that wide and generous classroom I learned how to read for a third time.

I also found new and brilliant friends in the northern hemisphere. From my time in Pennsylvania, I'd like to mention Sara Marzioli, Mich Nyawalo, José Alvarez, Maritza Davidson, Karl Davidson, Lisa Rosenblatt, Darwin Tsen, and Victoria Lupaşcu, as well as the various members of the Milton, Marx, and other reading groups that we have assembled during the years. In North Carolina, my gratitude goes to my colleagues in the Department of English at Appalachian State University. Most especially, I wish to acknowledge David Orvis, for his welcome and mentoring over the years, and my dear friends and fellow comparatists Başak Çandar and Chris Meade, for their intellectual comradery, sense of humor, and hospitality.

The research I conducted for this book received generous support from the Department of Comparative Literature and the College of the Liberal Arts at Penn State University in the form of an RGSO travel grant that allowed me to conduct archival research in multiple cities in South America. Likewise, a grant from the University Research Council at Appalachian State University gave me the opportunity to visit the General Archive of the Indies in Seville in Spain, and the British Library and the Cambridge University Library in the United Kingdom. Parts of this project were presented at the Universidad del Pacífico (Lima, Peru) and at Penn State University, and this book has greatly benefited from the comments I received at both venues.

I am very grateful to Georgina Leighton and Lily Mac Mahon at Bloomsbury Academic for their extraordinary diligence and their generous interest in this project. I am also indebted to the anonymous reviewers whose feedback on my book proposal and manuscript has been invaluable.

I finally wish to thank, with all my heart, my wife Caroline Egan—the brilliant interlocutor and comrade with whom every day I learn again how to read and write. Her impact on this book has been enormous—it is no hyperbole to assert that it would not exist without her.

Introduction: *Plus Ultra*

Plus vltra, mas Mundos ay.

Plus Ultra, there are more worlds.

Sor Juana Inés de la Cruz, "Loa" to *El mártir del Sacramento. S. Hermenegildo*

A fifteen-minute video film welcomes visitors every day to the Archivo General de Indias ("General Archive of the Indies") in Seville, the largest depository of original documents related to the overseas possessions of the former Spanish Empire. The film offers a compact history of the archive: the original construction and various uses of the edifice known as the Lonja, where the archive is located; its proximity to the Guadalquivir river; its superlative importance as historical repository, and so on. Two voice-overs take turns explaining these details, but while the second merely lectures viewers on factual information, the first voice speaks as though it emanated from the building itself, describing in the first person the series of mutations that have affected the structure since its initial edification in 1584. At one point, this talking archive proudly recalls a moment in the late eighteenth century when Juan Bautista Muñoz, Royal Cosmographer of the Indies, chose the Lonja building as the seat for the collection of colonial documents: "Juan Bautista Muñoz recorrió mis galerías, deterioradas por el paso del tiempo y mis nuevos usos, pero mi recia construcción en piedra y mis bóvedas coronadas por el emblema de *Plus Ultra*, símbolo mejor que ningún otro de lo indiano, debieron de convencerlo" (Gobierno de España 2010: 6:33–6:54) ("Juan Bautista Muñoz examined my galleries, deteriorated by the passage of time and my other uses, but my sturdy stonework and my vaults crowned with the emblem *Plus Ultra*, a symbol of the *indiano* better than any other, must have persuaded him").[1]

---

[1] Unless otherwise noted, all translations are mine (see further details on bilingual editions at the end of this introduction).

While the solemn voice, a personification of the Lonja building, ponders the persuasive appeal of its material and symbolic attributes, it does not elaborate on what renders the Latin phrase *Plus Ultra* such a quintessential symbol of the *indiano*—that is, things pertaining to the Indies. That the *indiano* appeal of *Plus Ultra* remains unexplained is perhaps telling, given that a good explanation of that symbolism might test visitors' patience. It would have to start with ancient tales of the Greek demigod Heracles—more specifically, those of his tenth labor, during which the hero fought the giant monster Geryon in Erytheia to take his famous cattle. Once the task was accomplished, Heracles took a moment to set two enormous pillars at the boundary of Europe and Africa, marking the westernmost limit of his journey, or the end of the world.[2] The pillars would then become a standard motif with recurrent presence in ancient, medieval, and Renaissance visual and literary arts. Around 1516, Charles V of Spain adopted the pillars as the central emblem for his coat of arms, and added the Latin caption *Plus Ultra*, which for him meant "further beyond," even though that message would have required slightly different phrasing in Classical Latin (Rosenthal 1973: 199).[3] Charles, who had just effectively inherited the vast territories of the nascent Spanish Empire and would soon become Holy Roman Emperor, saw his vast imperial authority perfectly captured in symbolically disregarding Heracles's restriction and surpassing the ancient boundary. On the one hand, *Plus Ultra* implied a modern triumph over the limits of the Classical imperial imagination— most especially, of Rome, the ancient paradigm of empire (after all, Hercules, the Latinized version of Heracles, was also a quintessential symbol of Romanness). On the other hand, the phrase recoded the conceptual value of the pillars: no longer the end of the world, they now signaled the new and unprecedented reach of the Spanish Empire, which had recently claimed jurisdiction over most of the territories recently "discovered"—variously called the Indies, America, and the New World.[4] Transhistorical and transatlantic, the pillars and their motto *Plus*

---

[2] The earliest references to this episode seem to come from Pindar's odes, which characterize the pillars as markers of material and conceptual limits. The *Nemean Odes*, for instance, describes them as "ναυτιλίας ἐσχάτας / μάρτυρας κλύτας" (3.23–4) ("renowned witnesses of the uttermost limit of seafaring"). The *Olympian Odes* notes that "τὸ πόρσω δ' ἐστὶ σοφοῖς ἄβατον κἀσόφοις" (3.44–5) ("what is beyond lies untrodden for both the wise man and the fool"). Other Classical sources include Diodorus Siculus (*Library* 4.12.2–5), Apollodorus (*Library* 2.5.10), and Strabo (*Geography* 3.5.5).

[3] It was long believed that Heracles' pillars also contained the inscription *non plus ultra* or *ne plus ultra*, and that, on the basis of that inscription, Charles V designed his own motto by removing the negative adverb. However, Rosenthal (1971, 1973) overturned this assumption in two essays about the adoption of the pillars emblem by the Spanish monarch.

[4] Here and throughout this book I use the terms "America" and "the Americas" indistinctly. The adjective "American" must therefore be read in a continental sense (I reserve the demonym "US American" for the United States).

Ultra epitomized the ideals and implications of the imperialism that Charles came to embody.

It is apparent that, in valorizing the motto *Plus Ultra* as pre-eminent symbol of the *indiano*, the personified Lonja building alludes primarily to the phrase's transatlantic appeal: Charles went "further beyond" the pillars when his empire invaded and occupied the Indies. But given its Greco-Roman lineage, the phrase *Plus Ultra* also comes to evoke a transhistorical affiliation between ancient Classical narratives (so inscribed in the early modern European imagination) and the seismic disruption that America brought into that imagination in the late fifteenth and early sixteenth centuries. In effect, once the pillars ceased to be a limit and instead became the limen between the "New" and "Old" worlds, their symbolism was altered—as were countless other elements associated with the antiquity deemed "Classical." In a paradoxical motion (typical of imperial imagination and its fascination with ever-receding horizons), the pillars traveled beyond themselves, quickly spreading across the New World the geopolitical message of Habsburg expansion. In fact, before the first half of the sixteenth century had ended, the pillars were already ubiquitous as the stamped emblem on the surface of the *macuquinas*, the first coins minted in the New World. The standard motto of this early currency was, of course, *Plus Ultra*.[5] By the start of the seventeenth century, Charles' motif was so universally recognized that the Andean writer Felipe Guaman Poma de Ayala could use it in his depiction of the city of Potosi, with a group of Incan lords who, holding the pillars, act as literal human buttresses of the imperial monument. Guaman Poma complemented the image with the caption *"PLVS VLTRA / EGO FVLCIO CVLLVNAS EIOS"* (c. 1615: 1057 [1060]) ("Further Beyond / I strengthen his columns"). The spelling "cvllvnas" instead of "collvmnas" reflects the lack of a phonological distinction between "o" and "u" in Quechua. Guaman Poma's addendum to Charles' imperial motto was, in other words, written in a Quechuacized Latin (see Fig. 0.1).[6]

The manifold convergences of an ancient Greco-Roman myth, a Habsburg imperial motto, and an Andean depiction of a New World city were already possible at a relatively early moment of the colonial period, with an illustration of five Incas holding Heracles's pillars and a caption in Quechua-inflected Latin. Striking as it is, the most remarkable aspect of this example may not be its

---

[5] See Hubbard 1968.
[6] See note 2 to the digital reproduction of this illustration on *The Guaman Poma Website* (Guaman Poma de Ayala). For a detailed examination of the transcultural implications of this image, see MacCormack 2007: 236.

Fig. 0.1 Civdad. La villa rica Enpereal de Potocchi. Courtesy of the Royal Danish Library, GKS 2232 kvart: Guaman Poma, Nueva corónica y buen gobierno (*c*. 1615), page 1057 (1060).

syncretic configuration, but its unexceptional quality. Indeed, the amalgamation of transhistorical and transatlantic motifs of Guaman Poma's illustration exhibits a typical gesture in the context of the New World: the creative adaptation of the intellectual inventory, mythological tropology, and ideological legacy of Greco-Roman motifs in the Americas. As this study will discuss, such adaptations span centuries. Latin American scholars working on the most diverse periods and areas of the region frequently refer to the pervasive presence of the Classics in cultural and artistic practices of all sorts. However, a dialogue among scholars of the Classics in the Americas working on different historical moments is, at this point, still at a formative stage. One is in fact prompted to ask, would a transhistorical approach of this sort be productive? Are there enough elements to propose genealogies of Latin American Classicisms, and would they matter at all? Can a transhistorical survey help us sketch a narrative of what has happened with the Classics in the New World since they surpassed the pillars of the demigod Heracles and journeyed across the Atlantic to the New World? And what could be learned from that?

This book is conceived as an attempt to deal with the broad implications of these questions. I contend here that the Classical tradition has played the role of interlocutor and agent in the perennial exercises of self-definition of the New World. Furthermore, I posit that the rhetorical productivity of the encounter between the Classical tradition and Latin American communities has surfaced with a particularly vivid impetus in key moments of the latter's history. This study chronicles five of these moments, articulated both as reports of this encounter, as well as theoretical and analytical interventions in it. It is in this sense that I opt from the outset for the notion of an "encounter with" the Classics, because the type of contact I trace in these pages was not imagined as mere influence. Rather, the approach to the Classics in the New World was a conscious attempt to retroactively and dramatically rewrite the implications that ancient texts and authorities had and could have in the configuration of the transatlantic polity inaugurated by the colonial invasion of the Americas. In the process, the Classics came to acquire a defining role in the idea of the New World.

For accidental and methodological reasons, the majority of cases studied in this book focus on the South American region—hence the book's title—but I believe they will prove evocative of phenomena affecting Latin America and even the Americas at large. More importantly, I will argue here, the cases analyzed in this book evince, despite their different chronologies, certain transhistorical trends in their relation with the Classics. Here I want to emphasize that my use of the adjective "transhistorical" places the accent on "historical" rather than its prefix, for I do not contend that the relative patterns that may be registered across the case studies explored in this book reveal any type of essential or transcendental "Latin American" way of being. If there are certain patterns it is because, due to very well-known geopolitical events, the regions we designate as part of "Latin America" have effectively been exposed to common political and ideological dynamics. A prominent example (one highlighted in several chapters of this book) is the impact of the world-famous and world-shattering label *mundus novus* or New World, so forcefully imprinted on the whole continent from the earliest contacts between Europeans and Americans. Whatever particularities are legitimately recognized in the different histories of America, we must also keep in mind that those individual, local, regional, and national histories had to allot an important degree of their institutional, material, and cultural energy to dealing with the implications of that title. Indeed, *mundus novus* would indelibly mark the continent's post-Columbian history in the shape of at least two lasting ideological "conditions": first, America's perennial newness—enunciated in different contexts as geographical *tabula rasa*, revolutionary geopolitics, and regeneration of essential forms of humanism; and second, America's entanglement between identity and alterity with respect to the Old World—an ambiguous sense of self clumsily yet effectively coded (even today) as both "Western" and "Non-Western," and occasionally negotiated (yet never fully solved) as colonial *oikoumene*, New World baroque, hybrid nature, racial synthesis, and transcultural space. What is "transhistorical" in this case is not, therefore, a particular cultural behavior or demeanor, but a common challenge—which would in turn elicit a myriad of different responses. Such responses provide the rudiments of a genealogy of apprehensions and dilemmas that American intellectuals have experienced when thinking of their own role in world history. In outlining the major contours of this encounter and analyzing its features and consequences, I seek to offer a partial yet hopefully functional revision of key moments in the cultural histories of Latin America articulated on the basis of the vital role the Classics played in that history. I intend to show, in short, that a critical glance through the horizon defined by Hercules's pillars and its inexhaustible gnome *Plus Ultra* provides us with a fresh perspective from which to re-evaluate not only well-known historical and cultural processes in Latin America, but also the rhetorical character and importance of the Classics in Americanist studies at large.

This expectation might seem to be at odds with the principle of chronological and geographical specificity that tends to define monographic studies. I hope to show that, despite the extensive temporal range of cases covered in this book, its composition is not contravening the basic wisdom of that axiom. In principle, this book does not have any comprehensive pretensions, not even with regard to the cases chosen for this study. While I have endeavored to foreground the historical specificity of each case I examine, no single analysis could exhaust their complexity. I am nevertheless interested in proposing linkages among these episodes, again not as evidence of immanent attributes, but as signs of the enduring legacy of the "New World" invention and other similar ideologemes, and I believe that studying the role of the Classics in this formation provides the rudiments for such a genealogical approach.

With these caveats in mind, I would like to elaborate on three important critical and methodological challenges for a project of this nature:

1. Since ancient Greek and Roman traditions are canonical sources of European knowledge, asserting that these traditions have had a permanent and systematic role in the cultural history of "Latin America" is effectively a truism. How can this assertion be transformed into something more than a futile confirmation of what is apparent?
2. The two categories at play, the "Classics" and "Latin America," are already powerful expressions of cultural, historical, and geographical synthesis. Indeed, the designation of the "Classics" not only gestures toward more than 1,200 years of complex writing and readership across the Mediterranean, but also reifies the hierarchical structure with which Europe consecrated that tradition. The formulae "Latin America" and "South America," no less compact, often find themselves used as catchalls that efface the substantial differences among the many histories, communities, and languages included under their umbrellas. How should we navigate the breadth of the categories "the Classics," "Latin America," and "South America" without ignoring the specificities their usage may conceal?
3. The most serious issue (and perhaps the main objection for the reader) is that even when admitting these two categories, "Classics" and "Latin America," their historical and conceptual vastness is such that the question of their interplay could well be the point of departure for a compendious project and even an entirely new discipline. Evaluating the relationship between the Classics and Latin America might have had some appeal for a humanist polymath or a Neoclassical encyclopedist, but it is perhaps too broad for contemporary academic standards.

Is the scope of this study, then, too unwieldy for a monograph?

To begin addressing this question, I would propose that the main challenge lies not so much in the categories "Classics" and "Latin America" themselves, but in the question of their interaction. After all, neither the ideologically loaded term "Classics" nor the blurry and problematic term "Latin America" has prevented the formation and endurance of the fields of Classical and Latin

American studies. The problem at stake is how to tackle the relationship between these two spheres of knowledge—that is to say, what methodological and analytical strategies might we assume to approach this encounter in a way that is manageable and meaningful?

We must first note that the connection between the Classics and Latin America is a phenomenon consubstantial with the arrival of Europeans in America. It could not have been otherwise: as the Classics were one of the main traditions on which European intellectual knowledge was based—along with the biblical and the patristic—being educated in the fifteenth or sixteenth centuries implied an acquaintance with the legacy of ancient Greece and Rome. The prestigious quality of the category "Antiquity" indicates the foundational character Europe attributed to the Greco-Roman traditions. The coinage of widely used antonomasias illustrates this: by the end of the High Middle Ages, a modestly educated European would easily identify Virgil as "the Poet" or Aristotle as "the Philosopher." The advent of the Renaissance would only amplify the range of European classicisms. Whether in the sphere of law, sciences, literature, religion, or others, it would be virtually impossible to find a European author from the early modern period who does not somehow allude to or reflect an influence from the Classics. The use of Latin as a scholarly language is another clear indication of the *sine qua non* status of the Classics in European academic discourse of the period.

Still, the early modern geopolitical configuration of late fifteenth-century Iberia presented, in the already complex panorama of Western Europe, a special scenario for the development of Classical humanism. As Kristeller remarked in his overview of intellectual practices in the Renaissance:

> [T]he world of classical antiquity, and especially its literature and philosophy, seems to possess a solid reality which, like a high mountain range, has remained above the horizon for many centuries. Yet on closer inspection, it becomes apparent that the use made of this heritage by later generations has been subject to many changes. Each period has offered a different selection and interpretation of ancient literature, and individual Greek and Latin authors as well as their individual writings have seen more or less deep ebbs and tides of popularity at different times.
>
> 1961: 5–6

Iberia was a privileged shore for those ebbs and tides. On the one hand, the long-standing practice of Muslim scholarship in the peninsula had produced thinkers as powerful and influential as Ibn Rushd (known as "the Commentator" because of his influential gloss of the works of Aristotle); the works of these Muslim thinkers would in turn propitiate an energetic movement (especially in Toledo) to translate Arabic treatises, which often transmitted Greek texts, into Latin.[7] On the other hand, the negotiation between Classical philosophy and Christian doctrine characteristic of Thomist theology and other forms of scholasticism had also taken deep roots in the Christian kingdoms of Iberia. These traditions imagined themselves in direct continuity with the literary and scholarly practices of Late Antiquity.[8] By the mid-fifteenth century, the messy networks of these multi-ethnic, polyglot, and often conflicted scholarly practices became further complicated, as new waves of humanism emerging from the influential circles of Italian scholars entered into Hispania, bringing along a reconsideration of the Classics defined by a new fascination with oratory and eloquence, a revival of interest in classical Greek and philology, and a surge of Castilian translations (via Italian and Latin) of Greek works largely unavailable in the Middle Ages (Lawrence 1990: 222). The Europeans who invaded the Americas at the end of the fifteenth century, whether educated or not, would inevitably carry the marks of this polymorphic Classicism. In fact, the Classics already designated the very path of access to the New World—as Ἀτλαντὶς θάλασσα (Atlantis thalassa), the "Sea of Atlas" that Herodotus located beyond Heracles' pillars (1.202.4).[9]

These circumstances explain, to a certain extent, the historical lack of critical attention given to the subject of this book. Since the presence of the Classics in the Americas was pervasive, the phenomenon has been, until recently, largely taken for granted—a linkage that no critic would have denied, but one that did not seem to substantially alter the understanding of Latin America. Furthermore, the ancient Greek and Latin corpus has occupied, and still occupies (despite canonical reconfigurations), a prominent position in the canonical idea of the "West." Because of this, the very question of the role of the Classics in Latin America could legitimately seem suspicious through certain theoretical

---

[7] Hasse (2014) provides an overview and bibliography of the fascinating history of the transmission of Arabic scholarship in Europe. His essay highlights the complex interaction of ancient Greek, Arabic, Hebrew, and Latin, as well as the crucial role that Spain's centers of translation played in the development of medieval and Renaissance philosophy.

[8] For a survey of the defining presence of Aristotelian philosophy in the works and legacy of Thomas Aquinas, see Curran 2013 and McGinn 2014. For a concise examination of the confluences and tensions of Aristotelianism, Thomism, and Averroism, see Burke 2016 and Giletti 2004. For a discussion on the role of a cultural bridge that scholasticism enabled between Iberia and the New World, see Gracia 1994.

[9] See also Kadir 1992: 40–61 for the suggestive hypothesis of a philological play in Greek and Latin by the cosmographer Martin Waldseemüller (*Cosmographiae introductio*, 1507) embedded in America's name.

lenses—I am thinking, in particular, of Latin American postcolonial and decolonial studies.

I will return to this concern, but for now, I hasten to note that this study is not interested in endorsing the cultural sacrosanctity long attributed to the Classics (see the "Class of the Classics" section below). As a matter of fact, the cases analyzed in the course of this study constitute eloquent examples of the authoritarian prescriptions, appropriative gestures, anxiogenic moments, and hazardous consequences that the pervasiveness and flexibility of the Classics have enabled in key moments of Latin American history. Yet the instances in which the encounter between the Classics and Latin America have come to bear on this history must not be taken at face value. The various uses of the Classical tradition in Latin America have never been simple subservient articulations of European paradigms in the New World; rather, they have always involved complex processes of ideological and cultural adaptation, negotiation, and recreation. Given the fundamental consequences they have had, an academic debate on these matters, especially regarding the South American subcontinent, is a pending task for our understanding of both Greco-Roman reception and the history of the region. This book addresses the necessity of reformulating our approach to the conjunction of these two fields. The following brief account of its academic precursors will illustrate some of the key issues at play in the study of the Classics in South America.

Prospective Classicisms on Latin America

In the US academy, the first explicit declaration of the importance of studying the Greco-Roman tradition within Latin American studies seems to date to 1939, in an essay by Tom B. Jones titled "The Classics in Colonial Hispanic America" and published in *Transactions and Proceedings of the American Philological Association* (*TAPA*). The opening statement highlights the lack of critical attention to this phenomenon:

> This paper deals with a neglected, if not unknown, chapter in the history of the classics in the Renaissance and Post-Renaissance period. Although in the past some attention has been paid to the classical revival in Spain, there has been almost no attempt to study the transfer of the classics to the Spanish colonies in the New World. Therefore, in this paper it is my purpose to indicate the importance of this latter subject and to lay a foundation for future work in the field.
>
> 1939: 37

The categories in which Jones situates his contribution speak to his conceptual assumptions. He understands the subject of the Classics in the colonial world in terms of the Renaissance and what he deems "Post-Renaissance," and he implicitly adopts the premise of *translatio imperii*, imagining the relationship between the Greco-Roman tradition and the New World as a "transfer" from the Spanish metropolis to its American colonies. In accordance with this analytical framework, the connection between the Classics and Latin America operates unidirectionally, always from East to West, from the textual practices of ancient Greek and Rome to their European *rinascimento*, and from Europe to the Americas. Jones argues for the relevance of his subject through a selection of samples, which he organizes as follows:

> In this paper four aspects of the history of the classics in colonial Hispanic America will be considered: (1) the classical influence in philosophy, science, medicine, and law; (2) colonial editions and translations of classical authors; (3) classical scholarship in the colonies; and (4) the influence of the classics upon colonial literature.
>
> 1939: 38

Following this outline, Jones dedicates the nine pages of his essay to a series of samples—for example, commentaries on Aristotle written in Mexico, descriptions of Peru included in a translation of Pliny's *Historia naturalis*, editions of Cicero's *Orationes* published in Mexico, instances of Homeric and Virgilian motifs in New World epics, and so on. None of these cases are glossed, for the purpose of the author is only to demonstrate that the Classics played an important cultural role in the colonial period. The conclusion of the essay, grounded in the consistent presence of Classical authors, texts, and motifs in the early colonial period, is that "the importance of the classics in the formation of the culture of the Spanish colonies is very clear, and, eventually, when the cultural history of Hispanic America is written, its classical foundations must be considered in detail" (1939: 45). These closing remarks are important, for even though Jones concentrates on colonial Hispanic America, he hints at the transhistorical implications of his subject.

It does not seem, however, that Jones's plea was readily heard—and in fact he himself left behind his work as a Latin American historian to become a full-fledged Mediterranean scholar, focusing largely on Sumerian and Roman histories later in his career. In the meantime, in the English-speaking world the question he posed went virtually unaddressed for several decades. It is only fifty-five years after the publication of Jones' essay on the Classics and colonial

Hispanic America that the theme he had suggested as constitutive of the "cultural history of Hispanic America" received sustained critical attention once again. Though a much broader attempt to engage with the connection between the Greco-Roman tradition and the New World, the title of this new project was as laconic as that of Jones's article: *The Classical Tradition and The Americas* (1994) (hereafter *CTA*), edited by Wolfgang Haase and Meyer Reinhold. In the prologue, Haase defines the study of the relationship between the Classics and the Americas as a multifocal "history of reception of antiquity" (where "reception of antiquity," he explains, functions as a more refined formula than "Classical tradition").[10] In highlighting the multiplicity of receptions of the Classics in the New World, Haase implicitly draws a distinction between the *CTA* project and the horizon defined by Jones (who is not mentioned in *CTA*), not only because of the larger temporal and geographical coordinates, but also because of the way the relationship between the Classics and the New World is reimagined—no longer as a unidirectional influence, but rather as a complex network of cultural and discursive exchanges. This different approach is consciously predicated in the selection of the conjunction "and" instead of the preposition "in" for the project's title. Haase marks the importance of that choice in his presentation of the structure of *CTA*:

> The classical tradition *in* the Americas ... constitutes the subject of one, and by far the larger of the two major parts of this work. The predominantly European perspective of the intellectual preparation for and comprehensive mental dealing with the encounter with the unknown lands and peoples is treated in the other, shorter part. Both together make up the panorama of *The Classical Tradition and the Americas*. Because of the temporal priority of Europe in the history of the "classical tradition," the shorter part is placed at the beginning; it consists of the present Volume I, entitled *European Images of the Americas and the Classical Tradition*. The second part will consist of the remaining volumes: Volume II on *The Classical Tradition in the Latin American Countries*, Volumes III and IV on *The Classical Tradition in Colonial America and the United States*, Volume V on *The Classical Tradition in Canada*, and Volume VI on *Classical Scholarship in the Americas*.
>
> 1994: VIII

Thus, while the taxonomy of Jones's essay (his four "aspects") was thematic (the Classics in the history, literature, philosophy, art, and scholarship in Colonial Hispanic America), the governing principle of the *CTA*'s subdivisions were

---

[10] For terminological considerations, see "The Class of the Classics" section below.

geographical (the Classics in Latin America, the United States, and Canada, in the European images of the Americas, and in American scholarship). Despite their differences, the classifying strategies in both cases shared a common rhetorical gesture: enumerations meant to demonstrate the ubiquity of the Classics in the New World. Furthermore, they were both announced as great opportunities for the re-evaluation of conventional academic fields—on the one hand, the Classics; on the other, the geographical and thematic areas of Hispanic American studies (Jones) and American studies broadly (*CTA*).

Considering these ambitious intellectual goals, the actual results of the *CTA* project are somewhat disappointing. Haase insists that "[w]ith its overarching theme, the reception of antiquity in relationship to the Western hemisphere, [this work] is devoted to a subject that has *in no way* been treated comprehensively or exhaustively to date" (1994: x; my emphasis). But the CTA project ended up being no less prospective than Jones's essay had been. Of the eight volumes Haase anticipated in 1994, not even the first one was fully realized. The single book that came to light from the project (in which Haase's prologue is included) comprises only the first part of the first volume—*European Images of the Americas and the Classical Tradition*—which, Haase had emphasized, constituted by far the smallest part of the project. Its smallness is, of course, relative to the entire plan, as this first half of the first volume already amounts to 681 pages. The studies compiled in this half-volume book, which deal mostly with the cartographic, ethnographic, and mythological transformations that Columbus's arrival to the Americas brought about in the European imagination, constitute an important contribution to our understanding of the early period of contact between the Old and New Worlds. The articles, however, are all confined (as the volume's title indicates) to "European Images of the Americas." The understudied nature of the Classics *in* the Americas, which the *CTA* preface diagnoses as urgent, remained unaddressed. This partial volume was published in 1994; two and a half decades later, there has been no sign of a new attempt either to complete that first volume or to resume the larger project.[11]

After the frustrated *CTA* project, attempts to provide a transhistorical panorama of the Classics and Latin America were taken up by South American scholars during the aughts: first, the two-volume compilation titled *América Latina y lo Clásico* ("Latin America and the Classical"), published in 2003 by the

---

[11] Dr. Gertrud Grünkorn (Editorial Director of the Classical and Ancient Near Eastern Studies series of Walter de Gruyter Press, which published the *CTA*) confirmed to me via e-mail that the project was abandoned after the first half-volume.

Chilean Society of Classical Studies and edited by Giuseppina Grammatico; and second, *La influencia clásica en América Latina* (2010) ("The Classical Influence in Latin America"), a six-essay volume edited by Carla Bocchetti on the impact of the Classics in different moments of Latin American cultural history (with a focus on the nineteenth and twentieth centuries). As I devote the entire fifth chapter of this study to Grammatico's edited volume, I refer the reader to that chapter (though a short summary is provided below). Bocchetti's compilation provides new insights into the subject, though it is relatively brief and each piece is independent from the other. The volume does not seek to postulate a comprehensive hypothesis.

In Anglophone academia, meanwhile, Andrew Laird raised the broader question of Latin American Classicism in his entry "Latin America" for Blackwell's *A Companion to the Classical Tradition* (2007). Laird foregrounded the distinctions between Classical "reception" (as the specific usage of Classical elements in a subsequent period and for a concrete purpose) and Classical "tradition" (as the relatively permanent use and transmission of the Classics in a certain region). In his entry, Laird compiles examples from diverse periods and regions in Latin America, from the early colonial period to the Latin American "boom" of the twentieth century. This survey allows him to illustrate the wide gamut of approaches to the Classics by key Latin American figures, from the revolutionary Hellenism of the Cuban José Martí to the conservative Latinism of the Colombian Miguel Antonio Caro. Tellingly, Laird could remark that his entry was "the first-ever guide to the classical tradition in English to give any consideration at all to Latin America" (2007: 228). As Tom Jones had done in 1939, Laird concludes yet again with a prospective statement: "As well as providing a new terrain for interdisciplinary enquiry, the cornucopia of classical traditions in the Hispanic or Latin American heritage could secure an important role for Greco-Roman studies in today's academic curricula" (2007: 235).

When I began working on this subject, about a decade ago, I encountered a scenario reflecting Laird's assessment: a remarkably rich and promising field of study that appeared, nevertheless, still largely untrodden. In very recent years, Laird's expectation has begun to materialize with visible strength—in what hopefully are the signs of the full establishment of an academic field in Latin American Classicisms. Consider, for example, this sequence: a volume titled *América Latina y lo clásico; lo clásico y América Latina* ("Latin America and the Classical; The Classical and Latin America"), edited by Nicolás Cruz and María Gabriela Huidobro, was published in Chile in August of 2018. In December of the same year, the compilation *Antiquities and Classical Tradition in Latin*

America, edited by Laird and Nicola Miller, appeared in the UK. And in January 2020, the volume *Greeks and Romans on the Latin American Stage*, edited by Rosa Andújar and Konstantinos P. Nikoloutsos, has joined this growing trend. In just two years, and on both sides of the Atlantic, these collections have taken on the common task of illustrating the broad geographical, chronological, rhetorical, and thematic spectrum of Latin American Classicisms. This is an exciting context for the publication of a monograph on the subject of Latin American Classicisms. Furthermore, it is my hope that the case studies explored in this book, mainly focused on South America, will complement and enter into productive dialogue with this new bibliography, which has so far tended to focus on North and Central America—especially Mexico.

Along with the transhistorical volumes listed above, others have explored the connection between the Classics and Latin America in more specific periods. These include Mario Briceño Pozo's *Reminiscencias griegas y latinas en las obras del Libertador* (1971) ("Greek and Latin Reminiscences in the Works of the Liberator"), which compiles the abundant usage of Classical imagery in the writings of Simón Bolívar; and the two-volume *Mitos clásicos en la literatura española e hispanoamericana del siglo XX* (2009) ("Classical Myths in Twentieth-Century Spanish and Hispanic American Literature"), edited by Juan Antonio López Ferez, with the second volume devoted to authors from throughout the Americas. Understandably, the colonial period has been the most attractive field for the examination of the Classics in the New World. Prominent monographs that take up this line of inquiry are David Lupher's *Romans in a New World: Classical Models in Sixteenth-Century Spanish America* (2003), which argues that ancient Greek and Roman paradigms of imperial behavior were adopted and critically interrogated during the conquest of Mexico in the early sixteenth century, not only as models to be emulated, but also as standards to be surpassed; and Sabine MacCormack's *On the Wings of Time: Rome, Spain, the Incas, and Peru* (2007), which evaluates the role of Roman historiography and literature in narrations of the history of the Incas written during the Colonial period. Most recently, Laura Fernández, Bernat Garí, Álex Gómez Romero, and Christian Snoey edited the volume *Clásicos para un nuevo mundo: Estudios sobre la tradición clásica en la América de los siglos XVI y XVII* (2016) ("Classics for a New World: Studies on the Classical Tradition in sixteenth- and seventeenth-century Americas"). This volume, a selection of the proceedings from a 2014 conference held in Madrid, includes a wide range of studies on the literary, geopolitical, historiographical, and juridical roles the Classics played in the first two centuries of Spanish presence in the New World.

We now have, I believe, the elements for a field of Latin American Classicisms that can draw on collaboration among scholars in Latin America, the United States, and the United Kingdom. Below I propose a few general and theoretical considerations that a project of that magnitude would demand.

The Class of the Classics

While the study of the Latin American Classicisms has been reinvigorated in the last decade or so, the larger field of the study of Classical receptions worldwide has grown steadily since the turn of the century. Here the term "reception," as defined by Lorna Hardwick and Christopher Stray, deals with "the ways in which Greek and Roman material has been transmitted, translated, excerpted, interpreted, rewritten, re-imaged and represented" (2008: 1). Under the banner of "Reception Studies," scholars have enthusiastically welcomed these efforts as an opportunity to challenge conventional assumptions about the "Classics" and to expand, over a wide range of regions, historical periods, and critical perspectives, the type of philological and cultural analysis previously restricted to the periods and traditions typically considered Classical (Martindale 2006: 1–2). These efforts have in turn led scholars to adopt a new terminology for the examination of intertextual phenomena.[12]

The same impetus has also led to an interrogation of the political and cultural implications of analytical categories formerly taken for granted. Hardwick, for example, comments on the way the term "legacy," for a long time associated with the presence of the Classics in subsequent periods, appeared to imply that "ancient culture was dead but might be retrieved and reapplied provided that one had the necessary learning" (2003: 2). Other terms that have merited critical re-examination have been "influence," "tradition," and "Classical" itself. For two reasons in particular, this last term poses serious challenges. First, it has been historically used by scholars of Greek and Roman antiquity to signify a corpus imagined as paradigmatic and foundational to a certain cultural identity (Western, European, etc.). Second, the narratives associated with that imaginary identity have often played a role in real processes of geopolitical reconfiguration (invasion and occupation, conquest, imperialism, colonization, etc.). As a result,

---

[12] Hardwick lists the following terms as a "working vocabulary for reception studies": acculturation, adaptation, analogue, appropriation, authentic, correspondences, dialogue, equivalent, foreignization, hybrid, intervention, migration, refiguration, translation, transplant, and version (2003: 9–10).

the term "Classical" appears to conjure a traditionalist approach to antiquity at odds with the declared attempts by contemporary Classicists to renovate our understanding of those same eras. Since the term Classical is effectively used throughout this book to refer to the body of texts, authors, and motifs typically associated with Greek and Roman antiquity, an explanation of what is understood here by "Classical" is in order.

While the word "Classical" has multiple meanings, the *OED* lexicalizes its association with the Greco-Roman corpus in its first definition: "Of or relating to the ancient Greek or Latin writers whose works form a canon of acknowledged excellence; of or relating to the works themselves. Hence: of or relating to ancient Greek or Latin literature in general" (s.v. "classical," definition A1a). But the term derives from the less restrictive Latin adjective *classicus*, which, according to the nineteenth-century Latin lexicon by T. Lewis and Charles Short, meant "of or belonging to a classis"—where *classis* is more or less akin to the contemporary social meaning of the word "class." The adjective *classicus*, Lewis and Short explain, also had a military sense: "[a soldier or a force] coming or belonging to a fleet" (Lewis and Short 1879: s.v. "classicus," definition II); and its nominal derivation, *classicum*, was used to denote "a field or battle-signal upon the trumpet" or, simply, a "war-trumpet" (Lewis and Short 1879: s.v. "classicus," definition IIB). Finally, in a more restricted sense, Lewis and Short present an acceptation closer to the current sense of "Classical," indicating that *classicus* could have also been used to refer to the principal or the highest social class (Lewis and Short 1879: s.v. "classicus," definition I) and, by extension, it later denoted "of the highest rank, classical, superior, standard" (Lewis and Short 1879: s.v. "classicus," definition IB).

The way these definitions are arranged suggests a tension between the historical use of Classical and its lexicographic codification. The *OED* reports this tension in a note to the variant "classic": "Classical Latin *classicus* 'of the highest class of citizens' is rare, and its metaphorical application to authors in the sense 'of high status (and therefore capable of providing guidance as to good usage)' occurs in one isolated case, Aulus Gellius 19.8.15" (s.v. "classic"). *Classicus*, it turns out, was mainly used as part of the military jargon in general, and in a naval sense in particular. The history of this word presents, therefore, an inversion: the least Classical denotation of *classicus*—"of the highest class of citizens," and by extension "superior, standard"—is included in the first definition of the entry *classicus* in Lewis and Short's authoritative lexicon. But this primary definition is substantiated by only one example—the isolated source also mentioned in the *OED*—from the *Attic Nights* by the second-century Roman grammarian Aulus Gellius.¹³ In contrast, subsequent entries (which define *classicus* in its more conventional senses in Classical Latin) include far more attestations. This means that Lewis and Short's arrangement of the different meanings of *classicus* is closer to the idiomatic sense of "Classical" in English, rather than a reflection of its historical Latin usage. The resulting conundrum is almost a tongue twister: the Classical sense of *classicus* was not "Classical," but classificatory and military. *Classicus* became properly "Classical" only in late and post-Classical Latin.

This explanation, while labyrinthine, nevertheless reveals that the relationship between "class" and "Classical" ends up affecting the scholarly ways the terms are understood. Even though the primary sense of both *classis* and *classicus* was descriptive and taxonomical—*classicus* meant "belonging to one of various classes"—the term somehow acquired the elitist restriction that still marks the word "Classical," and so *classicus* became, instead, "belonging to the first or highest class."¹⁴

These considerations may appear mostly technical, but they actually raise important questions when thinking about Latin American Classicisms. Does the use of the word "Classical" to refer to the Greco-Roman tradition inevitably imply a certain acquiescence to the classist significance that has inflected the term? Is the mere use of the term "Classical" a tacit iteration of those old cultural hierarchies? Would a different terminology be better in exploring the relationship between those two spheres? The lexicographic intricacies of the word Classical described above also echo ideological problems in the study of the reception of antiquity. After all, the geographical areas studied here—the Americas, Latin America, South America—have been profoundly marked by material and cultural exploitation and colonialism. Questions about the inherent elitism of the "Classical," then, are not merely abstract.

---

¹³ In this section from the *Attic Nights*, Aulus Gellius recounts an entertaining grammatical debate, between the scholar Cornelius Fronto and an anonymous poet, about whether two Latin nouns, *harena* ("sand") and *quadrigae* ("a team of four"), the former a collective singular and the latter a mandatory plural, could be inflected to indicate their opposite grammatical numbers (the results being *harenae* and *quadriga*). The passage in question says, "Ite ergo nunc et, quando forte erit otium, quaerite an 'quadrigam' et 'harenas' dixerit e cohorte illa dumtaxat antiquiore vel oratorum aliquis verl poetarum, id est classicus adsiduusque aliquis scriptor, non proletarius" (19.8.15) ("So go now and inquire, when you chance to have leisure, whether any orator or poet, provided he be of that earlier band—that is to say, any classical or authoritative writer, not one of the common herd—has used *quadriga* or *harenae*"; Rolfe 1967: 377). The fact that this usage of *classicus* is modified by a pleonasm of emphasis, *adsiduusque*, and by an antonym, *proletarius*, suggests that Aulus Gellius is ascribing a rather peculiar meaning to the word.

¹⁴ Cf. the different uses of the word "class" in modern English: while it is possible to talk of upper or lower classes, a phrase such as "a gentleman of class," or the adjectival derivations "classless" and "classy" denote instead a restrictive and elitist sense of the word.

The characterization of the word "Classical" in the *CTA* project (introduced above) illustrates this delicate issue. Haase, who writes at a time defined by the energetic revision of academic practices by Cultural Studies, hastens to define "Classical" not in terms of a superior heritage, but as a "neutral" mode of reception of ancient Greece and Rome:

> "Classical" here refers to Greek and Roman antiquity in Europe and the lands around the Mediterranean, and this in a twofold sense, both particular and general, either with reference to a selection of normative phenomena drawn from that antiquity, or as descriptive of antiquity in its totality. The "tradition" of the classical in its twofold sense is the relationship, continuing through the centuries, between each respective "present" and antiquity, a relationship determined at all times both by the conditions of each "present" and by the circumstances of the past, and assuming greatly different forms according to time and place.
>
> 1994: V

Haase does not nuance the distinction between particular and general senses of "Classical," but does elaborate on the term "tradition" to highlight the process through which ancient Greek and Roman cultures became acknowledged as Classical. In describing this Classicalization of Greece and Rome, Haase remarks on the role of "presents" as fundamental to the ideation of the Classics: the ancient tradition is conceived of as such so long as it operates in tandem with periods that look back onto that tradition—"each respective present," says Haase—and thereby render it Classical. Greek and Roman literatures, in this sense, were not and could not have been Classical in their own ancient Greek and Roman contexts (though the Greeks were authoritative sources for Latin authors, and this recognition often manifested itself as vivid cultural anxiety). Instead, their repeated use in different "presents" is what ultimately consecrated them as Classical. This consecration was well underway before the arrival of Europeans in the Americas. Late Classical, medieval and early modern "presents" had already both appropriated and transformed the Classical tradition and reflected on those appropriations and transformations. As a result, the first clause of the *CTA*'s title, *The Classical Tradition*, already entails a multitude of historical interventions, even before *the Americas* is attached to it.

These deliberations, which indicate Haase's nuanced sense of the implications of the study of Classical reception, make the following remark rather unexpected:

> [I]t could not be the intent for a project focused on a partial aspect of the emergence of European culture in America simply to join the growing chorus of

highly politicized negative criticism of the role of the European in the Americas. Despite full awareness of the fact that there is no such thing as pure objectivity, even in scholarly investigations, there will be no intention here to present, either in the whole work or in its parts, a preconceived positive or negative tendency.

1994: VIII

The phrase "the growing chorus of highly politicized negative criticism," which implicitly dismisses critiques of European colonialism, is paradoxically followed by the disavowal of any "preconceived positive or negative tendency." But more surprising is the brief footnote on the first page of the *CTA* prologue: "In principle, 'classical tradition' is understood here in the sense of the well-known and influential book by Gilbert Highet, *The Classical Tradition. Greek and Roman Influences on Western Literature*" (Haase 1994: v, n. 1). No more is said regarding this seminal work, though it is clearly central to the understanding of "Classical" advanced in the *CTA*.

An extensive survey ranging from Classical antiquity to modern literature and across an array of literary genres, Highet's *The Classical Tradition* provides a vast repertoire of what Haase might call the multiple "presents" of the Classics. But Highet does not explicitly delve into the implications of this word. "This book is an outline of the chief ways in which Greek and Latin influence has moulded the literatures of western Europe and America," begins his treatise, primarily assuming that the term "Classical" is tantamount to "Greek and Latin influences." However, the reader is soon able to surmise what Highet means by Classical. "Our world is in many ways a continuation of the world of Greece and Rome," he writes, and then explains:

> It is not always understood nowadays how noble and how widespread Greco-Roman civilization was, how it kept Europe, the Middle East, and northern Africa peaceful, prosperous, and happy for centuries, and how much was lost when the savages and invaders broke in upon it. It was, in many aspects, a better thing than our own civilization until a few generations ago, and it may well prove to have been a better thing all in all. But we are so accustomed to contemplating the spectacle of human progress that we assume modern culture to be better than anything that preceded it. We forget also how able and how willing men are to reverse the movement of progress: how many forces of barbarism remain, like volcanoes in a cultivated island, still powerfully alive, capable not only of injuring civilization but of putting a burning desert in its place.

1949: 3

The language and imagery of the Classicist Highet are themselves eminently Classical. In his seventh-century BCE *Works and Days*, the Greek poet Hesiod had already imagined a primordial time when the Olympic Gods, then ruled by Cronos, created the first stock of human beings, a "golden race" (χρύσεον γένος) free from toil and misery; when this generation finally came to an end, it was succeeded by a silver race, a bronze race, a race of heroes, and an iron race, each of these new generations signifying a more degraded stage of humanity (vv. 110–201). Taking on this tradition, Virgil proclaimed seven centuries later that the Age of the Emperor Augustus, Virgil's friend and patron and crafter of the *Pax Romana*, signified the return of the Golden Age of Cronos: "redeunt Saturnia regna; / iam nova progenies caelo demittitur alto" (*Eclogues* 4.6–7) ("the reign of Saturn returns; / a new generation descends from heaven on high"; Fairclough 1950: 29).[15] The recent Civil Wars, the fall of the Republic, the authoritarianism, and the imperialist expansionism promoted by Augustus did not seem to trouble (at least explicitly) Virgil's idyllic characterization.

Highet's description of Greco-Roman civilization seems almost like an invocation of the Classical motif of *Saturnia Regna*. Despite the discordance between this utopian image and the state of the world when *The Classical Tradition* was published—1949, only four years after the end of the Second World War, in which Highet himself fought as an officer in the British army—Highet rehearses a *Saturnia Regna* paean not only to characterize the Classical tradition itself, but also to ponder, apparently *en passant*, the degree to which Greco-Roman civilization was more or less similar to his own: "It was, in many aspects, a better thing than our own civilization *until a few generations ago*, and it may well prove to have been a better thing all in all" (1949: 3; my emphasis). Highet thus presupposes, in 1949, that his era recovered (to a degree, he concedes) a Classical splendor that had been lost. The linear degradation expounded by Hesiod becomes for Highet (as it had for Virgil) a story of cyclical regeneration. Highet then closes his remarks with a statement that ironically evokes the Classical sense of *classicum* as "war-trumpet," stridently warning his reader of the volcanic latency of "forces of barbarism," and picturing the consequences of the collapse of civilization in terms of an incandescent process of desertification.

These are the same categories through which, in 1994, Haase asked the reader to understand the word "Classical." In spite of his disclaimer, "there will be no

---

[15] The versatility of this particular motif for the purposes of self-defining Classicisms is discussed in Chapter 5.

intention here to present, either in the whole work or in its parts, a preconceived positive or negative tendency" (1994: VIII), the conceptual reference for Haase and his editorial work on the *CTA* is none other than Highet's highly idealized, heavily ideological, and distinctly political characterization of the Classical tradition.[16] The complexity of this genealogy shows that the lexical displacements in the definitions of "Classical" and *classicus* are not only linguistic phenomena. Highet's nostalgic glorification of the Greco-Roman tradition, along with Haase's conservative Classicism presented under the guise of neutrality, are both symptomatic of one of the main problems with which contemporary Classical studies still have to come to terms: a long history in which the legacy of ancient Greece and Rome has been used as the keystone of appropriative, civilizing, and ultimately predatory narratives of cultural and political superiority.

I have provided this lexical and disciplinary genealogy of the word "Classical" in order to address the issues posed earlier, which can now be summarized in a single question: how should we deal with the ideological resonances of the word "Classical" when talking about a region marked by a colonial history derived from the same ideology? My answer is, precisely, by emphatically acknowledging this conjunction from the outset and adopting a terminology that reminds us of that history. The implementation of allegedly more neutral terms, such as the "reception of antiquity," runs the risk, in my opinion, of comfortably avoiding an uncomfortable history. Because of the classism its own lexical root and scholarly usage predicates, "Classical" is an accurate descriptor not only of the Greco-Roman tradition, but of what has been done with and through that tradition. If I use the term in this book, stressing its perceived cultural value by capitalizing its initial, it is because I seek to constantly remind the reader that the appropriation of the Classical tradition in Latin America cannot and should not be divested of its problematic history.

---

[16] Indeed, Haase's prologue is only one of many in which Highet's book has been used as the fundamental reference for contemporary studies of the Classical tradition in the Americas. A more recent example appears in a catalogue of Classical motifs in twentieth-century Spanish and Spanish American literatures: *La tradición clásica en las literaturas iberoamericanas del siglo XX: Bibliografía analítica* (2004) ("The Classical Tradition in 20th-century Iberian-American Literatures: Analytical Bibliography"), by José María Camacho Rojo, from the University of Granada. The matter-of-fact tone of the opening line of Camacho's prologue distinctly echoes Haase's reference to Highet: "Como es bien sabido, por *tradición clásica*, expresión usualmente empleada desde la publicación en 1949 de la conocida obra de Gilbert Highet ... se entiende la recepción de un texto clásico, la influencia que la literatura greco-latina ha ejercido, como sustrato y modelo, en la cultura occidental, desde la Edad Media hasta nuestros días" (2004: 13) ("As is well-known, by *classical tradition*, an expression often used since the 1949 publication of the famous book by Gilbert Highet ... we understand the reception of a classical text, the influence that Greco-Roman literature has exerted, as substratum and model, in Western culture, since the Middle Ages until our days").

Greek and Latin America? A Summary of the Chapters

Resisting the temptation to delve into the category "Latin America" as I have done with "Classical," I simply want to clarify that "Latin America" is used in this book to refer to those areas of the Americas whose geopolitical formation was historically marked by the imperialist presence of mainly Spain and Portugal. The term "Latin" also ironically invokes a dimension of the Classical reception that this work seeks to trace. And even though the locution "Latin America" is not bereft of inconveniences, especially when it can be (and has been) used to efface the fundamental differences among the numerous communities comprised under its umbrella, it provides a synthetic term to approach the common features that relate the histories of all those nations. Since the cases presented here exemplify transnational and intercultural phenomena that often assumed a continental projection, and the root "Latin" resonates with the Classical tradition, "Latin America" seems an unavoidable term in the context of this book.

Within the larger context of Latin America, the majority of the cases studied in this book pertain to South America. I began this project through the writings of authors associated with the Viceroyalty of Peru, and while at a certain point I contemplated comparing these with writers from the northern regions of Latin America—especially colonial and republican Mexico, but also Guatemala in the nineteenth century and Cuba in the twentieth century, to mention a few—ultimately, I decided to keep the project mostly focused on South America, including authors and texts linked primarily to Peru, Venezuela, Argentina, Ecuador, Colombia, and Brazil. Of course, this is still quite a capacious horizon of analysis, but I also believe that the relative circumscription to the South American region brings important benefits to the study of the Classics in the New World. After all, within the still emerging field of Latin American Classicism, studies on North America, and most especially Mexico, seem to be preponderant.[17] There is not, to my knowledge, another book whose focus is that of South American Classicisms, even though the phenomenon presents traits in the region that are unique and cannot be equated with northern parallels—prominent examples of this are the importance that colonial Classicisms placed

---

[17] Colonial Mexico in particular has been the subject of a number of studies on Classical reception. See, for example, the essays by Dietrich Briesemeister (2000) and Andrew Laird (2006) on the practice of Neo-Latin in New Spain, and Anna More's book (2013) about the "Creole archive" as epitomized in Carlos de Sigüenza y Góngora's works. Other examples appear in the recent edited volumes by Cruz and Huidobro (2018), Laird and Miller (2018), and Andújar and Nikoloutsos (2020).

on the idea of the south or the "Antarctic" (as discussed at the end of Chapter 1), as well as the South American range of the Bolivarian campaign and subsequent debates about it in the early nineteenth century (as examined in Chapter 3). There are, furthermore, multiple cases in this book that complicate the South American geographical scheme: for example, Diego Mexia de Fernangil and José de Acosta, both studied in Chapter 1, eventually traveled from Peru to Central and North America, and those journeys had a defining role in the way they appropriated elements from the Classical tradition; some of Simón Bolívar's ideas about history, examined in Chapter 3, included his reflections on Latin America broadly and the geopolitical role that the United States was taking in the hemisphere in the early nineteenth century; the Brazilian composer Antônio Carlos Jobim, whose fascination with the myth of Orpheus is analyzed in Chapter 4, worked in the United States in the later part of his life; and the Classical scholars who attended the 2001 conference examined in the final chapter came from all different regions of Latin America. Still, while these instances explain why the term "Latin America" has been and will be used consistently in the course of this book, it is important to keep in mind that this study deals primarily with cases from the South American region.

The problems of the subject having been posed, its antecedents discussed, and its primary categories interrogated, the raison d'être of this book can be restated as follows: our understanding of the cultural and geopolitical formation of Latin America demands a consideration of the crucial presence of the Classical tradition in that history. This book examines the pervasiveness of this phenomenon—not through an impossibly comprehensive survey of Classical receptions in South America, but rather through a selection of important episodes that suggest one viable genealogy of New-World Classicisms, while recognizing that other genealogies could be drawn as well. This recognition explains the different methodologies at work throughout the chapters, which sometimes include historical and archival approaches, in other cases rely on close readings and literary and theoretical analysis, and in some others adopt a more narrative and even journalistic style. As a whole, the five chapters of this book articulate a diachronic survey of the creation and normalization of Latin American Classicisms, from the arrival of Europeans in the Americas until our own era, hopefully providing a vantage point for evaluating and expanding the complexity of that history. The cases selected illustrate the high degree of versatility in the appropriation of ancient narratives in the New World but also highlight the presence of transhistorical anxieties, especially Latin Americans' status as "New World" subjects and their conflicted self-imagination as Western and Non-Western. Ultimately, this book has been conceived as an essay laying critical foundations for further inquiries into the messy cultural history of South America. It is my hope that the variety of cases, periods, and regions considered here might help us define the contours of a network of Classical motifs, a network that has been central to the cultural history of the region.

The first chapter, "Avatars," begins by proposing that the imaginary categories of "New" and "Old" used to define the relationship between Europe and the Americas also served as fertile ground for thinking about the tension between both "Worlds" through Classical narratives. While authors in the New World assumed their position to be an opportunity to "write" the Americas and present themselves as founding figures, their own education as humanists, the audience to whom their writing was addressed, and the framework in which their cultural categories operated, imposed on them the imperative of preserving and rehearsing prestigious models that dated back to antiquity. The founding narrators of the Americas found themselves, in this sense, in the conundrum of having to operate as both old and new writers; their fictitious solution, I propose, was to become Classical. I analyze the works of three authors in whom this syncretic impetus is particularly vivid. First, I study José de Acosta's *Historia natural y moral de las Indias* (1590), his strategic allusions to the Roman scholar Pliny the Elder, and the Aristotelian premise in which his encyclopedic approach to the Americas is grounded. Then I examine Diego Mexía de Fernangil's prefaces to his two poetic volumes: his translation of Ovid's *Heroides*, titled *Primera parte del Parnaso antártico de obras amatorias* (1608), and his original compilation *Segunda parte del Parnaso antártico de divinos Poemas* (1617). In addition, I analyze the poem-prologue that precedes the first volume's translation, "Discurso en loor de la poesía," by the anonymous *criolla* or "Clarinda." Entangled in a dysfunctional dialectic between New and Old Worlds and overwhelmed by the forceful newness imposed on their identities, all these writers seek to negotiate their transatlantic position by conflating authority and authorship via the Classics, turning themselves into New World avatars of Greeks and Romans and rehabilitating their roles, predicaments, and achievements in their own works. These self-definitions lead them to a common conclusion: the recurrent use of the south, or the "Antarctic," as the defining element of their new Classical identities.

The second chapter, "Chorographers," explores the role of the Classics in the troubled configuration of *criollo* communities in the city of Lima in the mid- and late colonial period (late seventeenth and early eighteenth centuries). It surveys the adaptation of Virgilian motifs in a series of artifacts and texts dedicated to the celebration of the capital of the Viceroyalty of Peru—in particular, the first artistic maps of the walls surrounding Lima created by Pedro Nolasco Mere (1685 and 1687); and the hybrid Spanish-Latin epic poem *Fundación y grandezas de la ciudad de Lima* (1687) by the Jesuit Rodrigo de Valdés. I complement analyses of these two cases with brief sketches of related texts—the anonymous description of the 1590 arrival in Lima of Viceroy Garcia Hurtado de Mendoza; the 1639 *Historia de la fundación de Lima* by the Jesuit Bernabé Cobo; the epic poem *Vida de Santa Rosa de Santa María* (1711) by Luis Antonio de Oviedo y Herrera; and the epic poem *Lima fundada* (1732), by Pedro de Peralta Barnuevo. These authors and artists, I argue, coincide in imagining Lima and the Viceroyalty of Peru as endowed with enough autonomous history to merit the celebrations of a local *patria*, even within the coordinates of the Spanish Empire. The stigma of "brief history," however, encumbers Lima's self-glorification when compared to the ancestral claims of European cities. As a strategy of historical compensation, Limenian artists resort to the prestige of Virgil and his *Aeneid* as lenses with which to refract the glorification of their city within a larger sense of world history. The result is the transformation of the temporal prestige of Classical antiquity into the spatial commonality of a transatlantic *oikoumene*—one where Latin and Spanish, American societies and classical mythologies, and the past and the present all collapse.

While the first two chapters focus on the early and mid-/late colonial periods respectively, they also serve as the antecedents to the cases explored in the third chapter, "Personae," which examines the rhetorical and political use of Classical imagery during the turbulent early nineteenth-century Independence Wars or Age of Revolution, particularly regarding the figure of Simón Bolívar. Given the political turmoil of the period, the traditional temporal tension between old and new (which articulates the colonial dynamics examined in the first two chapters) is now metabolized as the geopolitical tension (never fully dialectical) between the Spanish and the American. Because Bolívar was the focus of much of the political and cultural debate of his time, this chapter provides abundant examples of how both partisans and enemies of the Liberator resorted to the histories of ancient Greece and Rome in order to promote or condemn his regime and political project. Two cases are at the core of this chapter: the first is one of the most important poetic pieces of the time, José Joaquín de Olmedo's *Victoria de Junín. Canto a Bolívar* (1825), a poem which, intending to celebrate the battles which consolidated the independence of most of Latin America from Spain, resorts to Classical epic and lyric models (in particular, Homer, Pindar, and Horace); the second is the series of attacks and slanders based on Classical images and motifs that were directed against Bolívar throughout his political and military career. This tradition of diatribes leads us to one of the most dramatic moments in Bolívar's life: the 1828 attempt to assassinate him. Literally based on the narratives of Cato the Elder, Julius Caesar, and the account of the fall of the Roman Republic, the 1828 conspiracy against Bolívar is one of the most astonishing rehearsals of ancient motifs in the political arena of post-revolutionary Latin America, one which, given Bolívar's role in the constitution of the new Latin American republics, had the potential to substantially alter the geopolitical structure of the region.

The fourth chapter, "Mythographers," relocates the contradictory history of Classicisms surveyed in the previous chapters within the coordinates of aesthetic modernism and identity construction, focusing on the instrumentalization of Classical mythological portrayals of local cultures in twentieth-century Latin America. I begin with a brief example of this phenomenon: the adoption of the myth of the Minotaur by Jorge Luis Borges as an icon for his own place within the history of Argentine letters. I discuss the ways Borges's particular understanding of the Minotaur, epitomized in his iconic "La casa de Asterión," was later adopted and developed by other Latin American writers, thus shaping a genealogy that echoes ancient protocols of mythography. The example of Borges's bio-mythography provides the elements for a theory of what can be called "mythological contamination," the process through which authors who adopt an ancient classical myth end up themselves entangled in the mythopoetic logic of the narrative they choose. Having defined the terms of this dynamic, the rest of the chapter tests its applicability in a much larger case: the multiple iterations of the myth of Orpheus in the scenic arts of Brazil. Covering a span of more than fifty years, through varied modes of writing and spectacle which include theatrical pieces, films, musicals, personal letters, memoirs, and musical movements, as well as pivotal Brazilian figures such as Vinícius de Moraes, Antônio Carlos Jobim, Carlos Diegues, and Caetano Veloso, the myth of Orpheus becomes one of the most prominent and pervasive motifs in the twentieth- and twenty-first-century debates on the representation of Brazil. In surveying these processes with an eye toward the ancient history of the transmission of the Orphic myth, I demonstrate that, as in the case of Borges, the protocols of ancient mythography are replicated in the construction of a modern yet truly mythological Brazilian Orpheus.

The fifth chapter, "Pedagogues," operates both as final chapter and conclusion to this book. It returns to the transhistorical questions on newness, self, and otherness, sketching a genealogical narrative that recapitulates the way those questions are rehearsed in the four initial chapters of the book. In order to better illustrate the features of this genealogy, the chapter examines its ideological resonances in the twenty-first-century movement organized by Chilean scholars to form a Latin American Federation of Classical Studies. The movement achieved its highest point at a conference held in 2001 in Erice, Sicily, titled *América Latina y lo Clásico*. As often happens at events of this nature, the conference included not only papers and publication plans, but also excursions, social and leisure activities, and artistic performances. Yet these activities become symptomatic when considered in the larger history of the New World Classicisms this book proposes, as the convention included the dramatic reading of classical hymns in Ancient Greek and Latin during pilgrimages to ancient ruins, letters to various Ministries of Education in Latin America demanding the mandatory teaching of Latin and Ancient Greek courses in high school, and even a collective manifesto, written in Latin under the auspices of Erice's local goddess, and signed by prominent scholars from throughout Latin America. I elaborate on the features and implications of these activities in connection to the Virgilian narrative of Aeneas descending into the Underworld to visit his father Anchises (a mythical quest that begins in the same town where the conference takes place, and which is explicitly alluded to in the event's opening session). By tracing the concomitances between epic and academic language, I demonstrate the rhetorical continuity created between this scholarly project and the mythical and ideological nostalgia already manifest in Virgil's poem and fully embedded in the history of South American Classicisms. The *América Latina y lo clásico* project provides, I argue, a contemporary and telling recapitulation of the history of the anxieties, appropriations, transformations, and self-definitions examined in the first four chapters.

Note on the Translations

All of the non-English citations used here are accompanied by English translations; unless otherwise noted, these translations are my own. However, many of the Greek and Latin texts cited come from bilingual editions, where the Greek or Latin texts appears facing the English translation, and those citations will show two parenthetical references: the Classical texts' parenthetical references are arranged according to their conventional format (e.g., "*Iliad* 1.1–7"), while the translations' parenthetical references follow Chicago style (e.g., "Murray 1999: 13"). In-text translations are provided in parentheses with quotation marks, immediately following the original reference; if the translation is not mine, the translation's reference is provided within the same parenthesis, preceded by a semicolon. In the Bibliography, names of the translators of bilingual editions cross-refer to the author translated (e.g., "Murray, A. T. 1999. In Homer 1999"), where full details of the edition are provided. These entries will also include the formula "Bilingual ed." (e.g., "Homer. 1999. *Iliad.* Vol. 1. Bilingual ed. Trans. A. T. Murray. Cambridge, MA: Harvard University Press").

1

Avatars

res ardua vetustis novitatem dare, novis auctoritatem.

It is a difficult task to give novelty to what is old, authority to what is new.
Pliny, Naturalis historia

[A]unque el Mundo Nuevo ya no es nuevo sino viejo, según hay mucho dicho y escrito de él, todavía me parece que en alguna manera se tendrá esta Historia *por nueva.*

[A]lthough the New World is no longer new but old, as much has been said and written about it, I still think that in some way this History *will be seen as new.*
José de Acosta, Historia natural y moral de las Indias

Preliminaries

Despite the maturity that Europe ascribed to its own history, despite the novelty with which Europe tantalized its own imagination when thinking of the Americas, the Old and the New Worlds, as such, were born at the same time. When thinking about the European crafting of the idea of the New World, scholars tend to emphasize the "invention of America" without considering the equally invented character of the Old World. But the characterization of America as new also transformed the authority and *locus* that decreed such newness—Europe—into the necessary Old World through which the New became meaningful. That is to say, *mundus novus* could only exist in correlation to a *mundus vetus*. Hence the cataclysmic effect of the conception of these categories in the European version of the world: on both sides of the Atlantic, each continent acquired a whole new political and historical sense, a redefined meaning of past and future. Ironically, this transatlantic simultaneity also shaped the contours of a paradox that more directly affects Europe than America. The epic bard of the Finnish *Kalevala* sang of a similar event: like Väinämöinen, the hero who was born after gestating for 730 years in the womb of his mother the Ocean, the Old World was—from the moment of its birth—an aged, wrinkled newborn.[1]

In 1606, more than one hundred years after Columbus's arrival on the shores of Guanahani, the Dominican friar Gregorio García would pithily capture the tension in this paradox—the conceptual tension between "Old" and "New." In writing the prologue to his investigation into the peopling of the Indies, the *Origen de los indios del Nuevo Mundo* (*The Origin of the Indians of the New World*), García would reiterate, as Columbus and his successors had done, that everything was new when the Spaniards reached America. In particular, nature: "Aguas no uſadas, Aire nuevo, Cielo nunca viſto, Animales, i Aves peregrinas, Frutas, Iervas, i Plantas de ninguno eſcritas" (García ((1606) 1725) 1981: Proemio) ("Waters unused, new air, a sky never before seen, foreign animals and birds, fruits, herbs, and plants of which nothing had yet been written"). Tellingly, García's wide-ranging catalogue of newness avoids the repetition of the epithet "nuevo" by creatively resorting to synonyms, as though even rhetorical redundancy were impertinent in a world where everything is meant to be new. This desire for even stylistic newness is not insignificant, for these "unused waters," "the sky never seen before," and so on presuppose a European post-Columbian and never an indigenous pre-Columbian observer— one who could have, say, previously used those waters, seen that sky, and catalogued those plants. García's treatise presents itself as an investigation into the origins of the New World peoples, but it departs from a radical sense of newness that paradoxically implies the eradication of indigenous subjectivity.

But that aporia was not García's primary concern. More pressing was the fact that, while the novelty he describes was spectacular, it was also dangerous, for the sole existence of a world regarded as radically new elicited a series of questions that touched on delicate matters of faith. Father García begins his treatise by pondering these difficulties: for him, there was no question (there could not be without committing heresy) that biblical history was universal, that humanity was the offspring of Noah, and that all beasts were descendants of those rescued from the destruction of the Flood. How could there be, then, animals in the

---

[1] The relationship between Old World and New World comes from a tradition of previous *mundi novi*, rooted in biblical eschatologies and repeatedly invoked during European antiquity and the Middle Ages. For a detailed account of the trope of the "New World" before 1492, and its defining role in the hemispheric version inaugurated by Amerigo Vespucci, see Kadir 1992, Chapter 3.

Americas that did not exist in the Old World? How did the descendants of Noah manage to traverse the Atlantic and inhabit the Americas centuries before the arrival of Columbus? The peoples of the New World: where did they come from?

Questions like these are symptomatic of the ideological and epistemological uncertainty that shaped the phenomenon analyzed in this chapter: the role of Classical paradigms in the self-fashioning of the intellectuals who wrote about the novelties of the Americas. Since the infallible character of the Scriptures made biblical history impervious to questioning, García and his contemporaries, anxious for answers, would turn their attention to the alternative, secular sources of knowledge available: the literatures of ancient Greece and Rome. Yet this task would prove a complex one: despite the wide array of utopias, *oikoumenai* (or versions of the inhabited world), and ends of the world that Classical authors had confected (sometimes with astonishing meticulousness), there was no secular prescription of a phenomenon with the magnitude of this *mundus novus*.

The Americas thus appeared incommensurable to the European colonial gaze precisely because they demarcated a serious textual and conceptual lacuna in Classical archives—and it is in this sense that the Classics became instrumental for the invention of the Western hemisphere's newness. Indeed, as Franklin Pease indicates in his introduction to García's treatise, "la imagen de la *novedad* de las Indias para los escritores europeos del siglo XVI era, como bien anota [Antonello] Gerbi al referirse a Oviedo y Américo Vespucio, 'únicamente en el sentido que los antiguos no las conocieron'" (Pease 1981: xvii) ("the image of the *novelty* of the Indies for European writers of the sixteenth century, as [Antonello] Gerbi correctly notes when referring to Oviedo and Americo Vespucci, was 'only in the sense that the ancients were ignorant of them'"). Pease and Gerbi coincide on an issue that profoundly affects any consideration of the founding narratives of the New World: in epistemological terms, the Americas were new primarily as a consequence of their absence in Classical literature.[2]

Yet the fact that Classical authorities had not known of the Americas did not render the Classics obsolete or useless. Rather, the appearance of the New World in the imagination of Europe brought with it a whole new rush of Classical scholarship. Eager to understand what they considered to be

---

[2] Pease insists on the general reach of this phenomenon, remarking that for García and others "América representa un nuevo y muchas veces difícil universo, pleno de sorpresas, de riesgos y desafíos, que lo obligaban a replantear los conocimientos clásicos y renacentistas sobre el mundo y el hombre" ("America represents a new and often difficult universe, full of surprises, risks and challenges, which forced him to reformulate Classical and Renaissance knowledge about the world and man") (1981: xvii).

geographical oddities in the Americas, their singular flora and fauna, their strange peoples, and their bizarre languages and habits, sixteenth-century writers, already immersed in humanist learning, turned their attention avidly to Classical texts, scrutinizing even the most obscure works and authors in an attempt to find any argument or evidence useful for their conceptualization of the New World. This obsessive search for answers led to a meticulous rereading of Greco-Roman theories and scientific methods. Moreover, the New World scholars found in Classical authors the perfect models for their own intellectual performance, as the first lines of García's treatise illustrate:

> Aristóteles, Príncipe de los Filófofos Naturales, i Morales, dice en fu Metafífica, que todos los Hombres defean naturalmente faber, i à esto con apetito natural fe inclinan ... Movidos de aquefte fin, refieren las Hiftorias (según dice S. Hieronimo) que algunos rodearon muchas Provincias, i pafaron tempeftuosos Mares, con grande riefgo, i peligro de la vida, para faber algunas Ciencias. Afí Pitágoras pasó a los Memphiticos Adivinos, o Profetas. Afi Platón caminó a Egypto, a do eftaba aquel Filofofo Archita Tarentino, i llegó a la Región de Italia, que antiguamente fe llamó la Gran Grecia; Y quien era Maeftro, i poderofo, cuia doctrina refonaba por los Generales, i Teatros de Atenas, fe hiço Difcípulo, i Eftrangero, queriendo más aprender de otros agenas, i no conocidas cofas, con verguença, que fin ella enfeñar las fuias propias.
>
> García ((1606) 1725) 1981: Proemio

> Aristotle, prince of the natural and moral philosophers, says in his *Metaphysics* that all men naturally wish to learn, and are inclined thus with a natural appetite ... Prompted by this goal, the Histories tell us (according to S. Jerome) that some [of these men] traversed numerous provinces and crossed stormy seas, at great risk and in life-threatening danger, in order to learn certain sciences. Thus did Pythagoras go to visit the Seers or Prophets from Memphis. Thus did Plato travel to Egypt, where the philosopher Archytas of Tarentum lived, and arrived in the region of Italy, which was formerly known as Magna Graecia. And thus he who was previously a powerful teacher, whose doctrines resonated across the lecture halls and theaters of Athens, became a student and a stranger, wishing more to learn unknown and foreign things from others, and with humility, than to shamelessly teach his own.

After highlighting the humbling metamorphosis of great Classical professors into foreign students of the unknown, García parallels this image with the experience of learned European scholars in approaching the New World: "Esto mismo, me parece à mi, les ha sucedido à muchos Hombres Doctos, i Curiosos, que al principio fueron à las Indias Occidentales, i Nuevo Mundo; los quales, aunque en las cosas que en el Viejo ai, eran Sabios, en las de aquel Orbe eran ignorantes" (García ((1606) 1725) 1981: 3-4) ("It seems to me that the same happened to many learned and curious men, who initially went to the West Indies and the New World; and who, though wise in matters of the Old World, were ignorant in those of that other Orb"). Of course, this parallel strategically misses one point, for he does not contend that the "learned men" who came to the New World sought native versions of Archytas of Tarentum or the Seers of Memphis who could teach them new lessons. What he wishes to clarify is that the Spanish invasion was not just a matter of military conquest and religious conversion, but also a revolutionary form of scholarship. Along with soldiers arrived new avatars of Plato and Pythagoras who, renouncing their previous intellectual status, weathered the elements and faced the same dangers and toils as the conquistadors had, longing to acquire the knowledge that Plato and Pythagoras could never have achieved. This intellectual paradigm sets the stage for further iterations of the tension described in the epigraphs of this chapter: in considering the novelties of the Americas, *mundus novus* scholars had to be both new and old, or rather new and ancient, to vindicate the originality of their "discoveries" while simultaneously asserting their authority as New World embodiments of Classical sages.

My purpose in this chapter is to interrogate this complex phenomenon: the use of the Classics as a mechanism for bridging the ideologemes of the Old and the New Worlds, and the consequent shaping of foundational academic figures after Greco-Roman paradigms—that is, as New World avatars of Classical authorities. I began this line of inquiry a few years ago, in an essay that foregrounded El Inca Garcilaso de la Vega's strategic use of the Neoplatonic philosophical apparatus and the literary figure of Julius Caesar in the construction of his authorial persona—especially in the *Comentarios reales de los Incas* ("Royal Commentaries of the Incas").[3] Here I propose an expansion of my conclusions on El Inca by examining three other prominent instantiations of the projection of the Classical tradition onto the authors of the New World. I first examine the strategic adoption of Classical authority in the self-characterization of the Jesuit José de Acosta, author of the influential treatise *Historia natural y moral de las Indias* (1590). Initially written in Latin during his stay in Peru and New Spain, and self-translated after his return to Spain, the text consciously casts its author's itinerant presence in the Old and New Worlds as the dual embodiment of Aristotelian empiricism and Roman

---

[3] See Campos-Muñoz 2013.

naturalism. This compound self-characterization would eventually make its way into the reception of Acosta as a foundational figure in natural philosophy and sciences in the Americas. I approach the second and third cases in tandem, looking at Diego Mexía de Fernangil's *Primera parte* and *Segunda parte del Parnaso antártico* (1608 and 1619), as well as the *Primera Parte*'s famous poetic prologue "Discurso en loor de la poesía," composed by an anonymous author known as "Clarinda." The Classical impersonations in these cases are collaborative: while Mexía profits from the Roman poet Ovid's vicissitudes as an exile to define the New World as a troubled horizon that can only be navigated through poetry, Clarinda employs mythological imagery and the Classical structure of poetic catalogues to claim her self-appointed role of New Muse, and to validate that role in an imagined continuity between the literary histories of the Old and New Worlds.

By comparing markedly different textual practices—natural philosophy in Acosta, and translation and poetry in Mexía and Clarinda—this chapter illuminates the performative dimension of intellectual self-fashioning in the nascent academic communities of the New World and the role of the Classics not only as archive but also as source of intellectual identity. In the aftermath of the Conquest, the instrumentalization of the Classics in the early cultural production of the New and the Old Worlds ironically helped consolidate the idea of newness at the heart of the colonial polity. The avatar roles adopted by Acosta, Mexía, and "Clarinda" allow us to witness a process in which the Classics are repeatedly evoked in a transatlantic exchange that is not only geographical but also temporal, conceptual, rhetorical, and political.

Acosta, the Elder

The Jesuit missionary and naturalist José (or the Latinized Joseph) de Acosta arrived in the New World in 1571 and remained there until returning to Spain in 1587. His years in the Americas were divided between his duties as professor of theology in a number of colleges and his itinerant activities between New Spain and Peru. Author of three Latin treatises written after his missionary and scientific experiences in the New World, as well as a number of theological essays, his name would become a key reference in international intellectual circles after the publication of his most famous work, the *Historia natural y moral de las Indias* (Seville, 1590) ("Natural and Moral History of the Indies").

As Acosta explains to his readers, his *Historia* went through two main compositional stages. The first two books were originally written and published in Latin as *De natura Orbi Novis* ("On the Nature of the New World") in Seville in 1588, as a prelude and, according to him, "decoy" to attract readers to the other Latin title included in the volume: *De Procuranda Indorum Salute* ("On Providing for the Salvation of the Indians").[4] Shortly afterwards, however, Acosta translated his *De natura Orbi Novis* into Spanish and added five more books to complete the final version, which he then titled *Historia natural y moral de las Indias*. The result of these additions and editions was an encyclopedic study of the nature of the New World. The first four books describe, in analytical order, the geocentric system of the universe, the four elements composing the earth, the habitability of the Indies, and its flora, fauna, and minerals. The last three books, the "moral history" of the Indies, analyze in proto-anthropological fashion the cultural habits of Aztecs (Nahuas) and Incas—their religious, social, scientific, and administrative practices. Of these, the very last book provides a general account of the ancient Mexicans, from the pilgrimage of the seven tribes until the arrival of the Spaniards.

In a recent examination of the reception history of Acosta's work, particularly his *Historia*, Jorge Cañizares-Esguerra has remarked that studies of the Jesuit's treatise are extensive but primarily focused on the sections devoted to the "moral history" of Aztecs and Incas (the last three books) at the expense of the naturalist matter of the first four (2018: 189). One way to redirect our critical attention to Acosta's natural philosophy is to consider the foundations of his authorial voice, and that leads primarily to Classical sources. In effect, Acosta's position as an author is shaped through strategic references to his two preferred precursors: Aristotle and Pliny. While critics acknowledge the presence of these authors in Acosta's work, they typically do so to explain the sources and epistemological mindset of the Jesuit. Here, instead, I am interested in considering the role those Classical writers play in the fashioning of Acosta's own authorship and authority as a natural historian. Acosta's treatise is not particularly abundant in citations of Classical and biblical sources (when compared, for example, to Gregorio García), but among those he cites, the Greek philosopher and the Roman naturalist have particular preponderance, especially in the first four books of the *Historia*.

---

[4] O'Gorman estimates that Acosta wrote the initial version of *De natura Orbi Novis* circa 1581, about six or seven years before he departed from the Americas for Spain (xxvii). For an account of the connection between *De natura Orbi Nobis* and the missionary treatise *De Procuranda Indorum Salute*, and the former's role of "salsa para el gusto" (lit., "sauce for the taste," i.e., a decoy or lure), see Lopetegui 1942: 220–2.

Acosta uses these two ancient authors not only in relation to his observations of natural phenomena, but also to characterize the tension between Classical knowledge and the New World experience that he himself embodies. The simultaneous reliance on and emendation of Classical sources, the transit (conceptual and physical) between the Old and the New Worlds, and the composite and multilingual writing of the *Historia* are all dynamics that converge in Acosta's writerly authority, rendering his authorial self (to paraphrase Mikhail Bakhtin's well-known category) something of a shifting chronotope—a coordination of time and space that is, in reality, multiple times and spaces at once. I will argue here that Acosta's eventual canonization as a New World avatar of Pliny depends on these carefully crafted convergences.

A passage in Aristotle's *Rhetoric* states that, contrary to what some writers opine, the reputation or *ethos* of an author may well be the most important element in achieving persuasion.[5] It seems that Acosta took this point to heart, as he finds in the *ethos* of Aristotle himself a primary model. From the start, Acosta is clear in defining this predilection: while El Inca Garcilaso, for example, had embraced Plato's legacy through the Neoplatonic tradition, first through the exercise of translation and then through the projection of Rome on his study of the Incan Empire, Acosta, consistent with his Jesuit education, repeatedly declares his fondness for Aristotle, "el filósofo excelente" ("the excellent philosopher") ((1590) 1962: 29), over Plato, whom at a certain moment he qualifies as suspicious and flamboyant: "Yo, por decir verdad, no tengo tanta reverencia a Platón, por más que le llamen divino" ((1590) 1962: 59) ("To tell the truth, I do not have too much reverence for Plato, even though they call him divine"; López-Morillas 2002: 67).[6] Acosta had interiorized this empirical lesson during the process of becoming a Jesuit. As Thayne Ford points out, "[a]ccording to Aristotle's method ... understanding and knowledge [were] valid only so long as they correspond to sensory experience ... Aristotelian empiricism meant that the Jesuits should use their senses to observe and accumulate data in order to ascertain the final or first causes of the natural world" (1998: 23). Aristotle shaped the empirical standpoint for those Jesuits,

---

[5] "οὐ γάρ, ὥσπερ ἔνιοι τῶν τεχνολογούντων, οὐ τίθεμεν ἐν τῇ τέχνῃ καὶ τὴν ἐπιείκειαν τοῦ λέγοντος, ὡς οὐδὲν συμβαλλομένην πρὸς τὸ πιθανόν, ἀλλὰ σχεδὸν ὡς εἰπεῖν κυριωτάτην ἔχει πίστιν τὸ ἦθος" (*Rhetoric* 1356a) ("for it is not the case, as some writers of rhetorical treatises lay down in their 'Art,' that the worth of the orator in no way contributes to his powers of persuasion; on the contrary, moral character [ethos] so to say, constitutes the most effective means of proof"; Freese 1926: 17).

[6] Ford examines the role of Plato and Aristotle as epistemological and academic paradigms in the sixteenth century, emphasizing that the Jesuits' preference for Aristotle was unusual for the times (1998: 22).

who, like Acosta, were progressively achieving more and more importance in the Americas, not only as missionaries but also as scholars. We should think about the Aristotelian influence on Acosta, then, in terms that are methodological rather than simply citational. By adopting an empiricist approach in the *Historia*, Acosta validates his first-hand experiences of the New World and uses these in order to create his authorly *ethos*.

The first sections of the *Historia* exemplify this attitude. Though the authority of Aristotle is invoked throughout the book, Acosta takes his most emphatic stand with respect to the Philosopher in discussing the first subject of his treatise: the nature and habitability of the Southern hemisphere. The matter had been studied by ancient and contemporary scholars alike, but Acosta distinguishes his approach by emphasizing the locus of enunciation from which he commences his treatise: "Estuvieron tan lejos los antiguos de pensar que hubiese gentes en este Nuevo Mundo que muchos de ellos no quisieron creer que había tierra de esta parte, y lo que es más de maravillar, no faltó quien también negase haber acá este cielo que vemos" ((1590) 1962: 15) ("The ancients were so far from thinking that this New World was peopled that many of them refused to believe that there was any land in these regions; and, what is more surprising, there were even some who denied that these heavens that we behold exist here"; López-Morillas 2002: 13). Here "the ancients" are distant not only in temporal terms, but also on account of their geographical position in the Old World and their inability to observe the New. As a consequence, even the best philosophers conceived of the world as if it were a house, "en la cual el techo que la cubre sólo la rodea por lo alto y no la cerca por todas partes" ((1590) 1962: 15) ("in which the roof that covers it encircles only the upper part and does not surround it everywhere"; López-Morillas 2002: 13). What constituted an enigma for the best minds of antiquity, the shape of the world, is for Acosta a self-evident reality, but only insofar as such truth manifests itself over "here"—a "here" from which the nature of the world can be confirmed by simply looking at the sky. Symptomatically, Acosta's first sentence reinforces this deictic certainty three times: "this New World," "this part," and finally, "this sky that we see." The immediacy of the deixis goes to the heart of his empirical authority.

Predictably, the most notable exception to the limited ancient understandings of the world was, precisely, that of Aristotle, who conceived of the sky as circular—a view which, Acosta reminds the reader, was later condemned as contrary to the Scriptures ((1590) 1962: 16). Acosta, however, only brings up this precedent to underscore again his own perspective as an inhabitant of the New World, with a diction that almost renders his voice autochthonous:

Mas viniendo a nuestro propósito, no hay duda sino que lo que el Aristóteles y los demás peripatéticos, juntamente con los estoicos sintieron cuanto a ser el cielo todo de figura redonda y moverse circularmente y en torno, es puntualmente tanta verdad, *que la vemos con nuestros ojos los que vivimos en el Perú*, harto más manifiesta por la experiencia de lo que nos pudiera ser por cualquiera razón y demonstración filosófica.

(1590) 1962: 17; my emphasis

But to come to our purpose: there is no doubt that what Aristotle and the other Peripatetics believed, along with the Stoics, as to the whole heaven being round in shape and moving circularly in its course, is so patently true *that we who live in Peru see it with our own eyes*, and it is made even more manifest by experience than it could be through any philosophical argument or demonstration.

López-Morillas 2002: 16; my emphasis

Acosta insistently presents himself as part of the place he describes. From his empiricist standpoint, this is the kernel of his authority: his capacity to use the adverb "here." The foundation of Acosta's knowledge with respect to the Classics is his ability to produce an utterance whose verifiability was not possible for any of the great minds of antiquity—not even Aristotle, who, despite having "felt" that the sky was spherical, still concluded that the area closer to the equator was a "Torrid Zone," uninhabitably hot. Though in a concessionary tone—"Este es el parecer de Aristóteles, y cierto que apenas pudo alcanzar más la conjectura humana" ((1590) 1962: 33) ("This is the opinion of Aristotle, and truly human conjecture could scarcely achieve more"; López-Morillas 2002: 6)—Acosta clearly signals the Philosopher's error—due, again, to the fact that he could not live in or speak from the New World. Only his experience in the Americas gives Acosta the confidence to correct Aristotle, as he readily admits: "no me determino a contradecir a Aristóteles si no es en cosa muy cierta" ((1590) 1962: 82) ("I cannot bring myself to contradict Aristotle unless on some very obvious matter"; López-Morilla 2002: 94). These corrections, however, do not compromise his affinity with the Greek thinker. Rather, in refuting Aristotle on the basis of his experience in the Indies, Acosta is being rigorously Aristotelian.

Acosta's approach to the Americas through the lens of his favorite philosopher is thus intimately associated with his time in the New World, where the shape of the earth and the habitability of the supposed "Torrid Zone" are "very obvious matters" of lived experience. The locus of enunciation is so defining that, when Acosta resumes writing his *Historia* in Spain, he feels compelled to warn the reader of changes in the way references are phrased in the remaining chapters. These changes are, precisely, of a deitic nature: "[L]os dos libros precedentes ... hablan de las cosas de Indias como de cosas presentes ... Pero en los libros cinco siguientes, porque los hice en Europa, fue forzoso mudar el modo de hablar, y así trato en ellos las cosas de Indias como de tierras y cosas ausentes" ((1590) 1962: 86) ("The two preceding books ... speak of things of the Indies as things present ... But in the five subsequent books, because I wrote them in Europe, I had to change the mode of expression, and so in those books I deal with things of the Indies as with lands and things that are absent"; López-Morillas 2002: 98). The treatise's narrative style is altered to reflect the referential shift: from the description of the present vicinity to the description of a recollection from overseas. If in the opening books Acosta's voice shows a tension between Classical speculation and his own concrete experiences, his diction in the next books registers a different fluctuation, this time from the "presence" of natural history while in the New World, to the memory of that history from the Old—in his own words, "tierras y cosas ausentes" ("lands and things that are absent"). In spite of his dislike for Plato, the broken composition of the treatise ends up performing, from Books 3 to 5, a demiurgic act: the textual recreation, in the Old World, of the absent New.

But the translation and expansion of Acosta's original treatise will also magnify the symbolic importance of his other Classical model: Gaius Plinius Secundus, better known as Pliny the Elder, the famous Roman encyclopedist of the first century CE. Acosta draws this connection from the start, knowing well that a book titled *Historia natural y moral de las Indias* would inevitably resonate with the model he constantly cites, Pliny's *Naturalis historia*—characterized by Numa Broc in his study on Renaissance geography as "the *de facto* encyclopedia of the Renaissance" (quoted in Butzer 1992: 544). Acosta was not the first author to employ the formula "natural history" and the model of Pliny to consolidate his own authority. About half a century earlier, Gonzalo Fernández de Oviedo had invoked the same model in his polemical *Historia general y natural de las Indias* ("General and Natural History of the Indies"), whose first part was published in 1535. Sabine MacCormack and other scholars have thoroughly explored the adoption of a "Plinian" role in the composition of Oviedo's *Historia general*, whose contents and thematic organization not only benefited from the treatise of the Latin savant, but also explicitly attempted to surpass it.[7] But not much attention has been given to Pliny's rhetorical influence on Acosta's *Historia*

---

[7] MacCormack examines Oviedo's insistence on presenting himself as outperforming Pliny (2007: 146). For other aspects of the relationship between Oviedo and Pliny, see also Lupher 2003: Ch. 5, and Beckjord 2007: Ch. 2.

beyond acknowledging his citations and references to the Roman, or noting that, 150 years later, Benito Jerónimo Feijóo would proclaim Acosta the New World Pliny. But Pliny, like Aristotle, was also fundamental in the development of Acosta's authority.

Firstly, it is important to remember that the association between Pliny and the New World reaches back to Christopher Columbus himself. Even though he makes no direct reference to the Roman savant, we know that his exploratory expectations were shaped by reading an Italian translation of Pliny's *Naturalis historia*—whose pages, incidentally, contain in a marginal note one of the few extant cases in which Columbus appears to write in his native dialect.[8] It is also worth noting that the call for a Pliny who describes the newness of America is, literally, as old as the term "New World." Indeed, in his famous 1503 pamphlet, *Mundus novus*, Amerigo Vespucci remarks that the marvels of the New World largely surpassed those described by the Roman scholar, implicitly stating the necessity of a new naturalist account: "Et certe credo quod Plinius noster millesim[a]m partem non attigerit generis [animalium]" (quoted in Küpper 2003: 369) ("And I think that our Pliny did not manage to cover a thousandth of the animal species"). Vespucci's possessive phrasing, "Plinius noster" or "our Pliny," alludes to the perspective of a European intellectual class that had long appropriated the Roman naturalist into its own domain. The domestic possessive, moreover, also hints at the need for "Eorum Plinius," their Pliny, the Pliny of the New World—which is precisely how Acosta would be remembered by posterity.

It is in the fluctuation between New and Old that Acosta's appropriation of Pliny takes place. The change of titles in his treatise articulates this movement. From the first version of his project, *De natura Novi Orbis* ("On the Nature of the New World"), to the expanded version, *Historia natural y moral de las Indias*, Acosta shifts from the general Latin *natura* to the Spanish *Historia natural*, a title which, though vernacular, is consciously styled after the paradigmatic Latin encyclopedia of Pliny. The politics of readership embedded in the treatise shift accordingly. If the original intention of the brief *De natura* was to entice the curious reader into an exposition of evangelist tactics, the purpose of the Spanish translation and the significant expansions, the new prologue states, is to provide a record of the "treasures" that God allotted to the new territories of the Catholic monarchs. This is an important change in the way Acosta imagines the reception of his work. No longer strictly subordinated to the missionary aims of the Latin

---

[8] For this and other linguistic aspects of Columbus's writing, see West and Kling 1991: 20.

version, the expanded Spanish text has a more encyclopedic impetus and targets a much larger audience.

Furthermore, Acosta declares that his self-translation is undertaken "usando más de la licencia de autor que de la obligación de intérprete" ((1590) 1962: 14) ("using more license as a writer than the accuracy of a translator"; López Morillas 2002: 11). The title's change already exercises that license. As noted above, instead of providing a more literal translation of *De natura Orbi Novis*, Acosta retitles his work with *historia* in the Latin, Plinian sense: a natural history. There is no doubt that the association between the phrase *historia natural* and Pliny's treatise was unavoidable, as Sebastián de Covarrubias's 1611 *Tesoro de la lengua castellana o española* ("Thesaurus of the Castilian or Spanish Language") proves. While Covarrubias first defines *historia* as a narration of the past or of events witnessed, he concludes with this clarification: "Y Plinio intituló su gran obra a Vespasiano Emperador, debajo del titulo de Natural historia" (Covarrubias 1611: s.v. "historia") ("And Pliny titled his great work to Emperor Vespasian with the title of 'Natural History'"). It is through the legacy of Pliny that the term *historia* comes to be associated with the natural (rather than strictly human) world. This is why, in the prologue to his edition of Acosta's *Historia*, O'Gorman remarks that some have found the use of the term *historia* in the title to be an inappropriate extension of the term (1962: cxli).

"Natural history" as a Classical genre is thus instrumental in the redefinition of readership that attended the process of translating *De natura Novi Orbis* into the first chapters of the *Historia natural y moral de las Indias*. There is a series of inversions here: the original text didn't yet present itself as a reformulation of Pliny's work, but it was written in Latin; the newer version does aspire to fulfill a Plinian role, but, in trying to reach a larger audience, it does so in Spanish, and at the same time adopts the distinctly Classical title of *Historia natural*.

This tension between ancient and modern also surfaces in the first lines of the "Proemio al lector" (Proem to the Reader):

> Del Nuevo Mundo e Indias Occidentales han escrito muchos autores diversos libros y relaciones, en que dan noticia de las cosas nuevas y extrañas, que en aquellas partes se han descubierto, y de los hechos y sucesos de los españoles que las han conquistado y poblado. Mas hasta agora no he visto autor que trate de declarar las causas y razón de tales novedades y extrañezas de la naturaleza, ni que haga discurso e inquisición en esta parte, ni tampoco he topado libro cuyo argumento sea los hechos e historia de los mismos indios antiguos y naturales habitadores del Nuevo Orbe... Así que aunque el Nuevo Mundo ya no es nuevo sino viejo, según hay mucho dicho y escrito de él, todavía me parece que en

alguna manera se podrá tener esta Historia por nueva, por ser juntamente historia y en parte filosofía y por ser no sólo de las obras de la naturaleza, sino también de las del libre albedrío, que son los hechos y costumbres de hombres. Por donde me pareció darle nombre de *Historia Natural y Moral de las Indias*, abrazando con este intento ambas cosas.

(1590) 1962: 13-4

Many authors have written sundry books and reports in which they disclose the new and strange things that have been discovered in the New World and West Indies and the deeds and adventures of the Spaniards who conquered and settled those lands. But hitherto I have seen no author who deals with the causes and reasons for those new things and natural wonders, nor has any made a discourse and investigation of these matters; nor have I encountered any book whose matter consists of the deeds and history of those same ancient Indians and natural inhabitants of the New World ... Thus, although the New World is not new but old, for much has been said and written about it, I believe that this history may be considered new in some ways because it is both history and in part philosophy and because it deals not only with the works of nature but with problems of free will, which are the deeds and customs of men. That is why I gave it the name of *Natural and Moral History of the Indies*, including the two things in this aim.

López-Morillas 2002: 10-11

Readers of Garcilaso may recall that El Inca begins his *Comentarios reales* with an analogous clarification—about the "learned Spaniards" who had already written about the New World. But whereas Garcilaso emphasizes his position of native chronicler as the foundation of his authority, Acosta here claims to be supplementing the writing of his predecessors with the most important object of research according to Aristotle: the discussion of the *causes* or origins—in this case, of the natural world and people of the Americas.[9] Acosta insists (with some degree of hyperbole) on his foundational role in articulating such etiologies: "I have seen no author who deals with the causes and reasons for those new things and natural wonders." His focus on causes not only adheres to the prescriptions of the Aristotelian *Metaphysics*, but also rewrites the beginning of Pliny's

---

[9] In *Metaphysics*, Aristotle is clear in pointing out that the study of causes (etiology) is the supreme discipline, even more important than the knowledge of ends (teleology): "μάλιστα δ'ἐπιστητὰ τὰ πρῶτα καὶ τὰ αἴτια· διὰ ταῦτα καὶ ἐκ τούτων τἆλλα γνωρίζεται ἀλλ'οὐ ταῦτα διὰ τῶν ὑποκειμένων), ἀρχικωτάτη δὲ τῶν ἐπιστημῶν, καὶ μᾶλλον ἀρχικὴ τῆς ὑπηρετούσης, ἡ γνωρίζουσα τίνος ἕνεκέν ἐστι πρακτέον ἕκαστον·" (982b) ("[A]nd the things which are most knowable are first principles and causes; for it is through these and from these that other things come to be known, and not these through the particulars which fall under them. And that science is supreme, and superior to the subsidiary, which knows for what end each action is to be done"; Tredennick 1962: 12).

Naturalis historia, which employs a similar trope in its dedication to Titus, son and heir of the Emperor Vespatian:

> [materiae meae] iter est non trita auctoribus via nec qua peregrinari animus expetat: nemo apud nos qui idem temptaverit invenitur, nemo apud Graecos qui unos omnia ea tractaverit. magna pars studiorum amoenitates quaerimus, quae vero tractata ab aliis dicuntur inmensae subtilitatis obscuris rerum in tenebris premuntur. ante omnia attigenda quae Graeci τῆς ἐγκυκλίον παιδείας vocant; et tamen ignota aut incerta ingeniis facta, alia vero ita multis prodita ut in fastidium sint adducta. res ardua vetustis novitatem dare, novis auctoritatem, obsoletis nitorem, obscuris lucem, fastiditis gratiam, dubiis fidem, omnibus vero naturam et naturae sua omnia.
>
> Praefatio 14–15

> [T]he path [of my subject matter] is not a beaten highway of authorship, nor one in which the mind is eager to range: there is not one person to be found among us who has made the same venture, nor yet one among the Greeks who has tackled single-handed all departments of the subject. A large part of us seek agreeable fields of study, while topics of immeasurable abstruseness treated by others are drowned in the shadowy darkness of the theme. Deserving of treatment before all things are the subjects included by the Greeks under the name of "Encyclic Culture"; and nevertheless they are unknown, or have been obscured by subleties [sic], whereas other subjects have become stale. It is a difficult task to give novelty to what is old, authority to what is new, brilliance to the common-place, light to the obscure, attraction to the stale, credibility to the doubtful, but nature to all things and all her properties to nature.
>
> Rackham 1938: 9, 11

If Pliny's predecessors (the learned Greeks, practitioners of the "Encyclic Culture" or ἐγκύκλιος παιδεία that would engender, after a false reading of Pliny and others authors, the word "encyclopedia") had not been able to articulate the all-encompassing project of the *Naturalis historia*, Acosta's own precursors—among them, Oviedo—had likewise failed to undertake a study of causes in the New World. Acosta invokes the importance of etiology, then, to justify his role as primary *scriptor* of the Americas (interestingly, the epistemological newness that the Jesuit claims is not compromised by the fact that he actually uses sources other than his own experience—the manuscripts of the Mexican Jesuit Juan de Tovar outstanding among them).[10]

---

[10] On the decisive role of Tovar's research in the composition of the last sections of the *Historia natural* and the consequent controversy over Acosta's originality, see O'Gorman 1962 ("Prólogo," xii–xxiii; "Apéndice tercero"; and "Prólogo a la primera edición," ci–cviii).

If the Plinian overtones of Acosta's *Historia natural* were already clear in its original Latin version, by the time Acosta prepares the Spanish, largely expanded version of that initial *De natura Novi Orbi*, his anxiety to make the connections between his work and Classical scholarship conspicuous become much more palpable. So much so that Acosta begins the third book in Spanish with a new general prologue, as a transition to the extension of the original two books written in Latin. Let us examine this process. First, at the conclusion of the second book, Acosta incorporates a short paragraph titled "Advertencia al lector," a brief "Note to the Reader," standing by itself between the second and the third books. In it, Acosta warns the reader of the change from the indexical "here" to the distant "there" in the referential terminology of his treatise—as explained earlier, a transatlantic index, for the "here" of the first two books referring to the New World was possible while Acosta was writing them, whereas the translation and expansions, written in Europe, shifted the location. But as if this stand-alone notice were insufficient, Acosta also felt compelled to elaborate on the rationale of his project at the beginning of its third book, providing what amounts to a second general prologue in all but name. This time, Acosta not only implies a new locus of enunciation, but he also explicitly relates his overall project to its Classical models:

> La relación de cosas naturales de Indias, fuera de[l] común apetito [de querer saber cosas nuevas], tiene otro, por ser cosas remotas y que muchas de ellas o las más no atinaron con ellas los más aventajados maestros de esta facultad, entre los antiguos. Si de estas cosas naturales de Indias se hubiese de escribir copiosamente y con la especulación que cosas tan notables requieren, no dudo yo que se podría hacer obra que llegase a las de Plinio, Teofrasto y Aristóteles. Más ni yo hallo en mí ese caudal, ni aunque lo tuviera, fuera conforme a mi intento, que no pretendo más de ir apuntando algunas cosas naturales que estando en Indias vi y consideré, o las oí de personas muy fidedignas, y me parece no están en Europa tan comunmente sabidas.
>
> (1590) 1962: 87

> Apart from [the] common desire [of knowing new things], the description of natural things in the Indies responds to another desire because there are very remote things and among the ancients even the most learned masters of this subject did not discover many or even most of them. If it were possible to write fully about natural things in the Indies, and with the consideration required by such notable things, I do not doubt that a work could be written equal to those of Pliny, Theophrastus, and Aristotle. But I do not find that vein in myself, nor would it agree with my aim even if I did, for I intend only to take note of some

natural things that I saw and contemplated while in the Indies, or that I heard from very reliable persons and which I believe are not commonly known in Europe.

López-Morillas 2002: 100

It is no surprise that the authorial paradigms invoked here by Acosta are his intellectual heroes, Pliny and Aristotle (as well as Aristotle's prestigious successor, Theophrastus). And while he assumes a rhetorical modesty, calling his own intentions humble in comparison to those of his predecessors, he simultaneously casts himself as their New World avatar, observing and recording that which the ancients could never witness. The playful dictum (used as this chapter's epigraph) "aunque el Nuevo Mundo ya no es nuevo sino viejo, según hay mucho dicho y escrito de él" ("even though the New World is not new anymore, but old, since there is so much said and written about it"), which appears in the first general prologue of the *Historia natural,* is echoed in this second "preface," where it takes on an epistemological dimension: early modern scholarship serves as a supplement to ancient knowledge. But declaring that the New World is now old not only gestures toward the already flourishing tradition of *novomundista* narratives with which the Jesuit contrasts his own contribution; ironically, such a statement also describes with laconic precision the juxtaposition of the two traditions that his treatise is articulating: the old, Roman scholarship of the Imperial Age, and the new naturalist historiography of the Americas in the sixteenth century. The New World can be the Old, a preface admits another preface, American scholarship can also be Classical, and here is there. There is room, then, for an American avatar of the Old-World *Plinius noster—Plinius eorum,* the one of the Indies.

If, in the opinion of later authors, it was the sober Acosta and not the effervescent Oviedo who finally became the Pliny of the New World for whom Vespucci so longed, this might be due in part to the express avoidance of political history in the writings of both the Roman and the Jesuit. Indeed, despite the fact that both Pliny and Acosta dedicate their treatises to royal patrons, they generally evade direct engagement with the power struggles of their day. Pliny, after Nero's death in the year 68 CE, had witnessed the turbulent "year of the four Emperors" and the civil turmoil of the aristocratic struggle for power, whose aftermath was the triumph of Vespasian and the rise of the short-lived Flavian dynasty (69–96 CE). For his part, Acosta had arrived in Peru in 1572, in the early years of the administration of Francisco de Toledo, at the time of the defeat of the neo-Inca state at Vilcabamba, and when the bloody conflict between the Spanish conquistadors that took place two decades earlier was still a fresh memory. And yet neither author pays heed to these crucial events. Pliny removes the remarkable deeds of his patrons from the *Naturalis historia*, reserving for them a different treatise: "Vos quidem omnes," says Pliny to Titus, "patrem, te fratremque, diximus opere iusto, temporum nostrorum historiam orsi a fine Aufidii" (Praefatio 20) ("As for your sire, your brother and yourself, we have dealt with you all in a regular book, the *History of our own Times*, that begins where Aufidius's history leaves off"; Rakhman 1938: 21). Likewise, Acosta starts his proem by contrasting previous accounts of the Indies, which mainly focused on "los hechos y sucesos de los españoles que las han conquistado y poblado" ((1590) 1962: 13) ("the deeds and adventures of the Spaniards who conquered and settled those lands"; López-Morillas 2002: 8), with his own project, centered instead on "las causas y razones" ("the causes and reasons") of the wonders of the New World.[11] These focalizations rhetorically distinguish the Roman and the Jesuit naturalists from other types of historians (from Livy, Aufidius, or Josephus, in the case of Pliny; and from Cieza de León, Oviedo, or even Las Casas, in the case of Acosta).

In accordance with Acosta's expectations, his *Historia* promptly achieved wide reception in Europe, and multiple translations soon followed its first printing in Spanish.[12] Predictably, the critical response to Acosta's treatise soon included comparison with Pliny. The first documented instance of this analogy was drawn by French translator Robert Regnault. Having translated the *Historia* only eight years after the publication of the Spanish original, Regnault would note in his dedication to King Henry IV that Acosta was "[un] homme certainement docte et fort curieux" who "peut estre appelé l'Herodote et le Pline de ce monde nouvellement descouvert" (quoted in Courcelles 2003: 312) ("a man certainly erudite and quite curious [who] could be called the Herodotus and the Pliny of that world recently discovered"). This early endorsement would inaugurate the much-repeated equation of Acosta and Pliny. More than a century after the publication of the *Historia natural*, another renowned Spanish encyclopedist, Fr. Benito Jerónimo Feijóo, would devote a section of his *Teatro crítico universal* ("Universal Critical Theater") to celebrating Acosta as

---

[11] The exception to Acosta's evasion of contemporary politics occurs in the few chapters that describe the encounter between Moctezuma and Cortés during the first stages of the Spanish Conquest of Mexico. For a comment on this oddity, see O'Gorman 1962: xxvii–xxviii.

[12] In 1596, only six years after the original publication, Giovanni Paolo Galucci would translate it into Italian. In 1598, two new translations appeared, in Dutch and in French. The first English version was published in 1604. For further details on this quick international circulation, see Cañizares-Esguerra 2018.

the Spanish reincarnation of Pliny. Echoing the formulation of Vespucci about *Plinius noster*, Feijóo suggests that because Acosta wrote about a *New* World, he actually achieved more than his Roman predecessor:

> El padre Acosta es original en su género y se le pudiera llamar con propiedad *el Plinio del Nuevo Mundo*. En cierto modo más hizo que Plinio, pues éste se valió de las especias de muchos escritores que le precedieron, como él mismo confiesa. El padre Acosta no halló de quién transcribir cosa alguna. Añádase a favor del historiador español el tiento en creer y circunscripción en escribir, que faltó al romano.
>
> (1726–40) 1924: 226

> Father Acosta is original in his genre and could be properly called *the Pliny of the New World*. In a way, Acosta did more than Pliny, for the latter took advantage of the findings of previous writers, as he himself admits. Father Acosta had no one from whom to transcribe anything. Also to the advantage of the Spanish historian was a characteristic caution and circumspection in writing, qualities that the Roman author lacked.

In contrast to Pliny, says Feijóo, Acosta did not rely on previous authors to compose his treatise—he himself was the source of his own knowledge. And even though the "originality" of Acosta's *Historia natural* and its relation to previous sources would become one of the most contested issues in the years to come,[13] the characterization of the Jesuit as the New Pliny in the New World became a commonplace. Feijóo eulogizes Father Acosta in the course of a catalogue whose purpose is to redeem the good name of Spain at a time when "the glories" of Spanish scholarship have been, according to Feijóo, unfairly underestimated. Through his foundational persona, Acosta furnishes an example ideally suited to a nationalist vindication. In the eyes of Feijóo, Acosta engenders *ex nihilo* the possibilities of the scientific tradition in the Americas; as the origin of a new naturalism in a New World, his work could not be deemed other than Classical.

In the complex process of composing the *Historia natural*, we see again and again that Acosta not only draws on the Classical world for citational authority, but that he consciously channels and dialogues with the ancients. The empiricist principles that Acosta learned from Aristotle serve to establish epistemological authority and even allow him to refute his predecessor; later, when translating his Latin treatise into Spanish, Acosta meticulously crafts his authorial persona

---

[13] See footnote 10.

in terms of another eminent Classical forerunner, the Roman naturalist Pliny. In both instances, we can identify an oscillatory logic that projects Acosta's narrative persona to a distant Classical authority and then brings it back to the immediacy of the present task. The treatise is written first in Latin, but then is translated into Spanish, yet retitled after the great Latin encyclopedia; in the first two books of the *Historia natural*, America is "here," while in the rest it is "there," yet the authority of the "here" is never compromised; Aristotle was wrong about the New World, but Acosta makes this point on the basis of his own empiricist formation. As Aristotelian avatar of Pliny, Acosta's authorial self-construction consolidates his place in the foundational narratives of the New World.

The Antarctic Ovid

While Father Acosta portrayed himself as a Classical authority on the natural history of the New World, the poets of the early colonial period were also exploring the adaptation of Classical paradigms in their literary endeavors and identities. Especially well known is the case of Alonso de Ercilla y Zúñiga, author of *La Araucana* (1569–89). In the spirit of Renaissance epic, this famous poem recovers motifs and tropes dating back to Homer, Virgil, Lucan, and Statius to depict the sixteenth-century confrontation between Spanish conquistadors and native Araucos.[14] Yet Ercilla was not, of course, a solitary figure. From very early on, lyric and epic writers found in the Americas fertile ground in which to rehearse ancient poetic practices.[15] Especially remarkable is the case of Diego Mexía de Fernangil, a Sevillian translator, poet, and bookseller who spent most of his life in the New World during the last decades of the sixteenth century and the early part of the seventeenth.[16] Mexía's case, examined at length here, provides an exemplary instance of how the New World would be conceptualized by a colonial poetic imagination defined by Classical paradigms.

Under the title *Primera parte del Parnaso antártico de obras amatorias* ("First Part of the Antarctic Parnassus of Works of Love"), Mexía collected a series of

---

[14] These Classical antecedents have to be understood, of course, along with the influence from medieval and other Renaissance epic poems—for Ercilla in particular, from Juan de Mena's *Laberinto de fortuna* (1444) and Ludovico Ariosto's *Orlando furioso* (1516–32).

[15] Some major studies of poetry in colonial Latin America include Hampe 1999; Kohut and Rose 2000; Coello 2001; Firbas 2008; Fernández et al. 2016; and Laird and Miller 2018.

[16] The first documented information about Mexía is his permission to enter the New World, dated in Seville on March 5, 1682 (Gil 2008: 68); he was probably a very young adult. The last document mentioning him, from Potosí, is dated February 7, 1625 (Gil 2008: 84–5). We can estimate, therefore, a life spanning from *c*.1565 to *c*.1630.

his own poetic translations, in Spanish hendecasyllables in *terza rima* o *rima incatenata* (the rhyme structure Dante invented for his *Commedia*), of most of the Roman poet Ovid's *Heroides*—a set of epistolary poems attributed mostly to female mythical characters addressing their lovers (Dido to Aeneas, Deianira to Hercules, Ariadne to Theseus, etc.). Additionally, Mexía translated the *Ibis*, a ferocious diatribe against an unnamed enemy, which Ovid wrote while in exile. Following the conventions of his time, Mexía also arranged the front matter for his book (dedication, proem, address to the reader, and congratulatory poems from his friends). This paratext is particularly special, as it became the stage for a crucial literary event in the Americas: the famous *Discurso en loor de la poesía* ("Discourse in Praise of Poetry"), an 808-verse vindication of poetry composed by an anonymous female poet often known as "Clarinda"—one of the earliest extant female voices in the literary history of the New World.

Documents show that the manuscript of the *Primera parte del Parnaso antártico* was sent from Lima to Seville in 1602 and eventually published there in 1608 (Gil 2008: 76). By 1617, Mexía had prepared the full manuscript of a *Segunda parte del Parnaso antártico*, qualified as *de divinos poemas* ("Second Part of the Antarctic Parnassus of Divine Poems"). This volume, instead of new translations, gathered a substantial collection of Mexía's original poetry, with 200 sonnets on the life of Christ and six long compositions on religious and philosophical matters (an epistolary biography of Mary, a poetic life of Saint Margaret of Antioch, a poetic praise of Saint Anne, a "memento mori" poem, and two substantial religious eclogues—one narrative and the other dialogic). But the manuscript of the *Segunda parte* was never published (and is currently held in the National Library of France). In the preface, Mexía mentions a *Tercera parte* fully finished, but this manuscript is lost.

Mexía and (to a lesser extent) Clarinda remained relatively obscure authors for a long time, but an important body of critical scholarship (almost exclusively in Spanish) has flourished around both writers in recent decades. The publication of a facsimile of the *Primera parte* in 1990 by Trinidad Barrera opened new avenues for critical inquiry. Clarinda, in particular, has received significant attention, with scholars examining her foundational role in the definition of a poetic system in the New World (Vélez-Sainz 2010); the importance of a female voice in colonial discourse (Chang-Rodríguez 1998 and 2011; Fernández 2017); her inscription in the tradition of *laudatio artium* or praise and defense of poetry (Rivers 1996; Fernández 2017); the question of her anonymity and the possible clues regarding her historical identity (Cornejo Polar and Mazzotti 2000; Perilli 2004–5; Vinatea 2012); and the literary strategies and implications of her engagement with Mexía

(Holloway 2013; Chang-Rodríguez 2003). The scholarship on Mexía has, in turn, mostly focused on his role as literary and cultural translator (Rose 1999; Gil 2008; Vélez-Sainz 2010), but we have also learned a great deal about his life thanks to a careful archival survey by Juan Gil (2008). Most of the criticism on Mexía has examined his *Primera parte*, with references to the *Segunda parte* that are sporadic or connected to Mexía's first volume, so we are still in need of major studies of the second volume—with the significant exception of Rodríguez Garrido's analysis of *El Dios Pan* ("The God Pan"), an eclogue with which Mexía closed his *Segunda parte* (Rodríguez Garrido 2011).

Across these studies, the parallels Mexía draws between his life and that of the Roman poet Ovid are always acknowledged. They are indeed impossible to ignore: from the proem to the *Primera parte*, titled "El autor a sus amigos" ("The Author to His Friends"), Mexía labors to present his experience in the New World, his literary interests, and his activity as a translator, as a vivid recreation of the life and works of the celebrated Publio Ovidius Naso. In fact, as Mexía's introductory account makes clear, these parallels gave rise to the translation itself. In 1596, Mexía recalls, the vessel in which he had embarked from Peru toward New Spain was assaulted by a violent tempest that almost shipwrecked it. After having lost all hope, the crew and Mexía himself barely managed to reach the shores of Sonsonate, El Salvador. Unwilling to test his luck one more time, Mexía decided to complete the rest of his trip to Mexico City by land. It is during this trip, described as an epic journey across the most inhospitable wilderness, that Mexía claims to have purchased, from a student in Sonsonate and "para matalotaje del efpiritu" ("for sustenance for my spirit"), a copy of Ovid's *Heroides*, which he translated on his way to Mexico City (Mexía (1608) 1990: 2r).[17] Mexía's adventures are thus framed as replicating Ovid's exile from Rome to the Black Sea outpost of Tomis, where the Roman was sent in the year 8 CE under the orders of the Emperor Augustus. Citing textual passages from Ovid's *Tristia* and *Ex Ponto*, both of which were written while in exile, Mexía not only recounts the difficult trip that led him, almost providentially, to encounter Ovid's *Heroides*, but also laments the "barbarian" life that he, like Ovid in Tomis, suffers in the New World. Mexía thus establishes the trope of the exiled poet as the foundation for an explicit biographical parallel that also serves as introduction to his rendering of Ovid's *Heroides*. The Sevillian presents himself, in sum, both as the itinerant translator and the living translation of the famous Roman poet.

---

[17] Barrera (1990) added a parallel pagination in brackets to her facsimile of Mexía's book. In this chapter, I follow the book's original folio notation.

Mexía's self-identification with Ovid is so blatant that it has been routinely noted by critical readers of his *Primera parte*. In fact, this phenomenon is the sole subject of an article by Bernat Castany Prado, who carefully examines the presence of Ovid in both Mexía's *Primera* and *Segunda parte* through the survey of abundant biographical, thematic, and formal parallels connecting both authors (Castany 2016). It has been clearly established, then, that Mexía is a full-fledged avatar of Ovid in the New World. I will contend, however, that some fundamental aspects of Mexía's Ovidian performance still need to be recalled—aspects which pertain, precisely, to memory and forgetfulness. In the course of his work as a poetic translator and writer, Mexía's Ovidian identity functions not only as an authorial device that allows him to reconstruct or re-member different episodes and experiences, but also as a way to strategically conceal or "forget" key social and political anxieties pertaining to life in the New World. This reading requires, then, paying attention to the obverse of Mexía's writing—to those things that are left unsaid and which are conspicuous only by their absence. The consideration of these omissions, I believe, provides the elements for a productive comparison with Clarinda—whose anonymity may not be unrelated to Mexía's own concealing drive. The comparative examination of these two key Classical avatars highlights, I will argue, a dynamic of additions and erasures constitutive of the foundational narratives of the New World.

Scholars have noticed that Mexía's activity as a translator is not merely linguistic or literary. Rather, it operates within the coordinates of *translatio studii et imperii*, the transferal of cultural values and political power typical of imperial and colonial occupation (Rose 1999: 397; Chang-Rodríguez 2011: 91; Vélez-Sainz 2010: 56). Indeed, as a major Classical author with a profound impact on European and especially Spanish humanists, Ovid served well the aspirations of Spain's geopolitical and ideological *translatio*.[18] But in addition to considering that general role, it must be noted that Mexía takes great pains in defining, time and again, his own understanding of his role as translator. A metatextual reflection on the act of translation occurs in the *Primera parte*'s prefatory address "El autor a sus amigos" ("The Author to his Friends"), where Mexía remarks on technical and stylistic aspects of his Spanish rendering of Ovid and admits that his many emendations and poetic liberties make him more an imitator than a translator (Mexía (1608) 1990: 3r).[19] But another reflection on the implications

---

[18] Ovid was immensely popular in medieval and early modern Spain, and editions and translations of his work circulated in colonial Peru (Gil 2008: 72–3). For a comprehensive history of Ovidian translations in Spanish, see Alatorre 1997.

[19] Regarding the phenomenon of *imitatio*, see Barrera 1990: 15 and Fernández 2017: 28.

of translating Ovid appears earlier, in the volume's dedication, where Mexía retrieves an anecdote from a life of Ovid composed by the Italian humanist Ercole Ciofano—a prominent biographer and commentator who, coincidentally, was born in Ovid's home town of Sulmona (Mexía (1608) 1990: Dedicatoria). Ciofano, Mexía explains, cites the legend of a golden reed-pen, allegedly found in the ruins of an ancient edifice and kept by Queen Isabella Jagiellon of Hungary, bearing the inscription *Ovidii Nasonis calamus* (Ovidius Naso's reed-pen). Mexía, who dedicates his book to Don Juan de Villela, *oidor* (judge) of the Royal *Audiencia* of Lima, comments on how this pen might have benefited his translation:

> Efta pluma, pues, quifiere yo (Señor) alcançar agora, afsi para con ella efplicar los fublimes concetos, q̃ ella mefma (guiada del Gallardo efpiritu de Ovidio) efcriviò en eftas fus epiftolas que yo mal traduzidas, a v.m. (como a fagrada ancora) confagro: como para poder con ella manifeftar al mundo antiguo, el grã teforo, q̃ efte nuevo alcança en tener a v.m.
>
> Mexía (1608) 1990: Dedicatoria

> Thus, I wish I could procure this pen now, both to use it to explain the sublime concepts that the pen itself, guided by the gallant soul of Ovid, wrote in these his epistles, which, albeit badly translated, I dedicate to you as my sacred anchor; and to manifest with it to the ancient world the great treasure that this new one has in the person of Your Excellency.

By fantasizing about holding Ovid's legendary pen, Mexia both seeks to assimilate the Roman's genius and submit to "the ancient world" the anachronistic example of a New World judge—Villela, his addressee. Mexía continues, "quando eftas Epiftolas no merecieren el nombre de Ovidianas, por fu umilde traduzion, fe les debe el de Criftianas, por la oneftidad, i moral dotrina con que las é traduzido" (Mexía (1608) 1990: Dedicatoria) ("though these Epistles may not deserve the title of Ovidian, due to their humble translation, they do merit that of Christian for the honesty and moral doctrine with which I translated them"). This Christian piety notwithstanding, Mexía admits his apprehension about submitting his translations to Spain: "Confieffo mi temeridad, en embiarlas a Efpaña a imprimir: Mas es jufto, que fe entienda, que aviendo ella con tanta gloria paffado fus colunas, con las armas, de los limites, q̃ les puso Alcides, también con ellas passò las ciencias, i buenas artes, en las cuales florecen con eminencia en eftos Reynos muchos ecelentes fugetos" (Mexía (1608) 1990: Dedicatoria) ("I confess my audacity in sending them to Spain to be printed. Yet it is fair to make known that as she [Spain] crossed with her arms the limits that Alcides imposed on her, so too crossed the sciences and fine arts, in which many excellent individuals eminently flourish in these realms").

The dedication thus outlines the version of *translatio studii et imperii* Mexía adopts. First, the translation enacts a temporal migration, from the present to the past, whereby the juridical order of the New World is submitted to Classical antiquity for the purpose of exhibition and validation. Second, the translation performs a religious transferal, Christianizing Ovid's controversial poetry and therefore adapting it to the salvationist discourse of the colonial regime.[20] Third, the translation recalls the transatlantic movement crystallized in Charles V's version of the Pillars of Hercules,[21] a motion that was both military and cultural, and inverts the orientation by sending back the translation of Ovid from the New World to the Old. Notice the remarkably dense *translatio* of Mexía's adoption of Ovid: in a short account elaborated around the virtual axis of Ovid's *calamus*, the translator defines his work as the textual rendering of the juridical, chronological, religious, military, cultural, and geopolitical translation of colonial order in the New World.

The manifold translation invoked by Mexía is titanic; no wonder, then, that the material performance of this *translatio* is figured as an epic sea and land journey—that is to say, in the shape of a conquistador narrative. Mexía first clarifies that his trip was motivated largely by intellectual curiosity—he wanted to see New Spain. During the journey, near the Gulf of Papagayo (in present-day Costa Rica), a terrible storm assailed his ship, destroying the rigging and taking a sailor's life, so it seemed that the vessel and all of its cargo would sink (Mexía (1608) 1990: 1r–1v). When all hope was gone, and even the pilot had given up, the ship miraculously made it to a harbor in Sonsonate (Mexía (1608) 1990: 1v). Mexía determines not to risk another sea trip and traverses the distance between Sonsonate and Mexico City by land. This second stage of his trip would not be much easier, however: "Fueme dificultofifsimo el camino por fer de trecientas leguas, las aguas eran grandes, por fer tiempo de ivierno; el camino afpero, los lodos, i pātanos muchos: los rios peligrofos, i los pueblos mal proueidos, por el cocolifte i peftilencia general q̃ en los Indios avia" (Mexía (1608) 1990: 1v) ("The journey was extremely difficult, for the distance to cover was 300 *leguas*;[22] the rain was intense, for it was winter; the road was rough, marshes and swamps

---

[20] After the Council of Trent, Romance translations of Ovid's *Ars Amandi* were forbidden by the Church (Castany 2016: 64).
[21] See the Introduction.
[22] According to the old Spanish measuring system, a *legua* was equivalent to 5,572.7 meters, about 3.5 miles. Therefore, Mexía estimates that his journey totaled more than 1,000 miles.

abounded, rivers were dangerous, and due to the illness and general pestilence that affected the Indians, towns were poorly supplied"). All these calamities, experienced at sea and on land alike, constitute the uncanny context of Mexía's encounter with Ovid's *Heroides*:

> Eſtas razones, i caminar a paſſo faſtidioſo de requa (q̃ no es la menor en ſemejãtes calamidades) me obligaron (por engañar a mis proprios trabajos) a leer algunos ratos en vn libro de las Epiſtolas del uerdaderamente Poeta Ovidio Naſon, el qual para matalotaje del eſpiritu (por no hallar otro libro) cõprè a vn eſtudiante en Sonſonate. De leerlo uino el aficionarme a el: la aficiõ me obligò a repaſarlo; i lo uno i lo otro, i la ocioſidad me dierõ animo a traduzir con mi toſco, i totalmente ruſtico eſtilo, i lenguaje, algunas epiſtolas de las q̃ más me deleitarõ.
>
> Mexía (1608) 1990: 2r

> These reasons, and the tedious pace of my asinine mount (which was not the lesser of such calamities) forced me (to escape my own hardships) to read from time to time a book of the Epistles by the true poet Ovidius Naso, which, as sustenance for my spirit (not having found any other book), I bought from a student in Sonsonate. Reading the book made me fond of it, and such fondness forced me to reread it. And through both the fondness and the rereading, and with the spare time, I felt encouraged to translate, into my rough and wholly rustic style and language, some of the epistles which most delighted me.

There appears to be something fated in Mexía's random finding of the Roman poet's work—and that is clearly a point Mexía wants to convey. Indeed, while the passage explicitly describes his serendipitous encounter with the *Heroides*, Mexía's account of his strained journey resonates (given Ovid's status as the quintessential Classical exiled poet) with very different books. The first is the *Tristia* ("Sorrows"), a series of lamentations in which Ovid surveys different stages of his exilic experience (his departure from Rome, the harrowing journey to the Black Sea, and the hard life in the remote town of Tomis, amid the local Sarmatians and Geats); addresses the wife and friends (both loyal and treacherous) he left behind; examines the accusations against him that led to his exile; and begs gods and the emperor for forgiveness. The second book, the *Epistulae ex Ponto* ("Letters from the Pontus"), rehearses similar issues in epistolary form, some years into his exile. And so, though Mexía had stumbled upon the *Heroides*, he describes his own maritime and land journeys in a way that more closely echoes the *Tristia* and *Ex Ponto*. Almost inevitably, Mexía cites *Tristia* and *Ex Ponto* directly as well. However, something peculiar occurs in this process: when he finally quotes those two other Ovidian books, he does not choose passages that would echo his fraught journey (though he could have done so easily). Instead, he cites passages describing the period when the poet was already settled in Tomis and had been in exile for a prolonged period.

This shift, from arduous exilic journey to settled life in exile proper, is subtle but significant. It begins as a form of *captatio benevolentiae*, where Mexía claims that his translations were more a way to pass the time than an attempt at virtuosic display, as his difficult life has him occupied with more material concerns (Mexía (1608) 1990: 3v–4r). In this context, Mexía laments his sorry physical and spiritual condition:

> pues à veinte años q̃ navego mares, i camino tierras, por diferentes climas, alturas, i temperamẽtos, barbarizando entre barbaros, de fuerte q̃ me admiro como la lẽgua materna no fe me à olvidado, pues muchas veze [sic] me acontece, lo q̃ a Ovidio eftando defterrado entre los rufticos del Ponto lo cual finifica el en el quinto libro de Triftes, en la decia feptima, cuãdo dize q̃ queriẽdo hablar Romano, habla Sarmatico, cuyos verfos fon eftos:
>
> *Ipfe ego Romanus vates, ignofcite Mufae*
> *Sarmatico cogor plurima more loqui*
> *Et pudet, et fateor: iam defuetudine longa*
> *Vix fubeunt ipfi verba Latina mihi.*[23]
>
> Mexia (1608) 1990: 4r

for it is now twenty years since I have been navigating the oceans and wandering the land, through different climes, altitudes and weathers, barbarizing among the barbarians, to the extent that I marvel that I have not forgotten my mother tongue, since many a time it happened to me what occurred to Ovid when he was exiled among the rustics of the Pontus,[24] as he points out in the fifth book of the *Sorrows*,[25] seventh section, where he declares that, upon trying to speak in Latin, he ended up speaking in Sarmatian, and these are his verses:

> *I, the Roman bard—pardon, ye Muses!—am forced to utter most things in Sarmatian fashion. I admit it, though it shames me: now from long disuse Latin words with difficulty occur even to me!*
>
> Wheeler 239[26]

---

[23] The passage Mexía cites belongs to Ovid's *Tristia* 5.7.55–8. See also *Tristia* 5.12.57–8.
[24] A region on the southeastern coast of the Black Sea.
[25] The *Tristia* or "*Sorrows*," composed in 10 CE, is the poetic lamentation of Ovid after having been exiled to the Pontus.
[26] The translation of Mexía's citation is mine—this parenthetical citation refers only to the translation of Ovid's *Tristia* by Wheeler.

Just before this, Mexía had been describing the traumatic journey from Peru to New Spain. But here, the specificity of that trip transforms, quite suddenly, into a reflection on twenty years spent in the New World. This transition is significant: instead of presenting his life in Peru as the mercantile displacement from Spain to the Indies it effectively was, Mexía appears to rewrite his own life in the New World in a way that matches more precisely the trajectory drawn by the *Tristia* and the *Ex Ponto*, with a harrowing "exilic" journey as the direct preface to life in exile. The pejorative "barbarians," Mexía appears to say, applies not only to the indigenous peoples, but also to the class of European adventurers who came to the New World only to become rich—the so-called *Peruleros* (Mexía (1608) 1990: 4r–4v). In this regard, Castany has made a suggestive argument: since the barbarians in Ovid's books are actually divided between the "semi-barbaric" Sarmatians (who were linked to Greek settlers) and the fully barbaric Geats, Mexía, following suit, arranges a pair in which the *Peruleros* operate as the semi-barbarians and the local indigenous communities are fully barbaric (Castany 2016: 59–60). This equivalence performs the same gesture as Mexía's fragmented and selective account of his New World "exile": it preserves the Classical narrative of Ovid at the expense of simplifying the rather complex social fabric of the Americas—where Mexía had already spent most of his life.

Perhaps this also explains why Mexía never abandons the motif of the tempest as a prefatory device. It is indeed remarkable that, some fifteen years after he had shipped the manuscript of his *Primera parte* to Seville for publication, Mexía again returns to this device—this time in the *Segunda parte*'s dedication to Francisco de Borja y Aragón, Prince of Esquilache and 12th Viceroy of Peru:

> Vna de las Empreſas, o Symbolos (que el excelentiſſimo Señor don Iuan de Borja, padre de Vuestra Excelencia ... hizo imprimir en Praga ...) es la de la nao, que esta desaparexada en el puerto esperando que pase el tiempo riguroso del invierno, como lo significa su mote, diciendo DVM DESAEVIT hiems. Empreſa tan significativa, para el estado en que me hallo, que ninguna otra, ni otras muchas lo pudieran mexor dezir a V. Ex. Pues aviendo por espacio destos ocho años últimos corrido por mis negocios tan deshecha tormenta, que aviendo me llevado los mas de los bienes que llamã de fortuna, me recogi en esta Imperial Villa con mi familia como en seguro puerto esperando pasasse el rigor deste airado invierno: donde cõ quietud he gozado de los bienes del entendimiento sobre quien no tiene la Fortuna dominio ni imperio alguno. He desembuelto muchos autores Latinos, i he frequentado los umbrales del templo de las sagradas Muſas.
>
> Mexía 1617: fr–fv

One of the emblems or symbols (which the most excellent Don Juan de Borja, father of Your Excellency ... ordered to be printed in Prague ...) is that of the ship unrigged in a harbor, waiting for the rigorous winter weather to be over, as is declared in its motto, which reads "Until winter abates"—a formula so representative of my current condition that no other, one or many, could express it better to Your Excellency. These last eight years my businesses have been through such a blustery storm that, after I lost most of those goods that are called fortune, I retreated with my family to this Imperial Town [Potosí] as though to a safe haven, waiting for the rigor of this furious winter to be over. Here I have quietly enjoyed the wealth of understanding, over which Fortune has no ruling or empire whatsoever. I have scrutinized many Latin authors and frequented the gateway of the Sacred Muses' temple.

Mexía's artful rehearsal of the storm motif begins with a citation from the *Empresas morales* ("Moral Emblems"), a collection of emblems or allegorical illustrations, each accompanied by a prose explanation, that Juan de Borja, father of his dedicatee, composed and published in Prague in 1581. The emblem that Mexía cites (number 25 in Borja's volume) depicts a ship without sails near a harbor. The Latin phrase "dum desaevit hiems," borrowed from Virgil's *Aeneid* 4.52, decorates the illustration. Mexía reads the motto as declaring "Until winter abates" (following Borja's gloss, which provides that same translation in Spanish: "Hasta que amanse el invierno"; Borja 1581: 24v), even though the Virgilian line, due to a degree of ambiguity in the verb *desaevio*, could instead be translated (as has often been the case) as "While the winter rages." The former reading focuses on the end of the storm; the latter, on its duration. In choosing the first, Mexía makes clear that he harbors, in this *Segunda parte*, the hope of finally overcoming the long "winter" whose narration began in the preliminaries of the *Primera parte*. But that expectation does not wash away the memories of things lost—the desired fortune that led Mexía to the New World in the first place. This material reminder, however, is yet again sublimated into a lofty endeavor, as the stay in Potosí ceases to be a survivalist quarantine, becoming instead an intellectual retreat that allows the poet to read the ancients and frequent the temple of the Muses. Clearly, Mexía has not abandoned his penchant for aestheticizing his material predicaments through the Classics.

Likewise, after decades spent in the New World, Mexía remains obsessed with a particular Classical image: a cataclysmic storm followed by a long exile in a barbaric land. But now, instead of the inhospitable shores of Sonsonate, the tempest has propelled him to the heights of Potosí in the Altiplano. Despite the distinct character of his two first books, then—one a set of translations from

Ovid, the other a compilation of original Christian poetry—the second volume is indeed a *Segunda parte del Parnaso antártico* that is closely tied to the *Primera parte*, and not at all an attempt to undertake a different enterprise. Even though his second book is fully focused on religious poetry, the tropes related to exile, shaped in the *Primera parte* under the aegis of Ovid, remain fundamentally intact in the *Segunda parte*. Castany, who follows Mexía's justification for his translations in the *Primera parte* as an anticipation of his self-fashioning as a Christianized Ovid in the *Segunda parte*, has proposed an equivalence between the 200 religious sonnets and the Ovidian *Metamorphoses* and suggested that the pious content of the whole volume be read as a declaration of spiritual exile from the realm of God (Castany 2016: 68, 71–2, 80–1). I concur with these hypotheses, with the addition that they must be read in tandem with the persistent use of the tempest motif traced here. This consideration is important because the tempest trope's resilience evinces that Mexía's Ovidian drive cannot be reduced to a mere humanist adherence to a Classical paradigm. It also implies something more serious: Mexía's recalcitrant determination to continue representing the part of the world where he has already spent most of life as an uncultured, wild, and barbaric otherness.

It is worth noting that Mexía also employs these Ovidian tropes in order to aestheticize or gloss over his social and professional status as a merchant. For example, when describing his Peru–Mexico trip in the *Primera parte*, Mexía felt compelled to clarify that the journey was less a business trip than a matter of intellectual curiosity: "[n]avegando ... d'el Piru, a los Reinos de la Nueva Eſpaña (mas por curioſidad de verlos, que por el interés que por mis empleos pretendía)" (Mexía (1608) 1990: 1r) ("[s]ailing ... from Peru to the realms of New Spain (more due to my curiosity to see them than for the interests of my businesses)"). However, as Gil's investigation makes clear, Mexía *did* have important deals to conduct in New Spain: his Sevillian family had contacts with Mexican booksellers, and the Anglo-Spanish War (1595–1604), specifically the Capture of Cadiz in 1596, had a severe impact on his transatlantic business (Gil 2008: 73). Of all this, Mexía simply states, "me martirizò vna cõtinua melancolia, por la infeliciſsima nueua de Cadiz i quema de la flota Mexicana, de q̃ fue [sic] ſabidor en el principio d'eſte mi largo viaje" (Mexía (1608) 1990: 1v) ("I was tortured by a permanent melancholy, due to the extremely sad news about Cadiz and the burning of the Mexican fleet, which I learned about at the start of this my long trip"). The line reads superficially as the lamentation for the troubles of his homeland, but it turns out to be directly linked to his own concerns as a merchant. This hint at his professional life also affects the anecdote of his purchase of Ovid's *Heroides*, which he supposedly acquired "por no hallar otro libro" (Mexía (1608) 1990: 2r) ("because I found no other book"). The episode leaves us with the odd image of a bookless bookseller, rescued from his troubles in exile by the troubled, exiled Ovid. In the *Segunda parte*, in which the luckless Mexía transforms his forced relocation to Potosí into an intellectual retreat, the pattern continues: Mexía Classicalizes his professional life as a *Perulero*, bookseller, and merchant, the very material conditions of his intellectual work.

Gil has pointed out another significant omission: for all his years in America and his declared intellectual curiosity, Mexía appears remarkably uninterested in the history of the Incan Empire, instead casting their legacy into the category of "barbarian" (Gil 2008: 86–7). Rodríguez Garrido has qualified this assessment by detailing how the last piece by Mexía we know of, the eclogue *El Dios Pan*, alludes to the Incan rulers' fate as a lesson for Spain on the ephemerality of power and the need to follow the design of God to sustain that power—and in fact, the eclogue itself is the dramatization of a conversion from paganism to Christianity (Rodríguez Garrido 2011). However, Rodríguez Garrido also acknowledges that the indigenous presence in Mexía's poem is fully subordinated to the project of Christianization of the Andes, and that Mexía has no real interest in the Incas, not even in seeing them through the lens of European humanism (Rodríguez Garrido 2011: 308). Indeed, Mexía does not even toy with the possibility of transatlantic equivalences between Classical antiquity and the indigenous New World (in the way El Inca Garcilaso would, for example, equate Rome and the Incan Empire). And this is true throughout his extant works, which evince no serious interest in indigenous American societies. This is why it is hard to agree with Chang-Rodríguez's suggestion that the figure of the sun in the *Primera* and *Segunda parte del Parnaso antártico*, which decorates the inside cover of both texts as an allusion to Apollo or Delius, can be somehow connected to the divine Sun worshipped by the Incas (Chang-Rodríguez 1998: 101)—or even worse, taken as a symbol of European/American *mestizaje*, as Vélez-Sainz proposes (2010: 63). In reality, Mexía invokes indigenous American communities only a few times and in very formulaic terms, as barbarous, lost pagans, or candidates for conversion.

The storm motif that Mexía is so fond of turns out to be not merely Classical (as those of Odysseus, Aeneas, or Ovid), but also biblical, for it washes away, in a diluvian fashion, both the indigenous communities that always problematized the newness of the New World, and Mexía's own material and professional life as *Perulero*. The omissions and arrangements embedded in Mexía's literary project reveal a particular form of anxiety and cultural violence that Classical narratives enable in a critical moment of the colonial enterprise. But there is one final important omission—or rather, an inconsistency—that inflects Mexía's work: the identity of the other major writer of the *Primera parte*: Clarinda, the author of the *Discurso en loor de la poesía* ("Discourse on Praise of Poetry").

The Austral Muse

If Mexía glossed over certain matters in his writing, his most famous prologist went further, hiding her own identity. Vinatea has described the various social implications of Clarinda's anonymity—most suggestively, the resonances with the Limenian *tapadas* or veiled women (Vinatea 2012: 93-4). Much can be said about Clarinda's poetic performance (and in fact she has received significantly more attention than Mexía), but here I would like to focus on her interaction with Mexía. In his introduction to her poem, Mexía writes that Clarinda insisted on writing anonymously. He then justifies the inclusion of her poem as preface to his translations of Ovid's *Heroides*: "con el qual discurso (por ser una eroica dama) fue justo dar principio a nuestras eroicas epístolas" (Mexía (1608) 1990: 9r) ("as she is a heroic dame, it is fitting that we initiate our heroic epistles with her discourse"). Here Mexía establishes a textual parallel between Clarinda and the female voices permeating Ovid's *Heroides*. The anonymous writer, already veiled as nameless, is thus further concealed in her association with mythological women.

While Mexía adheres to Clarinda's preferences for anonymity, he does not shy away from highlighting that she was "una feñora principal deste Reino, mui verfada en la lengua Tofcana, i Portuguesa" (Mexía (1608) 1990: 9r) ("a prominent lady of this realm, very well versed in the Tuscan and Portuguese languages").[27] These qualities are indeed consistent with the poem's contents. In addition to allusions to Torquato Tasso and Dante (which appear to substantiate the author's alleged proficiency in Tuscan), the metrical pattern of the *Discurso* matches the one used by Mexía in his translations: the *rima terza* or *terzine incatenate* created by Dante in his *Commedia*. The linguistic versatility of the author of the *Discurso* is supplemented by the erudition the poem deploys in almost every stanza, in a fashion which, despite a few errors, is truly formidable.[28] In the course of 808

---

[27] These and other elements have led Vinatea to propose that Clarinda was in fact the Italian intellectual Catalina Maria Doria, who would have arrived in the New World in the late sixteenth or early seventeenth century (2012).

[28] For a study of errors and typos in Clarinda's poem, see Vinatea 2016.

hendecasyllables, often composed in an intricate and lengthy syntax (the initial sentence alone runs to twenty-one lines), the *Discurso* skillfully weaves, in the name of a defense of poetry, an extensive collection of mythical characters and motifs; a catalogue of Classical, medieval and contemporary poets from the Greek, Latin, Hebrew, Italian, Portuguese and Spanish traditions; allusions to sacred characters as practitioners of poetry (most notably the Virgin Mary, on account of her *Angelus*); a condemnation of Luther and Calvin; a justification of Classical and mythological imagery in Christian writing; and a list of local poets in the Americas—among many other subjects. References to the Classical world abound. Clarinda's initial address to Mexía exemplifies the typical features of this poem:

> i ô gran Mexia en tu eſplandor m'inflamo
> ſi tu eres mi Parnaſo, tu mi Apolo
> para qu' a Apolo, i al Parnaſo aclamo?
> Tu en el Piru, tu en el Auſtrino Polo
> eres el Delio, el Sol, el Febo ſanto
> ſé pues mi Febo, Sol, i Delio ſolo.
>
> 1608: vv. 40–5

> and, o great Mexía, in your splendor I am inflamed;
> if you are my Parnassus, my Apollo
> what do I claim for Apollo and Parnassus?
> You in Peru, you in the Austral Pole
> are the Delian, the Sun, the holy Phoebus;
> be then my only Phoebus, my Sun, and my Delian.

There is nothing more natural than equating Mexía, the author of a text titled *Parnaso antártico*, with Apollo (and it seems that "Delio" was indeed Mexía's nickname).[29] Yet the way in which the equivalence is structured here appears to anticipate stylistically what will soon become the baroque of the Indies. Through a play of substitutions ("You [and not the Classical Parnassus and Apollo] are my Parnassus, my Apollo") and heteronyms (Delian, Sun, Phoebus), one chiasmus per tercet renders the attributes and epithets of the Greek divinity a mirror of the characterization of Mexía. By labeling Mexía "my Parnassus," moreover, Clarinda even renders him a synecdoche of his own work, the *Parnaso antártico de obras amatorias*. Amidst the titles and epithets, the fourth verse prompts the reader to remember that the jurisdiction of this new Apollo is the southern hemisphere: "You in Peru, you in the Austral Pole."

---

[29] See Gil 2008: 70.

This hemispheric reminder (so evocative of Acosta's diction examined earlier) will recur throughout the prologue-poem. Instead of the Heliconian Muses, the *Discurso*'s author summons the "Ninfas d'el Sur" (1608: v. 22) (Southern Nymphs); in addition to their European counterparts, the goddess Fame is asked to celebrate the feats of Peruvian female poets: "i aun yo conozco en el Piru tres damas, / qu'an dado en la Poeſia eroica mueſtras" (1608: vv. 458–9) ("and I also know in Peru three ladies / who have shown in Poetry heroic compositions"); the spirit of Poetry, moreover, has settled in the Americas: "O Poetico eſpiritu, embiado / d el cielo empireo a nueſtra indina tierra" (1608: vv. 760–1) ("O Poetic spirit, sent / from Empyrean heaven to our unworthy land"). In fact, there is a triple ambiguity in this line: "[N]uestra indina tierra," could mean "our unworthy Earth" or "our unworthy land." In fact, it could also say "our Indian land" if we conjecture that the manuscript read "indiana" instead of "indina." In any case, for the purpose of highlighting the regional identity of the "Antarctic Parnassus," much more important than all these allusions is the singular list of local authors in the *Discurso*. This record may well be the *raison d'être* of the whole poem. The preamble to this catalogue bridges the tradition of pagan and Christian poets across the Atlantic with those living in the Americas:

> Como es poſsible yo celebre a aquellos,
>   que aſido tienen con la dieſtra mano
>   al rubio intonſo Dios de los cabellos?
> Pues nombrallos a todos es en vano,
>   por ſer los d'el Piru tantos, qu'eceden
>   a las flores que Tempe da en verano.
> Mas Muſa di d'algunos ya que pueden
>   contigo tanto, i alça mas la prima,
>   qu'ellos ſu pletro, i mano te conceden.
>
>   1608: vv. 511–19

> How is it possible that I might praise those
>   who hold with a dexterous hand
>   the fair locks of the untonsured God?
> Naming them all would be a vain attempt
>   for there are in Peru so many that they exceed
>   the flowers blossoming at Tempe in summertime.
> But, Muse, sing of some, since they do so much justice
>   to you, and raise even more your first chord,
>   as they yield their hand and plectrum before you.

In addition to the references to "Tempe" (the bucolic vale in Thessaly, so cherished by Apollo and the Muses), the "prima" (the most acute string of the lire) and the "ple[c]tro" (that ancient device used to tune and pluck the strings of the harp), the Classical impetus of these lines is clear in the central question itself. The *dubitatio* ("How is it possible that I might praise . . .") and the new invocation of the Muse, followed by the enumeration of poetic heroes, inscribe the composition within the tradition of poetic catalogues that dates back to the Homeric *Boeotia* or Catalogue of Ships (*Iliad* 2.484–877).[30] The subsequent list begins with the Limenian poet "doctor Figueroa" and goes on to praise (as they are named) the poets Duarte, Fernandez, Montesdoca, Sedeño, Pedro de Oña, Miguel Cabello, Juan de Salzedo Villandro, Ojeda, Gálvez, Juan de la Portilla, Gaspar Villarroel, Diego Ávalos, Luis Pérez Angel, Antonio Falco, Diego de Aguilar, Cristóval de Arriaga, and Pedro Carvajal. An entire generation of early colonial poets is in this way situated in the Classical *locus amoenus* of the Rimac river valley of Lima—a New World Tempe in the City of the Kings.

With a few exceptions (like Pedro de Oña), the poets included in this list are mostly obscure—to the point that more than one is known only for having been mentioned here.[31] Such obscurity is actually indicative of the purpose of the poem. By listing so many local authors in a *Discurso en loor de la Poesía* that abounds in references to the most prestigious names in the Western tradition, Clarinda seeks to incorporate a generation of unknown *Indiano* poets into the lineages of Virgil, Dante, and Camões. Thus, while the author of the *Discurso* is a poet, she is also, as enunciator of a transatlantic history of poetry, a source of poetic authority—in a word, a Muse. Not surprisingly, the sonnet Mexía dedicates to his kind and learned prologist, printed right after her *Discurso*, substantiates this role:

L' Antigua Grecia con fu voz divina
Celebra por Deidades d'Helicona
Nueue Poetifas, dandoles corona
De yedra, lauro, rofa, i clavellina;

---

[30] In the Homeric *Iliad*, the *dubitatio* is expressed through a beautiful hyperbole: "πληθὺν δ᾽ οὐκ ἂν ἐγὼ μυθήσομαι οὐδ᾽ ὀνομήνω, / οὐδ᾽ εἴ μοι δέκα μὲν γλῶσσαι, δέκα δὲ στόματ᾽ εἶεν, / φωνὴ δ᾽ ἄρρηκτος, χάλκεον δέ μοι ἦτορ ἐνείη, / εἰ μὴ Ὀλυμπιάδες Μοῦσαι Διὸς αἰγιόχοιο / θυγατέρες μνησαίαθ᾽ ὅσοι ὑπὸ Ἴλιον ἦλθον" (2.488–92) ("But the common folk I could not tell nor name, nay, not though ten tongues were mine and ten mouths and a voice unwearying, and though the heart within me were of bronze, did not the Muses of Olympus, daughters of Zeus that beareth the aegis, call to my mind all them that came beneath Ilios"; Murray 1999: 87). Also cf. Hesiod, *Theogony* 22–8 (in *Hesiod. Homeric Hymns. Epic Cycle. Homerica*).
[31] For details regarding the identities of the authors listed in Clarinda's relation, see Tauro 1948, section VI ("Poetas elusivos de la Academia Antártica") and Barrera 1990: 22–4.

> Traxila, Mirti, Annites, Miro[,] Erina,
> Noßida, i Telefila, que s'entona
> Con dulce canto, i Safo, a quien pregona
> Su Lesbos, como Tebas a Corina.
> Mas o matrona onor d'el mifmo Apolo,
> La clavellina, rofa, lauro, i yedra
> En todo figlo, folo a ti fe deve.
> Pues fiendo la Deidad de nuestro Polo
> T' adorarán en fu Parnafia piedra
> Las nueve mufas, i las Griegas nueve.
>
> Mexía (1608) 1990: 26r

> Ancient Greece with her divine voice
> Celebrates as divinities of Helicon
> Nine Poetesses, giving them a crown
> of ivy, laurel, rose and carnation,
> Praxilla, Myrtis, Anyte, Moero, Erinna,
> Nossis, and Telesilla, who intones
> with her sweet song, and Sappho, whom
> her Lesbos extols, as Thebes does with Corinna.
> But, o mother, honor of Apollo himself,
> the carnation, rose, laurel and ivy
> in any time are only due to you.
> For, being the Goddess of our Pole,
> the nine Muses, and the nine fair Greeks
> will worship you in their Parnassian stone.

Mexía, citing from an epigram by the ancient writer Antipater of Thessalonica,[32] retrieves the names of nine female Greek poets, most of them rather obscure, and conflates them all with the nine Muses in the figure of the anonymous author of the *Discurso*. The synthesis might seem bombastic, but in terms of the function of Clarinda in the project of *Parnaso antártico*, it is rhetorically accurate. After all, the interactions among Mexía, the translation of Ovid, the *Discurso*, and its anonymous author, as well as the index of poets included in it, are eminently specular: the *Discurso* commences with an invocation to a local Apollo who is also a wandering Ovid, who invokes *a* Muse who, being also an Ovidian heroine of the *Heroides*, invokes *the* Muse to accurately deliver a catalogue of poetic heroes, all this in the context of a New World that is recreating the Classical Mount Parnassus and its poetic fertility.

---

[32] *The Greek Anthology* XI.26.

So much simultaneity—so much translation indeed—was not incidental. As the story goes, Mexía and his Parnassian cohort were members of the obscure "Academia Antártica" (Antarctic Academy), one of the first intellectual communities in the Americas. What we know of the Academia is very little— hence the documentary relevance of the *Discurso*, which has been one of the most important sources for studying this institution. We know that a group of learned poets tried to differentiate their literary practice, what Mexía called "la verdadera Poesia" ("the true Poetry"), from the popular poetry of the time, "que de hazer coplas a bulto, antes no ai quien no lo professe" ("for there is no lack of those skilled in crafting rhymes by the dozen"; Mexía (1608) 1990: 4r). The Academia Antártica was thus an elite intellectual and social circle, and this further explains the mechanics of exhibition and omission characteristic of Mexía's work. Indeed, ties between Mexía and Clarinda, and their ties with the other members of the Academia Antártica, constitute the fabric of that intellectual community. Within this logic of reciprocity,[33] the hermetic and foundational anxiety of the poets of the *Parnaso antártico* is directly related to the appropriation of Classical imagery to depict their foundational aspirations, for only through their self-Classicalization does "poetry" become "true Poetry." No wonder, then, that Ovid is designated by Mexía as "the true Poet Ovidius Naso." Julio Vélez-Sainz errs when he remarks that Mexía "convierte sus traducciones en unos espacios verbales donde Nasón puede reposar para siempre" (2010: 60) ("transforms his translations into verbal spaces where Naso can rest for ever"). What Mexía does is exactly the opposite: in performing his wanderings, the Sevillian wakes Ovid from his Classical slumber. Clad in the authority of their New World Parnassus, the anonymous Clarinda literally fulfills the task of Muse, while Mexía becomes the Antarctic avatar of Ovid.

And yet, how is all this abundant talent compatible with Mexía's lamentation about the barbarism of the New World in which he is exiled, repeated in both of his prefaces? Did he conceive of the Academia Antártica as an extraordinary intellectual bubble? If so, why does he never mention the academy? Why this further omission? Aside from the remarks and sonnet dedicated to Clarinda, the

---

[33] Raquel Chang-Rodríguez has described the eulogistic reciprocity between Mexía and Clarinda as the "ecos andinos" ("Andean echoes") that characterized the attitude of the early intellectual community in the New World (see in particular "Ecos andinos," but also the Introduction in her edition of the *Discurso*; Chang-Rodríguez 2003). The relationship between translator and prologuist is thus presented not only in terms of a master and a disciple, but also—reflecting a gendered version of the Americas—as the dialogue between an Apollonian Spain and a Muse of the Indies respectively. Via the concept of a "literary system" coined by Pierre Bourdieu, Vélez-Sainz arrives at a similar conclusion (Vélez-Sainz 2010).

only reference he might have made to his fellow poets of the Academia Antártica is in the preface's title, "El autor a sus amigos" ("The Author to his Friends").[34] I would like to close with an argument that addresses these questions by bringing together the four authors examined in this chapter: Gregorio García, José de Acosta, Diego Mexía, and Clarinda.

Conclusions: Culling, Cultivation, and Culture

As the examples discussed above evince, the phenomenon of New World avatars in the early colonial period reformulates an old binary, already characteristic of pastoral poetry and its tropes (the garden, the Arcadia, the *locus amoenus*, etc.): the duality of the "natural" and the "cultural." Hence García's proclamation of the newness of the New World (cited at the start of this chapter): "Waters unused, new air, a sky never before seen, foreign animals and birds, fruits, herbs, and plants of which nothing had yet been written," a declaration that symptomatically transitions from the not-yet-perceived (a sky never seen) to the not-yet-scripted (flora and fauna "of which nothing had yet been written"). Acosta, following suit, organizes his monumental *Historia* by moving from "the works of nature" to "the deeds and customs of men." Mexía, much more histrionic, dramatizes his own movement from nature to culture by weathering storms and crossing the wilderness in order to find his American Ovid and his Andean Muses. Clarinda, a poetic pontifex, bridges old culture and new nature through her encyclopedic tour de force.

"Nature" and "culture" operate as forms of colonial coding because, just like the term "New World," they served to elide previous practices of signification and overdetermined the political value of those things they designated—and so, the habits and practices of people could be deemed either "natural" or "cultural," or both, in accordance with the ideological parameters and agenda of those who authorized themselves to make such distinctions. That is why the illusory opposition between "nature" and "culture" constantly vanishes in the context of the New World, for both categories, inextricably entangled, are easily exchangeable in the colonial occupation, rewriting, and juridical codification that was commonplace by the late sixteenth and early seventeenth centuries. Through the analogy of ancient traveling sages, García presents himself as the

---

[34] The third sonnet, by Pedro de Soto, "Catedrático de Filofofia en Mexico" (Professor of Philosophy in Mexico), was most likely composed during Mexía's stay in Mexico City after his difficult trip. See Gil 2008: 73–4.

herald of a New Pliny, a New Ovid, and a New Muse, and these in turn authorize themselves to determine the parameters of New World nature—the stage on which their role as culture heroes could be performed.

To illuminate this process, it is useful here to extrapolate a few ideas developed by Djelal Kadir in his analysis of the controversial sixteenth-century Italian philosopher Giordano Bruno. Kadir focuses on the ironic linkages between memory, memorialization, mnemonics, and forgetfulness embedded in the life and works of Bruno, whose philosophical and theological peripeteias turned to be deadly, as he was infamously burnt by the Inquisition in 1600 (while Mexía was working on his translation of Ovid, Clarinda was perhaps arriving in the New World, and Acosta's recently published *Historia* was being released in German, Dutch, and, for the second time, French). In examining Bruno's case, Kadir reminds us of the etymology of ἀλήθεια (*aletheia*), Greek for "truth." Composed of an alpha privative attached to *lethe*, "forgetfulness," the term suggests that "truth" is "non-forgetfulness," a process (epistemological and political) of salvaging, selection, and recuperation (Kadir 2011: 87). Kadir then advances the following caveat:

> [C]ulture is by definition a process of cultivation, which means, in effect, a series of adjudicatory and managerial processes that forge consensus, hallucinatory or otherwise, by clearing the ground through exclusions and inclusions, which is another way of recalling the Latin verb *colere*, "to clear the ground" for cultivation ... [*Colere*] is the same verb from which we derive the terms *culture* and *colonization*.
>
> Kadir 2011: 89

If culture is both culling and cultivation, a "clearing [of] the ground through exclusions and inclusions," we may be entitled to suspect that very few "cultural process" (in its ominous signification as procedural removal, cultivation, and growth) match the radical colonial erasure memorialized in the term *mundus novus*. As a matter of fact, the geopolitical term "discovery," colonial in its origin and consecrated by historiography even to this day, insinuates itself as a cognate of a certain version of *aletheia*, inasmuch as *lethe* (forgetfulness), related to the verb λανθάνω (*lanthano*, to escape notice), is also a form of "covering"—and of course, the prefix "dis-" of "dis-covery" plays the role of an alpha privative. "Discovery," as revelatory truth or colonial *aletheia* unveiled by the intellectual class that emerged from the violence of European occupation, was instrumental in the incorporation of America into European cultural imagination. Cultural foundation as the "growth" of discovery is precisely the task of the Classical avatars examined here, inasmuch as they come to complete the cultivation that follows the violent clearing of ground—which is epistemological but also material.

That seems to be why each of the authors discussed above, in their own way, recapitulates the narrative of discovery as a preface to their cultural intervention. García evokes the learned men who "traversed numerous provinces and crossed stormy seas;" Acosta, having no Classical or contemporary etiological account of the New World, finds himself across the Atlantic and claims the empirical authority that Aristotle could never acquire; Mexía, a fully-fledged translator even when he writes original poetry, perennially performs the stormy journey to the shores of poetic self-consecration; Clarinda, in the guise of a voyager crossing the universal history of poetry, reconstructs and displays the Old World within the New. This is also why the barren wilderness of the barbaric *Peruleros* and indigenous people that Mexía never mentions except to decry appear to be completely at odds with the abundant intellectual membership of the *Academia Antártica*—so plentiful, says Clarinda, that "[n]aming them all would be a vain attempt / for there are in Peru so many that they exceed / the flowers blossoming at Tempe in summertime." Their two characterizations of the intellectual agents in the New World, apparently contradictory (Mexía sees none, Clarinda a myriad), simply constitute different stages of the same cultural process of culling and cultivation we still call colonization. Hence their collaborative engagement. It is no wonder that Clarinda introduces the bountifulness of the *Academia Antártica* with Mexía's favorite trope:

> Porque dilatas el dificil curſo?
> porque arrojas al mar mi navecilla?
> mar que ni tiene puerto, ni recurſo.
>
> vv. 505–7

> Why do you widen the difficult course?
> Why do you toss to the sea my puny ship?
> A sea with no harbor nor refuge.

It is important to notice that the trajectory or *translatio* enacted by Clarinda's "puny ship" leads irrevocably to the *Antarctic*. Tauro has noticed that, just like Mexía's *Parnaso antártico* and the *Academia Antártica*, multiple texts from the late sixteenth and early seventeenth centuries explicitly referred to the South in their titles—as is the case with Miguel Cabello de Balboa's *Miscelánea Antártica* (1586), Diego de Ávalos y Figueroa's *Miscelánea Austral* (1602), and Juan de Miramontes y Zuázola's *Armas Antárticas* (1615). For Tauro, these allusions,

... parecía(n) resumir una promesa de novedad e interés, pero también acusaba(n) la proyección del espíritu hacia los problemas y secretos de la tierra. Y así como los hombres trasladados a América eran llamados "indianos," en España, cuando anunciaban su familiaridad con lo antártico, no hacían otra cosa que blasonar de su penetración en la realidad cuyo conocimiento incorporaban a la opinión universal.

15

... seemed to condense a promise of novelty and interest, but also revealed the projection of the spirit toward the problems and secrets of the land. And when those men who were called "indianos" for having been transferred to America announced in Spain their familiarity with "the Antarctic," what they were actually doing was flaunting their acquaintance with a reality whose knowledge they incorporated into universal opinion.

In the process of transferring and adapting the epistemological categories that formed history and reality in Europe (history and reality are in fact two of these categories, along with natural science, poetry, and divine revelation), the Old World and the New World, both engendered simultaneously, are engaged in a paradoxical process that is also simultaneous—one that is both specular and differential. This dynamic is, of course, constitutive of all translations: as in the case Acosta's self-translation or Mexía's version of Ovid, the textual reality and the authorial construct that supports it both face the dilemma of conveying the same in a different language. The Old and the New in the transatlantic World of the late sixteenth century constituted the geographical and conceptual loci where these ideological collisions occurred. The Classics, which are meant to be both ancient and flexible enough to be actualized according to the necessities of the present, provided an incomparable instrument to dramatize the tensions that our Classical avatars exemplify. These founding voices articulate a dialogue that is simultaneously Old, New, and Classical, without any contradiction. The Classics thus become a formidable device to negotiate the dilemmas of the New and the Old in the early years of the invention of America—and as such, they proved their enormous functionality as the platform for the rhetorical coordination of clearable nature and colonial culture.

Hence the importance of the "Antarctic." In a world that is ready to be found and founded, but whose foundations are rendered Classical, the South becomes the mechanism that harmonizes the diverse chronological tensions sparked by those processes of cultural translation. The reason is that, as the cases of García, Acosta, Mexía, and Clarinda constantly prove, the "cognates" through which the New World becomes translatable into the Old and vice versa abound. The axial difference, the turning point that resists being translated and requires being founded, is instead directional, deictic. It is the South: as *terra incognita* or unknown land that is becoming *terra cognitura* or a land about to be known, the Southern hemisphere creates an epistemological imminence which, although reflective of ancient sapience, is also seen as genuinely original, because of the absence (or misinterpretation) of the South in the Classics. The Antarctic is what actualizes the foundational role of the avatars of the Classical—it is what makes them both new and Classical, recent and primordial. This would be, perhaps, our authors' message to posterity: the Classical in the New World is the South.

2

Chorographers

[Nuestra materia es] tan cierta, y tan virtuosa quanto la de [la Eneida de Virgilio es] incierta y prophana; y [la] Fundacion [de Lima] tan gloriosa, y tan noblemente executada por vn santo designio, como la de Roma dudosa, y hecha por vn Asylo o Junta Tumultaria.

[Our subject is] as true and virtuous as that of [Virgil's Aeneid is] uncertain and profane; and [Lima's] foundation is as glorious and nobly executed by a holy plan, as that of Rome was doubtful, and conducted by a group of delinquent refugees, or a motley crew.

Pedro de Peralta y Barnuevo, *Lima fundada*

Preliminaries

On the morning of the January 6, 1590 the Spanish nobleman Don García Hurtado de Mendoza y Manrique, 4th marquis of Cañete, made his solemn entrance into Lima, the "City of the Kings" and capital of the Viceroyalty of Peru, to be officially acknowledged as its new viceroy.[1] Protocol required that Don García cross beneath a triumphal arch during the ceremony,[2] so the Limenian

---

[1] Lima was founded on January 18, 1535 by the Spanish conquistador Francisco Pizarro. The *Libros de Cabildo de Lima* (the official city council books) contain the proceedings related to the city's foundation. Those records state that the new urban settlement (in a valley known by the Spaniards as "Lima" on account of the coastal pronunciation of "Rimac," the local river) would henceforth be called the City of the Kings (Lee 1935: 14). The *Libros de Cabildo* don't state explicitly the reason for this designation, but it was long assumed to be a reference to the biblical Three Kings (the Magi or the Three Wise Men), whose feast was two weeks earlier, on January 6. In 1639, the historian Bernabé Cobo writes that there are two names for the city, explaining that *Lima* was the most common designation in the local parlance even though official documents preferred the title *Los Reyes* ((1639) 1882: 25). The use of Los Reyes as the official name of the city remained the practice for a long time: by the end of the seventeenth century, viceroys and other authorities would sign their letters to the Spanish monarch from "Los Reyes."

[2] The symbolic and juridical importance of the entry ceremony and triumphal arch in the investiture of the viceroy is discussed in detail by Alejandra Osorio (2008: 62).

nobles commissioned one Mateo de Leon, an Augustine friar, to design the structure. On the basis of Leon's design, local artisans built a temporary arch of slaked lime and adobe, decorated with elaborate pictorial and textual motifs, and installed it in the streets of Lima, to greet the new viceroy. We don't know whether Don García took the time to examine the arch closely or not, but the anonymous manuscript that records the reception gives us a precise sense of what he would have seen. A series of Classically inspired images, combined with Latin captions and epigrams painted on the pilasters, doors, and the archway, would likely have caught his attention. But one detail in particular would have certainly aroused his interest (and perhaps his surprise): on one of the doors he would have seen himself, depicted as an ancient knight, together with his late father—who had also been Viceroy of Peru, three decades earlier. A hexametric Latin line would have informed him that, in the picture, he was the Virgilian Aeneas—while his father was, of course, the illustrious Trojan elder, Anchises.

The reception of Don García, with all its Classical paraphernalia, gives us a useful window into a specific way of thinking about the New World and its intricate relationship to the Classical tradition—one that greatly differs from what we saw in the previous chapter. As argued there, the newness of the New World provided a remarkable opportunity for writers in the aftermath of the conquest to embrace the trope of *terra incognita* to justify and develop a foundational authority, and they often did so by strategically taking on attributes of key figures in the Greco-Roman tradition—by fashioning themselves, I have posited, as avatars of Classical authorities. But if that newness provided a rhetorical opportunity, it also created a critical problem: how could the New World "compete" with the monumental antiquity of the Old? This question would become especially pressing in circumstances such as the reception of Don García, in which New World urban centers had to symbolically and officially present themselves, so to speak, to the Old World. More generally, this issue would critically inflect the terms through which local panegyrists would celebrate their own cities—a form of chorography that, as some scholars have noted, became very popular in the early Americas.[3]

---

[3] On the basis of a study by Ana María Rey Sierra, Pedro Guibovich provides a very useful overview of the conventions of chorography, which included "una descripción geográfica de la ciudad, la narración de su fundación a medio camino entre la leyenda y la realidad, el retrato de sus habitantes y de sus costumbres, el inventario de los personajes ilustres de la villa, o la especificación de los productos típicos de la zona, todo ello en lenguaje hiperbólico" (2007: 361) ("a geographic description of the city, the account of its foundation midway between legend and reality, a picture of its residents and customs, an inventory of the prominent members of the community, or the characterization of the typical products of the region, all of it in a hyperbolic language").

To illuminate the tension between old and new in these efforts, this chapter interrogates the symbolic and political value of Classical imagery in the early and mid-colonial self-depictions of Lima. I will argue that the newness of the capital of the Viceroyalty of Peru propitiated a form of colonial apprehension, a "New World anxiety" that would frequently re-emerge throughout the formative stages of its urban history. After all, how could a city like Lima, founded very recently and yet endowed with extraordinary political and economic importance, compare to the venerable urban centers of Europe? Furthermore, what would be the role of the Classical tradition, so constitutive of the European sense of antiquity, in complicating the colonial capital's desire to reach a sense of greatness in line with that of Europe?

The early seventeenth-century manuscript *Yndias de Birreyes y Gouernadores del Pirú* ("Indies of the Viceroys and Governors of Peru"), the source of the narrative of Don García's reception (*c.* 1600–50: 112v–126v),[4] begins with a description of Lima that succinctly captures this transatlantic anxiety:

> Amanecio el sabado y dia de los Reies la cibdad dellos tan vistosa y bien adereçada q̃ parecía no auer mas q̃ desear por q̃ en Riquezas, galas, curiosidad, Templos, Religion, y edificios no ay otra en las Yndias q̃ ygualar se le pueda, en tantas cossas juntas. Por q̃ ay suertes de caualleros y damas mucho termino, hidalguia y hermosura, la qual naturaleza quiso a porfia poner lo ultimo de su caudal, favoreciendoles dios con larga y prodiga mano depositando en ella damas acauadissimas, todas juntas y cada vna de por si y con razon meritissimamente celebradas no por apasionadas, ni aficionadas lenguas, sino por justicia q̃ quiere dezir dar a cada qual lo suyo ...
>
> *c.* 1600–50: 112v–113r

At daybreak on Saturday, the feast day of the Kings, their city appeared so splendid and well adorned that it seemed there was nothing left to desire, for throughout the Indies there is no other [city] that can compare in wealth, elegance, novelty, temples, religion, and edifices. For it has lineages of gentlemen and ladies of great condition, nobility, and beauty. In their beauty nature has sought to exhaust its choicest supply, for God has favored them with largesse and

---

[4] The manuscript of *Yndias de Birreyes y Gouernadores del Pirú* ("Indies of the Viceroys and Governors of Peru") is marked MS 2835 in the catalogue of the National Library of Spain in Madrid. The register lists the text as *Discurso sobre Virreyes y Gobernadores del Perú* ("Discourse on the Viceroys and Governors of Peru"), and provides a full digital reproduction of the manuscript, which has been used in this study. The full manuscript is also available in an 1867 transcription by Luis Torres de Mendoza, who dates the handwriting to the early seventeenth century and, based on internal evidence, attributes the text to a certain Tristán Sánchez (1867: 212–13, n. 1). I have not been able to corroborate this attribution.

generosity, placing there [in the city] the most perfect ladies, each and every one of them, and all together, celebrated not by partial or biased tongues, but by justice that gives each one her due . . .

Something about this urban paean exceeds the merely laudatory. If the estimated date (*c.* 1600–50) of the manuscript is correct (and this seems likely, given its meticulous account of the events of 1590), our anonymous chronicler is contemporary with the authors discussed in the previous chapter. There is, nevertheless, a crucial rhetorical difference between those authors and this writer. While the former present themselves as authorities in the natural history and poetry of the New World, adopting Classical identities as devices through which to articulate their founding voices, the author of the passage transcribed above implicitly relegates the foundational moment to the distant past. Instead, the society of Lima is represented as culturally and materially mature. Rather than the images of an ancient civilization, a wild land, or a blank slate that characterize other contemporary accounts (like Mexía's trials and tribulations across Mesoamerica or García's exaltation of America's radical newness, seen in Chapter 1), the picture of Lima conveyed here is one of a new yet fully-grown city, with a sophisticated social fabric, an impressive architectural landscape, and wealth unrivalled across the Americas.

Perhaps the most thorough examination of such characterizations of the Peruvian capital has been Alejandra Osorio's 2008 *Inventing Lima*—a study of the cultural and material development of Lima as a "great city" and New World center. In this book, Osorio argues that the rise of Lima must be understood in terms of early modern and imperial urban ideals. Osorio, who locates those ideals in the 1588 treatise *Le cause della grandezza e magnificenza della città* by the Italian thinker Giovanni Botero, proposes that population, location, and economy were the main criteria for determining a city's greatness—a vision that in turn de-emphasized traditional conceptions of great *urbes* based on antiquity and physical dimensions (2008: 4–7). Osorio thus claims that colonial Lima is defined by a form of "urban baroque modernity," a reconfiguration of the ideals of the "great city" derived from the geopolitical demands of the imperial expansion of Spain (2008: 145–6). Osorio's analysis demonstrates the ways in which Lima transformed its newness into a functional structure for its urban development. However, the complex and often contradictory character of colonial self-imagination, I argue here, still leaves room for the obverse of Osorio's assessment: that Lima's newness was *also* a cumbersome and anxiogenic property.

The lavish characterization of Lima cited above already hints at that. After all, for all its claims to be a great city, by 1590 Lima was effectively a very young place, with barely half a century of colonial existence. As María Antonia Durán Montero explains in her architectural and urban history of colonial Lima, very few major civic buildings had been constructed by the end of the sixteenth century (1990: 36).[5] This is very much the image that Fray Diego de Ocaña, a Hieronymite from Extremadura who was in Lima from 1599 to 1601, conveys in his subsequent travel account. Fray Diego praises the development of religious institutional life in the city, but remarks that it is "muy falta de fiestas de plaza" ("very much lacking in public square celebrations"), and that, aside from the numerous churches, "en lo demás es como una aldea, en lo que es saberse cosas muy menudas que pasan en una calle, dentro de una hora se sabe por toda la ciudad" (2010: 150) ("in every other aspect it is like a village in which the little things that occur in one street are within the hour known by the whole city").

The *Yndias de Birreyes*'s report is therefore somewhat intriguing in its portrait of abundance. Its stress on Lima's affluence could be related to popular perceptions about the extraordinary natural wealth of the New World—as Osorio remarks, the two tropes about the natural wealth of Peru and the newness of Lima consistently appear in chroniclers' reports (2008: 7). By emphasizing Lima's opulence, the author of *Yndias de Birreyes* might be synthesizing these tropes, suggesting that the City of the Kings is reaching a degree of cultural wealth that matches Peru's transatlantic reputation as natural cornucopia. In fact, the passage would have worked especially well as a corrective to a common image that European readers had of American cities—as rudimentary towns in a fertile land (as Ocaña's description suggests), instead of the sophisticated urbs the chronicler is interested in portraying.[6] In listing "wealth, elegance, novelty, temples, religion, and edifices," the report does not omit any aspect of the picture: it strives to comprehend all the spheres of a great city: material, spiritual, and civil. The anxiety to valorize Lima as an urban center, then, gives rise to the superabundant description in *Yndias de Birreyes*.

Not all American cities, however, would be afflicted by this particular form of anxiety—or at least not to the same degree. Anna More (2013) has demonstrated,

---

[5] For a synoptic description of this early stage in the development, see Durán Montero 1990: 32–6.
[6] Many colonial-era *criollo* authors would seek to correct the long tradition of European misrepresentations and prejudices regarding American communities. A tradition of encomiastic prose and poetry devoted to the New World *criollo* communities and their cities sprouted as an emphatic (though not necessarily heeded) counter to those prejudices. For a recent examination of this phenomenon in relation to epic poetry about baroque Lima, see Mazzotti 2016.

for example, that colonial Mexican writers (notably Carlos de Sigüenza y Góngora, the focus of her study) resorted to what she calls a "Creole archive" in their self-representations as inhabitants of Mexico City in New Spain. This "archive" carefully assimilated the pre-Hispanic legacy into local narratives through a strategic metabolization of Amerindian artifacts, documents, and ruins—for example, the pre-Columbian city of Tenochtitlan, on whose ruins Mexico City was founded. In the case of Peru, El Inca Garcilaso could perform analogous historiographical acrobatics in his approach to Cuzco, not only because of the providentialist linkages he drew between the Incan and Spanish histories, but also because the imposing structures in the imperial capital of the Incas effectively became the foundations of colonial Spanish buildings. Indeed, Garcilaso, born in the aftermath of the conquest, personally remembers Cuzco not as an Incan but a colonial city—hence his chorographic reconstruction on the basis of Cuzco's most prominent Spanish residents.[7] Like Mexico City, Cuzco could adopt the dignity associated with urban antiquity and claim a continuum between its pre-Colombian and colonial histories. But unlike Mexico City, Cuzco was *not* the capital of the Viceroyalty of Peru, nor did it possess the rank of "head" of the kingdom—in fact, this became the point of contention in a well-documented legal battle between Lima and Cuzco.[8] The capital of Peru was Lima, a new city with no major pre-Hispanic antiquities to borrow for the purpose of its self-glorification.[9] Lima could not make claims about monumental ancestries, but if it aspired to find a place in the colonial urban imagery, it could not avoid the pressing need for a genealogical narrative or some sense of deep history for the construction of a diachronic identity.

Don García's arrival in 1590 was admirably suited to this purpose. Coincidentally born in the same year Lima was founded, 1535, Don García had had a chance to visit the capital briefly during his youth, when his father, Don Andrés Hurtado de Mendoza, became the 3rd Viceroy of Peru in 1556. The then twenty-one-year-old Don García remained in the twenty-one-year-old city for a short while before leaving for Chile, so he saw the capital of the new viceroyalty

---

[7] See Campos-Muñoz 2013: 135–6.
[8] See Osorio (2008: 35–55) for an overview of the dispute between Cuzco and Lima for the title of "head city." While the advocates of Cuzco invoked its dignity as royal city of the Incan Empire, Lima's defenders dismissed the Incas as a "defunct monarchy" (2008: 40), and made their case on the grounds of the political and religious primacy of Lima in the new Spanish imperial order.
[9] This is true even though Lima was very close to Pachacamac, an ancient oracle that flourished for hundreds of years until the sixteenth century. Epic poet Pedro de Peralta Barnuevo (discussed later in this chapter) imagined that the oracle ceased to speak the moment Christians arrived in the area.

in its initial layout. But his father's administration did not fare well; in fact, Don Andrés was forced to unceremoniously end his appointment as viceroy after a bitter controversy with local powers led to his deposition.[10] Don García's appointment decades later served, in this sense, as a form of genealogical reparation, and the authorities of Lima in charge of the reception seized on this. The imagery inscribed on the doors of the triumphal arch built for Don García, painstakingly described in *Yndias de Birreyes*, illustrates their understanding of its familial significance.[11]

The chronicle reports that the left door of the arch depicted Don García as a captain in full armor helping a royally clad damsel, a representation of Lima, to stand up from amid the ruins of edifices (an allusion to the earthquake of 1586). A Latin caption read, *Delia suscitas de Pulvere populum / et de cinere eregis* [sic] *Patrem*, a couplet that the verbose chronicler translates paraphrastically: "quiere desir Pidiendo la leuantase de su cayda con tu venida levantas esta cibdad de su poluo y caida y junto con esto Refrescas las Cenizas y memorias gloriosas de tu Padre muerto" (*c*. 1600–50: 113v) ("it means, asking to be raised after her fall, the city, by your arrival, is lifted from her dust and fall, and likewise, you revitalize the ashes and memories of your deceased father").[12] To that motif, the design also added a depiction of Don García's father, Don Andrés, who, though reposing in a sepulcher, could still communicate with his son by means of another Latin message, which he held in his hand: *Nunc magis adventu revocas me nate sepulcro / Regia quam lacrimis flens America suis*—translated by the chronicler as follows: "no menos o hijo mio despiertas tu mi memoria en estos Reinos con tu venida q̃ suele esta provinçia y quarta parte de el mundo llamada America despertarla y celebrarla con sus lagrimas llorando siempre mi perdida y tu

---

[10] For details about Don Andrés Hurtado de Mendoza's controversial administration, see Busto Duthurburu 1963: Chapter 4.
[11] For a detailed examination of the European tradition of triumphal arches and their complex adaptation in the New World, see Estabridis Cárdenas 2002: Chapter 6 (221–3 for a reference to Don García's reception); Ramos Sosa 1992: 48–70 (and 56–60 for his comments on Don García's reception). Other descriptions of Don García's triumphal arch (all on the basis of the *Yndias de Birreyes* manuscript) include Durán Montero 1990 and Lohmann Villena 1999: 124–6. For prominent instances of triumphal arches in Mexico, see Parodi 2008 and More 2013: Chapter 3.
[12] A more literal translation of *Delia suscitas de Pulvere populum / et de cinere erigis Patrem* would read "You raise the people from the Delian dust / and lift your father from the ashes." I have not been able to ascertain the meaning of the obscure clause *Delia pulvere*, "Delian dust" (none of the scholars who describe the arch remark on this strange adjective). The translation does not offer clarification. The chronicler incorrectly transcribes *eregis* instead of *erigis*, so perhaps the manuscript should have read *De Lima* (not "*Delia*") *suscitas de Pulvere populum*, but assuming such a serious error in the name of Lima in a text about that city seems very unlikely; furthermore, the resulting construction, with its two ablatives, would hardly be grammatical, and if so, unidiomatic (I thank Dr. Maya Feile Tomes for her kind assistance with this question).

ausencia" (*c.* 1600–50: 118r) ("no less, oh son of mine, do you awaken my memory in these kingdoms with your arrival, than does this province and fourth part of the world called America awaken and celebrate it [my memory] with tears, continually crying for my loss and your absence").[13] Mendoza the Elder thus presents himself as a talking memory awakened by the arrival of Mendoza the Younger.

The combination of allegories and Latin captions arranged on the left door suggest both Don García's filial devotion to his father the former viceroy and his chivalric devotion to the city of Lima. Furthermore, the older Mendoza, galvanized by the presence of his son, is able to make a post-mortem address. As the meeting point of father and son, Lima itself enables the impossible dialogue of the two Mendozas, and, in doing so, assimilates within its own historical narrative the intergenerational and dynastic dynamic the two viceroys represent. No wonder, then, that the complex temporal and transatlantic juxtapositions embedded in the images of the left door are mirrored and strengthened on the right door of the arch through a quintessentially Classical image—that of Aeneas, the hero of the famous Virgilian epic:

> en la otra Puerta estaua Pintado Eneas y su padre Anquises sobre sus hombros en lo alto estaua una letra q̃ dezia
>
> *Honor onusque Paternum*

q̃ dize honra y carga Paternal era de aqueste lugar esta letra

> Padre y honrra llevas junto
> carga bien auenturada
> mas Para ti reservada.

El Anquises tenia otra en la mano q̃ desia

> *Pietas filiorum*

Piedad y Respeto de hijo a padre.
El eneas q̃ representaua la persona de el Virrei yua caminando Por medio de la mar con Vna espada desnuda por baculo. El mote dezia

> *Aquae multe non Potuerunt*
> *extinguere Pristina.*

---

[13] A more literal translation would read, "Now you summon me back from the sepulcher in this royal city—more with your arrival, son, than weeping America [could do] with its tears" (I take *regia* as a shortened version of *regia civitate*, "in this royal city," given Lima's official name, the "City of the Kings").

q̃ dise ni la muchedumbre de las aguas que auia de por medio ni la distancia del lugar fueron bastantes para causar en mi algun oluido de este Reino al qual e llegado por el Valor de mi braço y virtud.

c. 1600–50: 118v–119r

On the other door Aeneas was painted with his father Anchises on his shoulders; above, a caption which said:

Honor onusque Paternum

which means "Honor and Paternal Burden." There should have been a caption that read:[14]

You carry both your father and your honor
a most blessed burden
but reserved only for you.

The Anchises figure held another caption in his hand that read:

Pietas filiorum

Piety and respect from son to father.
The figure of Aeneas that represented the viceroy appeared walking across the ocean with a naked sword as a staff. The caption read:

Aquae multe non Potuerunt
extinguere Pristina.

meaning: "not even the multitude of intervening waters nor the distance was enough to make me forget this kingdom, to which I have arrived by means of my strength and virtue."

The Classical image selected for the episode could not be more common. In fact, while we now associate Virgil with the famous portrayal of the Trojan Aeneas carrying Anchises on his back (*Aeneid* 2.721-4), the image was already conventional even in his time: it was used in a range of scenarios, from ancient Greek black figure pottery made centuries before Virgil's birth to North African coins minted by Julius Caesar. In the early modern period, representations of standard mythical episodes like this had promptly made their way into the New World—and specifically to the Viceroyalty of Peru—shortly after the Spanish

---

[14] Not all the images and captions originally planned for the arch were added to the actual monument, due to a lack of space. However, the anonymous chronicler often reports, as he does here, on those missing elements. For more about this, see pp. 82–83 below.

invasion, and not once but many times.[15] It is not surprising, then, that in the late sixteenth century, Aeneas and Anchises once again rehearsed their famous escape, this time crossing the Atlantic Ocean to attend the reception of Don García in Lima.

But if the Classical motif of Aeneas carrying Anchises was itself a commonplace, its association with the image on the left panel of the arch complicates its symbolic value. As explained above, the left door showed Don García helping a Lady Lima stand up while his deceased father greeted him from the grave. By itself a symbol of intergenerational loyalty, when placed next to the survivalist episode of Aeneas carrying Anchises, the image of the encounter between the living viceroy and his dead father recalls yet another episode of the *Aeneid*: the *descensus ad inferos* or quest into Hades through which Aeneas is reunited with the deceased Anchises. It is through this extraordinary meeting with his father that Aeneas learns about metempsychosis, or the transmigration of souls. In the propagandistic economy of the poem, the episode is especially important, as it allows Virgil to configure the rise of Rome as a reconstitution of the city of Troy, and Emperor Augustus's regime as the fulfillment of a prophecy. The rendering of Aeneas/Anchises as Don García/Don Andrés recasts the underworld interview of the Virgilian epic, and transfers its significance for Rome onto the city of Lima—a capital that also wishes to legitimize itself by means of a venerable ancestry.

Given the transatlantic context of the New World encounter, however, the axis of the hero's movement has to be strategically adjusted. Don Garcia, in his role of *figura Aeneae*, translates the original verticality of the Trojan's descent into a horizontal crossing—literally, as he appears (in a not-so-subtle Christological image) to be ambling across the ocean waters, with a sword as walking staff. In this manner, Lima takes on the exceptional role of a New World Elysium—the space in which past, present, and future collapse, metempsychosis is enabled, and *pietas* is both Limenian and transatlantic. These resonances are heightened when we consider details, recorded by the diligent anonymous chronicler, that were included in the original plans for the arch but did not make it to the final version due to insufficient space. One is especially relevant for this analysis: while describing and explaining the Virgilian motifs, the chronicler reveals that the right door of the arch was supposed to reproduce a line from the *Aeneid*,

---

[15] See Lohmann (1999) for a series of examples of these early colonial adaptations.

in which Aeneas first contemplates the splendid construction of Carthage. The verse in question, however, would have appeared with a slight alteration in the arch: "Miratur molem Gartia magalia quondam" (c. 1600–50: 120r) ("García marvels at the greatness [of the city's edifices], formerly small huts"). "Gartia," the Latinized name of Don García, substitutes—of course—the original "Aeneas" (*Aeneid* 1.421).

This virtual verse, ultimately not included in the final version, nevertheless contains the logic of the entire arch. No longer bound to the specificity of the reception of Don García, the arch becomes a transatlantic threshold through which Classical imperial motifs can be translated into American realities, and the significance of Lima as a New World urban center offers itself for the consideration of European metropolises. As Don García was returning to the city he saw in his youth, the Limenian citizens wanted to excite his admiring observation: *miratur Gartia*. They imagined the viceroy acknowledging the development of the City of the Kings by 1590 with the admiration and perhaps envy that Aeneas showed before the marvelous rise of Carthage. In fact, the Limenians could have argued that the Virgilian line was more appropriate for Don García than for Aeneas. After all, in the *Aeneid* the Trojan contemplates Carthage for the first time and didn't know how the Tyrian city looked originally (the huts mentioned as the original structures of the city were known by the poet, not the hero). By contrast, Don García, who had visited Lima for the first time thirty-four years earlier, could actually compare its former and present states— his *admiratio* would have reflected the contrast between his youthful recollections and his return. That was, at least, what the Limenians anticipated— and prescribed.

The Virgilian citation adopted by the Limenians who welcomed Don García is, in sum, an early yet clear sign of Lima's developing self-consciousness as a New World city with respect to the antiquity of European cities, and a primary example of the way the Classics could be used to translate and negotiate that anxiety. As Don García was returning to the New World after decades in Spain, whatever he had to say about the development of Lima in that time would have been a gauge of the image projected by the New World capital to Europe, and the Limenians wished to control that image. Latent in the use of Classical paraphernalia is a desire to assert a degree of cultural commensurability: the *criollo* denizens of Lima were showing themselves to be as acquainted as any other learned European with the Greco-Roman lingo of the Renaissance. But more important is their eagerness to assert a degree of urban commensurability:

their city was, despite its youth, quickly adopting the features of a great urbs, in a process that could be refracted through the figure of Aeneas, the founding father of Rome (paradigm for any city wishing to acquire world status). The lack of sufficient space in the arch to fit all the decorations planned in the original design ironically appears to replicate the brief period in which Lima had become a great city. These literary and ideological dynamics only grew stronger as time passed, since the newness of Lima became, paradoxically yet predictably, more burdensome as the city grew.

As this example illustrates, the study of Classical motifs in the characterization of colonial Lima goes well beyond the mere identification of cultural influences. They often illuminate the self-perception of colonial subjects, both in local and transatlantic terms. The critical task for those colonial subjects was that of creating the terms for a New World chorography, a portrayal of Lima as a site of cultural and historical wealth that would attain transatlantic urban prestige even without the antiquity associated with comparable European cities. The cases examined throughout this chapter respond to the same premise, inasmuch as they all constitute instantiations of New World anxiety in Lima, and the diligent attempts of its chorographers to negotiate that anxiety through the Classics. Even more specifically, all these cases develop the symbolic, rhetorical, and ideological affiliations between Lima and antiquity through the paradigmatic imperial poet Virgil and his magnum opus, *The Aeneid*.

First, I will discuss the Classicalization of Lima as a New World space by considering late seventeenth-century maps of its walls (built to protect the city from piracy), paying special attention to the linkages between New World imagination and the motifs from the *Aeneid* present in those maps. Second, I will consider Lima's Classicalization as the site of a New World language, examining the uncanny adaptation of Latin in the 1682 epic poem *Fundación y grandezas de la muy leal y noble ciudad de Lima* by the Limenian Jesuit Gregorio de Valdés, paying special attention to the Virgilian ancestry assigned to the poem by its editors. Finally, I will consider the continuity of Virgilian motifs in later colonial chorographies, looking briefly at two major eighteenth-century epic poems: José Antonio de Oviedo y Herrera's *Vida de Santa Rosa de Santa María* (1711), and Pedro de Peralta y Barnuevo's *Lima fundada* (1732). The conjunction of these cases distinctly illustrates the degree to which what I am calling here New World anxiety, already present in the 1590 reception of Don García, is by the eighteenth century truly constitutive of Lima's colonial self-representations—particularly those adopting Classical motifs.

The Borders of the New World: Pedro Nolasco Mere's Maps of the Walls of Lima

The history of Lima's physical borders sets the parameters of the city's conceptualization as a New World space. This approach takes us to the year 1685, almost a hundred years after the elaborate reception of Don García. At this point, Lima is one of the wealthiest cities of the Americas, and don Melchor de Navarra y Rocafull, Duke of Palata and 22nd Viceroy of Peru, is leading the ongoing project to erect the system of walls that would eventually surround the capital city. The project followed decades of intense debates about the need to protect Lima and its treasures against frequent pirate attacks on the Pacific coast, and the viceroy had invested his considerable energy and influence to justify, both in Lima and in Madrid, the contriving of the most expensive structure in the 150 years of the city's history.[16]

The task was neither simple nor uncontroversial. The question of the need to wall Lima had been debated by influential members of society time and again in the seventeenth century.[17] In fact, Limenian authorities and notables had, on several occasions, managed to reach a consensus for the construction of a wall system, only to be frustrated by dissenting voices at the highest levels of the colonial administration (most prominently by the government of Charles II in 1673, and then by the Viceroy-Archbishop, Melchor Liñán de Cisneros).[18] Despite this resistance, reports of pirate attacks periodically reignited the debate about walls. When Melchor de Navarra y Rocafull, the Duke of Palata, became Viceroy of Peru in 1681, the demands for a defensive wall echoed throughout the city. This is how, in his 1689 memorial, the Duke of Palata remembered the social and political context that motivated the construction:

> [Las] repetidas entradas de esquadras de enemigos en este mar hicieron perder la confianza en que reposaban los vecinos de esta ciudad, y se dispertó el cuidado y los discursos de ponerla en defensa con murallas y baluartes, sobre que desde entonces se escrivieron muchos papeles y se formaron plantas que se han

---

[16] For comprehensive historical and technical accounts of the walls project, see Lohmann 1964 and Burneo 2012.
[17] For an examination of accounts of the construction of the wall, see Lohmann 1964: 151–67 and Burneo 2012: 89–98.
[18] See Burneo 2012: 117–18.

> hallado el archibo; pero concluyendo todos los discursos en la dificultad de fortificar una ciudad que es el depósito de toda la plata que enriquece el orbe, se suspendian ... con que cessaron estos discursos y quedaron sepultados en el olbido por muchos años, asta que en el año de 1683 llegaron a esta ciudad las noticias de aver entrado y saqueado los piratas á la Veracruz en la Nueba España.
>
> Este lastimosso sucesso dispertó en todos los estados de esta ciudad aquellas antiguas ansias de assegurarse con la defensa de las murallas, y sin reparar el costo ni en lo grabosso de los medios que se pudiessen aplicar para la obra, se hablaba en ella por todo género de personas, y subió al pulpito la instancia con tanto esfuerzo, que en todos los sermos á que asistí por aquel tiempo no habia asunto que no se rodeasse para parar en fortalezas, torres y muros con lugares de Escriptura, y como si yo no deseasse lo mismo que daba á entender resistia para empeñarlos mas, me predicaban y se esforzaban á combertirme con tan públicas y sagradas exhortaciones.
>
> Navarra y Rocaful (1689) 1859: 366

The repeated arrival of enemy fleets in these waters made the residents of this city lose the security they used to have, and roused an interest in defending the city with walls and bastions, and since then many papers were written on the topic and plans were contrived—all of which are now in the archives. But since all the treatises agreed on the difficulty of fortifying a city that is also the storehouse of all the silver that enriches the world, the initiative was suspended ... and thus, treatises ceased to be written, and were relegated to oblivion for many years, until the year 1683, when the news that pirates had entered and sacked Veracruz in New Spain reached this city.

This sorrowful event awoke in all echelons of the city the old anxiety for safeguarding themselves with defensive walls, and so, in spite of the onerous costs and demanding measures required for the project, the matter came to be widely discussed among all sorts of people, even reaching the pulpit with so much zeal that, in every sermon I attended during that time, there was no theme that was not ultimately spun into a discussion about fortresses, towers, and walls, even with citations from the Scriptures, as if I did not wish the same thing (for they thought I resisted in order to incite them even further), and so they kept preaching and endeavoring to convert me with public and sacred exhortations.

The social pressure the Duke of Palata describes here is significant. When the viceroy finally overcame the fierce opposition to the project by powerful individuals —most especially his own predecessor, the Viceroy-Archbishop Melchor Liñán y Cisneros, who enjoyed direct correspondence with the Spanish

Crown[19]—it was due in large part to the growing panic reflected in this passage, a fear that would be renewed each time the residents of Lima heard further news about the assaults occurring on the coast of Chile, Panama, and other Spanish ports. The atmosphere strengthened the resolution of the Duke of Palata, and he devised a complex plan to tackle, against all odds, the considerable difficulties of raising the 120,000 pesos initially estimated for the project. According to Josephe de Mugaburu's *Diario de Lima*, the construction officially began on Friday, June 30, 1684 (1918: 150). The project was concluded in 1687— a remarkable feat, achieved in part through the constant pressure applied by the Duke.[20]

The erection of the walls was, in sum, a highly politicized event responding to specific local circumstances—the chronic news of pirate attacks, the position of Lima at the center of the flux of silver in the Spanish Empire, years of debates about the erection of military defenses, and the tremendous pressure the citizens were putting on the Duke. An awareness of all these pragmatic motivations allows us to better assess, by contrast, the singularities of the earliest pictorial representations of those walls. In 1685, about a year after the construction work began, a French Mercedarian friar named Pedro Nolasco Mere was completing a map depicting how Lima would look once the project was complete. While his illustration (and even more so a second one he created a few years later) has often been studied on account of its cartographic value, the decorative, artistic, and symbolic decisions made by Nolasco Mere have been largely overlooked. I will argue, however, that this iconic apparatus offers singular insights into Lima's Classical self-imagination, and therefore also merits critical examination.

Considering the difficulties of his life in the New World, one can only wonder how Nolasco Mere might have imagined his relationship to the city he would come to depict in 1685. Nolasco Mere had arrived in Lima from France in the early 1660s, where he later joined the Mercedarian order. Perhaps he then adopted the surname

---

[19] An examination of the *legajos* ("document bundles") containing the official correspondence between Limenian authorities and the Spanish Crown from 1681 to 1687 reveals that many of the letters focus on or at least mention the ferocious rivalry between the Duke of Palata as Viceroy of Peru and Liñán y Cisneros as former viceroy and current archbishop of Lima (see *Signaturas* Lima 81–Lima 87, Archivo General de Indias). There is, in fact, an entire file on a controversy over jurisdictional power concerning these two authorities (see *Signatura* Lima 296, Archivo General de Indias).

[20] The Duke proudly foregrounds the speed of this project in his memorial to the King, even calling it miraculous ((1689) 1859: 317). While the Duke presents the project as though it was concluded smoothly and without any difficulty, there are signs indicating the opposite. For example, Mugaburu notes that in 1686 workmen had to be conscripted from other projects to hurry the walls along (1918: 176).

"Nolasco" in tribute to his patron saint.[21] In 1672, a French invasion of the Low Countries precipitated a war between Spain and France (1672–8). Consequently, a 1674 viceregal decree ordered all Frenchmen in the Spanish colonies to be sent to prison. Nolasco Mere, who was on board a ship destined for France at the time, was detained in Panama, forced to return to Peru, and placed in custody for at least four years (Vargas Ugarte 1968: 292; Günther 1983: 9).[22] During his imprisonment in Lima, Nolasco Mere gained a reputation as an efficient illustrator and engraver, and so, in 1685, the Duke of Palata chose him to draw a prospective map of the walls, which would be included in a report for Charles II (Vargas Ugarte 1968: 293). In 1687, Nolasco prepared a second, more refined map, rehashing some of the elements of the 1685 version, but also adding many more details, adjusting the perspective, and correcting inconsistencies between the prospective design and the actual construction (see Figs. 2.1 and 2.2).[23] Some 150 copies of this second print were prepared, and, as had happened with the first illustration, the second map

[21] Rubén Vargas Ugarte estimates that Nolasco Mere became a Mercedarian in 1663, but he cites a legal appeal from 1678 in which Nolasco Mere claims to have been living in America for fifteen years, nine of which had been spent in the Mercedarian order—meaning that his ordination would have taken place around 1669 instead (1968: 292). Günther corrects the math, explaining that 1663 was the year Nolasco Mere arrived in Lima, and that his induction in the Mercedarian order occurred six years later (1983: 9). Medina calls him "Father Mere," suggesting (as Vargas Ugarte points out) that "Nolasco" was a later addition—a hypothesis compatible with his affiliation to the Mercedarians, whose founder and patron is Saint Pedro Nolasco (Medina 1904: lxxiii; Vargas Ugarte 1968: 292, n. 1).

[22] Günther indicates that Nolasco Mere's detention occurred in 1674, whereas Vargas Ugarte dates the episode to January of 1675.

[23] Father Pedro Nolasco Mere designed two prints of the new walls of the city of Lima. The first was made in 1685, when the construction was still at a very early stage. The second map was drawn in 1687, when construction had practically been completed. These dates appear in peripheral sections of the original prints (see Figs. 2.1 and 2.2). But the central images, the map grids, of both illustrations were subsequently reprinted in different publications that also altered the decorations around those grids. Thus, the 1688 publication, *La estrella de Lima convertida en sol sobre sus tres coronas* (a commemoration of the beatification of Toribio de Mogrovejo), reproduced only the 1685 map's urban grid, substituting Nolasco Mere's peripheral decorations with a series of religious motifs. Likewise, the 1748 *Relación histórica del viage a la América Meridional* by Antonio de Ulloa reproduced the 1687 map's urban grid alone, also removing Nolasco Mere's original surrounding decorations (and adding to the original design a new neighborhood, the Rimac district, across the river of the same name). This series of prints, reprints, adaptations, and alterations explains why there has been some confusion about the chronology of the original maps—a problem that even affected their cataloguing in the Archivo General de Indias. For example, both Medina (1904) and Vargas Ugarte (1968) seem to be aware of the existence of the 1685 map only, as they make no mention of the second. Günther mentions both of them, but dates both to 1685 (1983: 10). This was probably because he was working with subsequent adaptations that only conserved the central grids, and since Nolasco Mere included the dates of his maps in peripheral illustrations, none of those later versions recorded the original dates. A recent essay by Serrera and Elvás follows Günther and repeats the same dating mistake (2015: 86). Even the catalogue of the Archivo General de Indias had until recently dated both maps to 1687 (probably because they were once stored in the same file along with the 1687 letter from the Duke of Palata reporting the completion of the work), though an informal communication I had with AGI archivists might have facilitated a correction. In any case, the correct sequence—one map from 1685, the other one from 1687—has been properly acknowledged by other scholars, among them the former director of the Archivo General de Indias, Pedro Torres Lanzas (1902: 13); Fernando Chueca Goitia and Leopoldo Torres Balbas (1951: 290–1); Lohmann (1964: 203–4); and Ramos Sosa (1992: 66).

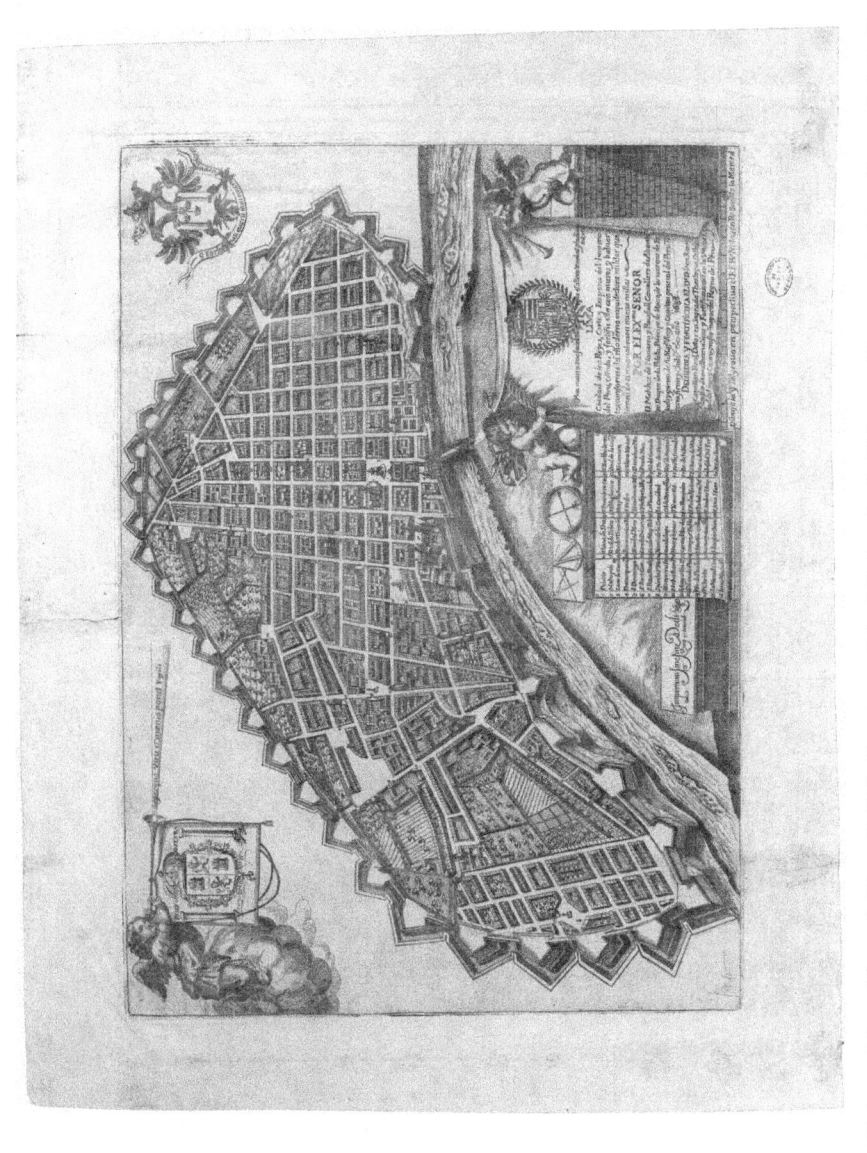

Fig. 2.1 Pedro Nolasco Mere, *Plano de Lima* (1685). Courtesy of the Ministerio de Cultura y Deporte. Archivo General de Indias. AGI, MP-PERU_CHILE,13BIS. Plano de la ciudad de lima y sus fortificaciones.

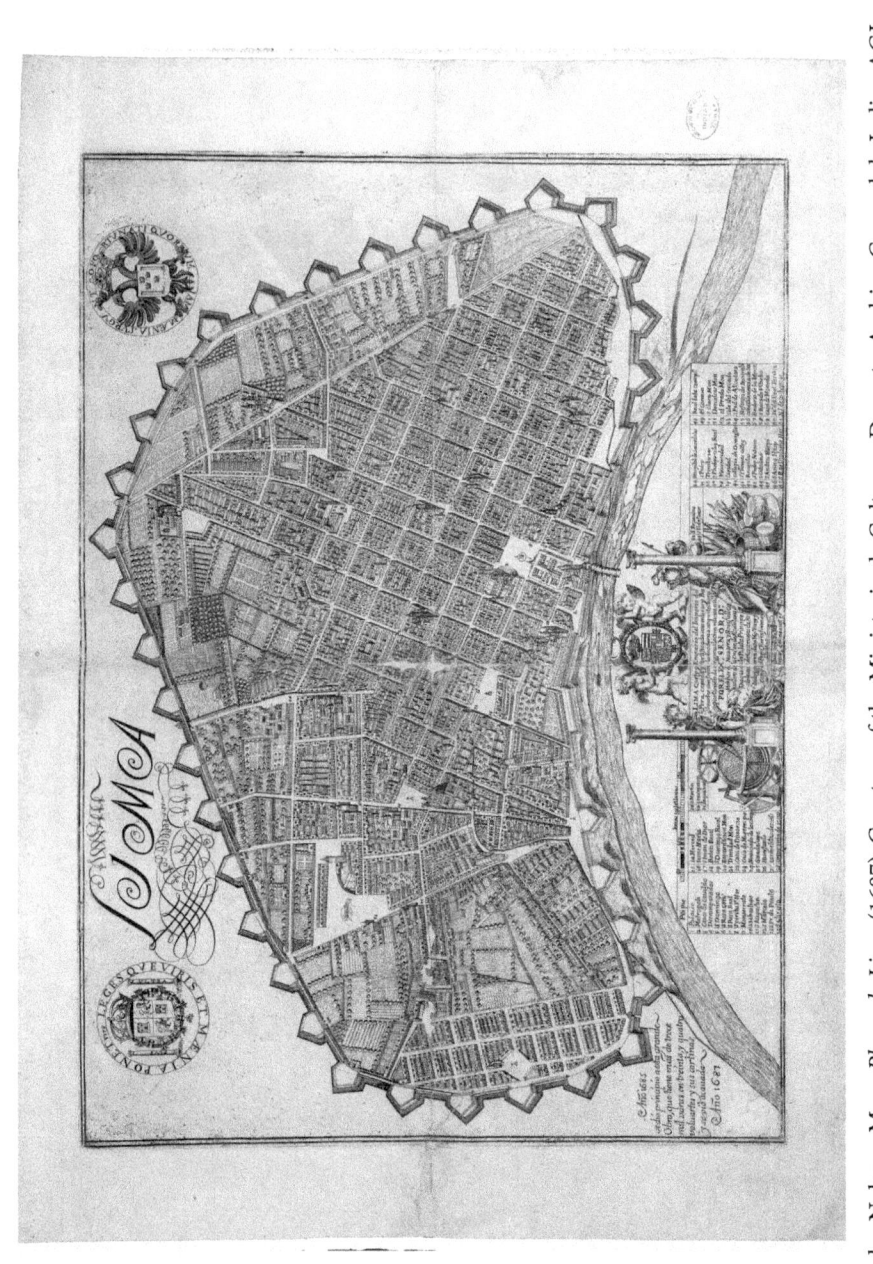

Fig. 2.2 Pedro Nolasco Mere, *Plano de Lima* (1687). Courtesy of the Ministerio de Cultura y Deporte. Archivo General de Indias. AGI, MP-PERU_CHILE,13. Plano de la ciudad de lima y sus fortificaciones.

was included in a letter to the king. This document, signed by the Duke of Palata on October 14, 1687, announced that all that was needed to complete the construction of the walls was the installation of doors, which would be accomplished by the time the monarch received the missive (Navarra y Rocaful 1687).

Scholars who have compared both maps usually favor the second version, remarking that the first fails to adequately represent the urban structure of the city. Günther, for example, argues that "desde el punto de vista de calidad artística y de valor documental, el último plano de Nolasco Mere, por su realismo y profusión de detalles, es superior al primero, cuyas manzanas, simples esquemas, no son sino un ocasional relleno intermuro" (1983: 10) ("from the point of view of artistic quality and documentary value, Nolasco Mere's second map is superior to the first, whose streets, mere outlines, are no more than an occasional intramural filling"). Serrera and Elvas agree (2015: 86). Lohmann remarks that the "imaginary" and "illusory" drawing of the walls in the first map in no way corresponded to the definitive edification (1964: 203). These modern disapprovals of the 1685 map may well echo a long history of objections. The Duke of Palata himself would acknowledge, in the 1687 letter accompanying the second map, that with the construction work finally over, "[h]ase hecho una nueba estampa mas bien explicada que la primera" (Navarra y Rocaful 1687) ("a new print has been made, more accurate than the first one").

But the mimetic and chorographic inadequacies of the first map are precisely what render it a privileged testament to the values and aspirations captured by Nolasco Mere. After all, the 1685 map, drawn at the early stage of a project that would only be completed years later, was neither a representation of a reality nor a technical design. As a proleptic statement, rather, the first illustration represents an expectation, the projection of an urban desire that is focused overwhelmingly on the dense walls themselves. Günther's characterization of that inner urban grid as an "occasional intramural filling" is suggestive, for the emphasis in Nolasco Mere's early map is clearly placed on the walls, not the city within them. One could argue, in fact, that the 1685 map is less a depiction of the city and its walls than a picture of the walls surrounding a city. This impression is apparent in a comparison between the two maps (Figs. 2.1 and 2.2 above). While the later one shows more attention to detail in the city's urban grid, the different perspective in the first map makes the walls the defining feature, especially along the riverbank. The formidable system of walls and bastions in the first map surrounds a de-emphasized urban layout, as though that "occasional intramural filling" were hurriedly designed, meant to suggest rather than depict the streets of Lima.

But this vague urban grid is not the only oddity of the first map. For an illustration intended to show the Spanish king a solution to the crisis of piracy, it is remarkable that, aside from a brief caption indicating that the walls' design followed "la moderna aquitectura militar" ("modern military architecture"), Nolasco Mere's first map makes no other allusion to the protective function of the walls. Looking at this first map, it seems that the defensive role of the construction, which the Duke of Palata repeatedly described as the main justification of the project, is not the primary motif of Nolasco Mere's illustration. The map includes no hint of battle, no allusions to the dangers that motivated the project, or even explicit references to the strength of the construction. Instead, in all their baroque glory, the walls are supplemented with other standard Renaissance ornaments: cherubim, the emblems of Spain and Lima, a few nautical icons (a compass, a sextant, etc.), a legend listing the edifices of the city, a banner indicating the names of the viceroy and the architect, and—here, perhaps, is the key detail—three citations in Latin, placed around the city's image. The result is a somewhat ironic illustration that, even though expressly created to flaunt a brand-new system of walls, highlights them without alluding to their defensive purpose. This omission extends to the three Latin citations, which also seem to overlook, as we will see below, the defensive concerns that so agitated the Duke of Palata and the Limenians who favored the construction.

The three Latin captions appear to follow a certain geometrical logic. In the upper-left corner, an angel holding a horn decorated with the arms of the Spanish Crown blasts the following statement: "Legesque viris et moenia ponet," Latin for "He will set up laws and walls for his people" (1.264); on the opposite, upper-right corner, the eagles of Lima's coat of arms hold in their talons a banner with the inscription "O fortunati quorum iam moenia surgunt," meaning "O happy those for whom the walls already rise" (1.437). Under the map, on the upper surface of a lonely pedestal drawn in the middle lower section of the illustration, a third Latin citation reads, "Imperium sine fine dedi," or "I have given [them] an empire without end" (1.279). The three sentences are complemented by the bibliographical reference "Virg. i" or "Virgil. i," and the one in the lower section adds "æneid." Like the Limenian reception of Don García Hurtado de Mendoza almost a century earlier, the three citations are again all extracted from the *Aeneid*—more specifically, from the first canto. Strategically placed in the upper-left and -right corners, and the middle lower section of the illustration, the Virgilian citations form a virtual triangle around the fortification (at the time, equally virtual) of the city. The triangulation of these three statements defines the walls not as an expression of military technology, but as a cultural and sociopolitical sign associated with legislation (*leges*), happiness (*fortunati*), and imperial expansion (*imperium sine fine*). Such a symbolic (rather than pragmatic) character is heightened when we consider the function of the Virgilian citations within the storyline of the *Aeneid*.

The first citation (in the upper-left corner) is the first of the numerous prophetic statements that populate the *Aeneid*. As the poem begins, a violent storm instigated by Juno forces Aeneas and his ships to beach on unknown shores. We soon find out that the land is Carthage. Above, in Olympus, Venus bitterly reproaches Jupiter for not fulfilling his promise of restoring the greatness of Troy through the lineage of her son Aeneas and the foundation of Rome (1.234–7). Jupiter smilingly explains that nothing has changed regarding Aeneas's fate. The god's reply provides the context of Nolasco Mere's first citation: "Hic tibi (fabor enim, quando haec te cura remordet, / longius et volvens fatorum arcana movebo) / bellum ingens geret Italia, populosque feroces / contundet, *legesque viris et moenia ponet*" (1.261–4) ("This thy son—for, since this care gnaws at thy heart, I will speak and, further unrolling the scroll of fate, will disclose its secrets—shall wage out a great war in Italy, shall crush proud nations, and *for his people shall set up laws and walls*"; Fairclough 1950: 259; my emphasis).[24] Jupiter's speech seems to give a straightforward answer to his daughter's grievance, but closer examination of the "legesque viris et moenia ponet" clause reveals a construction that combines two intricate rhetorical devices. The first, identified by Maurus Servius Honoratus in his famous fourth-century Latin commentary on the poem, is known as *hysteron proteron*, literally, "the latter earlier." Servius's postil on this line reads, "hysteroproteron in sensu; ante enim civitas, post iura conduntur" ("There is a *hysteron proteron* in the meaning [of this clause], for the city was established first, and then came the laws"; 1878: 97, commentary 264).[25] What Servius means is that, while the line places *leges* before *moenia*, the *moenia*, or walls (which, for Servius, means the city itself), should have been mentioned first, because the construction of walls would have preceded the establishment of *leges* or laws. A second trope is also identifiable in the same clause: the so-called *zeugma*, a figure of speech in which a single word affects two other words simultaneously, but in different senses.[26] The zeugma in this case is performed by

---

[24] Standard editions of the *Aeneid* transcribe this line as "moresque viris et moenia ponet." Evidently, Nolasco Mere was working with an edition with the variant *leges* (laws) instead of *mores* (mores, customs).

[25] In the same entry, Servius notes the variant *leges* for *mores*, favoring the latter.

[26] Consider, for example, the zeugma of the phrase "I called him a fool and myself a cab," where the single verb "to call" modifies two objects, "him" and "myself," simultaneously but in different senses.

the verb *ponet*, literally, "he put," which for *moenia* (walls) connotes "to erect," while for *leges* (laws) means "to arrange."[27] With characteristic semantic density, Virgil combines two different tropes in a single clause, yet the effect is more than a mere display of verbal acrobatics. The compound trope exemplifies the complex political dynamics often embedded in his style: the poet both merges (with the zeugma) the abstract creation of a legislative structure with the material construction of walls, and also subordinates (by dint of a *hysteron proteron*) the logical temporal precedence of edifices to the formal legal apparatus. These conceptual relocations and amalgamations are consistent with the political mythos of the poem. It is not an accident that the fratricide that signaled the mythic foundation of Rome happens precisely during the construction of its fortification: as the myth goes, Remus pokes fun at the trenches his brother Romulus is digging around the Palatine Hill, but is then killed by Romulus for jumping over—thus transgressing—the new perimeter. Inobservance of the walls, even nascent ones, is a grave form of lawlessness.[28] Virgil's double figure is a reminder of this axiom: as foundational elements of imperial masonry, laws and walls are inextricably bound in the creation of *civitas*—which means both "juridical community" and "walled city."

Nolasco Mere's second citation, *O fortunati quorum iam moenia surgunt*, "O happy those for whom the walls already rise" (in the upper-right corner of the map), occurs in a passage that is mirror and antitype of Jupiter's prophecy. Led by Venus in disguise, Aeneas and his Trojans leave the beach and head toward the new city of Carthage, ruled by the fated Queen Dido. Through the awe-struck eyes of Aeneas, the reader sees the labors of the Tyrians who, "qualis apes aestate nova" (1.430) ("like bees in early summer"), carry out the multiple tasks related to the construction of the city.[29] The concomitance of walls and laws is once again highlighted: some Carthaginians roll up stones to build the walls, while others institute laws, act as magistrates, and participate in the senate. At this moment, looking at the diligent rise of the city, Aeneas exclaims, "Oh happy those for whom the walls already rise!" Standing in front of Carthage, Aeneas eagerly expresses his desire for the fulfillment of his fate in the erection of the New Troy. The rising walls are a sign of *fortuna*, prosperity and good fate. That is why Aeneas' remark seems to betray a degree of envy: the budding Carthage is a

---

[27] The English phrasal verb "to set up" enables the same trope.
[28] For Classical sources of this episode, see Dionysius of Halicarnassus, *Roman Antiquities* 1.87.4; Livy, *History of Rome* 1.7.1–3; and Plutarch, *Lives*, "Romulus" 10.
[29] This is the same context from which a line of the *Aeneid* was borrowed and slightly adapted for the reception of Viceroy Don García Hurtado de Mendoza examined at the start of this chapter.

painful reminder of his lost city of Troy, of his deferred fate, and of the fact that he has not yet founded Rome, the New Troy.

The final citation, "imperium sine fine dedi" (at the center-bottom of the map), returns us to the conversation of Jupiter and Venus, to the conclusion of the former's prophecy. Once the Trojans finally manage to settle in the Latium, explains Jupiter, Aeneas' son Iulus "longam multa vi muniet Albam" (1.271) ("will with much vigor build the walls of Alba Longa"; Fairclough 1950: 261). From Iulus' stock, in turn, will come Romulus, who "Mavortia condet / moenia Romanosque suo de nomine dicet" (1.276–7) ("will found the walls of Mars and call the Romans after his own name"; Fairclough 1950: 261). Jupiter sets neither territorial nor temporal limits on Rome: "his ego nec metas rerum nec tempora pono" (1.278) ("For these I set neither bounds nor periods of empire"; Fairclough 1950: 261). This chronotopic boundlessness, paradoxically signaled by the transcendental properties of the city walls, is finally crystalized in the phrase Nolasco Mere borrows for his map: "imperium sine fine dedi" (1.279) ("dominion without end have I bestowed"; Fairclough 1950: 261). Symptomatic of the imperial self-imagination that Virgil is articulating in these lines, Jupiter's transcendental legislation treats the fate of Rome as *res judicata*. That is, the Romans have already been given an endless empire, even though there are no Romans yet and their city has not yet been built. Hence the shift in the verbal tenses, from the series of future simple verbs used in the early part of the prophecy (*fabor, movebo, geret, contundet,* and *ponet*) to the conclusive perfect tense of his final statement, *dedi*, "I have given."

Let us now return to our main subject and compare the allusions embedded in the three Virgilian lines discussed so far to the features and oddities of the map in which they are cited. There is nothing new, of course, in exalting the greatness of a city by comparing it to ancient Rome, but the grounds for comparison are usually a sense of shared monumental antiquity. That is, for instance, what allows Garcilaso to advance his characterization of Cuzco as "another Rome," as both are distinguished by a similarly ancient prestige. But that is not what Nolasco Mere's map suggests—he could not have exalted Lima's antiquity, for the city had not even reached its 150th anniversary when he made his map. Indeed, as the Virgilian citations embedded in the 1685 map suggest, Nolasco Mere develops a very different comparison between the cities. It is not that Lima all of a sudden acquires the antiquity of Rome, but rather, that Rome, the Eternal City, is drawn back to its earliest stages, to the times when it only existed as an expectation in the protests of Venus, the melancholy contemplations of Aeneas, and the prophecies of Jove. Circumscribed within that mythical and poetic incipit, the captions selected by Nolasco Mere present the paradigm of *civitas* and its walls not as a reality, but as an urban desire for which *pater* Aeneas could only sigh—not unlike the walled Lima that Nolasco Mere and the Limenian notables were still just envisioning in their first map of 1685. The selection of passages from the opening section of the *Aeneid* remind us that, at a certain point in time, Rome was a new community, just like young Lima. For Virgil, writing at the end of the first century BCE, the account of Aeneas's foundational quest supplied Imperial Rome and especially Emperor Augustus with a noble ancestry that, via its affiliation to the Trojans, matched that of the Greeks themselves. On the other side of the spectrum, the three *Aeneid* citations selected for the 1685 map of Lima, narratively oscillating between wandering survivalism and prophetic zeal, ironically render Rome, just for an instant, a new city—almost a New World city, one could argue, from the perspective of someone like Nolasco Mere, who had lived in Lima for about a quarter of a century, and who was, just like Virgil, designing a virtual picture for his political patrons—in this case, the Duke of Palata and, by extension, the King of Spain.

The equating of Rome's antiquity and Lima's novelty through the mythological and epic ground of the *Aeneid* hints, yet again, at a form of New World anxiety. Time and history play a defining role in the achievement of urban dignity; time and history are, consequently, systematically reformulated in the context of the New World—and this negotiation of antiquity is constitutive of the map drawn by Nolasco Mere. The Limenian polymath Pedro de Peralta y Barnuevo would later argue that 200 years for Lima were equivalent to the thousands of years of European history.[30] As if anticipating that equation, Nolasco Mere's citations are also inflected by the manipulation of temporal coordinates. Upon seeing the fortification of Carthage, Aeneas cries "Oh happy those for whom the walls *already* rise" (my emphasis), highlighting the present time of his contemplation (which, in the logic of the poem, anticipates the walls that Romulus, his descendant, will eventually erect). While comforting his daughter, Jupiter states, "I *have given* [the Romans] an empire without end" (my emphasis), rendering the imperial infinity of a Rome that doesn't exist yet a fait accompli. "He *will* set up the walls and the laws" (my emphasis), the third of the citations, finally presupposes an extraordinary future tense in which the creation of architecture and governance are simultaneous processes. The three citations propose, in this way, a complex amalgamation of past, present, and future; of history and prophecy; and of material and ideological values. They are perfectly suited to the

---

[30] For more on this, see the discussion of Peralta at the end of this chapter.

characterization of a New World city that bypasses traditional evolutionary stages, turning rustic *magalia* or huts into a monumental urban grid in a matter of mere decades, and erecting its surrounding walls in just three years—so swiftly that the Duke of Palata could proudly boast that the construction "has seemed a miraculous accomplishment."[31] And so, if the New World space is at odds with the paradigms of antiquity structuring Old World self-imagination, it only makes sense that the circumscription of that space—for the walls are a literal *definitio*— ends up inscribed with signs of the consequent need to adjust the notion of imperial time. The pithy Latin captions become, in this way, subtle reminders to the Spanish monarch about the role of Lima in the modern configuration of the transatlantic empire.

I have so far suggested a series of conceptual associations between the Classical citations on Nolasco Mere's first map and certain apprehensions constitutive of Lima's self-imagination. The degree to which Nolasco Mere is conscious of those anxieties is, of course, impossible to determine, but deeming the selection of captions from the *Aeneid* a mere ornamental gesture—a banal set of citations only determined by the mention of walls in a famous poem—would be a crude simplification. In tune with the baroque principles of the period, authors were ready to invest considerable energy in assessing the manifold implications of their literary choices. Word plays, puns, puzzles, acrostics, anagrams, and so many other popular devices depended on an intense and even extreme examination of texts—so much so that one is tempted to define the spirit of the baroque as a heightened form of close-reading. The erudite, inquisitive intellectual community of the Lima in which Nolasco Mere lived would have readily embraced the most extravagant implications of his Latin captions on the map of their city.[32]

---

[31] See footnote 20, above.

[32] This may also illuminate the significance of the fourth Latin caption in the map, which was not extracted from the Classical *Aeneid*, but from the biblical book of Nehemia (which Nolasco Mere identifies, following the Vulgate Bible, with the second book of Esdras). This fourth caption reads "Una manu sua faciebat opus & altera tenebat gladium. Es. 25" ("One of their hands did the work while the other hand held a sword"). The citation originally refers to Nehemia, a cup-bearer to the fifth-century-BCE king Artaxerxes of Persia. As the tradition has it, Nehemia, with the consent of his monarch, moved to Jerusalem and rebuilt its ruined fortification in record time: fifty-two days. The extraordinary feat was supposedly accomplished by forcing the masons into a non-stop rotation while maintaining a permanent state of alert because the project encountered the strong opposition of neighboring communities. To defend the walls from those potential threats, the workers were also ready to act as soldiers, laboring, as the caption states, with "one hand, while the other held a sword." In choosing this caption, is Nolasco Mere alluding to the expediency of the construction and the looming threat of the powerful nobles opposed to the project, or even potential attacks by pirates the walls were meant to keep out? Is he conflating the paradigm of Jerusalem with that of ancient Rome in the depiction of Lima, as part of his idea of a New World capital? If so, is this insinuating or imagining a potential reformulation of the empire, as synthesis of the Christian and Pagan centers of the Old World, now consolidated through the City of the Kings? While these questions go beyond the scope of this chapter, they do merit critical examination.

There is, however, an important degree of irony in Nolasco Mere's map that does not seem to be accidental. After all, the eternity Jupiter promised to Venus as an attribute of Rome in the first chapter of the *Aeneid* was, by 1685, simply vestigial and rhetorical. And yet, Nolasco Mere does rehearse the dictum "Imperium sine fine dedi" in his map, even if that prophecy had proved wrong. While it could be argued that the Holy Roman Empire supposed an imaginary continuity between Augustan Rome and seventeenth-century Europe, Imperial Rome was by then an ancient and ruined polity located in a mythical past. There is a critical contradiction, or at least a heavy tension, between the claims of a *civitas aeterna* and its circumscription *in illo tempore*—and a New World version of *translatio imperii* would have offered a tantalizing solution to that ideological knot. The following section might shed further light on this possibility.

The Language of the New World: Rodrigo de Valdés's *Fundación y Grandezas*

Secluded from the noisy debates about the walls and other public matters in Lima, the Jesuit Rodrigo de Valdés (Lima, 1609–82) composed one of the most peculiar—and still rather obscure—pieces of poetry ever written in the New World. The title reads, *Poema heroyco hispano-latino. Panegyrico de la Fundación y Grandezas de la muy Noble, y Leal Ciudad de Lima* ("Heroic Spanish-Latin Poem. Panegyric to the Foundation and Splendors of the Very Noble and Loyal City of Lima"). Published posthumously in 1687, the frontmatter includes the typical censors' approvals, a dedication to Charles II, a "Prologue to the Reader," a series of elegies, sonnets, romances, epigrams, and acrostics in Spanish and Latin, and a long "Carta de edificación" (a biographical eulogy originally delivered by a Jesuit colleague after Valdés passed away—a standard procedure in the Society of Jesus).[33] All these prefaces are followed by the *Fundación y Grandezas* itself, composed of 572 assonant quatrains numbered and distributed in thirty-eight sections.[34] Internal evidence suggests a relatively long process of

---

[33] The prologuist (whose role will be discussed at length later) introduces this biographic document by explaining its procedural character (Garabito 1687a: 11–12). It has no pagination, but since it is only twelve pages long, I have suggested these myself.

[34] Throughout this work I abbreviate the poem's title as *Fundación y Grandezas*. See footnote 42 for an explanation of this abbreviation.

composition—sometime between 1660 and 1682 (the year Valdés died).[35] The poem was intended as a miscellaneous panegyric on the foundation and the natural, architectural, social, and religious greatness of Lima, but its most remarkable characteristic is its language, which, as described by the designation "hispano-latino," consists of an artificial amalgamation of Spanish and Latin.[36]

Scholarly bibliography on this remarkable text is scarce. For centuries, the few scholars who took notice of the poem treated it as a mere curiosity—as an example of the extremes of the gongorist style so popular in the New World baroque.[37] Those same few critics coincided in disparaging the literary qualities of the text, calling it a "jerigonza bárbara" ("barbaric gibberish"), "aberración" ("aberration"), a display of "erudición indigesta" ("indigestible erudition"), and so on. Only in the early twentieth century did the poem begin to receive (albeit sporadically) more serious attention, first within general studies of the tradition of baroque Spanish-Latin poetry practiced on both sides of the Atlantic, and then, in the last three decades, in relation to the development of *criollo* identities.[38] These studies have recently been consolidated in Neal A. Messer and Jerry Williams's modern edition of Valdés's poem, published in 2017 (the first

---

[35] Messer and Williams point out that the earliest verses date back to the first years of the 1660s and identify references to a living Phillip IV (who died in 1665) as *terminum post quem* for the poem's composition (2017: 9–10). There is, however, a more precise early reference: the successful embassy of Luis Méndez de Haro, who represented Spain in the negotiation that led to the signing of the Treaty of the Pyrenees on November 7, 1659 (which put an end to a long territorial war between Spain and France). The poem dedicates an entire section to congratulating Méndez de Haro for this achievement, in a way that suggests that the event was still fresh (Valdés 1687: viii, stanzas 100–13). Furthermore, Méndez de Haro died on November 26, 1661—which might be a more accurate *terminus post quem*, since the poem clearly alludes to him as a living figure.

[36] Messer and Williams indicate various signs that Garabito, the editor, chose the title (2017: 10). Garabito explicitly takes responsibility for calling the poem "heroic": "aunque el numero de fu metro no lo permita, lo piden lo heroyco, y fublime de fus affumptos, y de las fentencias, y vozes cõ que fe explican" (1687d: 11) ("even though its meter does not allow it, the title is demanded by the heroic and sublime character of its subjects, as well as the concepts and voices with which those subjects are explained").

[37] For a detailed history of harsh critical assessments of the poem, see Messer and Williams 2017: 37–43 and Mazzotti 2009: 2.

[38] On the tradition of Spanish-Latin writing, see Buceta 1925 and 1932 (Valdés is examined in the second). Dietrich Briesemeister (1986) reads Valdés's poem in relation to the early modern sense of competition between, on the one hand, imperial Spain and its language, and on the other, ancient Rome, Italy, Latin, and Italian. Studies of the poem in relation to expressions of *criollo* identity include Mazzotti 1996 and 2009, which see Valdés's text as formulating *criollo* notions of identity with respect to both the multi-ethnic make-up of the New World and the imperial and intellectual cultures of Spain and Europe; Guibovich 2007, which examines the poem's instrumentalization of the chorographic genre for the vindication of Lima and *criollo* communities within the Spanish Empire; and Vinatea 2017, which considers the imperial character of Spanish and Latin used in the poem, and the stakes of New World communities in defining such attributions. While not focused on the case of Valdés, other important studies of the tradition of Spanish-Latin composition are Ruiz 1991 and Woolard and Genovese 2007.

republication of the text since its original publication in 1682).[39] Messer and Williams provide an annotated edition of the poem, with translations of the Latin sections, and a lengthy introduction that reviews scholarship on the work, examines the frontmatter of the *editio princeps*, and summarizes the contents of each of the "paragraphs" or cantos into which the text is divided.[40]

While this recent revalorization of the poem is a salutary turn, it is worth reflecting on the resistance that the poem encountered. Indeed, the long critical denigration or neglect of the poem responds primarily to its immersion in the aesthetic and intellectual trends of the moment it was composed, which did not translate at all well in subsequent eras. The *Fundación y Grandezas* is truly a product of its time, and the rejection it suffered later is not a mere reflection of the trite tale about neoclassical repudiations of the baroque. While such aesthetic and poetic shifts played a role, it is also clear that the transatlantic expectations of cultural validation this poem articulates, so meaningful within the viceregal community of seventeenth- and early eighteenth-century Lima, became illegible once the Spanish colonial order had been dismantled—it is no accident that the most acerbic criticism comes from the post-independence decades. The poem's revalorization requires, therefore, examination of its role as representation and symptom of the complex political, religious, and social dynamics of the viceroyalty and its position in the Spanish Empire.

As an elaborate commendation of the capital of the Viceroyalty of Peru, Valdés's poem fully participates in Lima's chorographic tradition of self-glorifying literature explored in this chapter. Moreover, by dint of its engagement with the Classical tradition (both accidentally and intentionally, as explained below), the poem also provides an excellent vantage point for further exploring the development of what we are calling New World anxiety. However, here I would like to redirect our attention to the preliminaries of the *Fundación y Grandezas*, rather than the poem itself—and this for two reasons: those sections provide precious evidence about the stakes that the original readers had in the

---

[39] While completing the final revisions of this book, I learned about a second modern, critical edition of Valdés's poem—prepared by Martina Vinatea and published in 2018. Unfortunately, I was not able to consult this important contribution to Valdés's bibliography in time to incorporate it within the narrative of this chapter.

[40] One sign of the incipient stage of criticism on Valdés's poem is the fact that scholars have not yet agreed on a standard abbreviation for its title. Buceta (1925 and 1932), Brisemeister (1986), and Messer and Williams (2017) call it *Poema heroico* or (following the original spelling) *heroyco*, the title given by Garabito; Mazzotti (2009), considering what seems to be Valdés's original intent as represented in the heading that precedes the poem, calls it *Fundación y Grandezas*; Vinatea (2017), focusing on the language of the poem, calls it *Poema hispano-latino*. I follow Mazzotti, as it appears to reflect the author's wish and is more distinct than the other two solutions.

poem, and their content remains insufficiently studied despite the recent renewal of interest in the poem in general.[41] Thus, while I offer below a brief introduction to the poem itself, I will focus primarily on the frontmatter, foregrounding two strategies the prefatory authors use to connect *Fundación y Grandezas* to the Classical tradition: a parallel between Virgil and the poet Rodrigo de Valdés and, more especially, a valorization of the Spanish-Latin language that Valdés created.

Indeed, the prologue to *Fundación y grandezas* quickly defines a connection between the poem and the Classics through an explicit comparison between Valdés and the Roman epic poet Virgil. While such a rhetorical parallel was quite common in epic poetry, comparisons are usually textual or tropological. The perspective adopted by the prologuist Francisco Garabito de Leon is, however, biographical. Garabito, nephew of Rodrigo de Valdés—responsible for editing the poem and posthumously publishing the work—describes in his "Prologo al lector" ("Prologue to the Reader") the fraught composition, acquisition, and editing of the poem's manuscript, highlighting in the process the unmistakable echoes between his uncle's last days and those of the renowned Virgil:

> [A]ñade nueva recomendacion [a Valdés] la mano agena [del editor], que ſaca à luz eſta obra poſtuma tan contra la voluntad del Autor, que auiendo ſoſpechado el intento de dàrla à la Eſtampa en los Deudos, y Amigos, que ſe la pedimos en ſu vltima enfermedad, la raſgò, y deſpedazò en muy menudas piezas, ſepultandola debaxo de vna tarima de el cancel, ò retrete de la cama ; y à no auerla eſcapado la induſtria de vn Padre Eſcholar, caſi de las braſas, y cenizas, como la Eneyda de Virgilio, lloràramos en eſta el incendio, que ſolo en amenazas hizo llorar, en aquella, à los mayores Poetas, como ſi vieran de nuevo conſumirſe en llamas à la meſma Troya. Y fuè la dicha, que paſſando el Padre Eſtudiante (que quiſiera nombrarlo de agradecido) por el corridor, y puerta del difunto à tiempo que ſe barria, y componia para otro suceſſor el apoſento, le impeliò la curioſidad, ò inſpiracion divina à reconocer entre la baſura vn monton de papeles deſmenuzados, y advirtiendo por algunas clauſulas de los verſos, que era la celebre Poeſia Hispano-Latina del comun Maeſtro en todas letras, recogiendo tanto deſperdicio de perlas, y flores de erudicion, con vn prolixo trabajo de muchos meſes, fuè vniendo, y componiendo toda la obra, aunque perdiendo à vezes el hilo de tan dorada eloquencia en eſte laberinto de tan cõfusos retazos.
>
> 1687d: 6–7

---

[41] Messer and Williams (2017: 44–50) provide a description of the poem's preliminaries, paying particular attention to the prologue and the biographical letter—as Guibovich 2007 and Mazzotti 2009 also do. The multiple poems also included in the frontmatter have received, however, minimal critical attention.

> The alien hand [of the editor] constitutes a new commendation [for Valdés's poem], as it brings to light this posthumous work very much against the author's will, who, suspecting that relatives and friends intended to give his poem to the press (as we had requested it from him during his last illness), decided to shred and tear it apart in very small pieces, burying it under a plank in the niche or recess where his bed was placed; and if the diligence of a priestly scholar had not rescued it from the flames and ashes, as it happened to Virgil's *Aeneid*, we would be now lamenting this fire, just as the mere threat [of burning the *Aeneid*] made the greatest of the poets cry about the Mantuan's poem, as if they saw Troy itself again consumed in flames. And it was a happy accident that, when the aforementioned priestly scholar (whom I wish I could name out of gratitude) happened to pass by the corridor and the door of the deceased, just as the bedroom was being swept and arranged for a successor, was compelled by curiosity or divine inspiration to notice amid the garbage a pile of shredded papers, and realizing, on account of a few clauses in the verses, that it was the famous Spanish-Latin poem of that master in all letters, collected such a squandering of pearls and flowers of erudition, and after diligently working on them for many months, he united and recomposed the entire piece, although occasionally losing the thread of such golden eloquence amid the labyrinth of those puzzling fragments.

Garabito is right: the timely rescue of Valdés's manuscript distinctly recalls the well-known tradition that tells of a moribund Virgil wishing to have his *Aeneid* destroyed—a deathbed wish ultimately overruled by Emperor Augustus himself. These resonances were too tempting to be ignored. It is true, of course, that Garabito had no need to resort to this episode to identify Valdés with Virgil, insofar as the *Fundación y Grandezas*, partially devoted to the foundation of the city of Lima, was already thematically located within the Virgilian epic tradition. Moreover, the comparison with Virgil was practically obligatory in praises and eulogies of Renaissance and baroque epic poems, and the need for a New World Virgil singing of the foundation of Lima by Pizarro and his conquistadors had been explicitly enunciated already half a century earlier in Fray Buenaventura de Salinas's *Memorial de las historias del Nuevo Mundo, Piru* (*Memorial of the Histories of the New World, Peru*) of 1630 (Guibovich 2007: 363; Mazzotti 2009: 167). And yet, the narrative of the precarious survival of the *Fundación y grandezas* manuscript, which Garabito describes in great detail, decidedly enhances what might have otherwise been a procedural invocation of Virgil. In fact, while the story of the *Aeneid*'s near-destruction and providential rescue was well known, one wonders whether Garabito might have taken a moment to consult ancient reports of the episode while composing his prologue.

The examination of two Classical passages suggests so. Pliny the Elder, in his report on eminent Romans (and in what may be the oldest reference to the story) briefly remarks that "Divus Augustus carmina Vergilii cremari contra testamenti eius verecundiam vetuit, maiusque ita vati testimonium contigit quam si ipse sua probavisset" (*Naturalis historia* 7.114) ("His late Majesty Augustus overrode the modesty of Virgil's will and forbade the burning of his poems, and thus the bard achieved a stronger testimony than if he had commended his own works himself"; Rackham 1942: 581). For Pliny, the survival of the *Aeneid* by the action of *Divus Augustus* and against Virgil's desires constitutes the highest recommendation, since the publication of the poem does not result from the request or even consent of the author, but rather, imperial endorsement in the face of an extraordinary act of *verecundia* ("modesty," "humility," and even "shyness"). These are also, with suggestive precision, the terms of Garabito's praise of Valdés: the rescuing of the *Fundación y Grandezas* from oblivion, by "an alien hand," is in itself a "a new commendation" that confirms "the rigor of the author's humility" (1687d: 6).

Garabito's narrative also resonates with details contained in the brief "Life of Virgil" penned by the fourth-century grammarian Aelius Donatus—a transcription or expansion of a lost *Vita Vergilii* by the Roman historian Suetonius (*c.* 69–130 CE). In his version of the story, Donatus provides a slightly different context for Virgil's radical decision, highlighting the struggle between the poet and his executors:

> [Vergilius e]gerat cum Vario, priusquam Italia decederet, ut siquid sibi accidisset, "Aeneida" combureret; at is ita facturum se pernegarat; igitur in extrema valetudine assidue scrinia desideravit, crematurus ipse; verum nemine offerente nihil quidem nominatim de ea cavit. Ceterum eidem Vario ac simul Tuccae scripta sua sub ea condicione legavit, ne quid ederent, quod non a se editum esset. Edidit autem auctore Augusto Varius, sed summatim emendate, ut qui versus etiam inperfectos sicut errant reliquerit; quos multi mox supplere conati non perinde valuerunt ob difficultatem, quod Omnia fere apud eum hemistichia absolute perfectoque sunt sensu ...
>
> Aelius Donatus 39–42

[Virgil] had arranged with Varius, before leaving Italy, that if anything befell him his friend should burn the "Aeneid"; but Varius had emphatically declared that he would not do such [a] thing. Therefore in his mortal illness Vergil constantly called for his book-boxes, intending to burn the poem himself; but when no one brought them to him, he made no specific request about the matter, but left his writings jointly to the above mentioned Varius and to Tucca, with the stipulation that they should publish nothing which he himself would not have given to the world. However, Varius published the "Aeneid" at Augustus' request, making only a few slight corrections, and even leaving the incomplete lines just as they were. These last many afterwards tried to finish, but did not wholly succeed owing to the difficulty that nearly all his half-lines are complete in sense and meaning ...

Rolfe 1959: 479

In a study of the textual sources of the famous episode, Fabio Stok remarks on a key difference between Pliny's account and that of Suetonius/Donatus, as the latter source does not mention a testament proper, but rather situates the narrative in an ongoing oral exchange—almost a debate—between Virgil and his executors, Varius and Tucca, in addition to Augustus (2007–8: 202–3). This distinction is also significant in Garabito's preface, as he similarly describes a tension between the dying Valdés and his "Deudos" ("relatives") and "Amigos" ("friends"), whose eagerness for the manuscript betrayed their desire to publish the poem. But as opposed to Virgil, who had already entrusted his "book-boxes" (*scrinia*) to Varius before his trip abroad, Valdés was still in possession of his poem when the controversy occurred, and was therefore able to do what Virgil could not: he ripped up the text ("shredded and tore it apart in very small pieces," says Garabito with dramatic pleonasm), hiding the remains under a plank in his cell. Still, the fact that the two manuscripts were rescued against the will of their authors left a mark in both cases—and Garabito does not miss the chance to suggest that parallel as well. As Donatus points out, the publication of the *Aeneid* without Virgil's consent had left the poem with a number of incomplete lines that his contemporaries (and later poets) found impossible to mend. Garabito, in turn, admits that the anonymous rescuer and editor of Valdés's papers sometimes loses the thread of the original poem—an effect of the fragmentary condition in which the manuscript was found.[42]

---

[42] Briesemeister states that Garabito himself tried to recompose the draft (1986: 99). Garabito, however, alludes to a third person, "vn Padre Escholar" ("a priestly scholar") or "Padre Estudiante" ("father student"), as responsible for both the rescue of the papers Valdés ripped apart and the reconstruction (or at least, initial reconstruction) of its fragments. Garabito also implies that this editor preferred to remain anonymous, as suggested by the parenthetical remark, "I wish I could name [him] out of gratitude." Furthermore, says Garabito, this anonymous first editor consulted separate drafts of the poem's quatrains, found by Valdés's secretary after the poet's death (1687d: 6–7). It is not impossible that Garabito created the fiction of another editor to hide his own intervention, and it is clear that he had the last word on the publication of the *Fundación y Grandezas*, since the cover presents him as the person who "sacó a la luz" ("brought to light") the poem— something that the "Licencia" or printing permission signed in Madrid corroborates. However, since many of the preliminaries suggest that Valdés was something of a cult figure admired by a generation of students, it is more likely that, as Garabito recounts, the process of reconstructing his poem garnered a collective interest. A plurality of hands is also suggested in the aforementioned

It is impossible to say for certain whether Garabito reviewed Pliny's and Donatus's accounts about Virgil's dying wish (though he does cite three passages from Pliny's *Naturalis historia* elsewhere).[43] Nevertheless, the resonances between Virgil's and Valdés's final wishes, which Garabito carefully draws out through the "precarious manuscript" trope, suggest an investment in the biographical parallels between the Roman and the Limenian poet that goes beyond the mere rhetorical gesture. The wider significance of these parallels is clear in another prefatory document: the "Aprobacion" ("Approval") of the Jesuit Pedro de Fomperosa, who rhetorically attributes the salvaging of Valdés's poem not to specific individuals but to the entire city of Lima. This gesture is significant because even though Garabito correlates the Roman Virgil with the Limenian Valdés, he does not explicitly compare Lima with Rome—in the way the Inca Garcilaso's *Comentarios reales*, for example, had done with Cuzco. But Fomperosa begins his praise of the *Fundación y Grandezas* with a question that is also an equation between the poet Valdés and his home city Lima: "Mándame V.S. cenſurar eſta obra, que màs que de cenſura, hallo digna de elogio. Pero de quien? De el Padre Rodrigo por ſer hijo de la Patria, ù de Lima por Madre noble de tal hijo?" (1687: n.p.) ("Your Lordship orders me to censor this work, but rather than censure, I find it worthy of praise. But whose praise? Father Rodrigo's, for being the child of this nation, or Lima's for being the noble mother of such a son?"). After this, he congratulates the whole city for the survival of the manuscript. Tellingly, Fomperosa's remarks also coincide with Garabito's in concluding that, just as it happened to Virgil, Valdés's deathbed wish aggrandizes the value of his poem:

> No ſolo parabienes, gracias debemos dàr à la Ciudad de Lima, de que aya reſcatado del incendio, ù del polvo de el olvido, eſtos fragmentos, honrando afsi la memoria de ſu Author, como lo hizo Auguſto con el Poema del Principe de los

---

"Carta de edificación" by Francisco del Quadro (written shortly after Valdés died): "no han faltado curioſos, ò eſtudioſos, que vniendo con muy prolija, y loable codicia los retazos de vnas dicciones con otras, ayan logrado la mayor parte de eſte teſoro" (§ VII) ("there has been no lack of scholarly researchers who, bringing together with a very diligent and commendable energy some of the text's fragments with others, have managed [to reconstruct] the larger part of this treasure").

[43] See the second and third pages of Garabito's prologue. The passages from Pliny include information about a contest between the Greek painters Protogenes and Apelles to determine which of them was capable of painting the thinnest possible line (*Historia naturalis* 35.83); the anecdote of an *Iliad* fully copied on the concave insides of a nutshell (7.21); and a proverbial citation: "Rerum natura numquam magis, quam in minimis tota est" (11.1) ("Nature is never so great as when it is fully contained in its smallest [element]"). The point of all these citations is that the relative brevity of Valdés's poem only magnifies its greatness.

> Poetas, contra fu vltima voluntad, pues le dexaba condenado à la hoguera. Afsi lo acreditò para fus aplausos no menos la aprobacion de Augufto, que de Virgilio el defprecio.
>
> 1687: n.p.
>
> The City of Lima deserves not only our congratulations, but also our gratitude for having rescued from the fire or dust of oblivion these fragments, thus honoring the memory of its author, as did [the emperor] Augustus with the poem of the Prince of Poets, against his last will, as he [Virgil] had left it condemned to burn on the pyre. Thus, the poem was acclaimed no less for Augustus' approval than for Virgil's disdain.

The actions of Garabito and the other rescuers of Valdés's poem turn out to be, by metonymy, the actions of the whole city. Once Lima has been credited as the agent responsible for the rescue of the poem's fragments, the metonymical principle of the passage also infuses the language Fomperosa uses, inasmuch as the "fire" and "dust of oblivion" from which the manuscript was salvaged becomes reminiscent of the actual flames that more than once ravaged the ancient city of Rome and left it in ruins. In a similar vein, Garabito's prologue remarks (in the passage quoted earlier) that the mere threat of destroying the *Aeneid* was tantamount to seeing Troy in flames for a second time. Could we discern, then, in this intricate web of allusions that repeatedly conflate city and text, an identification of the fragments of Valdés's manuscript with urban ruins—as perhaps a sort of textual parallel of the ruined city?

In a city like Lima, perennially anxious on account of its newness, such an identification made a great deal of sense. Guibovich describes the premise of the poem in these terms: "[p]or su historia pasada y presente, Lima emula a Roma y, por consiguiente, puede reclamar con justicia el título de 'reyna del Nuevo Mundo'" (2007: 356) ("because of its past and present history, Lima emulates Rome and can reclaim, with justice, the title of 'Queen of the New World'"). But to do so, the poem must first grapple with a profound sense of difference, because the past of Rome could not be immediately commensurable to that of Lima. A prominent sign of Rome's monumental deep history is the omnipresence of ruins scattered across the city, a feature that renders the Roman urban landscape, even to this day, a superimposition of architectural layers from different periods that constantly reminds the citizens of the dense history of their city. As a matter of fact, the popular Renaissance tradition of *Antichità di Roma* treatises, meticulous descriptions of former monuments and streets of Rome which were by then only ruins, bears witness to this antiquarian urban nostalgia.⁴⁴ But late seventeenth-century Lima lacked such layers.⁴⁵ In comparing poets and cities, the rhetorical challenge of Garabito and his colleagues was, pace Guibovich, that of negotiating the discrepancy between the Limenian present and the Roman past so that the parallel could be achieved.

This consideration suggests one way of understanding Garabito's account of the *Fundación y Grandezas* manuscript—damaged, torn into pieces, and stuffed under a plank. The tatters containing the poem and their rescue by a providential editor, both piously celebrated by Garabito, can be read as a textual substitute for the absence of monumental ruins in the City of the Kings. The episode possesses special importance because it allows Lima to age vicariously through the manuscript itself, with the textual ruins of *Fundación y Grandezas* serving as the living vestiges of Lima, somehow comparable to the remnants of ancient edifices in the great city of Rome. Messer and Williams have stated their puzzlement about the appeal such a broken poem had for its original editors: "Given all the intricacies of the provenance of *Poema heroyco*, the greater mystery is that despite the editor's acknowledgement in the prolog [sic] that we can only scope partial snippets and cloudy reflections of Valdés's true genius, the poem was still published" (2017: 13). As I contend here, the answer to this "mystery" is that the incomplete character of the poem actually *adds* an importance to the text that it wouldn't otherwise possess. Valdés's Virgilian wish, the destruction of the poem, its reconstruction, its inevitable incompleteness: all these episodes create an extraordinary symbolic surplus for Valdés's early readers. The fragmentariness of his manuscript invests it with the same precariousness of ancient cities, especially those that possess foundational consequence. A vestigial value: that is the significance Garabito and his colleagues are attempting to assign to the peculiar linguistic artifact that Father Valdés composed and then tried to destroy.

The vestigial value ascribed to the *Fundación y Grandezas*—that is, the transferal of the historical prestige of Roman ruins to the textual fragments narrating the foundation of the city of Lima—will in turn frame the value of the Spanish-Latin language that Valdés created. As the epithet "Hispano-Latino" conveys, Valdés's composition attempts to produce a new language through the amalgamation of seventeenth-century Spanish and ecclesiastical Latin. Written

---

[44] For more details about this genre, see Campos-Muñoz 2013: 134–6.
[45] Lima did not lack, however, its own share of ruins, as the late seventeenth century registered some of the most destructive earthquakes the city (situated in a very seismic area) had experienced. The consequent ruins, however, obviously lacked the history we are discussing here.

entirely in this artificial diction, theoretically legible to readers proficient in either Latin or Spanish, the poem is supposed to be devoted to the foundation and description of Lima, which had been capital of the Viceroyalty of Peru for about 150 years. Yet the voracity of the poem, supplemented by copious marginalia, greatly exceeds those parameters. While some cantos are indeed devoted to the City of Lima, many others—in a confused sequence that combines extravagant metaphors and Classical imagery—cover a miscellanea of international topics, from the celebratory characterization of various members of the Spanish royal family to the discovery of the Strait of Magellan, the stars visible from the Southern hemisphere, recommendations for the King of England, and even the holy signs hidden in the pulp and seeds of the fruits of the New World. The polymath character of the poem, a full rehearsal of the hyperbolic drive of the baroque, also seems to anticipate the encyclopedic zeal and miscellaneous interest of future Enlightenment scholars.

To craft his hybrid language, Valdés relies on the morphological kinship between Spanish and Latin—archaizing the orthography, actively seeking identical cognates, accumulating gerunds and cultisms, adopting parataxis as a syntactical standard, adding occasional Latin case endings to Spanish words, omitting definite and indefinite articles, and systematizing the use of hyperbatons. This method imposes a number of formal limits, as Briesemeister has noted:

> El repertorio léxico, morfológico, estilístico y formal de la poesía mixta hispano-latina forzosamente es pobre, pues aparte de la primera persona del singular del presente, apenas puede usar formas conjugadas de verbos, teniendo que reemplazar las conjunciones por gerundios y empleando vocativos y un orden asyndético [sic].
>
> 1986: 116

> The lexical, morphologic, stylistic, and formal repertoire of the hybrid Spanish-Latin poetry is inevitably poor—aside from the first person singular present, it can barely use conjugated verbal forms, having to substitute conjunctions with gerunds, and rely on vocatives and an asyndetic order.

"Poverty" is, however, a relative term. In the spirit of the baroque, so fascinated with the morphological and typographic challenges of acrostics, anagrams, chiastic arrangements, labyrinths, and similar formal tropes (many of these rehearsed in the preliminaries of the *Fundación y Grandezas*), constraints were in fact seen as enticing literary problems rather than uncomfortable restrictions. Valdés's poetic style is a characteristic offspring of this tradition, and, as mentioned earlier, his Spanish-Latin language already had a genealogy on both sides of the Atlantic.⁴⁶ But even though Valdés did not invent the genre, the *Fundación y Grandezas* is unique on account of the sheer extent to which the Limenian poet stretched the Spanish-Latin format: as said above, the poem comprised thirty-eight cantos of 572 quatrains, and that does not include the material that was lost after Valdés ripped up his own manuscript.⁴⁷ This may be, in fact, the longest Spanish-Latin poem ever composed.⁴⁸ This extension, added to the foundational subject of the poem, associates Valdés's poem more with the epic genre than to the short exercises in prose and poetry carried out by his predecessors.⁴⁹ The considerable difficulties of producing such a long piece explain in part the extensive period of composition—almost two decades, as Messer and Williams have estimated (2017: 9–10).⁵⁰

Because of the heterogeneous subjects covered by the poem, a full assessment of its thematic and figural content would demand a more extensive study. But a quick examination of the opening lines (Valdés 1687: I, stanzas 1–2) should provide a fair illustration of the poem's general features:

Canto beneficas luces,	Canto [las] luces benéficas.	I sing of the benevolent lights,
heroycas ſublimes cauſas,	[las] heroicas causas sublimes,	the sublime heroic causes,
immortales altas glorias,	[las] inmortales, altas glorias,	the immortal, high glories,
divinas immenſas gracias,	[las] divinas e inmensas gracias,	the divine and immense graces,
De Metropolitam Regia,	de la regia metrópolis que,	of the regal metropolis which,

---

⁴⁶ See footnote 38 above.
⁴⁷ Garabito estimates that about a fifth of the poem was lost: "paſſan de ciento las [quartetas] que quedaron ſepultadas, ſegun los numeros, que en los borradores vltimos ſe reconocen" (1687d: 7) ("the quatrains that remained entombed amount to more than a hundred, according to the numbers that can be identified in the last drafts of the poem").
⁴⁸ Buceta states that, indeed, Valdés's poem "tiene la distinción de ser el empeño más continuado y amplio llevado a cabo en esta clase de composiciones" (1932: 400) ("has the distinction of being the lengthiest and most continuous instance of this type of composition").
⁴⁹ Garabito explains that the *Fundación y Grandezas* deserves the title of "heroic poem" for its sublime subject and diction, even if it does not use the metric and stanzaic structure of the *octava real* (which in the Spanish tradition was the considered the "metro heroico" or "heroic meter" par excellence). See footnote 36 above.
⁵⁰ See footnote 35 above. The heterogeneous character of the cantos and their dilated composition made Messer and Williams hypothesize that maybe some of the quatrains were not originally part of the *Fundación y Grandezas* project, but rather accidentally inserted from other manuscripts into the printed edition of the poem.

quae inclita Colonia Hiſpana	tal como ínclita Colonia hispana	as if it were a Spanish Cologne
tres Orientales Coronas	posee tres coronas orientales,	(illustrious Cologne having three eastern crowns)
oſtenta occiduas Thiaras.	ostenta tiaras occidentales.	displays western tiaras.
[Spanish-Latin text]	[Modern Spanish]	[English translation *ad sensum*]

While the first quatrain, celebrating the lights, glories, and graces of the city, is a rhetorically standard epic proem, the second quatrain demands a much more challenging exegesis. The "metropolitam regia" ("regal metropolis") of the first line of the second stanza is of course the capital city. The adjective *regia*, not merely formulaic, alludes to Lima's foundational epithet and alternative name, "the City of the Kings"—which was still a standard way to refer to Lima in official documents at the time the poem was composed. The subsequent line, designating Lima as a "Colonia Hispana" ("Hispanic Cologne"), is an elaborate reminder that the label *regia* and the designation "City of the Kings" derive from the *Tres Reyes Magos*, the Three Kings or Magi on whose holiday, January 6, the city's foundation was decided. The European city of Cologne, which was by then a free city within the Holy Roman Empire, was famed for hosting the remains of the Magi, buried in the Cathedral of Cologne or *Kölner Dom*. And just as the Magi's sepulcher exhibited (as it still does) three commemorative crowns, so had Lima adopted three crowns in its official coat of arms. Valdés alludes to this heraldic feature with yet another metaphor: "occiduas Thiaras" ("the western tiaras"). The tiara, the papal headpiece, was made of three crowns piled one upon the other; its "western" iteration is, therefore, embodied in the triple crown of the emblems of Lima. The poetic hieroglyph of this second stanza consists, in short, of the following: the three crowns of the coat of arms of Lima, a "western tiara" because of its tripartite structure reminiscent of the papal headpiece, connect Lima to Cologne, where the Three Wise Men are buried and for whom the city is called "The City of the Kings"—and this kingly attribute justifies the proper designation of Lima as "a royal metropolis." To ensure that this series of similes, synecdoches, and compound metaphors is properly decoded, Valdés adds two marginal notes that clarify the intention of the references. Regarding the mention of Cologne, the first note states, "(1) En Colonia reposan las Sanctas Reliquias de los Reyes Magos; y por esta causa tiene por Armas tres Coronas como Lima" ("The Holy Relics of the Three Magi rest in Cologne, and this is the reason why its coat of

Arms has three crowns, like that of Lima"). Regarding the image of "western tiaras," the second note explains, "(2) De tres Coronas se compone la Thiara" ("The [Papal] tiara is made of three crowns").⁵¹

The style of these lines is exemplary of the entire poem. Throughout its thirty-eight cantos, Valdés deploys a purposely cryptic language whose interpretation requires a slow process of decoding and frequent recourse to his explanatory notes (which are not always illuminating).⁵² Once the tropological value of the references is determined (and that value is always univocal: the references always have a specific meaning), the result is a fundamentally epideictic and descriptive poem. While devoted to many different subjects, the vast majority of the quatrains operate under the same referential economy, based on an intricate system of allusions in a Spanish-Latin language and complemented by marginalia written in Spanish prose. As a result, the main challenge for the reader is working out the figurative algebra to determine the literal sense of the veiled yet precise poetic references—a process that requires stopping frequently to examine the verses in tandem with the notes and external reference works.⁵³

Valdés refers briefly to his own artificial diction in the opening canto, requesting that an "ambidextrous Muse" provide him with "sonorous voices" that, "resonating in conformity," may be able to "hold in suspension both Hesperides" (Spain and Italy), which would in turn be able to recognize "identical assonances" in the "dissonant claims" of "contrary metric lyres" combining "high bilingual phrases" (1687: I, stanzas 8–11). Aside from these remarks about its own poetic

---

51 Valdés, Garabito explains in his prologue, added the marginal notes at the urging of his pupils, to facilitate their comprehension. Garabito remarks that some had asked him to remove the notes from the edited version to make the experience more challenging for erudite readers, but he refused to do so, judging it a "crimē de invidiofo facrilegio" ("crime of envious sacrilege") to compromise any part of a text tantamount to "Reliquias de tan divino ingenio" (1687d: 9–10) ("Relics of such a divine genius").

52 The exegetic efficiency of the poem's marginalia has been called into question several times. Already in 1861, Juan Antonio de Lavalle complained that "algunas [notas] contienen noticias curiosas sobre Lima; pero las mas no tienen mas objeto que ostentar una erudicion indijesta, segun era costumbre de los escritores de la época, que en cada una de sus obras depositaban cuanto habian aprendido en su vida" (1861: 2) ("some of the notes include interesting details about Lima, but most of them have no purpose other than exhibiting an indigestible erudition, as was common among the writers of the period, who would pour into each of their works all that they had learned in their lives"). Mazzotti remarks that the notes are somewhat counterproductive, as they complicate the already difficult reading of the poem (1996: 64). Messer and Williams find that "many of the notes clarify little the meaning of the poem, and a few are misleading" (2017: 15). Furthermore, in spite of Garabito's point about Valdés's authorship of the marginalia (see footnote 51 above), Messer and Williams caution that "[t]here are good indications in the text that Valdés did not write some (if not most) of these marginal notes. More than to elucidate the poem, the majority of the notes merely add mastery to the author and the endeavor, leaning as heavily as they do on the service of Latin" (2017: 15).

53 Mazzotti similarly acknowledges that *Fundación y Grandezas* "requiere de una lectura sumamente lenta, por lo entrecortado de sus versos y la extrema erudición de sus imágenes" (1996: 64) ("demands a very slow reading, because of the halting character of its verses and the extreme erudition of its images").

language, the poem is devoted to encyclopedic, political, and social issues concerning Lima and the transatlantic world. In some instances, the poem takes on a diplomatic tone, requesting, for example, that the Portuguese kingdom reconsider its independence and reclaim its place within the Spanish Empire (a reminder of the sixty years during which Portugal was ruled by the Spanish Habsburg Crown, between 1580 and 1640); or that Charles II of England, in the aftermath of Oliver Cromwell's Protectorate and in emulation of the "Prodigal Son," abandon the Anglican creed and reinstate his kingdom within the jurisdiction of the Catholic Church and papal authority. On other occasions, the poem alludes in epic key to historical events like the discovery of the Strait of Magellan; or criticizes early chronicles—regarding, for example, rumors about the conquistadors' motivations in executing Atahualpa, the last Incan monarch. Among these various themes, the poem reserves many sections to the chorographic characterization of Lima and the New World, in a style always defined by the hyperbolic and narcissistic praise of the new metropolis, whose attributes frequently surpass those of the Old World. In Lima, flora, fauna, and climate are consistently better, the cases of madness or diabolical possession are extremely rare in comparison to European nations, and even its guiding constellation, the Crux or Southern Cross, is superior in accuracy to Polaris or North Star. Rare fruits and minerals, religious edifices and public monuments, and military fortifications and academic institutions further distinguish Lima, the thrice-crowned city, from the cities of the Old World.

Other than the brief references noted above, Valdés himself makes no further allusion to his Spanish-Latin language. His early readers, however, made it their primary focus. In spite of the many subjects the *Fundación y Grandezas* discusses, the various authors who contributed prefatory elements to the *editio princeps* of the poem do not pay much attention to its themes or episodes (even though some cantos touched on important contemporary matters). Instead, they tend to concentrate their energy on celebrating the skill of fusing Latin and Spanish, to the point that they appear more invested in the nature of the poem's language than the poem itself (even though, as mentioned earlier, the Latin-Spanish language already had prominent antecedents). Their investment in this point is especially important for understanding the social value of the poem: this fascination with the Latin-Spanish versification constitutes the ideological ground where the signs of Lima's New World anxiety flourish.

The first attribute Garabito assigns to the Spanish-Latin language is universality. In an address to the king at the start of the volume, he reasons the following: "la lengua Latina, que fuè particular, y propia de vna Provincia limitada de Italia, no lo es de effa, no de otra ninguna del Mundo, dexando de fer particular en vna, para fer vniuerfal en todas" (1687a: 4) ("the Latin language, which was particular and pertaining to a single limited province of Italia, belongs no longer to her or to any other province of the world, ceasing to be particular to one in order to become universal in all of them"). The same properties of universal jurisdiction and legibility of the Latin language are consequently ascribed to Valdés's poem, whose cantos are written, says Garabito, "con tal vnion, è identidad de frasses y vozes, que se haràn entender de las Naciones mas agenas, y estrañas de la lengua Española, si saben la Latina" (1687a: 4–5) ("with such unity and identity of phrases and words, that they will be legible for Nations most foreign and distant from the Spanish language, so long as they know Latin"). Once the poem has been endowed with such plasticity, Garabito can conclude that, even though Italy once owned the Latin language, the combination of Latin and Spanish reveals the latter's superiority to Italian: "Con todo fe fingulariza en Efpaña lo raro de efte privilegio de la prouidencia, que ni à la mifma Italia, y Roma, cabeça del Mundo, y de la Iglefia, fe concede: viendo equivocarfe tan reciprocamente la lengua Latina con la Española, que lleguen à fer vna mifma" (1687a: 4) ("Still, Spain is singular in this rare and providential privilege, conceded not even to Italy, or Rome itself, head of the World and the Church: that the Latin and the Spanish tongues coincide with each other so reciprocally that they end up becoming a single language").[54]

Garabito rehearses a complementary argument in the other preliminary texts he pens. In his dedication to the Belgian Charles de Noyelle, Father General of the Society of Jesus, Garabito associates the poem with the multilingual miracle of Pentecost, and characterizes the comprehensive reach of the Spanish-Latin text as equivalent to the Jesuit order's work as global promoters of the Catholic faith (1687b: 3–4). As Messer and Williams point out, Garabito's description of Valdés's bilingual construct shares a vision of Spanish-Latin writing endorsed for almost two centuries by Spanish writers, for whom "[t]he Hispano-Latin format tie[d] Spain and its language to the religious center of Rome and Roman Catholicism, and the secular center of the glorious Roman Empire, both part of a heritage of which Spain was proud" (2017: 18). But this dual affiliation to Rome, as both Catholic and imperial paradigm, reaches new dimensions in the context of the New World, since Valdés's hybrid language is now presented as a transatlantic sign of territorial expansionism and cultural circulation, with

---

[54] Garabito is following a long-practiced tendency in Spain, one that Thomas deemed the "intransigent patriotism" of sixteenth-century Spanish humanists, who tried to show that Spanish could more easily accommodate Latin syntax than Italian (1909: 38).

a universal intelligibility so superlative that it merits the title—according to Garabito in his prologue—of a *Non plus ultra* of poetry, the phrase borrowed from the caption inscribed on the columns of Hercules that decorated the arms of Lima. All this explains the remarkable corollary that Garabito proposes in the Latin elegy he composed honoring the death of his uncle—this time with an allusion to Virgil's home town of Mantua, rather than Rome:[55]

> Nec quo diremptum[56] ſingultu Mantua Vatem
> Planxerat, orba ſuo ſidere Lima dolet.
> Plus moeret; pluris facta est iactura;
> Mantua, cauſa tibi eſt, copia, Lima tibi.
> Virgilium Latiae, teſtudinis illa, flet iſta
> Virgilium Hiſpanae, Virgilium Auſoniae.
>
> 1687c: vv. 7–12

> Nor had Mantua mourned for the Poet,[57] when he was carried away
> With such sobs as Lima, orphaned of her star, now mourns.
> Lima mourns the more, for a loss of what is greater has occurred:
> You, Mantua, have a cause to grieve; You, Lima, have a multitude [of causes for which to grieve].[58]
> The former mourns the Virgil of the Latian lyre, the latter
> The Virgil of both the Hispanic and the Italian lyre.
>
> Braidotti and Rosso 2017: 147

In Garabito's opinion, the grief of Lima turns out to be quantitatively greater than that of Mantua: while Mantua had one cause to grieve with the loss of Virgil, Lima has multiple causes, because the death of the Spanish-Latin poet Valdés constitutes the death of "the Poet" of both Spain and Italy: *Virgilium Hiſpanae, Virgilium Auſoniae.*[59] This is the sense of the opposition between *cauſa*

---

[55] For the Latin poems included in the preliminaries of the *Fundación y Grandezas*, I use the English translations by Erminio Braidotti and John P. Rosso included in Messer and Williams's edition (2017: 145–52). I occasionally make amendments in my citations, which I explain in footnotes.

[56] The original says *direptum*. It should be *diremptum*, participle of *dirimo*.

[57] Braidotti and Rosso translate *Vatem* as "its poet," but in the original, the word is capitalized and has no possessive. Garabito is probably thinking of the antonomastic title "the Poet," which typically designated Virgil.

[58] Braidotti and Rosso translate *copia* as "[grief's] full flood": "You, Mantua, have cause to grieve, You, Lima, grief's full flood." I believe that with *copia* Garabito wants to suggest a comparison rather than simple abundance: if Rome had one cause for which to mourn, Lima has many. This sense is compatible with the subsequent two verses.

[59] Servius explains that *Ausonia* (a word he says derives from Auson, son of Odysseus and Calypso) is a designation first used for a section and then for the whole of Italy (1878: 374, commentary 171). Lewis and Short's dictionary indicates that *Ausones* (i.e., the inhabitants of Auosonia) is "a very ancient, perhaps Greek, name of the primitive inhabitants of Middle and Lower Italy" (1879: s.v. "Ausones").

and *copia* (v. 10): for Garabito, Valdés is not just an avatar of Virgil (in the sense proposed in Chapter 1), but rather a transatlantic compound of the Roman poet that comprehends both its Old World past and its New World present.

The rest of the items included in the frontmatter follow the logic set up by Garabito. Several of them are Latin poems, labeled *Epigramma* even when they usually contain a fair number of lines (instead of the brevity characteristic of Classical epigrams). Sometimes they do not indicate an author (some may be by Garabito, though he only claims to be the author of the Latin elegy, and his prologue says that friends and admirers supplied the other poems compiled in the preliminaries). One of these unsigned Latin *epigrammata*, titled "Ervditissimo Patri Roderico de Valdès Limano ..." ("To the Most Erudite Limenian Father Rodrigo de Valdés ..."), celebrates the mechanics of sameness and difference embedded in the Latin-Spanish language:

> Qvam mirum, Auctor, opus, caelandum[60] marmore condis,
> Vno cùm duplex fundis ab ore melos?
> Quifque (vel Hifpano, Latio vel perfonat, ore)
> Legerit hoc mirae laudis, & artis opus;
> Efferet ad Superos, iteratis ebibet horis,
> Nec fua verba leget, dum fua verba leget:
> Hifpano canis, Hifpanus fua perleget ore
> Ipfe canis Latio, nec fua verba leget.
> Ore fluis Latio, leget hic sua verba Latinus;
> Effluis Hifpano, nec fua verba leget.
> O decus aeternum! quam fuavi voce maritar,
> Et nectit linguas vna Latina duas!
>
> vv. 1–12

> How wondrous a work, worthy of being carved in marble, you establish,
>   O Author,[61]
> When you forge[62] a double song from single mouth!
> Every person (whether he speaks from Spanish or from Latin mouth)

---

[60] The original says *coelandum*. It should say *caelandum*, gerundive of *caelo*.
[61] Braidotti and Rosso omitted a clause in their translation: in the first verse, the adjectival phrase *caelandum marmore* (that which ought to be engraved in marble), whose gerundive modifies the word *opus*. I have supplied a translation for this omitted section. I have also changed their rendering of *condis*, from "you are composing" to "you establish," since I believe that the poem seeks to evoke the foundational connotations of the verb *condere* (lexicalized in the chronographic convention *ab urbe condita*).
[62] Braidotti and Rosso translate *fundis* as "you pour forth." I prefer "you forge" to suggest the process of smithing, which the verb *fundo* connotes.

Shall have read this work of wondrous praise and skill,
Shall exalt it to the Heavens above, and savor it again in later hours,
Nor shall he read his own words, as his own words he reads:
If you sing from Spanish mouth, a Spaniard here will read his words,
But if you sing from Latin mouth, he will not read his words.
If you flow forth in Latin tongue, a Latin here will read his words.
But if in Spanish you flow forth, his words he will not read.
O everlasting ornament! With voice how sweet does the one
Latin marry and combine the twofold tongues!

Braidotti and Rosso 2017: 148

The poem begins with an interesting verbal choice: the word *condis*—literally "you put together," used in Latin historiography to indicate the founding or establishment of a town or a city. In composing his poem (a process of smelting and forging, as the verb *fundis* in the second line suggests), Valdés performs a foundational gesture—associated, of course, with the city of Lima. But it is in the rhetorical parallels between imaginary Spanish and Latin speakers, and their respective languages (vv. 7 to 9 in the citation), where the author of this *epigramma* emphasizes the transcultural appeal of Valdés's poem. A Spaniard or a "Latin" (i.e., a person who speaks Latin) listening to the *Fundación y Grandezas*, according to the *epigramma*, may or may not recognize their own language at first: *Nec sua verba leget, dum sua verba leget*. Understanding requires, instead, a deliberate act and expectation: speakers must decide to see their own languages in the Spanish-Latin diction in order to access it, which means that legibility does not depend on an immutable linguistic identity, but rather, on the strategic flexibility of the reader. All this, interesting in poetic and philosophical terms, contains a special message for colonial readers struggling with the impossibility of establishing an equilibrium between Old World prestige and New World identity. Hence the foundational gesture in the opening line of "Ervditissimo Patri": the linguistic "self-alterity" that this *epigramma* assigns to Valdés's Spanish-Latin language ultimately translates into a political reality in the urban space of Lima, in which the imperial order can also recognize itself, despite the city's newness—as long as it wishes to do so. This key message, subtly embedded here, becomes explicit in a later *epigramma*, "Ad Urbem Limam Americae Meridionalis Regiam" ("To the Royal City Lima, of South America"). These are its opening lines:

Lima, novi Regina poli, quae ditibus aruis
Auriferas profers inter aratra ſpicas:
Vt gaudes famula Hiſpano, Regique Latino!

Legibus ille patrijs, imperat iſte ſacris.
Vtraque lingua tuas effert ad ſidera laudes,
Laudi namque tuae non erat vna ſatis.

vv. 1–6

Lima, Queen of the new pole,[63] who from your rich plow lands
Bring forth among the plows the golden heads of wheat,
How you rejoice as handmaid of the Spanish and the Latin King![64]
The former rules with patriarchal laws, the latter, those of God.
Each of the two tongues bears forth your praises to the stars,
For one alone was insufficient for such praise.

Braidotti and Rosso 2017: 151

Here, the epithet "City of the Kings" is transformed into praise for Lima as both a queen (in the New World) and a handmaid of two kings (the Spanish monarch and the Pope). This ambiguous transatlantic social performance, simultaneously royal and servile, synthesizes Lima's complex position in the political imagination of Valdés's society. And just as the Spanish-Latin language of the *Fundación y Grandezas* harmonizes the political and the religious (represented here by the Spanish and the Latin tongues, characteristic of the king and the Pope respectively), colonial Lima, no less dual, is subject to imperial and divine jurisdictions through its New World twofold tongue, as *non erat una satis* (one alone was insufficient). In other words, Lima is also Spanish-Latin, with all the symbolic implications that status implies: universal, ecumenical, imperial, and Catholic. A few lines later, the poem also characterizes Valdés's role in these transatlantic exchanges in apocalyptic terms: "Has acies vibrante manu Rodericus agebat" (vv. 11–2) ("These two edges [i.e., Latin and Spanish] Rodrigo handled with brandishing hand"). As the poem's subheading explains, the author of the "Ad Urbem Limam" *epigramma* borrowed the image of the tongue as a two-edged sword from a line of the biblical book of Revelations: "de ore eius gladius utraque parte acutus exiebat" (Vulgate Bible, Revelations 1.14) ("from its mouth came out a sharp double-edged sword").[65]

---

[63] Braidotti and Rosso translate *novi poli* as "new sky." I prefer the more literal "new pole," as I believe this term is part of the axial lexicon (along with austral, meridional, Antarctic, etc.) with which, as we saw in the conclusion of Chapter 1, colonial writers emphasized the idea of the south as a New World differential.

[64] As Braidotti and Rosso point out, the *rex latinus* alluded to here is the Pope.

[65] The poem indicates that the image appears in Chapter 4 of the Book of Revelations, but—as Braidotti and Rosso point out—the original source is Revelations 1.16.

The other prefatory poems largely adopt the same idea, modulated in different ways but always highlighting the transatlantic importance of Valdés and the qualities of his poetic conflation of Spanish and Latin. The "Ervditissimo Patri" *epigramma* discussed above notices that an anagram of Valdés's name produces the Latin word *Lavdes*, "praises." Another *epigramma* imagines Death choosing for Valdés the same arrow she had used to kill Horace, Virgil, Cicero, John Duns Scotus (or perhaps John Scotus Eriugena), Durandus de Saint-Pourçain, and Saint Thomas Aquinas ("Falce minax ..").[66] Another has Valdés requesting his own funerary services from Lima by speaking to his beloved city in Spanish-Latin ("Hic vbi ..."). And another states that Valdés's language united the formerly divided twin peaks of the Muses' Mount Parnassus ("Vnius ecce ..."). The poems in Spanish follow suit. One sonnet ("Al meſmo padre ...") calls him a "nuevo Apolo" ("new Apollo") who sings "en una y otra lengua, peregrino" ("in one and another tongue, a pilgrim"). Another, signed by Esteban Cruzado y Aragón, hails Valdés as a new Homer and new Virgil, a Spanish Horace and a Latin Góngora ("Mvda de abſorta ..."). These compositions, all celebrating the qualities of Spanish-Latin by presenting Valdés as a synthesis of the great poetic and intellectual luminaries of the Ancient and Renaissance worlds, are not only rhetorical praises, but also ideological statements. Valdés and his beloved Lima, all these poems point out, embody the universalist and transhistorical properties of the Spanish-Latin hybrid. Hence the revelatory importance of a caveat included in a celebratory sonnet in Spanish (signed by Esteban Cruzado y Ferrer), worth reproducing in its entirety:

> A La Fama diò Roma ſus blaſones
> En ſu Latina lengua dominante,
> Que, en periodos terſa y elegante,
> Eterniza ſus Marios, y Catones.
> En vno y otro Mundo ſus pendones
> Tremola Eſpaña con poder pujante,
> Y en ſu idioma Eſpañol dà luz brillante
> A Pizarros, Corteſes, y Colones.

---

[66] The closing line of this *epigramma* lists the other victims of Death's arrow by only one name each: "Flacce, Maro, Cicero, Scote, Durăde, Thoma." Messer and Williams suggest that the vocatives "Durăde" and "Thoma" stand for "Durante, aka Dante (Durante degli Alighieri)" and Sir Thomas More (Messer and Williams 2017: 48, 91, n. 62). I believe, however, that they more likely refer to the French Dominican Durandus de Saint-Pourçain (c. 1275–1332/4) and the *Doctor Angelicus* Thomas Aquinas (1225–74). This would concord with the inclusion of John Duns Scotus (or John Scotus Eriugena), as the first three names identify three great Latin poets, while the other three, prominent theologians of the Middle Ages.

A Eſpaña transformò en Mahometana
(ò! lo que eſta memoria nos laſtima)
Vn ignorante Rey, vn infiel, digo.
Mas tu pluma, en deſpique, haze Chriſtiana,
Romana à vn tiempo, y Eſpañola à Lima.
O vaſſallo diſcreto! ò fiel Rodrigo!

                                                1687b: n.p.

Rome gave her accolades to Fame
in her imperious Latin language,
which, smooth and elegant in its constructions,
eternalizes her Mariuses and Catos.
Spain, in one World and the other
waves her banners with mighty power,
and gives shining light in her Spanish language
to Pizarros, Cortezes, and Columbuses.
Spain was turned Muhammedan
(alas! how much this memory hurts us!)
by an ignorant King—an infidel, I mean.
But your quill, in reprisal, renders Lima
at once Christian, Roman, and Spanish.
O discreet vassal! O faithful Rodrigo!

The opening quartets establish, once again, a parallel between Roman and Spanish imperialisms mediated by their languages. The tercets, however, introduce a crucial (and, in the eyes of the poet, painful) reminder: there was a time when Spain was not Christian, but Muslim. In the context of celebrating the multilingualism of *Fundación y Grandezas*, this point is particularly delicate. As Garabito and his colleagues exhaustively insist, a fundamental attribute of the hybrid Spanish-Latin is its capacity for transcultural intelligibility, but this comes with a qualification: not all ideologies are equally welcomed in Spanish imperial universalism. Garabito had subtly made his point in his dedication to the king: Valdés's verses, he says in lines cited earlier, are composed with "such a union and identity of phrases and voices that they will be understood by the nations most alien and foreign to the Spanish language, as long as they know Latin" (1687a: 4–5). The final caveat, "as long as they know Latin," is not incidental; rather, it delimits the imaginary permeability of Valdés's poem, the borders of its universality. If the *Fundación y Grandezas* is endowed with an extraordinary legibility on account of its multilingualism, its Roman and Spanish attributes also perform the role of discriminating filters for those beyond the margins of transatlantic Christendom. While a subtle gesture in Garabito's "Dedicación," this is the explicit thesis of the sonnet by Cruzado y Ferrer. As an act of historical revenge against the Muslim heritage of Spain—and more specifically, as a counterpoint to the exchanges between Castilian and Arabic that crystallized in the modern Spanish language, which so afflicted Spain's Catholic zeal and its anxiety for European self-definition—Valdés's Latin-Spanish is cast as a belated Reconquista tactic to "cleanse" the imperial language of its "Moorish impurities." The hybrid diction of Valdés's poem turns out to be, paradoxically, a purist hybridity.

This bizarre property is fundamental to the symbolic value of Valdés's poem, and illuminates the special character that a *criollo* Spanish-Latin poem possessed with respect to its peninsular antecedents. Briesemeister has noticed that the first instances of Spanish-Latin compositions in Spain date back to the late fifteenth century and coincide with theories about the "corruption" of the Latin spoken in Spain—a supposed consequence of "barbarian" and Arabic incursions in the Iberian peninsula (1986: 108).[67] The identification between Latin and Spanish was thus read as a nostalgic recuperation of an illusory original language, a fiction that was compounded by the historical and religious values associated, via Latin, with Rome. Valdés's poem, written in the late seventeenth century, returns to all these ideological questions, adding into the fanciful mix an insoluble component: the peripheral voice of a Limenian struggling to unencumber himself of the newness of the New World. In effect, as the scholars who have written on the *Fundación y Grandezas* in recent years tend to agree, Valdés and his colleagues were part of an ongoing tradition of *criollo* self-vindication—the recurrent aspiration of colonial writers to provide an image of the New World free from exoticized exaggerations and misrepresentations, to combat European prejudices about American intellectuals, to demonstrate the potential value of American communities in the renewal of the Spanish Empire, and to prove a cultural commensurability with respect to Europe.[68]

Hence the uneasy coexistence of variegated goals in the *Fundación y Grandezas*: expression of both loyalty to the Crown and devotion to the local *patria* (in the restricted, pre-nationalist sense of *patria* or place where one was

---

[67] As the anonymous grammar printed in Louvaine (1555) states, the category of "barbarian" here included, among others, Carthaginians, Goths, Vandals, Chatti, Huns, and the Alani (qtd. in Briesemeister 1986: 110).

[68] See Briesemeister 1986: 100–4; Guibovich 2007: 357; Mazzotti 1996: 60; and Mazzati 2009: 135, 138–9, 148–9; Vinatea 2017: 195; and Messer and Williams 2017: 32–6.

born); written in both a comprehensive *lingua franca* and a discriminating *sermo Latinus*; both ancient monument and modern novelty; with Lima as both acquiescent periphery and (borrowing a key insight by Mazzotti) American *axis mundi*.[69] Martina Vinatea comments that Valdés's poem partakes in efforts to define Spanish as an "ecumenical language" (2017: 197). It does not seem out of place to elaborate on the implications of the term "ecumenical," derived from the Greek οἰκουμένη (*oikoumenē*), and used (as documented by the Liddell–Scott–Jones *Greek–English Lexicon*) first to refer to any inhabited region and then (without ever fully losing its original meaning) restricted to the Greek world, as opposed to "barbarian lands" (definition A). The strategic flexibility of the word *oikoumenē*, comprehensive and exclusivist in accordance with the rhetorical needs of its user, reflects a recurrent trait of imperial imagination: its universalist appetite and, at the same time, its perennial desire for homogeneity. In the viceregal capital of Peru, so afflicted by its newness, this paradoxical ecumenical circumscription was only exacerbated. In effect, the colonial Spanish-Latin language, already universalist and restricted in the sense explained above, also needed to be elastic enough to articulate the desired urban commensurability between the European past and the American present—not unlike the walls of Lima, finished the same year Valdés's poem was published.

Conclusions

The *Historia de la fundación de Lima* ("History of the Foundation of Lima," 1639), by the Andalusian-born Jesuit Bernabé Cobo, begins with this anxious desire: "Es la ciudad de Lima el Imperio y Corte de este reino de la Nueva Castilla del Perú, y tan esclarecida por muchas excelencias que en ella concurren, que solo le faltan los años para poder competir en grandeza y majestad con las mas nobles de Europa (calidad que sin sentírsele irá dando el tiempo)" ((1639) 1882: 7) ("The city of Lima is head and court of this kingdom of New Castile of Peru, and is so illustrious in its many excellences, that it is only lacking in years to be able to compete with the greatness and majesty of the noblest cities of Europe (though this quality will quietly appear as time passes)"). Cobo had first arrived in Lima in the early months of 1599, when he was seventeen years old, and was about forty-seven years old by the time he was penning his *Historia*,

---

[69] See Mazzotti 2009: 141, 144, 168.

having spent thirty years in Peru (most of them in Lima).[70] His treatise, a diligent chorography that combines foundational documents and a description of its edifices, institutions, and offices, monumentalizes the capital of the viceroyalty at a time when the city was reaching its first century of existence. Responding to that centennial milestone with his *Historia*, Cobo clearly wishes to begin with an enthusiastic commendation of his adoptive city. Nevertheless, he also feels compelled to make a caveat that rehearses the fundamental problem we have seen throughout this chapter: as a New World city, Lima remained, in spite of all its splendid features, still incommensurable with great European cities because it was "lacking in years"—it did not possess their venerable antiquity.

Father Cobo published his treatise in 1639, about forty-nine years after the reception of Don García Hurtado de Mendoza and forty-eight years before Valdés's poem was published and the walls of Lima were completed. Equidistant from the two moments of Limenian history examined above, this opening remark is a revealing textual link in a genealogy of the New World anxiety that began in the aftermath of the conquest and continued through the mid-colonial period. While his lionization of Lima does not make explicit comparisons between his adoptive city and Classical antiquity, it could have done so, since Cobo was schooled in such matters—as he had declared in the statement for his examination as a student of the Jesuit order (which he took in 1601, at age nineteen), "He estudiado en la Compañía de Jesús latinidad, arte de Manuel Álvarez,[71] epístolas de Cicerón, Tullio de officiis, Virgilio, Lucano, Oraciones de Ciceron, Salustio Quinto Cursio, Retórica del Priano[72] y otros autores y paréceme que tengo facilidad en el uso de la lengua latina" (1601: xix) ("In the Society of Jesus I have studied Latin, the grammar by Manuel Alvarez, the epistles of Cicero, *De Officiis* by Tullius [Cicero], Virgil, Lucan, the *Orations* by Cicero, Sallust, Quintus Curtius, *Rhetoric* by Priano and other authors, and it appears to me that I have aptitude in the use of the Latin language"). This roster of Latin authorities, another illustration of the role of Classical texts in the intellectual formation of young Jesuit scholars in Lima, reverberates strongly with the cases we have evaluated in this chapter. In particular, the presence of Virgil in the curricular

---

[70] For a biography of Cobo, see the prefatory study M. González de la Rosa included in his edition of the *Historia de la fundación de Lima* (1882: ii–xvi).

[71] Manoel Alvarez was the author of *De institutione grammatica libri tres*, a popular introduction to Latin grammar adopted by the Jesuits as part of their *Ratio Studiorum*, their official curriculum, in the sixteenth century.

[72] "Priano" is the apheresis or an incomplete transcription of "Cypriano"—for Cypriano de Soarez, the author of *De Arte Rhetorica*, a sixteenth-century textbook on rhetoric included in the *Ratio Studiorum* and used for almost 300 years by the Jesuits as an introduction to the subject.

report of someone like Cobo, who would become a foundational historiographic authority for Lima, resonates again with the singular role of "the Poet" in the city's periodic exercises of self-imagination.

Cobo was confident that New World anxiety would dissipate "as time passes." As we have seen, the cases of Nolasco Mere's maps and Valdés's poem, belonging to the later part of the seventeenth century, proved him wrong. Not only did the question of Lima's newness continue to haunt projects as illustrious as the construction of its fortification and the Latin epic narrative about its foundation, but the arrival of the eighteenth century, far from allaying the anxiety, only exacerbated it. Indeed, against Cobo's estimations, the steady expansion of Lima, its growing geopolitical power, as well as its cultural and material wealth, pressed its prideful citizens to search for more compensatory images to shore up their self-perception with respect to the prestigious urban centers across the Atlantic. The Classics typically provided a formidable set of pretexts and motifs that could be deployed in these efforts. Evidence of this is the flourishing of lyric and epic poetry focused on the city of Lima in the second half of the seventeenth and the first half of the eighteenth century. Virgil's *Aeneid* would, of course, constitute a primary reference for the development of these encomiastic forms of chorographic poetry.

An example of this literary development, ideologically linked to Nolasco Mere's maps and Valdés's poem, will serve to conclude this chapter. As mentioned above, the *katabasis* or descent into the Underworld, one of the most famous passages of the *Aeneid*, furnishes the poem with a pretext to recapitulate the monumental history of Rome, from its mythical foundation to the age of Emperor Augustus. Upon meeting the shadow of his father Anchises, Aeneas is given a "prophecy" of the great events and figures who will come after the time of the narrative (a few years after the end of the Trojan War) and before the time of the composition (Virgil's own era). This "prophecy motif" would become an almost unavoidable trope in the subsequent tradition of epic poetry, including that produced in the New World. But how could the centuries of events reported by Anchises translate into the brief history of a city like Lima?

This question clearly emerged while Don Luis Antonio de Oviedo y Herrera, Conde de la Granja, was composing his epic poem *Vida de Sta. Rosa de Santa Maria, Natvral de Lima, y Patrona del Peru. Poema heroyco* ("Life of Saint Rose of Saint Mary, born in Lima, and Patron of Peru. Heroic Poem"). The poem, published in 1711, is a twelve-canto biographical epic narrative about Saint Rose of Lima, the first saint in the Americas, but it is also a lionization of her city— which is characterized as an extraordinary *locus amoenus* and compared with the old capitals of Asia (Aleppo and Tauris), Africa (Carthage and Cairo), and Europe (Amsterdam and Geneva). Amid its recurrent praise of the city, the poem describes the growth of Saint Rose, a precociously pious child who amazes the Limenians with her miracles. Midway through the story, Rose decides to join the convent. The devil, furious about her decision (for it threatens his nefarious influence in Lima), descends into the depths of the Pichincha volcano. In the cavities of the volcano live two survivors of the Incan Empire: an old wizard called Bilcaoma and a beautiful prince named Yupanqui; the latter, a combination of Prometheus and Segismund, is fettered to a rock without knowing why. The devil's descent inspires a dream in Bilcaoma; the wizard then releases Yupanqui and reveals to the young prince that he is the last descendant of Incan royalty, and that he has been kept a prisoner until the moment when he would be ready to lead a rebellion against the Spanish and Christianity in the New World. Bilcaoma thus performs the role of Anchises in the *Aeneid*, recapitulating to the young Yupanqui the myths and history of the Incan Empire, providing an extensive account of the civil war between the Incas Huascar and Atahualpa, and the clash between Spaniards and Incas that brought down the latter's empire.

In 1732, twenty-one years after the publication of Oviedo y Herrera's *Vida de Sta. Rosa*, the polymath Pedro de Peralta Barnuevo Rocha y Benavides published *Lima fundada* ("The Founding of Lima"), another epic poem about the foundation and the greatness of the city, written in ten long cantos in two volumes. The epic hero is Francisco Pizarro, founder of the city. Peralta's poem includes the early clash between Spanish conquistadors and Incas, the internecine fights among conquistadors, the final victory of Pizarro's men, and the foundation of Lima as capital of the new realm. But, as his precursor Rodrigo de Valdés had done, Peralta also reserves a substantial number of lines for the meticulous description of all aspects of Lima and Peru—including details about flora, fauna, minerals, climatic conditions, edifices, institutions, historical episodes, prominent citizens, religious authorities and saints, intellectuals and artists (including Valdés himself), and so on. The device that justifies this wealth of information is, again, a version of the prophecy motif of the *Aeneid*, presented in this way: while taking a walk, Pizarro finds himself lost in the clearing of a forest, where a young male figure waits for him. The strange character reveals himself to be the "spirit of Lima," youthful as a reflection of the New World. After prophesizing to Pizarro the foundation of Lima, the youth begins an extensive report of the almost 200 years of natural, social, cultural, and political history of Lima, from the time of Pizarro's arrival to the year in which the poem was being composed (*c*. 1731). The prophecy is so meticulous that it occupies almost half of the entire poem (with the strange effect that the epic hero of the story remains still and listening to a prophet for about half of his quest).[73]

These two complex poems deserve far more attention than can be afforded here, but the brief summaries given above do illustrate how the heavy urban archives of the Old World, epitomized in the millenarian prophecy of Anchises to his son Aeneas, are still taxing for the anxious chorographers of the New World by the start of the eighteenth century. Self-conscious about that incommensurability, and yet pressed into the production of prophetic episodes for their epic narratives, both poets resort to a strategy of literary negotiation. Oviedo, in the conservative tradition of "extirpation of idolatry," transfers the prophecy motif to the Incan past—as a subterranean vestige of an indigenous paganism affiliated with the devil, and as a latent threat to the Christian Spanish order. Peralta, perhaps more creatively, proposes a new arithmetic: 200 years of Limenian history are tantamount to the millenarian history of European cities, since those two centuries have been enough to produce the extraordinary cultural wealth of Lima—garrulously reported by the young prophet across hundreds of verses. In one way or another, Lima's lack of monumental antiquity is literarily metabolized, and Anchises's prophecy is given a place within American newness. These late colonial instances prove that the passing of time only further inflamed Lima's New World anxiety. Even with 200 years of colonial history, the city is still unbearably new.

---

[73] For a detailed consideration of this poem and the implications of the prophecy motif, see Campos-Muñoz 2015.

3

Personae

*Mi aflicción no tiene medida porque la calumnia me ahoga,
como aquellas serpientes de Laocoonte.*

*My affliction is boundless, for calumny suffocates me,
like the serpents of Laocoön.*
Simón Bolívar, letter to Joaquín Mosquera, Fucha, March 8, 1830

Preliminaries

On the July 20, 1846, in the main square of Bogotá, the world's first public statue of Simón Bolívar was unveiled. Bolívar had passed away sixteen years before, on December 17, 1830. The final stage of his life had been marked by both a long and difficult respiratory illness and intense controversy over his political ideas for the new Latin American republics. Yet by 1846, much of the virulent criticism had receded, and Bolívar began to recover his reputation as the crafter (along with Argentine José de San Martín) of South American political independence from Spain. It was in this atmosphere of renewed favor that his close friend, influential philanthropist José Ignacio París Ricaurte, could commission in 1844 a commemorative statue of the Liberator, to be crafted by Italian sculptor Pietro Tenerani.

The first matter that Tenerani had to solve was how Bolívar's facial features should look—a difficult decision, since even during the General's lifetime several highly varied textual and visual versions of his face were in circulation.[1] Tenerani

---

[1] These would play an important role in the long debate on the racial and ethnic origins of Bolívar, one of the issues that most obsessed his partisans and political enemies, as well as his biographers. For more on this topic and debate, see Vicente Lecuna (1956, 1: 1–44). While Lecuna goes to great lengths to "defend" Bolívar's whiteness against the "accusations" of being mestizo, John Lynch has noted that "[t]he family lineage has been scoured for signs of race mixture in a society of whites, Indians and blacks, where neighbours were sensitive to the slightest variant, but, in spite of dubious evidence dating from 1673, the Bolívars were always white" (2006: 2).

Fig. 3.1 *Bolívar*, by Pietro Tenerani, Plaza Bolívar, Bogotá, Colombia (1846). Alamy Stock Photo.

finally chose to base the head on a portrait by the French illustrator François Désiré Roulin, began the designs and maquettes, modeled the statue in Rome, and cast it in Munich in 1844. When the work was done, Tenerani had sculpted an imposing 8.5-foot bronze statue of the General in military dress, holding a sword in his right hand and a rolled document in the left. Tenerani dressed his *Bolívar* in attire typical of a general of the Patriotic army, while the sword and document clearly alluded to his military, political, and juridical role in the constitution of the new republics. The sculptor, however, allowed himself the license of adding one element that was not part of Bolívar's conventional iconography: a long, Roman-like toga covering most of the General's uniform. An aura of antiquity marks the statue: even today, in one of the busiest areas of

Bogotá, the world's first public monument dedicated to the Venezuelan Liberator endures, exhibiting his Classical senatorial garment to the many visitors of the former "Main Square"—since renamed, of course, "Bolívar Square."

This Classicalization of Bolívar was no accident. In rendering his *Bolívar* an ancient character, Tenerani was continuing the practice of his master, the renowned Italian artist Antonio Canova (often regarded as the most important European sculptor of the eighteenth century). Canova had achieved fame in Europe for his numerous representations and adaptations of Classical myths and motifs. Moreover, his Neoclassical predilections had enjoyed the patronage of important figures—including Napoleon Bonaparte, whose face became the model for a spectacular marble representing a victorious Mars.[2] Tenerani, consequently, adapted the techniques of his master Canova in his depiction of the Liberator. However, it would be a mistake to reduce his senatorial *Bolívar* to a mere iteration of the European Neoclassical taste that so influenced Latin American artistic preferences of the late eighteenth and early nineteenth centuries. Tenerani's depiction also conveyed, intentionally or not, the features of a phenomenon that remains understudied in scholarship on the Latin American Age of Revolution: the pervasive utilization of the Classics as a mechanism of representation and intervention in the political arena of the time. As seen in the first two chapters, an erratic tradition of Classicisms had been brewing in the region for centuries by the time the wars began, and that tradition, far from vanishing, found its way into the language and political demands of the new period. By way of synecdoche, this chapter approaches the impact of the Classics during the emancipatory era through the pivotal figure of Simón Bolívar, taking the Liberator as exemplary actor, object, motif, agent, commentator, and victim— in short, as a *dramatis persona*—of the Classical impetus of his era.

During the first three decades of the nineteenth century, the period of Bolívar's main activity, three main concerns dominated the political debates of the time: a) the position of Latin American communities with respect to Europe—regarding not only Spanish colonial power, but also the cultural and ideological influence of France and the economic presence of the British Empire in the Americas; b) the relationship among different Latin American communities, both during the revolution and, to an even greater extent, in its aftermath (a question that included the organization of new nations, the formation of confederacies, the separation of territories previously conjoined, etc.); and c) the form of government (centralist or federalist, republican or monarchist) to be

---

[2] For an exhaustive analysis of this case, see Johns 1998.

adopted by each of the new nations. These difficult and often intertwined debates become all the more complex when considering the various ways in which they were articulated—in the rationalist language of the Enlightenment, the grandiloquent rhetoric of Romanticism, and the transcendentalist nationalism embedded in various forms of *caudillismo*. While not engendered by the revolution, these ideological and discursive paradigms were nonetheless heightened both by the struggle against Spain and the internecine wars among Latin American leaders for control of the emergent nations.

The Classics would be continuously present in these various processes: whether as symbols, categories and motifs used in debates, or as models of political constitution, the tales and characters of ancient Greece and Rome ceased to be the province of erudite specialists and became widely popular mechanisms for the representation, discussion, and analysis of political events. Motifs that once required acquaintance with the histories of Livy and Plutarch, the poems of Pindar and Virgil, the commentaries of Dionysus of Halicarnassus and Horace, or the mythologies of Ovid and Apollodorus began to move beyond the academic sphere. Now, as part of popular knowledge, those same motifs were one day deployed in a political speech; another, in a libelous inscription posted on the walls of a town; and the next, in a satiric poem published in one of the many burgeoning newspapers. Little by little, the Classics began to pervade the most diverse social and cultural realms. In all this, the key figure of Bolívar promptly became entangled in a myriad of Classical references, crafted by his friends and enemies alike, both criticizing and celebrating his role in the revolution.[3]

Not that the Classics had ever been absent from the intellectual endeavors of the New World. The Classics, as noted in Chapter 1, had been at the core of the foundational narratives of the Americas, taking a prominent role in the conceptual negotiation of the New and Old Worlds, and in the creation of American textual authorities. Likewise, throughout the colonial period the most

---

[3] For a survey of the history of the Classics in the emancipatory period, and particularly on the teaching of Ancient Greek and Latin during the revolution and in its aftermath, see Taboada 2014. Albeit not focused on the impact of the Classics in popular culture, the article explains the ideological and political coordinates through which the Classics were involved in debates about the emancipatory process—examples include the preference some intellectuals expressed for a new education in Spanish as a substitute for colonial and ecclesiastical instruction in Latin; perceptions of the "conservative" character of Latin education versus the more "disruptive" appeal of ancient Greek; and the role of a French bourgeois-type of Classicism in the American reception of the Classics. As Taboada points out, the Classics were important points of reference in the French Revolution, and their role in the Age of Revolution in Latin America carried with it those contemporary transatlantic echoes (2014: 210–11).

renowned authors of the New World produced versions of the Classics adapted to the Americas. At times, indigenous languages would blend with ancient motifs, as is the case with *El rapto de Proserpina y sueño de Endimión* (mid-1650s) ("The Abduction of Proserpina and the Dream of Endymion"), written in Quechua by the Cuzquenian poet Juan Espinoza Medrano, "El Lunarejo" (also known by his contemporaries as "the Demosthenes of the Indies"). At other times, Amerindian mythologies merged with those of ancient Greece and Rome, as happens in the interaction between the play *El divino Narciso* (1685) ("Divine Narcissus") and its dramatic prelude, both by Sor Juana Inés de la Cruz—often hailed by critics and publishers as "the Tenth Muse." This fascination with the Classical tradition often articulated critical anxieties emerging from the communities of the New World—as Chapter 2 illustrates, such was the troubled case of Lima, whose Virgilian adaptations exemplify the city's perennial attempts to define its status as New World capital within the transatlantic empire. By the end of the eighteenth century, when the first signs of what would become the revolution were noticeable, there was an already old and uninterrupted tradition of self-reflective Latin American narratives inspired by the legacy of the Classics. Whether for missionary and ecclesiastical purposes, the dramatization of *mestizaje*, the articulation of the *criollo* imagination, or the negotiation of cultural anxieties with respect to the Old World, the language of the ancients was ingrained in the imaginary of Spanish America.

The main difference between colonial uses of the Classics and their iterations in the era of Bolívar was determined, of course, by the project of emancipation. The narcissistic and intellectualized dialogue with the Classics characteristic of the colonial period was replaced by the politically explicit, intentionally provocative Neoclassicism of the early nineteenth century, invoked sometimes in the name of the king and sometimes in the name of independence (sometimes by the same people, in the constant political shifting and turncoat partisanship of the age). Thus, the tension between old and new, already constitutive of the exercises of discursive foundation and anxious vindication of the New World seen in the first two chapters, now came to be metabolized as the geopolitical struggle between monarchic Spain and colonial America. And, as had happened before, this renewed tension could never be, in spite of its ferocious antagonistic rhetoric, fully dialectical. The symbolic and semantic flexibility of the Classics, already exponentialized in the transatlantic *oikoumene* of the Spanish colonial system, continued its fluctuations and ambiguities in the Age of Revolution—constituting, yet again, a highly contradictory threshold in Latin America's historical imagination. In a further twist on Hercules' pillars, the cultural heritage of Europe—both Classical and Enlightened—was confusedly appropriated by the main actors of the New World both to challenge colonialist hegemony and to formulate a new political order that explicitly aimed to emulate other colonialist models (some of which, like the British, were no less ferocious and predatory than the Spanish).[4] At the core of these contradictions was the figure of Simón Bolívar, Liberator of the Americas, whose works and days, as well as fortunes and vicissitudes, epitomized the role of the Classical tradition in the turbulence of his time.

Bolívar himself would remark that the Classics played a seminal role in his conception of the revolution. When in 1824 the US Navy officer (and future admiral) Hiram Paulding visited the Liberator shortly before the decisive Battle of Junín, he asked Bolívar when he had become interested in the independence project. Bolívar replied, "Desde mi niñez no pensaba en otra cosa: yo estaba encantado con las historias de Grecia y Roma" (Lecuna 1956, 1: 153) ("Since I was a child I did not think of anything else: I was fascinated by the stories of Greece and Rome"). Bolívar did not explain the correlation between independentist ideals and the Classical tradition on this occasion—and perhaps the absence of explanation is already a sign that the link between them was obvious for him. For us, it helps to reproduce Manuel Pérez Vila's report on some of the references to figures and authors of ancient Greece and Rome present in Bolívar's private and public writings: Plutarch, Tacitus, Polybius, Alexander the Great, Julius Caesar, Brutus, Sila, Catiline, Cato, Cicero, Hannibal, Quintus Curtius, Dionysus of Syracuse, Epaminondas, Fabius Maximus, Marc Anthony, Miltiades, Pompey, Romulus, Seneca, Socrates, Titus, et cetera—not to mention the equally vast list of mythical and literary characters to whom he frequently referred.[5] Spanning history and mythology, the common thread in these examples is their pivotal role in social, ideological, and political transformations in antiquity. As a desired mirror of the present, the Classics became, in Bolívar's memory, inseparable from his earliest concerns for independence.

A quick glance at critical episodes in Bolívar's personal and political history, especially regarding the revolution, proves that he never abandoned that youthful enthusiasm for the Classics: his early education under the tutelage of Simón Rodríguez, whom he would later remember as his personal Socrates; his active

---

[4] For a consideration of these aporias and their latency in postcolonial studies, see Kadir 1995.
[5] These catalogues are extracted from Pérez Vila 1971—especially Chapter V (137–69), which provides a detailed account of the authors, movements, and intellectual tendencies with which the Liberator engaged in the course of his life. Other studies of Classical references in the works of Bolívar include Briceño 1971 and Hernández Muñoz 1998–9.

participation in the early Neoclassical debates with the aristocratic youth of Caracas—the so-called *mantuanos*; his trip through Spain, France, and Italy, culminating in his sacred oath in the name of the freedom of Latin America at the birthplace of ancient revolts, the top of Monte Sacro on the outskirts of Rome; the troubles and fall of the United Provinces of New Granada, during which he was often likened to the monsters of ancient bestiaries; his exile and famous "Carta de Jamaica," in which he compared Latin America to the territories of the Roman Empire after its fall; his most famous speech, the controversial "Discurso de Angostura," which presents Sparta and Athens as political antecedents informing his idea of the Latin American nation; the epic account of the battles that decided the final victory over the Spanish colonial powers; the design of his infamous "Constitución Boliviana," whose life-term presidency was promptly equated with the autocratic movement that brought to an end the Roman republic; the project of Great Colombia, which, in unifying the territories of Ecuador, New Granada (now Colombia), and Venezuela, fueled suspicions of an imperialist, even monarchist project; the 1828 conspiracy to assassinate him, literally modeled after the famous murder of Julius Caesar; and even the passionate debate on his political role in the years after his death.[6] In all these events the Classics serve as a register of the fortunes of Bolívar. The statue fashioned by Tenerani reflects, in this sense, not only the vogue of European Neoclassicism, but also the specter of the Classics that so haunted the Liberator throughout his existence.

Bolívar thus epitomizes the way the Classical tradition—in particular, its mythical icons and poetics—came to dramatize the turbulent Age of Revolution. The present chapter examines this phenomenon by considering two defining moments in the political life of the Liberator. The first occurred at the peak of his popularity: shortly after the battles of Junín and Ayacucho (August 6 and December 9, 1824), decisive in achieving South American independence from Spain, Bolívar requested that the writer and politician José Joaquín de Olmedo compose a poem to commemorate the victories. A Neoclassical revolutionary paean inflected by Horatian and Pindaric motifs, the poem was composed alongside a fascinating literary conversation between Olmedo and Bolívar himself. This correspondence certainly illustrates the Liberator's robust Classical

---

[6] To this long list, we could also add the case of Bolívar's famous precursor, Francisco de Miranda. Miranda already possessed a solid Classicist foundation when he traveled to Greece in 1786—a visit that exposed him to the plights of modern Greeks under the Ottoman Empire in a way that strongly resonated with the colonial reality of Americans under the Spanish Crown. For a detailed examination of this fascinating case, see Bocchetti 2010a.

training. But more importantly, the history of the poem's composition foregrounds a fundamental incompatibility between Bolivarian history and Classicist poetry, a mismatch that ultimately exhibits Olmedo and Bolívar's anxiety when imagining how they would be inscribed in future historical accounts of the military achievements of 1824. The second case is much more somber: four years after Ayacucho, a group of young intellectuals tried to assassinate the Liberator, in a conspiracy literally inspired by and articulated through the Classical narrative of the assassination of Julius Caesar. The uncanny poetic elements of this conspiracy are rarely discussed, and if so, only anecdotally, even though Bolívar barely escaped alive, and the attempt could have radically altered the political history of the time. These two cases, I argue, reveal much more than the loaded invocation of the Classics in the development of the revolution. They show that the Classics played a key role in the transformation of the revolutionary present into a new foundational history, but also that these harmonious ideals often fell victim to the unyielding complexities of the Latin American Age of Revolution.

Hypermetric History: José Joaquín de Olmedo's *Victoria de Junín*

On January 6, 1825, after hearing the news of the decisive Battle of Ayacucho (fought less than a month before, on December 9, 1824), the Ecuadorian politician, philologist, and poet José Joaquín de Olmedo (1780–1847) sent a note to Bolívar from his residency in Guayaquil, congratulating him on the victory of the Patriotic army over the Spanish forces. Olmedo's haste, however, did not prevent him from reminding Bolívar of the poetic potential of the victory: "En este momento me dicen que sale un buque para el Perú, y no quiero perder la primera ocasión de felicitar a usted por la memorable victoria de Ayax-cuco. Con mi licencia poética transformo así el nombre de Ayacucho, porque suena desagradablemente, y ninguna cosa fea merece la inmortalidad" (Olmedo 1960: 239) ("In this moment, I have been told, a ship is heading for Peru, and I do not want to miss the earliest opportunity to congratulate you on the memorable victory of *Ayax-cuco*. With poetic license I thus transform the name of *Ayacucho*, for it sounds unpleasant, and ugly things do not deserve immortality").

It is unclear what Olmedo meant by "Ayax-cuco," or how this hyphenated, analytical metamorphosis was supposed to embellish the original Quechua term "Ayacuchu" or "Ayacucho"—the geographical area in southern Peru where the battle that largely determined Spanish American independence was fought. "Ayax," of course, could refer to the gigantic Homeric hero Ajax, who—the story goes—was one of the greatest warriors of the Achaean army, second only to Achilles. Since the main leader of the Patriotic army in the Battle of Ayacucho was not Bolívar but his lieutenant, José Antonio de Sucre, Ajax's legendary subordination to Achilles might be hinting at Sucre's subordination to Bolívar. But the lexeme "cuco" does not concede even this unsatisfactory explanation. Its dual lexical definitions do not help: "cuco" is in Spanish the "bogeyman"; as an adjective, it can mean "cute" or "sly"—attributes which, of course, hardly apply to Sucre or Ajax. Finally, reading it as the Spanish rendering of the rare Latin term *cucus*, "jackdaw," would produce something like "the jackdaw of Ajax"—a semantic extravagance which clearly leads nowhere.

Regardless of its obscurity, both *Ayax-cuco* and its scant gloss evince an important attitude toward the crucial Battle of Ayacucho: Olmedo's sense of urgency to aestheticize the events that were bringing to an end the almost 300-year-long political subjugation of Peru, and most of the Americas, to the Spanish Crown. The hasty appropriation of Ayacucho as *Ayax-cuco* hints at Olmedo's desire to ensure for himself a distinct role in the construction of a historical record that he correctly perceived as imminent; that is why, only four weeks after the battle, Olmedo quickly sanctions the victory as "memorable" and "immortal" in his letter to Bolívar. The Liberator's response to this particular letter has disappeared, but later correspondence reveals that in that lost reply, the General did commission the poetic project that Olmedo was already hinting at. Indeed, only a few months later, Olmedo sent Bolívar the first draft of what would become one of the most representative poetic pieces composed in the context of the Age of Revolution: his *Victoria de Junín. Canto a Bolívar* ("Victory of Junín. Song to Bolívar").

In an article that close-reads the design of *Victoria de Junín*, Jorge E. Rojas Otálora has foregrounded the clear structural echoes between the ancient Greek epinicion (particularly the Pindaric type) and Olmedo's poem, as well as the way in which the mythopoetic elements in the latter incorporate political propositions for the welfare of the nascent nations. In this section, I follow a parallel route to that of Rojas Otálora, approaching instead the political and ideological elements of the poem from the perspective of the poem's compositional process—an exceptionally well-documented one that provides an extraordinary example of the nexus of history, literature, and politics in this critical period. The history of the composition of *Victoria de Junín* is convoluted but exemplary, for the resulting poem attests to the many discourses that converged in the reception and understanding of the crucial battles of Junín and Ayacucho. I trace that compositional process through the correspondence between Olmedo and Bolívar. By examining the Classical motifs invoked throughout their exchanges, I discuss the problematic relationship between the poem and the historical events that inspired it and I explain how the poem attempts to respond to the competing interests surrounding the glorification of Junín and Ayacucho. These dynamics all converge on the Liberator himself, for Bolívar's characterization as the literary hero of the military events of 1824, his poetic persona, enters into acute tension with Bolívar's other personae—as political agent, historical actor, and even literary critic. The composition of *Victoria de Junín* thus becomes a critical lens through which to assess the crisis embedded in the attempt to consolidate the Bolivarian project in the new republics in Latin America, and to guarantee the prominent role of the Liberator in the histories to be written about the emancipatory present.

With more than 900 verses, *Victoria de Junín* is a long and complex poem. Olmedo imagines a mythological account of the Battle of Junín, where his poetic Muse, after having roamed over the Andean battlefield, accompanies the march and offensive of the Patriotic army, describes the action of individual heroes—in particular, Bolívar—and celebrates their victory over the Spaniards. Suddenly, a voice from the sky interrupts the triumph: it is the Inca Huayna Capac, who, after recalling the loss of his ancient empire to the Spanish invaders, hails the victory of the Patriots and prophesizes the future and definitive victory in the Battle of Ayacucho. The Inca's vision is precise: as the Muse had done with Junín, Huayna Capac provides an account of the main heroes of Ayacucho, concluding with a celebration of Bolívar. Huayna Capac's prophetic intervention closes with a celestial performance honoring the Liberator, in which mythological virgins, the muses, the arts, and even the sun participate in the triumph. At the end of the poem, contemplating the enormity of the events described, the poet promises to return to simpler, more bucolic topics, happy to receive as a reward "una dulce sonrisa de la Patria, / y el odio y el furor de los tiranos" (Olmedo 1960: 279) ("a sweet smile from the Fatherland, / and the hatred and fury of tyrants").

Different Classical motifs figure in the poem, but the most noticeable, because of its recurrence and structural function, is the Homeric *aristeia*, the moment in which an epic narrative focuses on a particular hero's military prowess. Emulating the individualizing eye typical of ancient epic poets—particularly Homer, whom the poem alludes to multiple times—Olmedo scarcely pays attention to the larger battle between the two armies, concentrating instead on the actions of the main officers of the Patriotic army. The names of the heroes resonate along with their actions: General William Miller, the British officer who assisted Bolívar in the last stage of his campaign, is compared to Achilles charging his enemies and making them flee (v. 229); the single order that General Mariano de Necochea receives is to "win the battle" and so, forgetting his rank, he faces a hundred enemies alone until he is wounded (vv. 141–8); General José María Córdoba, crowned with Venus's myrtle and Mars' laurels, crosses mountains and abysses in pursuit of the defeated Spanish forces (vv. 527–34); Bolívar, of course, rises above everyone else: his sword eclipses all other warriors, on his forehead shines the name of Colombia, and his sole presence makes the Spanish army panic and run away (vv. 258–304).

The grandiloquent style of Olmedo was designed to both glorify the victory and attribute it to particular agents; his elaborate imagery, however, also ran the risk of becoming a caricature, something that Bolívar, in reading the poem, perceived immediately. In a letter signed on June 27, 1825, the Liberator assesses this double edge with meditated irony:

> Todos los calores de la zona tórrida, todos los fuegos de Junín y Ayacucho, todos los rayos del Padre de Manco-Cápac, no han producido jamás una inflamación más intensa en la mente de un mortal. Ud. dispara ... donde no se ha disparado un tiro; Ud. se hace dueño de todos los personajes: de mí forma un Júpiter; de Sucre un Marte; de La Mar un Agamenón y un Menelao; de Córdoba un Aquiles; de Necochea, un Patroclo y un Ayax; de Miller un Diomedes, y de Lara un Ulises ... Ud, pues, nos ha sublimado tanto, que nos ha precipitado al abismo de la nada, cubriendo con una inmensidad de luces el pálido resplandor de nuestras opacas virtudes. Así, amigo mío, Ud, nos ha pulverizado con los rayos de su Júpiter, con la espada de su Marte, con el cetro de su Agamenón, con la lanza de su Aquiles, y con la sabiduría de su Ulises.
>
> 1964: 18

> All the heat of the torrid zone, all the fires of Junín and Ayacucho, all the beams of Manco Capac's father, have never produced a more intense inflammation in the mind of a mortal. You shoot ... where there were no shots; you make yourself owner of all of the characters: you fashion a Jupiter out of me; of Sucre, a Mars; of La Mar, an Agamemnon and a Menelaus; of Córdoba, an Achilles; of Necochea, a Patroclus and an Ajax; of Miller, a Diomedes; and of Lara, a Ulysses ... You have made us so sublime that you ended up hurling us into an abyss of nothingness, covering with an immensity of lights the pale glittering of our opaque virtues. Thus, my friend, you have pulverized us with the rays of your Jupiter, with the sword of your Mars, with the scepter of your Agamemnon, with the spear of your Achilles, and with the wisdom of your Ulysses.

Responding to his poet, Bolívar describes the high pitch of Olmedo's poem with an ironic but also remarkably sophisticated assessment. Under the veil of rhetorical banter, the first sentence articulates a full version of Andean history by means of three fiery images: a) the Aristotelian concept of the "torrid zone," used by Europe to imagine the Western hemisphere, and refuted (see Chapter 1) by Acosta in his *Historia natural*; b) the beams of Manco Capac's father, the Inti or Sun of the Incan mythology; and c) the military "fires" of the campaigns of Junín y Ayacucho, presented here as both the end of the colonial era and the start of a new age. Bolívar's use of Classical, Incan, and emancipatory references artfully comprises in a single statement the main motifs of Olmedo's poem, only to inflict his caustic accolade ("[such fires] have never produced a more intense inflammation in the mind of a mortal") with a sudden reminder of a poetic inaccuracy: "You shoot ... where there were no shots." Bolívar is maliciously precise: the Battle of Junín, the main object of Olmedo's poem, was an encounter of the Spanish and Patriotic vanguards, fought exclusively with spears, bayonets, and swords—indeed, not a single shot was fired. The indictment is clear: the embellishments with which Olmedo renders Junín are not only hyperbolic, but also historically impertinent. Bolívar further refines the irony with a meticulous tongue-in-cheek catalogue of correspondences between his officers and the Homeric heroes—which he knew well, since he often carried with him, even during his military campaigns, a copy of the Homeric poems.[7]

The rest of the critique sustains the same sardonic tone: "Si yo no fuese tan bueno y usted no fuese tan poeta, me avanzaría a creer que Ud. había querido hacer una parodia de *La Ilíada* con los héroes de nuestra pobre farsa. Mas no, no lo creo" (1964: 18) ("If I were not so kind and you were not so poetic, I would be inclined to think that you intended to make a parody of *The Iliad* with the heroes of our pitiful farce. But no, I do not think so"). Bolívar thus shifts from questioning the characterization of heroes to what appears to be the most delicate point for him: the rhetorical value of the account, which seems to fluctuate between the epic and the parodic. Bolívar resolves the issue by suggesting that it will ultimately be a question of the reader: "Un americano leerá el poema de Ud. como un canto de Homero; y un español lo leerá como un canto del *Facistol* de Boileau" (1964: 18–9). ("An American will read your poem as a Homeric song, while a Spaniard will read it as a song from Boileau's *Le Lutrin*"). The comparison had to be acerbic for Olmedo, who knew well the famous mock-heroic poem *Le Lutrin* (1674), in which one of the highest authorities of Neoclassicism, the Frenchman Nicolas Boileau-

---

[7] See Pérez Vila 1971, "Apéndice," items 50, 204, and 239. Likewise, the *Diario the Bucaramanga*, the daily account of the life of Bolívar one of his aides-de-camp, Luis Peru de Lacroix, composed in 1828, reports on Bolívar spending part of the day (June 6, 1828) reading a French translation of the *Odyssey*.

Despraux, derided what he considered the bad taste of the inflammatory epic of his time. One wonders how Olmedo, after all these ironic comparisons, read the ambiguous declaration with which Bolívar concludes his biting commentary: "Por todo doy a Ud. las gracias, penetrado de una gratitud sin límites" (1964: 19) ("For all this I extend my thanks to you, filled with boundless gratitude").

The ambiguity of these remarks, by turns critiquing and applauding Olmedo's poetic efforts, is not simply an instance of intellectual playfulness. Much more importantly, they articulate the complexities of Bolívar's self-perception as a historical, military, and political actor, and his vision of the wars and the revolution in general. On the one hand, his criticism was entirely justified from a pragmatic point of view: an over-the-top Homer-like version of Junín and Ayacucho officially endorsed by him could easily have become a target for his political enemies.[8] On the other hand, however, Bolívar could not disassociate himself from the Classical imagery he was also so fond of. As biographer John Lynch reminds us, "Classical Republicanism tripped easily off the tongue of Bolívar," while the histories of Greco-Roman antiquity often constituted "sources of useful quotations" (2006: 32). Furthermore, Bolívar's affection for the Classics was not only discursive, but also performative. Multiple anecdotes reveal that he had a penchant for spectacular demonstrations associated with ancient motifs, something that his collaborators often commented on (Lynch 2006: 27). They had, for instance, heard and repeated the story of Bolívar's 1805 pilgrimage through Spain, France, and Italy, when he was only twenty-two years old, accompanied by his friend Fernando del Toro and his former mentor Simón Rodríguez. Upon arriving in Rome, Bolívar and his two companions walked the three miles from their lodgings near Piazza Spagna, in the center of Rome, to Monte Sacro, the hill on which the Roman Plebeians organized a revolt against the Patricians in the year 494 (Livy, *History of Rome* 2.32–3). Atop the hill, Bolívar would rehearse the ancient challenge to the Roman aristocracy by pronouncing a famous oath: not to rest until he had "broken the chains with which the Spanish power oppresses us" (Lynch 2006: 26).[9] Classical paraphernalia was also present

---

[8] Entire works have been written simply to record the many libels, attacks, and denunciations against Bolívar. See Rodríguez Demorizi 1966 and Lecuna 1956.

[9] The story of Bolívar's oath has produced a singular debate between those who argued that the event took place at the top of Monte Sacro versus those who believed it happened at the summit of the Aventine Hill—not to mention those who conflate the two. A chronicle of the dispute and defense of the Monte Sacro version can be found in Díaz González 1958. In his biography, Lynch confuses the Aventine Hill with Monte Sacro (2006: 26). In any event, an equestrian statue of the Liberator was placed in 1934 in the Via Flaminia in Rome to celebrate the episode—and, according to a note written on a photograph taken by a *Chicago Tribune* reporter, signed May 13, 1934, "Premier Mussolini was among the notables present at the unveiling" ("Rome Italy Simón Bolívar Statue" 1934). In 2005, an obelisk commemorating Bolívar's oath was erected in the actual hills of Monte Sacro.

in his public appearances, not only in his speeches, but also in the triumphs and parades with which he was many times received after his military campaigns. On August 6, 1813, for example, he made a splendid entry into Caracas after concluding the "Admirable Campaign" that had restored its independent republican government, and proclaimed to the people that "[their] liberators ha[d] arrived" (Lynch 2006: 26).[10] Bolívar and his officers were then crowned with laurels. Two months later, on October 13, a meeting of prominent citizens of Caracas officially conferred upon Bolívar the title that he most cherished in his life, "Liberator of Venezuela," which he called "[un] título más glorioso y satisfactorio para mí que todos los imperios de la tierra" (1970: 71) ("[a] title more glorious and satisfactory for me than all of the empires of the Earth").

Bolívar, in short, clearly perceived the overwrought dimension of Olmedo's poem, but was also fully aware of the rhetorical potential of the Classics when it came to social and political performance. He had, moreover, witnessed the value of intellectual prestige back in 1811, during his ambassadorship to England with Andrés Bello. Perhaps it was with this experience in mind that, while the 1825 correspondence on the *Victoria de Junín* was taking place, he also entrusted Olmedo with an embassy in England, to be conducted the following year, in order to establish official diplomatic relations between the new Republic of Peru and the British government. And so, after critiquing the diction of Olmedo's poem, Bolívar also takes a moment to remind him of his upcoming commission, playfully citing the proverbial blindness of Homer, in a comment that reads as both praise and a warning: "Uní a Ud. un matemático, porque no fuese que llevado Ud. de la verdad poética, creyese que dos y dos formaban cuatro mil; pero nuestro Euclides ha ido a abrirle los ojos a nuestro Homero" (1964: 19) ("I asked a mathematician to accompany you, lest you believe, carried away by poetic truth, that two plus two are four thousand; but our Euclid is also on his way, to open the eyes of our Homer"). "Euclid" here is the Peruvian mathematician, astronomer, and physician Gregorio Paredes, sent to aid Olmedo in his mission. While joking about Homer and Euclid, Bolívar reminded Olmedo of the seriousness of his delegation: the military campaign for the independence of Peru had just ended, and Bolívar considered diplomatic recognition from European powers a matter of political urgency.

---

[10] "Admirable Campaign" is the title given to the brief period of military action conducted between May and August 1813 and through which, under the leadership of Bolívar and with very few resources, Venezuela was re-recovered from the Spanish control that had followed Venezuelan's First Republic (1810–12). Detailed accounts can be found in O'Leary 1953, 1: 167–85 and Lynch 2006: 72–6.

Bolívar sent his initial, mixed impressions of Olmedo's poem without knowing that the poet had somehow anticipated his ambivalent reaction and had already sent Bolívar a new letter, criticizing his own poem and trying to justify himself to his patron. The content of this letter—dated May 15, 1825—is distinctly melancholy. Olmedo begins by paraphrasing an ancient deprecation: "Ya habrá usted visto el parto de los montes. Yo mismo no estoy contento de mi composición, y así no tengo derecho de esperar de nadie ni aplauso ni piedad" (1960: 252) ("I suppose you have already seen what the mountains have given birth to. I myself am not satisfied with my composition, and therefore, have no right to hope for either applause or mercy from anyone"). Olmedo here alludes to the famous admonition of the *Epistula ad Pisones* or *Ars poetica*, in which the Roman poet Horace (65–8 BCE) warns against the bombastic announcement of a poetic theme, lest the poem itself fail to fulfill the expectations created:

nec sic incipies ut scriptor cyclicus olim:
"fortunam Priami cantabo et nobile bellum."
quid dignum tanto feret hic promissor hiatu?
parturient montes, nascetur ridiculus mus.

vv. 137–40

And you are not to begin as the Cyclic poet of old:
"Of Priam's fate and famous war I'll sing."
What will this boaster produce in keeping with such mouthing?
Mountains will labour, to birth will come a laughter-rousing mouse!

Fairclough 1970: 463

The purpose of Olmedo in this letter is to vindicate his creation, whose main shortcoming, he concedes, is the lack of concordance between the plan of the poem ("[a] great and beautiful [plan], even though it's mine," says Olmedo) and its realization. The problem is not the concept, he argues, but the length of the poem, which makes the "beautiful plan" difficult to grasp. "[Quise a]brir con una idea rara y pindárica" (1960: 253) ("[I wanted] to start with a strange and Pindaric idea"), begins his explanation, alluding to the lightning and thunder that, at the very start of the poem, announce Bolívar's victory and God's endorsement. But the episodes following this pompous beginning, he admits, ended up delivering Horace's "laughable mouse." While pondering the underwhelming effect of his work, Olmedo realized the fundamental difficulty of his project. The "great plan" of his poem was (in keeping with the dictates of his Classical mentor Horace) originally monothematic: the celebration of the victory at Junín. However, the subsequent triumph at Ayacucho, unanticipated but also unavoidable in an account of the Patriotic army's victory, compromised the poetic unity of the project. Olmedo openly describes the discrepancy between his initial plan and the end result: "Como el fin del poeta era cantar sólo a Junín, y el canto quedaría defectuoso, manco, incompleto sin anunciar la segunda victoria, que fue la decisiva, se ha introducido el vaticinio del Inca lo más prolijo que ha sido posible para no defraudar la gloria de Ayacucho" (1960: 253) ("Since the goal of the poet was to sing only of Junín, and the song would be deficient, unfinished, incomplete without announcing the second victory, which was the decisive one, the prophecy of the Inca was introduced with as much prolixity as possible, so as not to undermine the glory of Ayacucho").

"Deficient, unfinished, incomplete"—the pleonasm seems to dramatize the exasperation Olmedo felt when the military victory of Ayacucho disrupted his poetic project on Junín. This was a delicate problem indeed. It made sense to compose a poem to glorify only Junín, because in that battle Bolívar had been the commander—hence the political equation implicit in the poem's title, *Victoria de Junín. Canto a Bolívar*, where celebrating the victory at Junín is tantamount to a song to the Liberator. At Ayacucho, however, Bolívar was absent: it was his lieutenant, José Antonio de Sucre, who played the leading role in that battle. According to the original arithmetic of the poet, the "Victory of Ayacucho" would have required a "Song to Sucre," but Olmedo could not have conceded such a parallel without eroding the heroic primacy of Bolívar. The task that Olmedo imposed on himself was the poetic assimilation of Ayacucho—arguably the more decisive battle, in which the Spanish viceroy was captured and the "Capitulación de Ayacucho" ("Capitulation of Ayacucho"), the official Spanish surrender, was signed—within his composition on Junín, so that credit for the final victory could be attributed to the Liberator as well. In other words, the challenge was to include the events of Ayacucho in the poem about Junín without eclipsing in any way the "Canto a Bolívar."

For Olmedo, the difficulty of conjoining Junín and Ayacucho was more than a matter of political etiquette: it was also a poetic conundrum diagnosed centuries earlier by Classical authorities for whom he held much respect. While Bolívar always had a copy of *The Iliad* at hand, Olmedo used to carry with him a pocket-sized edition of the works of Horace (1960: 232), which he not only feverishly read but also translated.[11] As Espinosa Pólit has noted, it is likely that

---

[11] Olmedo, an enthusiastic reader of Horace, translated at least one of his odes: the famous address "To the Ship of State" (I.XIV). The translation, available in his *Obras completas* (1960: 93), was published for the first time in Andrés Bello's *Repertorio Americano* of 1828 (Olmedo 1960: 371, n. 35).

the "Canto a Bolívar" was informed by Olmedo's readings of Horace (1980: 92). Indeed, in the ode "In the Praise of Lollius" (to the Roman Consul M. Lollius, friend of Augustus), Horace had commented on the crucial role of poetry in the consecration of heroes—in a manner that seems specifically designed for someone like Olmedo:

> vixere fortes ante Agamemnona
> multi; sed omnes inlacrimabiles
> urgentur ignotique longa
> nocte, carent quia vate sacro.
>
> *Odes* 4.9, vv. 26-9

> Many heroes lived before Agamemnon; but all are overwhelmed in unending night, unwept, unknown, because they lack a sacred bard.
>
> Bennett 1952: 321

A zealous disciple of Horace, Olmedo firmly believed in the role of the poet in the construction of memorable heroism—so much so that he makes this point in one of the first letters he sent to Bolívar about the poem, dated January 31, 1825: "[M]e atrevo a hacer a usted una intimación tremenda: y es que, si me llega el momento de la inspiración y puedo llenar el magnífico y atrevido plan que he concebido, los dos, los dos hemos de estar juntos en la inmortalidad" (1960: 245) ("I will dare to make an immense confession to you: if the inspirational moment comes to me and I am able to fulfill the magnificent and bold plan that I have conceived, the two of us, you and I, will live together in immortality"). Poetry, Olmedo insists to Bolívar, is the mechanism that would ensure their fame in the history soon to be written. The Liberator's inscription in history thus follows the Horatian prescription: Bolívar is the *vir fortis*, the great man; Olmedo, his *vates sacer*, the divinely inspired poet.[12]

The problem for Olmedo—to return to Junín and Ayacucho—is that the inclusion of two different places in one poem, and the desire to consecrate a single individual above everyone else, was also at odds with the prescriptions of Horace's *Ars poetica*, whose very opening states that a condition of good poetry

---

[12] Curiously, Horace's "Ode to Lollius," which introduces the relationship between the *vir fortis* and the *vates sacer*, has also been a site for a critical confrontation between the heroic and the parodic. John Ambrose's "The Ironic Meaning of the Lollius Ode" (1965) assesses this double edge: the poem is literally a praise to Roman politician Marcus Lollius, good friend of Emperor Augustus, Consul in 21 BCE and imperial governor of Gallia Comata in 17-16 BCE. But this Lollius did not deserve any praise: in 16 BCE he was defeated by German tribes, dishonorably leaving behind the emblems of the fifth legion as a trophy for the Germans. Given this record, Ambrose concludes that the poem must not be taken literally, but rather as a veiled scornful indictment of Lollius's ineptitude.

is maintaining a thorough sense of unity in a work (vv. 1–13). Horace in turn echoed the authority of Aristotle—whose *Poetics* emphasizes the importance of a unified structure in theatrical plots (1450b). In Olmedo's plan to consecrate the close of the campaign for independence, the aspiration to unity was impeded by the necessity of dealing with two different events in two different times and places, and with two different protagonists—while only one could play the epic hero. Conveniently, Horace also provides a solution to this conundrum by admitting the intervention of a divine agent—a *deus ex machina*—if the plot of a narrative cannot be solved otherwise: "nec deus intersit, nisi dignus vindice nodus / inciderit" (*Ars poetica*, vv. 191–2) ("And let no god intervene, unless [there is] a knot worthy of such a deliverer"; Fairclough 1970: 467). The problem of Junín and Ayacucho, a *dignus nodus* indeed, was both aesthetic and political. The remedy was, in turn, historical and mythological: the Inca Huayna Capac suddenly appears in the sky, first to hail the victory of Junín and then to prophesy the upcoming victory of Ayacucho, thus combining both battles within his discourse, and rhetorically ensuring that the glory of the entire military campaign was attributed to the leader present at Junín—Bolívar.

While the prophecy of Huayna Capac operates as a Horatian concession to the need for a *deus ex machina* to solve the Junín/Ayacucho conundrum, Olmedo's structural incorporation of this device follows another Classical authority: the Theban poet Pindar (*c.* 518–438 BCE), devotedly read by Horace and hailed by Quintilian in his *Institutio oratoria* as the greatest of the Greek lyric poets.[13] Olmedo's fascination with Pindar was most likely rooted in the Theban's exquisite *epinikia*, poetic celebrations of the achievements of athletes in the Panhellenic festivals of the fifth century BCE. Taking the battlefield as an athletic arena, Olmedo looks to the Theban poet as a model for his song of triumph, whose beginning, he explicitly declares, was meant to be "strange and Pindaric." Indeed, Huayna Capac's apparition echoes a compositional strategy typical of Pindar: the incorporation of mythical narratives as a structural mechanism to organize the contents of the poem. Through this mechanism, described by some scholars as a "ring composition," the poet first introduces the athlete to be praised; then, he announces a myth potentially akin, both

---

[13] Indeed, Quintilian's remarks on Pindar appear to endorse the opinion of Horace: "Novem vero Lyricorum longe Pindarus princeps spiritus magnificentia, sententiis, figuris, beatissima rerum verborumque copia et velut quodam eloquentiae flumine; propter quae Horatius eum merito credidit nemini imitabilem" (*Institutio oratoria* 10.1.61) ("Of the nine lyric poets, Pindar is far the greatest, for inspiration, magnificence, *sententiae*, Figures, a rich stock of ideas and words, and a real flood of eloquence; Horace rightly thinks him inimitable for these reasons"; Russell 2001: 283).

genealogically and thematically, to the athlete;[14] he then narrates the myth in detail, finally returning to the praise of the athlete, making explicit the connections between athlete and myth.[15]

Olmedo, fascinated by this effective appropriation of myths, likewise attempts to supply the victory of Junín with a historical yet also metaphysical endorsement through Huayna Capac, twelfth Incan ruler in Garcilaso de la Vega's chronology and eleventh in Guamán Poma de Ayala's. Olmedo's selection of this particular Inca is not accidental, as Huayna Capac already plays a prophetic role in El Inca Garcilaso's *Comentarios reales*—in particular, regarding the inevitable arrival of the Spaniards ((1609) 2000: 402–4). In the "Canto a Bolívar," the oracular skills of the spectral Inca also harken back to those of the Classical otherworldly soothsayer—as Tiresias was for the Greeks and Anchises for the Romans. In tune with the practice of incorporating Incan imagery into anti-Spanish rhetoric, the Pindaric ring composition enables the creation of a virtual link between the Incan Empire destroyed by the Spanish conquistadors, and the revolution led by Bolívar against their political descendants (the inconvenient fact that Bolívar and Olmedo were not detached from that genealogy did not go unnoticed, as we will see). But there is a crucial difference between Pindar's use of myths and Olmedo's mythical Inca. Pindar borrows heroic references from the myth in order to project them upon the athletic victories of his present time—so ultimately the present is the frame of the poetic associations. Olmedo, instead, invokes the Inca as the embodiment of an impossible third space in which to coordinate the troublesome dyad of Junín and Ayacucho. In doing so, he relinquishes any historical present, creating instead an epic atemporality that satisfies, somehow ironically, both the poetic requirement of temporal and spatial unity, and the political imperative of heroic exclusivity. In appearing at the close of the Battle of Junín to meticulously describe the future and decisive Battle of Ayacucho, the Inca anachronistically circumscribes Ayacucho within Bolívar's victory, but also within a new version of history. Indeed, by voicing the victory of Ayacucho through an Incan monarch and inscribing its significance within the Bolivarian project, both pre- and post-Hispanic Latin America embrace each other to legitimize, in a fictitious continuity, a cultural vindication that is also an anti-Spanish version of history.

---

[14] For more on the "ring composition," see William H. Race's introduction to his edition of Pindar's Olympian and Pythian odes (1997b: 20–1).

[15] For a more detailed analysis of the impact of Pindar's technique on Olmedo's poem, see Rosas Otálora 2010. Taking Olmedo's claims about his "Pindaric idea" as a point of departure, Rosas Otálora analyses the correlation among different passages of the *Victoria de Junín* and arrives at a conclusion similar to mine about the influence of Pindar's epinicion in the structural role of Huayna Capac's affiliation of Junín with Ayacucho.

Writing his pre-emptive defense of the over-the-top poem, Olmedo justifies himself with a remark that echoes the bucolic taste of Virgil and Horace: "si hubiera podido retirarme al campo quince días, habría hecho más que en tres meses" (1960: 254) ("If I had been able to retire to the country for fifteen days I would have done more than in these three months"). He then finishes his letter by requesting some feedback from Bolívar (not knowing that such feedback is already on its way): "Deseo que usted me escriba sobre esto con alguna extensión, diciéndome con toda franqueza todas las ideas que usted quisiera que yo hubiera suprimido. Lo deseo y lo exijo de usted" (1960: 254) ("I desire that you write to me about this in more detail, telling me with complete frankness all the ideas you wish I had suppressed. I want it and I demand it of you"). Such a request, despite its affectation, communicates a sincere desire: Olmedo is seeking not only the Liberator's approval, but also his criticisms. Like Odysseus when he begins singing of his own misfortunes in Book IX of *The Odyssey*, Bolívar is here asked to be not only protagonist and reader of *Victoria de Junín*, but also its editor.

Bolívar seems to have been delighted to take some time away from the duties of his everyday political and military life to talk about poetry, and responded eagerly, playfully citing the authorities of Horace and Boileau while recommending that Olmedo take some distance from the poem before revising it. In his review, Bolívar criticizes the very solution that Olmedo had conceived for the dilemma of Junín and Ayacucho—the apparition of the Inca:

> Ud. ha trazado un cuadro muy pequeño para colocar dentro un coloso que ocupa todo el ámbito y cubre con su sombra a los demás personajes. El Inca Huayna Cápac parece que es el asunto del poema; él es el genio, él la sabiduría, él es el héroe, en fin. Por otra parte, no parece propio que alabe indirectamente a la religión que le destruyó; y menos parece propio aún, que no quiera el restablecimiento de su trono, por dar preferencia a extranjeros intrusos, que, aunque vengadores de su sangre, siempre son descendientes de los que aniquilaron su imperio ... La naturaleza debe presidir a todas las reglas, y esto no está en la naturaleza. También me permitirá Ud. que le observe que este genio Inca, que debía ser más leve que el éter, pues que viene del cielo, se muestra un poco hablador y embrollón ...
>
> 1964: 34

> You have drawn a frame too small to place inside such a colossus, one that occupies all the space and whose shadow looms over the rest of the characters. Inca Huayna Capac seems to be the theme of the poem; he is the genius, he is the wisdom—he is, in short, the hero. Besides, it does not seem proper that he praises indirectly the religion that destroyed him; and even less proper that he does not

seek the re-establishment of his throne, but rather gives preference to foreign intruders who, although avengers of his blood, are still descendants of those who annihilated his empire ... Nature must govern all the rules, and this is not in accordance with nature. You will also permit me to point out that this Inca genie, who should be lighter than ether—since he comes from the sky—appears to be a bit verbose and jumbled ...

The "unnaturalness" that Bolívar diagnoses in placing the Inca at the core of Olmedo's poem is just as rooted in Horatian precepts as his object of criticism, the poet's *deus ex machina*. Olmedo had read the first section of *Ars poetica* and defined the idea of poetic proportion in terms of spatial and temporal unity. Bolívar is less technical and more conceptual: poetic proportion—any poetic rule for that matter—must be governed by "nature," and the support of the Inca for the revolutionaries does not seem natural to Bolívar.

The Liberator probably had in mind an analogous case when highlighting this conflict: early in the revolution, during the first months of 1809, a pamphlet entitled "Diálogo entre Atahualpa y Fernando VII en los Campos Elíseos" (Monteagudo 1977: 64–71) ("Dialogue between Atahualpa and Ferdinand VII in the Elysian Fields"), attributed to the soon-to-be radical revolutionary Bernardo de Monteagudo, circulated widely among liberal intellectuals who studied in the university of the city of Chuquisaca (in present-day Bolivia). In May 1808, during a critical moment of the Peninsular War (famously depicted by Francisco de Goya), the French army had invaded Spain and Napoleon had imprisoned King Ferdinand VII in the Château de Valençay (France). While the king would eventually be released in 1813, the 1809 "Diálogo" instead imagines that the he dies in prison and his soul goes to the mythical Elysian Fields, where he accidentally comes across the Inca Atahualpa. The two engage in a debate about the legitimacy of the Spanish invasion of America, which the Inca skillfully parallels with the French invasion of Spain. After an intense dialogue, the eloquent Inca manages to convince the king of Spain of the unlawfulness of the conquest of America, hailing the project of revolution as a historical vindication.[16]

---

[16] In his "Carta de Jamaica" (1815), Bolívar also reflected on the fate of the Incan Empire vis-à-vis the French invasion of Spain. His interlocutor, Sir Henry Culler, had deemed the Napoleonic usurpation "an act of divine retribution"; Bolívar, more critically, replied that "[e]xiste tal diferencia entre la suerte de los reyes españoles y de los reyes americanos, que no admite comparación; los primeros son tratados con dignidad, conservados, y al fin recobran su libertad y trono; mientras que los últimos sufren tormentos inauditos y los vilipendios más vergonzosos" (1970: 120) ("the difference between the fortune of the Spanish Kings and the American Kings is such that it does not admit comparison; the former were preserved and treated with dignity, and they have recovered their freedom and throne; while the latter suffered unheard of torments and the most shameful offenses").

Thus, the "Diálogo" had already tested the trope of "Incan endorsement" of the revolutionary project when Olmedo, assisted by Horace, conjured the phantom of the Inca Huayna Capac on the battlefield of Junín. The "Diálogo," moreover, would also test this trope with a Classical accent, since the impossible dialogue between Atahualpa and Ferdinand VII, and the even more impossible support of the king of Spain for the American revolutionary project, take place in the Elysian Fields. The revolution had, from the very beginning, embraced the idea of indigenous vindication to fuel resistance against the Spaniards and create an identity for the nascent countries—a trope that became a constitutive element of nationalist discourses throughout the first century of republicanism in Latin America.[17] Bolívar, however, was always aware of the artificiality of this construct. His remarks on Olmedo's poem, in fact, call into question the nativist claims of the revolution he himself led, assessing the phenomenon in terms of poetry, rhetoric, history, and *realpolitik* (duly assisted by the postulates of Horace). Sarcasm is not absent in this judgment: in Bolívar's opinion, the grandiloquent Huayna Capac, the *deux ex machina* invoked precisely to disentangle the knot of Junín and Ayacucho, ends up being confusing and verbose, with an extensive speech at odds with his ethereal form.

The Liberator cannot declare it explicitly, but it is clear that his objections to the role of the Inca were also related to his concern about the promotion of the Bolivarian cult. The overshadowing character of the Inca Huayna Capac, "the genius, the wisdom, in a word, the hero" of the poem, affected his own pivotal role, which Bolívar felt should have greater precedence in a composition called "Canto a Bolívar." Olmedo had tried to compensate for the absence of the Liberator in Ayacucho by making the Inca deliver the prophecy of the second victory on the battlefield of the first, but, as a consequence, the very mechanism of compensation became destabilizing. Bolívar the reader does not recognize himself in Bolívar the hero, who, despite a thunderous characterization, ends up being mostly an allusion rather than the agent of the victory. Consequently, the *Victoria de Junín* seemed to him an epic song to someone who was barely in the poem. Bolívar diagnoses the disproportion that Horace censures at the start of his poetics not only in the unnatural relations between the Inca and the revolution, but also in the lack of proportion between a literary device, the *deux ex machina,* and his own persona as Liberator.

---

[17] Rebecca Earle (2007) offers a survey of the different ways in which American pre-conquest communities were symbolically incorporated into nationalist discourses crafted by the creole elites of Latin American during and after the Age of Revolution.

But if Bolívar's letter begins with criticism, it ends with commendations. Elegantly, the Liberator reserves his good opinions for his final lines: "Confieso a Ud. que la versificación del poema me parece sublime; un genio lo arrebató a Ud. a los cielos" (1964: 35) ("I confess to you that the versification of the poem seems to me sublime; a genie snatched you to the heavens"); "[l]a estrofa 130 es bellísima; oigo rodar los torbellinos y veo arder los ejes; aquello es griego, es homérico" (1964: 36) ("stanza 130 is extremely beautiful: I hear the whirl of the twisters and I see the axles burning; that is Greek, Homeric"). Bolívar does not forget the deputation he commissioned to Olmedo either, and advises him, in a new game of Classical juxtapositions, to profit from his stay in London—alluded to as a new mythical Greece—to polish the poem: "La torre de San Pablo será el Pindo de Ud. y el caudaloso Támesis se convertirá en Helicona" (1964: 35) ("The tower of Saint Paul [in Saint Paul's Cathedral] will be your Pindus [the chain of mountains in northern Greece], and the abundant Thames will be your Helicon [the Mount in central Greece which, according to the myth, was the home of the Muses]").

Olmedo would answer Bolívar's objections almost a year later from London, in a letter dated April 19, 1826, but he received no more replies from the Liberator. In any case, the conversation was at that point concluded: since the poem, Olmedo explained, found wide acceptance in the European intellectual circles where the drafts were read, he decided to publish it as it was, with minimal corrections. But it is worth briefly summarizing the events of 1825 and their importance for thinking about the role of the Classics in memorializing revolution. When news of the victory of Ayacucho reached his ears, on April 6, Olmedo hurriedly wrote to Bolívar, hinting that he was already writing a poem. In his anxious historical awareness, Olmedo wished to consolidate himself as the poet of the revolution. It is precisely on account of that tremendous historical gravity that Olmedo relies on Classical prescriptions, which, through authorities such as Homer, Pindar, and Horace, supply the literary and historical paradigm of the *vates sacer* or sacred poet necessary for the consecration of the hero. The purpose of Olmedo is, in this sense, not precisely historical, but rather historiographic: his poem aspires to be an axial point, a distinctive mark of a history that is about to be translated into writing. The process is analogous to the grammatical structure of the verbal tense known as the future perfect: the present time of Olmedo—the time of the revolution, the time of Bolívar—is imagined as an already Classical event, canonized through the application of ancient poetic prescriptions, and then projected onto a future which then looks back to declare its value. Thus, Olmedo's project predicts, declares, and retrospectively confirms its own consecration. Olmedo aspires to supply a poetic and mythic milestone for an upcoming (but already imagined) periodization of the history of the revolution. By crafting the contiguity of Junín and Ayacucho to gravitate around the supreme figure of Bolívar, Olmedo sought to arrange a certain version of history.

It is at this point, however, when the asymmetries of history compromise the rigors of poetic declamation—when the Horatian principle of unity enters into conflict with the unbalanced significance of two battles, an Incan *deus ex machina* turns out to be impertinent and logorrheic, and the epic hero looks askance at his own epic poem. To further exacerbate the irony, and despite the Liberator's objections, Olmedo's aspirations were not completely unsuccessful, for the two battles were indeed translated by successive historians, chroniclers, and fiction writers as the two sides of the same coin—a coin, of course, cast by Bolívar's hand. Still today, in cities like Lima and Buenos Aires, Junín and Ayacucho are the names of adjacent streets.

In playfully navigating the Classical codes deployed by Olmedo, Bolívar was in turn symptomatizing his chronic contradictions. On the one hand was the histrionic and idealistic orator who performed a sacred oath at the top of a historic Roman hill, risked his life countless times in military campaigns, and one day gave up his possessions to the point of destitution to become, the next day, the most powerful figure in the revolution; in sum, the man who claimed, both in the public forum and in the intimacy of a letter to a close friend, that his title and achievements as Liberator were all the recompense he sought. On the other hand was the pragmatic manipulator, the republican who sympathized more with lifelong political office than with democratic elections, the ironist who could mock and publicly ridicule his most faithful partisans, and the man who scorned an alliance with José de San Martín because he wanted to be the absolute hero of the revolution. The ironic meanderings of his criticism of Olmedo's poem reflect in an exquisite manner the many contradictions of Bolívar himself. No wonder that the Classical tradition of which he was so fond and which he so frequently invoked was also effectively used to launch a formidable and sustained attack against him, so much so that it could have literally taken his life.

An Ides of March in September: The 1828 Conspiracy Against Bolívar

Antonio Cussen (1992) offers one of the earliest analyses of the relationship between poetics and politics in the Age of Revolution. Cussen focuses on key independence figure Andrés Bello (Caracas, 1781–Santiago de Chile, 1865), who, having traveled with Bolívar to England in 1811 to request economic support for the revolutionary project, remained exiled in London for almost twenty years to collaborate intellectually and poetically with the revolution from afar. Upon returning to America, Bello settled in Santiago de Chile for the rest of his life, where he became one of the creators of Chile's legal system, the author of a Spanish grammar, *Gramática de la lengua castellana destinada al uso de los Americanos* (1847) ("Grammar of the Castilian Language, Intended for the Use of Americans"), and, all in all, arguably the most important intellectual figure in the Chile of his time.

One of Cussen's main arguments is that Bello relied frequently, though often implicitly, on the figure of the Roman Emperor Augustus in the poetic representation of power. Heavily influenced by the Roman literature of the Age of Augustus and particularly obsessed with Virgil (to the point that he taught himself Latin to read Virgil in the original), Bello began his literary career long before the revolution, writing a series of poems which, influenced by the models of the *Georgics* and the *Eclogues*, praised the king of Spain as a new Augustus. When Bolívar became the central figure of the revolution, explains Cussen, Bello readapted the Augustan motif to the new political order, sometimes strategically applying the adjective "augusto" (august) to Bolívar, and sometimes suggestively employing the patterns of Roman imperial poetry to herald the new political era. By carefully playing with this motif, Cussen argues, Bello managed to simultaneously recognize the historical importance of Bolívar and warn against the risks of imperialism and authoritarianism.

A survey of the poetry related to the Age of Revolution suggests that the operative concept of Cussen's argument—the ambivalent use of the Classics to both celebrate Bolívar and caution him against potential excesses—extends to a larger context and to many more poets and intellectuals, including some more anonymous and less sympathetic toward Bolívar than Bello. As an instrument of political and historical commentary, poetry was consistently used by Bolívar's supporters and detractors alike; and so, if authors like Bello and his good friend Olmedo put their poetic skills and Classical knowledge at the service of Bolívar, his fiercest detractors also resorted to ancient history and mythology to launch sustained attacks against him and his political project. But while Bello's and Olmedo's poetry circulated through sophisticated circles and careful editions, much of the poetry against Bolívar and the revolution found fertile ground in public and informal venues. The revolution incited an intense popular poetry movement, in which partisans of all affiliations participated. It is particularly illuminating to read what nineteenth-century author Arístides Rojas, anthologist and commentator on the pasquinades produced during the Venezuelan revolution, once wrote in this respect:

> Cuando las bóvedas de [la prisión de] La Guaira fueron refaccionadas, todas las paredes estaban llenas de letreros políticos, de versos, sentencias e imprecaciones de todo género. Cada preso, según la importancia que se daba, creía que debía escribir en las paredes algún pensamiento alusivo a su permanencia en aquel lugar. Patriotas y realistas se disputaban el placer de dejar algo en los envejecidos muros.
>
> 1891: 185

> When the vaults of La Guaira [Penitentiary] were repaired, every single wall was full of political messages, poems, proverbs, satires, and all sorts of imprecations. Each prisoner, according to the importance he attributed to himself, believed that he had to write on the walls some thought regarding his stay in such a place. Patriots and Royalists often seemed to compete for the pleasure of leaving something on those aged walls.

While the authors of these graffiti were confined in jail, many of their poetic creations managed to escape the walls where they were originally composed and ended up reproduced in newspapers, flyers, on city walls, or simply in conversations. Tellingly, the proliferation of popular political poetry made a quick alliance with the jargon of Classicism, conjoining the symbolic strength of the latter to the wide public presence of the former. Bolívar was a frequent theme and motif: throughout the fourteen years of the Wars of Independence, and continuing in their aftermath, Bolívar became the object of an entire catalogue of grim Classical similes, often voiced through the most occasional or informal means. A few examples will suffice to illustrate this phenomenon: he was Pandora's Box, the source of all evils (including false hope); the infamous Sinon, the Achaean who treacherously convinced the Trojans to bring the famous wooden horse (secretly loaded with Greek warriors) into their city; a destructive and raging monster that came out of Tartarus—the section of the Greek Underworld where the wicked were punished for their sins; Pausanias, the fifth-century-BCE Spartan general who intended to betray his countrymen by making a deal with the Persian king; and, as an interesting counterpoint to Augustus, Bolívar was also Nero, the Roman emperor who, so says the legend, set fire to the ancient city of Rome for his personal aesthetic pleasure.[18]

---

[18] All these examples come from Rodríguez Demorizi 1966. By organizing chronologically the poetry against the Liberator produced between 1811 (when Bolívar became an activist in the revolutionary project) until 1831 (one year after his death), Rodríguez Demorizi composes a fascinating chronicle of the symbolic and political vicissitudes the Liberator had to navigate during the course of his public life. The majority of the poems and libels referred to in this section can be found in Rodríguez Demorizi's compilation; given its anthological character, however, I have provided original or alternative sources where possible, in order to expand the bibliographical context of this research.

One Classical reference, however, would play an especially dramatic role in the life of Bolívar: the persona and story of Caius Julius Caesar (100–44 BCE). Of course, the rise and tragic fall of Julius Caesar, so frequently depicted by sculptors and literary artists over the course of the centuries, was in the early nineteenth century widely known; yet few instances reveal the powerful impact of the misadventures of Caesar on modern history as the case of Bolívar. The history of this analogy, culminating in an actual conspiracy that almost ended the life of the Liberator, constitutes an extreme example of the crucial necessity of reflecting on the role of the Classical and Neoclassical traditions during the turbulent years of the revolution. By approaching the Caesarean version of Bolívar as a response to the Augustan version that Cussen identifies, I offer a counter-example of how the Classics in the Age of Revolution became a mechanism used not only to interpret the convulsive *realpolitik* of the time, but also (and more importantly) to actively attempt to transform such a reality. Far from a simple rhetorical device, the history of Julius Caesar became an index of Bolívar's presence in public affairs, as well as a galvanization to encourage radical resistance to this presence. The events of the Classical Ides of March ultimately became a script for history and political activism in the Age of Bolívar—a theatricalization of the Classical tradition which could have fundamentally altered the political formation of the new South American nations.

Before examining these events, it is first important to note that, as for the composition of Olmedo's *Victoria de Junín*, the association between Bolívar and characters and motifs extracted from the Classical repertoire was a phenomenon he himself encouraged—in fact, he did so throughout his political and military life. As early as 1814, toward the end of the short-lived United Provinces of New Granada (a precursor of present-day Colombia, created in 1811 and reconquered by Spanish forces in 1816), Manuel del Castillo, a colonel in the Patriotic army of New Granada, published in Cartagena a vicious letter against his former collaborator, Bolívar. As Rodríguez Demorizi reports, the diatribe was, even at that early stage in the political life of Bolívar, "una de las más violentas e implacables arremetidas contra el Libertador" (1966: 17) ("one of the most violent and implacable attacks against the Liberator"). Despotism, the first of the three main imputations of Castillo's letter—the other two being thievery and immorality—would become the primary charge against Bolívar for the rest of his life.

It was not Bolívar, but his army chaplain, José Félix Blanco, who responded to the accusations. Blanco found inspiration in Homer and replied to Castillo by comparing him with a minor epic character—Thersites (Rodríguez Demorizi

1966: 17–18).[19] This reference to the episode of Thersites, from the second book of *The Iliad*, was a shrewd one. After Achilles abandons the Achaean army, Agamemnon proposes launching a new attack against Troy (2.53–75); while everyone agrees and prepares for the battle, Thersites, described as "ugly beyond all men who came to Ilios [Troy]" (2.216) and "of measureless speech" (2.212), accuses Agamemnon of being ambitious, imprudent, and cowardly, and recommends that the army ignore the king's call. To everyone's satisfaction, Odysseus steps in, ordering Thersites "not to take the name of kings in [his] mouth" (2.250) and imposing silence on him by striking his back with the royal staff of Agamemnon (2.265).[20] For Blanco, this anecdote provided a useful parallel: even though both Castillo and Bolívar, like Thersites and Odysseus, belonged to the same army, the confrontation of these Greek precursors worked as a reminder of the ranks of the contenders—diminishing Castillo's value as accuser while raising Bolívar to a loftier, more royal position. When Bolívar heard of Castillo's attack and Blanco's reply, he not only accepted the equation Thersites=Castillo, but also completed the image by presenting himself, in a protest addressed to the President of New Granada on January 22, 1815, as the Homeric Odysseus: "Yo, es verdad, podría contestar al Coronel Castillo; pero esto sería justificarlo, dando yo pruebas de bajeza, degradándome hasta la esfera del Coronel Castillo, que no merece entrar en lid conmigo sino como Tersites con Ulises" ("In truth, I could respond to Colonel Castillo; but that would be to justify him, evincing baseness, degrading myself to the sphere of Colonel Castillo, who does not deserve to quarrel with me except as Thersites with Ulysses"; 1970: 106).

Bolívar's self-characterization as Odysseus was not a refutation of the charges levied against him by Castillo, but a rhetorical injunction meant to protect the reputation that his many accolades were, already by 1815, steadily consolidating. Indeed, most of the document is an *ad hominem* reply—a thinly veiled threat not only against his accuser, but against anyone who may antagonize him. By taking on the role of Odysseus, Bolívar not only defends himself in an official and public arena, but also hints at his ability to strike back—rhetorically but also in

---

[19] Interestingly, it seems that Blanco was an illegitimate son of María Belén Jerez de Aristiguieta y Blanco—one of the famous Aristiguieta, the nine Venezuelan sisters who were second cousins of Bolívar, and whose intelligence and beauty were celebrated with the title of "the nine muses" (see "José Félix Blanco" 2009 and Casanova 2008).

[20] Odysseus's silencing of Thersites is indeed definitive: he will never again appear or be mentioned in the Homeric poems. (In other accounts of the Trojan cycle, Thersites would reappear to mock the body of the Amazon queen Penthesilea after Achilles had slayed her. Achilles, who fell in love with the Amazon at the very moment when he killed her, also kills Thersites in retaliation.)

actuality—at his opponent. Hence the subtle but effective allusion to violence: "he does not deserve to quarrel with me except as Thersites with Ulysses."[21]

A second early example completes this picture. On September 7, 1814, Bolívar composed a self-defense, filled with philosophical reflections, as the United Provinces of New Granada were falling back under the control of Spanish forces. The document, known as the "Manifiesto de Carúpano" ("The Carúpano Manifesto"), remarked that it was "an evil stupidity" to blame the disasters occurring in a republic solely or principally on public figures (1970: 99). He argued that history would judge whether the "august title of Liberator" he had received was rightful or not (1970: 100). While Bolívar insisted on embracing the ambivalent title of "august Liberator," even during those disheartening times, a popular *décima* attributed to the Bogotá priest Juan Manuel García Tejada proposed an alternative imperial allusion:

> Bolívar, el cruel Nerón,
> este Herodes sin segundo,
> quiere arruinar este mundo
> y también la religión.
>
> qtd. in Rodríguez Demorizi 1966: 20
>
> Bolívar, a cruel Nero,
> this Herod without match,
> seeks to ruin this world,
> as well as its religion.

The concept was not original: as Rojas points out, "cuando Bolívar fue contra Bogotá a fines de 1814, circularon tantos dichos con los cuales se le hacía aparecer como un Nerón que sacrificaba sacerdotes, que profanaba templos, etc., etc., que al fin todo el mundo le juzgó como espíritu del mal" (1891: 187) ("when Bolívar marched against Bogotá toward the end of 1814, there were so many sayings in which he appeared as a Nero who sacrificed priests, who profaned temples, etc., etc., that in the end everyone judged him an evil spirit"). García Tejada knew that the Nero trope in his *décima* would have an impact on public opinion, maybe

---

[21] On April 24, 1815, Bolívar tried to arrange a conciliation between his and Castillo's factions, but Castillo responded two days later with a military attack against the Liberator's camp (Lecuna 1965, 1: 350). Although this attempt was unsuccessful, on May 5, 1815, Bolivar, who needed Castillo's support against the Royalist army, sent him another reconciliatory note (Grases and Pérez Vila 1970: 111). By the time they finally signed an accord, it was too late (Corrales 1889: 47). On May 8, Bolívar resigned his political command in the United Provinces of New Granada and set sail for exile in Jamaica the next day (Lecuna 1965, 1: 350–1). Castillo died less than a year later, shot by a firing squad of the Spanish army that reconquered New Granada.

because it also functions as a precise counterpoint to the Augustus reference that people like Bello and Bolívar himself were beginning to popularize around the same time (Cussen 1992: 73–84). The poem had been written in the last months of 1814 in Santa Fe de Bogotá, while Bolívar and his army camped on the outskirts. When notified of García's poem and the rumor of his portrayal of Bolivar as a destructive and sacrilegious despot, Bolívar relied on the same strategy he had followed in the Castillo/Thersites episode, embracing (in a public letter dated December 9, 1814) the infamous role of Nero that his enemies had imposed on him:

> Santa Fe va a presentar un espectáculo espantoso de desolación y muerte: las casas serán reducidas a cenizas, si por ellas se nos ofende. Llevaré dos mil teas encendidas para reducir a pavesas una ciudad que quiere ser el sepulcro de sus libertadores ... Esos cobardes tanto como fanáticos me llaman irreligioso y me nombran Nerón; yo seré pues su Nerón.
>
> qtd. in Rodríguez Demorizi 1966: 23

> Santa Fe will offer a frightening spectacle of desolation and death: houses will be reduced to ashes if they dare offend us. I will bring two thousand flaming torches to reduce to cinders a city that wishes to be the sepulcher of its liberators ... Those cowards and fanatics call me irreligious and dub me "Nero"; I shall be, then, their Nero.

The incendiary reputation of Nero provides Bolívar not only with an opportunity for rhetorical retaliation, but also with a clear threat to the people of Santa Fe de Bogotá. The people understood that the warning was not vain, and Bolívar's army occupied Bogotá three days later, on December 12, 1814 (Lynch 2006: 89). Although the independence of New Granada was close to its end, the Patriotic army's campaign between 1811 and 1815 had been sufficient to popularize the use of ancient parallels to characterize Bolívar. It did not matter if the simile was relatively obscure (Thersites) or well known (Nero): by translating Classical references into current political affairs, by rendering them in popular poetry widely distributed in letters, newspapers, pamphlets, graffiti, and oral performances, Bolívar, his partisans, and his fierce detractors were transforming the affectations of Neoclassicism into a recurrent and familiar language, increasingly available to everyone.

In the course of the following years, rumors about Bolívar's authoritarianism remained common currency, as did the Classical apparatus used to depict it. On March 16, 1818, the Venezuelan newspaper *Gaceta de Caracas* announced the defeat of Bolívar's forces in the valley of Aragua. The columnist reminded the readers that, despite his misfortune, "el insensato Bolívar ... según noticias, no se contenta ya sino con el título de *Emperador*, porque en material de títulos los dedos se le antojan huéspedes" ("En el preciso momento ..." 1818: 1875) ("the foolish Bolívar ... according to some news, is not content now except with the title of *Emperor*, because, when it comes to titles, each of his fingers holds a different one"). A lustrum later, in August 1823, Bolívar compared his political opponent, the Peruvian president José de la Riva-Agüero, with Catiline, the Roman conspirator against whom Cicero delivered his most famous diatribe (Rodríguez Demorizi 1966: 45). The following year, in August 1824, the Peruvian Marquis of Torre Tagle, formerly under Bolívar's orders, accused him of being a tyrant who sought to enslave the recently created Republic of Peru (Rodríguez Demorizi 1966: 47); the same imputations appeared a short time later in the Peruvian newspaper *El Desengaño* ("The Disillusion") (Rodríguez Demorizi 1966: 48–9).

The victorious outcome of the December 1824 campaign in Ayacucho, far from alleviating the doubts about Bolívar's authoritarianism, only aggravated them. The victory had taken the Liberator's reputation to its peak, but there was still the question of the role he would play in the aftermath of the wars. While some members of the local aristocracies worried about the power of the Liberator, ever-growing even after the wars, Bolívar's closest allies (especially from the army) were inclined to consolidate his political leadership through a dictatorship, and some even endeavored to install an imperial absolutist state under his command. María Antonia Bolívar, the Liberator's sister, wrote to him (on July 19, 1824) denouncing a rumor about an upcoming coronation, which she constantly had to refute: "[la] malignidad y envidia [de los difamadores] ha llegado hasta el exceso de decir que te vas a coronar al Perú ... [S]iempre les digo a todos que es una calumnia, que tú ni lo has pensado, que tú eres más grande sólo con el título de Simón Bolívar que de emperador" (Lecuna 1956: 2: 86) ("[the] malice and envy [of the slanderers] have reached the excess of saying that you will crown yourself in Peru ... I always tell everyone that that is a calumny, that you have not even thought of it, that you are greater with the sole title of Simón Bolívar than that of emperor"). María Antonia's fear increased when General José Antonio Paez, in a letter to Bolívar from Caracas, dated October 1, 1825, implicitly proposed the formal creation of an empire under the Liberator's rule, suggestively reminding him of the role of Napoleon in post-revolutionary France. The argument was that the political situation of Great Colombia was chaotic to the point that only absolute rule could restore order. Consequently, María Antonia took another moment to caution her brother, this time against the proposal of Paez: "Mandan ahora un comisionado a proponerte la corona. Recíbelo como merece la propuesta que es infame ... di siempre lo que dijiste en Cumaná el año de 1814, 'que serías Libertador o muerto'" (Lecuna 1956: 2: 86–7) ("They are now sending a commissioner to propose that you take a crown. Receive him as the infamous proposal he carries deserves to be received ... always say what you said in Cumaná in 1814, that you 'would be Liberator or dead'"). To underline her point, María Antonia reminded her brother of the recent failures of Napoleon Bonaparte in France (between 1804 and 1815) and Agustín de Iturbide in México (between 1821 and 1823).[22]

Rhetorically, Bolívar had always been opposed to imperial projects. In his response to Páez he repeated the examples proposed by his sister, adding to them (as he had done before) the Classical case of Julius Caesar: "Ni Colombia es Francia, ni yo Napoleón ... Yo no soy Napoleón ni quiero serlo; tampoco quiero imitar a César; aun menos a Iturbide. Tales ejemplos me parecen indignos de mi gloria. El título de Libertador es superior a todos los que ha recibido el orgullo humano" (Lecuna 1956: 2: 82) ("Colombia is not France, nor am I Napoleon ... I am not Napoleon nor do I intend to be him; nor do I seek to imitate Caesar, and even less Iturbide. Such examples seem to me unworthy of my glory. The title of Liberator is superior to all those that human vanity has received"). The heroic intonation of this response, which moves from France to Mexico and from Ancient Rome to Gran Colombia, outlines the historical significance Bolívar saw in his title of Liberator—the greatest achievement in the history of humanity, in his opinion. Yet this self-panegyric did not preclude him from highlighting the pragmatic reasons that made the imperial project nonsensical: "Son repúblicas las que rodean a Colombia, y Colombia jamás ha sido un reino. Un trono espantaría tanto por su altura como por su brillo" (Lecuna 1956: 2: 82) ("The nations surrounding Colombia are republics, and Colombia has never been a kingdom. A throne would be frightening for both its loftiness and its brilliance"). Colombia's stability depended not only on its own necessities but also on its relations with other nations: a certain political homogeneity or at least a basic agreement was imperative for the development of the region. The Horatian demand for proportion, applied here to the international role of Colombia in the aftermath of independence, could have well summed up the response of the Liberator.

---

[22] More than a century later (1921), in a discourse in the house of the Liberator, the Venezuelan presbyter Carlos Borges commented on the parallels drawn by María Antonia with a Classical analogy: "¿Dónde encontró, señores, esta sublime caraqueña, la pluma de Plutarco?" (Lecuna 1956: 2: 87) ("Where did this sublime *Caraqueña*, gentlemen, find the quill of Plutarch?").

Nevertheless, and despite the grandiloquent republicanism of Bolívar, his political actions had given very different and troubling signs. The Angostura Address, the Bolivarian Constitution, the conception of Great Colombia: in all of these projects, the Liberator kept advancing an idea of central power that became progressively more personalist and absolutist. The 1819 Angostura Address proposed the creation of a lifelong, non-democratic and hereditary senate to counterbalance the power of authorities elected by the people (Bolívar 1970: 159–61); the 1826 Bolivian Constitution, conceived by Bolívar himself, alternatively proposed a life-term presidency ("Constitución política de Bolivia de 1826," Art. 77);[23] meanwhile, Bolívar also strove to consolidate the geopolitical unity of the territories of Ecuador, New Granada (now Colombia), and Venezuela under the title of *Gran Colombia* (whose president, of course, was Bolívar himself). The local aristocracies thus had sufficient reason to be worried: their support for the revolution had been designed to facilitate the preservation of the privileges they held during Spanish colonial rule—which had diminished when the Spanish Crown began to apply the controversial Bourbon Reforms during the second half of the eighteenth century. The revolution had the support of the aristocrats who wished to recover their fiefs, but the Bolivarian doctrine, centralizing power on the one hand and promoting liberal policies (such as the abolition of slavery) on the other, was no less dangerous for the aristocrats than the Bourbon Reforms. Such anxieties would be translated into the nationalist rhetoric that, recycling the despotic tendencies attributed to Bolívar by the Spaniards during the war, characterized him as a terrible danger for the newly achieved independence of the Latin American republics.

These were the antecedents of the verse that would be composed toward the end of 1826 by the young Colombian poet Luis Vargas Tejada (1802–29), at first a strong supporter of Bolívar and later a radical dissident. Vargas Tejada, a self-taught polyglot, had entered Bogotá in 1824 (according to his first anthologist, José Joaquín Ortiz) knowing German, Latin, French, English, and Italian (Ortiz 1857: iv). In his early twenties, he became the secretary of the vice-president of New Granada (the president was Bolívar), General Francisco de Paula Santander. Vargas Tejada had only been seventeen when the Patriotic army, led by Bolívar and Santander and assisted by a British contingent, defeated Spanish troops in the crucial Battle of Boyacá (August 7, 1819), which marked the definitive independence of Colombia and most of northern South America. Seven years

---

[23] Both a lifelong senate and a life-term presidency were ideas conceived by Bolívar long before, as attested in the famous "Carta de Jamaica" of 1815, where he drafted the first versions of the political project advanced in the Angostura Address, and in the Bolivian Constitution of 1826 (see, in particular, Bolívar 1970: 129).

later, Vargas Tejada would recapitulate the military achievements of the Liberator in his "Recuerdos de Boyacá" ("Remembrance of Boyacá"):

> "Bolívar" truena el viento,
> "¡Al arma, americanos!"
> Lo oyeron los tiranos,
> Su faz palideció.
> ...
> Celebra, ¡oh Patria! el día
> De Boyacá, su pompa
> Pregone heróica trompa,
> Cante marcial clarín.
> En ecos de alegría
> Ya resonando escucho
> Las glorias de Ayacucho,
> Los truenos de Junín.
>
> 1857: 5, 11

> "Bolívar!" roars the wind,
> "To arms, Americans!"
> The tyrants heard it,
> Their countenance paled.
> ...
> Celebrate, oh fatherland!, the day
> Of Boyacá, and let a heroic
> Horn proclaim its splendor;
> Let the martial bugle sing.
> In echoes of joy
> I can hear resounding
> The glories of Ayacucho,
> The thunders of Junín.

In tune with the poetic style of the revolution, Vargas Tejada's composition also reflects the tropes that Olmedo rehearses in his famous 1825 poem. As in the *Victoria de Junín*, Bolívar is here capable of frightening the Spanish army with his sole, thunderous presence, while the Junín and Ayacucho victories are prophetically echoed in Boyacá. Vargas Tejada also refers, as usual, to the Spaniards as tyrants, opposed to the liberating force that Bolívar represents. Very soon, however, the attributes of Bolívar in Vargas Tejada's poetry would change radically, and the derogatory epithet "tyrant," this time singularized, would become his most frequent imputation against the Liberator.

Exactly when Vargas Tejada moved from singing the praises of Bolívar to condemning his autocracy is difficult to pinpoint, particularly because the chronology recorded in the primary sources of his poetry appears to signal an overly abrupt transformation. José Joaquín Ortiz's 1857 anthology of Vargas Tejada (published twenty-eight years after the poet's death) dates the laudatory "Recuerdos de Boyacá" to August 6, 1826 (a logical date to commemorate Boyacá, since the battle took place almost exactly seven years earlier, on August 7, 1819). Yet according to Rodríguez Demorizi, it was during the last months of the same year of the composition of "Recuerdos de Boyacá" (probably late in November) when Vargas Tejada's most famous composition, "Catón en Útica" ("Cato in Utica") was performed for the first time (Rodríguez Demorizi 1966: 64). Completely contrary to the pro-Bolivarian spirit of "Recuerdos," "Catón en Útica" characterizes Bolívar as an irredeemable tyrant. Is it possible that in the course of three or four months the young poet dramatically changed his perception of Bolívar? Was "Recuerdos de Boyacá" a poem written much earlier and only published afterwards? The documents do not provide a precise explanation of this phenomenon. At any rate, the proximity of the dates is certainly peculiar, for Vargas Tejada's "Catón in Útica" could not be more antithetical to his previous panegyric.

The Classical character alluded to in the later poem is Cato the Younger, renowned in Roman historiography as a model of honor, honesty, and political consistency. The main Classical source of his biography is Plutarch, whose *Life of Cato* recounts a series of passages from the early life of the Roman politician until his assumption of a position in the Roman Senate, all of them intended to illustrate his political responsibility, his abhorrence of bribery and corruption, and his contempt for wealth and power. A fervent defender of the republican regime, Cato became one of the main opponents of Julius Caesar, aligning himself with Pompey when the Roman Civil War that would bring the republic to its fall began. According to Plutarch, when Pompey was defeated in 46 BCE, Cato fled to the city of Utica, located in what was then the Roman province of Africa. Aware that Julius Caesar's arrival was imminent, Cato preferred to commit suicide rather than surrender to the man he considered a traitor and a tyrant. The anecdote of the death of Cato may have left its mark in the bloody events of Shakespeare's *The Tragedy of Julius Caesar*; certainly, it inspired the English playwright Joseph Addison to compose his *Cato, A Tragedy*—the same play that George Washington used to stoke the patriotic zeal of the Continental Army (Stockdale 1995: 75).

While Washington used the story of Cato for revolutionary purposes, Vargas Tejada appropriated the misfortunes of the Roman senator to represent post-revolutionary political anxieties. Since the rumors about Bolívar's imperialist tendencies were widespread, Vargas Tejada knew he could recount the tale of Cato and Caesar without explicitly referring to the Liberator or any other contemporary figure, and indeed, that the implicit comparison would be more effective.[24] That is precisely what he did. "Catón en Útica" recreates, in a poetic monologue with romantic tones, the very last moments of the heroic Roman senator. In the course of 109 verses (and a four-line chorus), a sorrowful Cato grieves for the destruction of the republic and announces his own demise. The first stanzas of the poem combine a series of lamentations for the tragic fall of the republican regime (which Cato equates with "Liberty") with a passionate accusation against Caesar, who is indicted as the tyrant, traitor, and impostor who came to destroy his own fatherland. Both components, sorrow and indignation, infuse the poem's beginning:

> Inútiles han sido mis esfuerzos:
> al fin triunfar el despotismo logra,
> y delante de César abatida
> yace en el polvo la soberbia Roma.
>
> 1857: 20

> All my efforts have been futile:
> finally, despotism has achieved its victory
> and before the eyes of Caesar
> the proud Rome lies defeated in the dust.

Throughout the poem, Cato emphatically insists on his constant yet failed attempts to defend the republic. The poem's message is arranged to define the synecdochic relationship between Cato and Rome: Cato's imminent suicide corresponds to the fall of Rome, executed both by a treacherous Roman citizen (Julius Caesar) and his wretched partisans. And so, while Cato kills himself, the Romans destroy their republic in blind devotion to Caesar—significantly, the synecdoche does not include Caesar himself, for the tyrant has no general correspondence: he alone encompasses all the political significance of his acts. The poem thus continues with formulaic lamentations over the loss of freedom and the horrors of tyranny. Some passages, however, are much more specific:

---

[24] It is possible that Vargas Tejada also had in mind the works by Italian playwright Vittorio Alfieri (1749–1803), whose *Bruto Primo* ("The First Brutus") and *Bruto Secondo* ("The Second Brutus") portray Brutus as the liberator of Rome and a model of republican behavior. Incidentally, the *Bruto Primo* is dedicated to George Washington, whom Alfieri identifies with Brutus (1966: 771).

El nombre de monarca has evitado:
¿un vano nombre a tu poder qué importa?
Y al pueblo necio engañas fácilmente,
de libertad dejándole la sombra.

1857: 25

The title of monarch you have avoided:
what could a vain name matter for your power?
And the foolish masses you deceive easily,
leaving for them only a shadow of liberty.

In declaring that Caesar has avoided the title of monarch, Vargas Tejada's Cato alludes to Caesar's famous triple rejection of the crown that Marc Anthony offered to him—an image that, in turn, could evoke any of the multiple times when Bolívar had theatrically offered to resign the various political positions he held, only to be refused and reinstated by the Congress. Yet, even more precisely, Caesar's rejection of the crown has a literal correlation with a particular episode in the life of Bolívar. Six months after the victory of Ayacucho, on August 6, 1825, aristocrats of the lands called "Alto Perú" (High-country Peru) decided to separate from Peru and constitute a new republic, called "Bolivia" as an eternal celebration of its eponymous hero. When Bolívar entered the new country twelve days later, on August 18, he was offered a beautiful crown of gold and diamonds to commemorate his victory. In a dramatic gesture that rehearsed his previous resignations, the Liberator declined it and offered it instead to Sucre, whom he publicly deemed "the victor" and "the hero of Ayacucho" (O'Leary 1953: 5: 100–1). Bolívar could not appreciate that, in rejecting the crown, he was also supplying a superb image to corroborate the parallel with Caesar insistently advanced by Vargas Tejada.

But the more serious elements of Vargas Tejada's poem are reserved for its conclusion. Noticing that Caesar and his forces are coming for him, Cato decides to put an end to his own life, but not before delivering a somber prophecy:

No será largo tu fatal imperio;
del pueblo el sufrimiento al fin se agota,
y hay un pecho en que palpita todavía
de un Junio Bruto el alma generosa.

1857: 26

Your fated empire shall not last for too long;
the suffering of the people will eventually be exhausted,
and there's still a chest in which
the generous soul of a Junius Brutus beats.

In describing the fatal predictions of a Cato who was on the verge of death, Vargas Tejada perhaps wanted to allude to the prophecies of dying heroes that mark the evolution of dramatic action in *The Iliad*—in particular, Patroclus's announcement of the death of Hector (XVI.843–54) and Hector's reiteration of the fated death of Achilles (XXII.355–60). A conventional trope, the moribund hero seems capable of announcing the death of his killer because of the transitional stage that connects his last moments of life with his destiny in the Underworld (where foretelling is also not uncommon). But Vargas Tejada's ultimate message was much more empirical and dangerous than literary. In his clear allusions to Bolívar, his Cato prophesying the advent of the avenger Junius Brutus was also an invitation to consider the possibility of a serious rebellion against the Liberator.

Not by chance, the poem promptly received precise and suggestive glosses. Shortly after its first public performance, the anti-Bolivarian journalist and publisher Vicente Azuero wrote a review of the poem in the Bogotan newspaper *El Conductor*, posing questions such as this: "¿Quién no se siente enardecido e indignado al ver a César esclavizando a la gloriosa Roma, arrebatando para sí solo el fruto acopiado de tantos guerreros y de tantos héroes, de tantos sabios y de tantas virtudes, fascinando al pueblo con sus triunfos y su fortuna, con su fingida clemencia y su falaz moderación?" (qtd. in Rodriguez Demorizi 1966: 64) ("Who does not feel infuriated and indignant in watching Caesar enslaving the glorious Rome, seizing for himself the fruits gathered by so many warriors and heroes, so many wise and virtuous men, captivating the people with his victories and his fortune, with his false clemency and his fallacious moderation?"). Because Azuero's comments repeated the quotidian imputations against Bolívar, the message was, *mutatis mutandis*, completely apparent. The long history of deploying Classical similes to criticize Bolívar facilitated even more the already legible allusion of Vargas Tejada's Cato. Not surprisingly, the text became immensely popular among the opponents of Bolívar.

Between 1826 and 1828, press attacks against Bolívar became much harsher. Pamphlets and newspapers had by then recovered much of the Classical repertoire used to deride the Liberator during the wars. And, while school students in the city of Bogotá memorized and publicly performed the monologue "Catón en Útica" (hailing liberty and clamoring for the death of the "tyrant"), Vargas Tejada composed a new (and no less verbose) dramatic monologue. This time, however, the Classical character was a female patriot, "La madre de Pausanias" ("Pausanias' Mother"). The Pausanias referred to here is the fifth-century Spartan general who betrayed his people by negotiating an alliance with the Persian king. In the poem, Pausanias' mother publicly repudiates her son on account of his disloyalty and joins the crowd that intends to execute him.[25] As with "Catón," the performance of this Classical episode in Bogotá was not simply an act of denunciation, but also a serious call for rebellion and even execution.

It is not clear how much Bolívar knew of the Classical versions Vargas Tejada was crafting, either of himself (as Caesar or Pausanias) or his enemies (as Cato or Pausanias' mother). But, as had happened before, when he seized upon the comparisons with Ulysses and Nero, Bolívar again took ownership, in personal correspondence with his collaborators, of the similes that his rivals were popularizing. In fact, he had already considered the figure of Cato long before Vargas Tejada's poem—ironically, when declaring his desire to resign to his political power. In a letter to Santander (dated June 10, 1820), after having made clear that he was resolved to relinquish his position, Bolívar compares his own determination with that of Cato (1964–9: 2: 192); in another letter to Santander (dated September 13, 1820), in which he repeats the same purpose, he compares the vice-president of Venezuela, Germán Roscio, with "un Catón muy prematuro en una República en que no hay ni leyes ni costumbres romanas" (1964–69: 2: 258) ("a most premature Cato in a Republic in which there are neither Roman laws nor Roman habits"). In a third letter, this time to Salvador Jiménez, Bishop of Popayán, he commented that "el heroismo profano no es siempre el heroismo de la virtud ni de la religión ... Catón y Sócrates mismo, los seres privilegiados de la moral pagana, no pueden servir de modelo a los próceres de nuestra sagrada religión" (1964–69: 3: 40) ("profane heroism is not always the heroism of virtue and religion ... Cato and Socrates himself, the privileged beings of pagan morality, cannot serve as a model for the heroes of our sacred religion"). As Vargas Tejada surmised, there was indeed a difference between the Liberator and Cato the Younger: while Bolívar admired the Roman senator's proverbial resolution, he did not consider him an appropriate model for contemporary political behavior.

Bolívar could not have anticipated how correct his evaluation of Cato would prove to be. While "Catón en Útica" was repeated by students and republished in newspapers opposed to the Liberator, Vargas Tejada was hosting a series of clandestine meetings in his house, which included professors and students from the prestigious Colegio de San Bartolomé, journalists (including Azuero), and some army officers. The topic: how to assassinate Bolívar. To enhance the Classical irony, the group assumed the collective title of "Sociedad Filológica"

---

[25] For details and Classical sources related to this episode, see Pomeroy 2002: 58.

(Philological Society) as a façade for their conspiracy. A leak of information precipitated events: on September 25, 1828, the conspirators met at Vargas Tejada's house in Bogotá before heading to the presidential palace of San Carlos, where Bolívar was staying with his lover, Manuela Sáenz. Divided into three groups, they managed to kill the three soldiers and the dogs of the Liberator's personal guard and access the palace, but at the most critical moment Sáenz somehow helped Bolívar to jump out of a window before the conspirators could reach him (Lynch 2006: 240–1).[26] The Liberator had escaped with his life; the following day, most of the plotters were captured, and later executed by firing squad. The poet Vargas Tejada managed to escape from the city and hide in a cave for an entire year. Popular legend has it that the period in the cave, which he spent writing poetry, was irreparably deleterious to his mental health. It may be true. At any rate, in 1829, when he was just twenty-seven years old, Vargas Tejada left the cave only to die a short time later—according to some versions, drowning in a river while trying to escape to Venezuela or Guyana (Ruiza 2010; Mendéndez y Pelayo 1894: xl).

The story of the misfortunes of Vargas Tejada and his collaborators appears, with its radical romanticism, a rehearsal of the Classics so uncanny that it almost seems farcical. Hence the impression of Marcelino Menéndez y Pelayo, who, in his 1894 anthology of Spanish American poets, sardonically commented, "En Vargas Tejada es más interesante la vida que los escritos. Era un tipo perfecto de conspirador de buena fe, de tiranicida de colegio clásico, admirador de Bruto y de Catón, en cuya boca ponía interminables romanzones endecasílabos contra el dictador y la dictadura" (1894: xl) ("Vargas Tejada's life is more interesting than his writing. He was the perfect type of well-intentioned conspirator, a tyrannicidal character of the Classical school, an admirer of Brutus and Cato, in whose mouths he put endless hendecasyllabic *romanzones*[27] against the dictator and the dictatorship"). And yet, despite the tragic irony of Vargas Tejada's project and death, the almost literal re-presentation of the events surrounding Julius Caesar's death, poetically announced and insistently repeated by those who would really

---

[26] In what seems an excess of irony, the window through which Bolívar escaped now has a plaque that commemorates the event with a Latin epigram: "Siste parumper spectator gradum / si vacas miratus viam salutis / qua sese liberavit/pater salvatorque patriae / Simon Bolivar/in nefanda nocte septembrina / An. MDCCCXXVIII" ("Stop for a moment, / spectator. If you are idling, contemplate / the exit way through which the father / and savior of the nation / Simón Bolívar / saved his own life on a nefarious / September's night / in the year 1828").

[27] *Romance* is a designation applied to a series of compositions in the Spanish poetic tradition. In this case, Menéndez y Pelayo uses it in the general sense of "rhymes"—the augmentative variant *romanzón* is obviously pejorative.

dare to attempt the assassination of the Liberator in the name of Liberty, could have effectively transformed the political balance of his time. Imagining potential history entails obvious dangers, but it may not be too difficult to picture the expedient political and symbolic appropriation of the figure of Bolívar that would have resulted if the conspiracy had been successful.

Yet the frustrated conspiracy, one of the wildest instantiations of Greek and Roman adaptations in the history of South America, was not only Classical because of the iteration of the infamous episode of Julius Caesar, but also because of the heroic pathos invoked to galvanize the seditious movement. An extreme example is the poem that Azuero composed and delivered in prison shortly before his execution. The poem takes the shape of a pre-mortem dirge, in which Azuero laments the failure of the conspiracy and justifies it in the name of Liberty. The bombastic verses of his final poem distinctly echo, almost verbatim, the lines that Vargas Tejada attributed to his Cato:

> ¡Compatriotas! No temo la muerte,
> sólo llevo al sepulcro el dolor
> de dejar a mi Patria en cadenas
> agobiada con cruel opresión.
>
> qtd. in Rodríguez Demorizi 1966: 109

> Countrymen! I fear not death.
> I only bring to my tomb the pain
> of leaving my Fatherland in chains,
> overwhelmed by cruel oppression.

Fearless before imminent death and lamenting the Fatherland's destiny over his own: in almost all aspects, Azuero interprets his own fate as Cato had done. The only difference, of course, is the lack of a new prophecy, which is instead replaced by the repetition of the romantic desideratum that drove the conspirators' actions:

> Arrancar al tirano la vida
> siempre fue mi primer intención;
> libertar al Estado de un monstruo,
> de un soberbio, de un vil opresor.
>
> qtd. in Rodríguez Demorizi 1966: 110

> To snatch the life of the tyrant
> was always my first intention;
> to free the Nation from a monster,
> from an arrogant, wicked oppressor.

Azuero's depiction of Bolívar condenses, in the extreme circumstances of its composition, the implacable appropriation of Classical commonplaces in what could have been the most dramatic event in the Age of Bolívar. Biographers affirm that the conspiracy had a tremendous impact on the Liberator, who did not outlive his enemies for too long. He died only two years later, on December 17, 1830. In the meantime, Bolívar's enemies relentlessly invoked the conspiracy in connection with its Roman antecedent as an actualization of the heroism of Cato and Brutus.

Vargas Tejada (along with Azuero and the rest of activists who attempted to assassinate Bolívar) was not relying on the Classical tale of Cato, Julius Caesar, and Junius Brutus as a mere allusion. He was crafting, in a manner similar to Plutarch's *Parallel Lives*, a political understanding of Bolívar through the mirror of the Roman general. There is, however, a fundamental difference between the ancient Greek biographer and the young Colombian poet: for Plutarch, the parallelism was a means for a personal, almost psychological analysis of key figures—a characterization which was not meant to be taken as a historical approach, as he himself warned: "οὔτε γὰρ ἱστορίας γράφομεν, ἀλλὰ βίους … οὕτως ἡμῖν δοτέον εἰς τὰ τῆς ψυχῆς σημεῖα μᾶλλον ἐνδύεσθαι καὶ διὰ τούτων εἰδοποιεῖν τὸν ἑκάστου βίον, ἐάσαντας ἑτέροις τὰ μεγέθη καὶ τοὺς ἀγῶνας" (*Life of Alexander* 1.2–3) ("For it is not Histories that I am writing, but Lives … so I must be permitted to devote myself rather to the signs of the soul in men, and by means of these to portray the life of each, leaving to others the description of their great contests"; Perrin 1919: 225). For Vargas Tejada, instead, the distinction between ἱστορία (history) and βίος (life) is dysfunctional: history is constructed by exemplary lives, and consequently both categories are structurally interdependent. Parallelism, in this sense, is a prescriptive mechanism to identify historical agency, which is conceived, in turn, as the exercise of a personal action capable of molding or transforming history. Such a capacity is reserved for extraordinary characters—extraordinary but not unique, since their attributes are constantly rehearsed through key moments of history. Hence the possibility of parallelism.

Vargas Tejada's reproduction of the conspiracy of Julius Caesar is, in the end, an attempt to take a part of the extraordinary agency attributed to Bolívar, because that was the only way (according to a reading of the Classical tradition that took it as casuistry) in which to turn reality into history. Thus, history ends up in the hands of those who perform historical roles—recognized as such through the parallelism, verification, account, and performance of their iterations. In other words, between Bolívar and Julius Caesar, or between Vargas

Tejada and Cato, there is a principle of identification operative in two senses: one is specular—the mirroring of one character onto another (identical); the second is indexical—one character permits the recognition (or identification) of his counterpart. This double-edged identification consolidates a grammar of history actualized in the personal features and agency of extraordinary individuals, and sanctioned by ancient accounts. Hegel's theorization on the "individual as subject of history," embedded in his lectures on the philosophy of history (contemporary to the Age of Bolívar), had laid the foundations for this dialectical understanding of individuality and universality. The premise with which Thomas Carlyle would open his famous *On Heroes, Hero-Worship and the Heroic in History* (published in 1841, only thirteen years after the failed conspiracy), symptomatizes the same ideological apparatus: "[A]s I take it, Universal History, the history of what man has accomplished in this world, is at bottom the History of the Great Men who have worked here" (2014: 91). No wonder that Plutarch's distinction between "τὰ τῆς ψυχῆς σημεῖα" ("the signs of the soul") of men and "τὰ μεγήθη καὶ τοὺς ἀγῶνας" ("the great deeds and contests") in which those men participated (*Life of Alexander* 1.3) is invisible for Carlyle, who fuses both categories: "[T]he soul of the whole world's history, it may justly be considered, were the history of these [great men]" (2014: 91). Under the umbrella of the Classics (though against Plutarch's warning), history in the Age of Revolution is personal, compact, and even theatrical. Provided that the right *dramatis personae* are available, history is performable.

Conclusions: History, Impersonation, Prosopopoeia

In 1822, Bolívar sent his twelve-year-old nephew Fernando Bolívar to the United States of America, to be educated in the preparatory school of Germantown Academy in Pennsylvania. The Liberator also wrote to those who would tutor his nephew a brief pedagogical note titled "Método que se debe seguir en la educación de mi sobrino Fernando Bolívar" ("Method that Must Be Followed in the Education of my Nephew Fernando Bolívar"). In just two pages, and through a series of concise statements (atypical, considering his usual verbosity), Bolívar lists the program of study he considers appropriate for his nephew. A general statement opens the document: "La educación de los niños debe ser siempre adecuada a su edad, inclinaciones, genio y temperamento" (1993: 157) ("The education of children must always be appropriate for their age, inclinations, personality, and temperament"). Bolívar then recommends the learning of languages (first the modern and then the ancient, "not neglecting his own [native Spanish]"); geography and cosmography, in turn, should be the basic courses of his instruction (1993: 157). He finally addresses the subject of history, whose acquisition is compared to that of languages: "La historia, a semejanza de los idiomas, debe principiarse a aprender por la contemporánea, para ir remontando por grados hasta llegar a los tiempos oscuros de la fábula" (1993: 157) ("History, similar to the learning of languages, must be taught starting with contemporary events, to then go back in time, gradually, until reaching the dark times of fables"). Other educational aphorisms, framed in the same style, complete this peculiar letter.[28]

Bolívar's idea of history taught backwards closely matches the analytical method Edgar Allan Poe attributed to his archetypal detective, Auguste Dupin, only eleven years after the Liberator's death. In "The Murders in the Rue Morgue" (1841), Poe imagines the possibility of explaining an apparently accidental thought through the methodical tracing of preceding ideas—a rationalization (or "ratiocination," as Poe preferred) that eliminates the possibility of randomness. Ideas, in this sense, are anything but casual—rather, they are fundamentally causal, always embedded in a rigorous logic that can become apparent through the exercise of (usually extraordinary) analysis. For Bolívar, the present time can be conceptualized in the same rationalist fashion: in requiring the pre-eminence of contemporary events in a course of history taught backward, Bolívar is defining the present as the *telos* of the past. Almost as a decree or *fatum*, the Bolivarian present is the realization of the necessary condition of events that could otherwise be seen as aleatory. Aware of the importance of the Age of Revolution in which he played such a central role, he admonishes the tutors of his nephew to teach "la historia contemporánea" ("contemporary history") as the point of departure from which to study the past. Previous histories become a preparation for Bolívar's own times.

The counterbalance of Bolívar's severely logical retrospection was, in turn, his mania for prospection. A quick glance at his most important documents—an illustrious example is his "Carta de Jamaica"—demonstrates his propensity for predictions, especially geopolitical. More often than not, his anticipations happened to be well aimed—as was the case with his oft-repeated prognosis on

---

[28] This pedagogical note should perhaps be compared with the writing of Bolívar's former mentor, the pedagogue Simón Rodríguez—particularly with Rodríguez's fascinating treatise titled *Sociedades Americanas* ("American Societies"), whose extravagant orthographic choices, provocative selection of different fonts and font sizes, unconventional layout, and aphoristic style seem to anticipate the graphic experimentalism of twentieth-century avant-garde movements.

the role of the United States in Latin America, included in a letter to Colonel Patrick Campbell, British Chargé D'affairs, where Bolívar distinctly identifies the rhetoric of liberty that would characterize the imperialist behavior of the United States.[29] Bolívar, in sum, often imagined his present, his Age of Revolution, as literally a pivotal or axial time at which the past arrived and from which the future departed.

This fondness for historical prospection and retrospection explains the contents of what is perhaps the most bizarre text Bolívar ever composed, "Mi delirio sobre el Chimborazo" (1822) ("My Delirium upon the Chimborazo").[30] In concise poetic prose that seems like the report of a dream, or perhaps an actual delirium, Bolívar imagines himself reaching the top of Ecuador's highest summit, Chimborazo, where he holds a hallucinatory dialogue with the Classical personification of Father Time, "un viejo cargado de los despojos de las edades" ((1822) 1833: 244) ("an old man weighed down with the remains of the ages"). While Bolívar observes in the face of Time "la historia de lo pasado y los libros del destino" ((1822) 1833: 244) ("the history of the past and the books of fate"), Father Time scolds the Liberator: "¿Por qué te envaneces, niño o viejo, hombre o héroe? ¿Crees acaso que el universo es algo? ¿Que montar sobre la cabeza de un alfiler, es subir? ¿Pensáis que los instantes que llamáis siglos pueden servir de medida a los sucesos?" ((1822) 1833: 244) ("Why do you persist in your vanity, child or elder, man or hero? Do you believe your universe is anything at all—that climbing to the top of a pin is an ascent? Do you think that the instants that you call centuries can be used to measure events?"). But even though Time reminds Bolívar of his puny condition, he still entrusts him with a prophetic mission: "no escondas los secretos que el cielo te ha revelado: di la verdad a los hombres" ((1822) 1833: 244) ("Do not conceal the secrets that Heaven has revealed to you: bring the truth to mankind"). The prosopopoeia of Time seems to imply the historical insignificance of Bolívar and his revolution, yet at the same time it grants him transcendental access to the highest framework of history, and charges him with the supreme oracular task of transmitting Truth to mankind.

---

[29] In this letter, dated August 5, 1829, Bolívar comments on a project aiming to name a "European prince" as his successor in the Colombian government: "¿Cuánto no se opondrían todos los nuevos estados americanos, y los Estados Unidos que parecen destinados por la Providencia para plagar la América de miserias a nombre de la Libertad?" (1964-69: 7: 260-1) ("Can you imagine the opposition that would come from the new American states, and from the United States, which seems destined by Providence to plague America with miseries in the name of Freedom?"; Fornoff 2003: 172-3).

[30] For details about this peculiar document and its allegorical value, see Ojeda, Martínez, and Ortiz 2005.

Through his own poetic hand, Bolívar's various personae simultaneously compete and collaborate in the schizophrenic construction of his role as living fulcrum of historical validation. It seems indeed impossible to imagine the Liberator's interaction with history and time in terms other than "delirium."

The presence of the Classics in the Age of Revolution examined throughout this chapter is a symptom of the extent to which not only Bolívar, but his detractors and allies as well, all devoted themselves to the constant rehearsal of such a delirious conversation. The two main poets of the chronicles narrated above, Olmedo and Vargas Tejada, approach the political persona of Bolívar as a figure whose utterance, depending on its inflection, is capable of molding both the history concentrated on him and the meaningfulness of their poetic voices. In spite of their political differences, both develop a common form of consciousness that could be called "historical hyperawareness," which would be defined as the anxious need to achieve an epochal performance suitable for posterity—in a context that, they knew with absolute certainty, was radically defining for Latin American geopolitics. Bolívar, in this sense, provides the means to realize their desiderata: Olmedo aspires to be the Poet of the Revolution; Vargas Tejada, instead, wants to be the Poet of the Rebellion. While the validation of such aspirations could only come from the future, their strategy consists of metabolizing the tropes, prescriptions, structures, and episodes of the ancient Classical tradition. Olmedo actualizes the role of the Horatian *vates sacer* to weave, with his proverbial "poetic license," a series of difficult pairs: the battlefield and victory of Junín with those of Ayacucho; the royal and metaphysical Inca Huayna Capac with the triumphal Simón Bolívar; and the fall of the Incan Empire with the American renovation brought by the Patriotic army. Each of these items is, of course, conveniently modulated by the Classics, whose divinities and epic heroes, mythologies and *dei ex machina*, and prescriptions and poetics, serve to hail the revolution. This Classicalization, for good or for bad, ensured for Olmedo a place in the history of Ecuadorian letters, as a founding father and the creator of national literature.

These antecedents, in turn, informed Vargas Tejada's selection of Julius Caesar as model for Bolívar. As attested by El Inca Garcilaso, who, through the manipulation of genealogy and the analogies proposed in his *Comentarios reales*, had claimed literal and rhetorical inheritance from the Roman general, the figure of Julius Caesar had been hailed several times as a model of soldier and writer applicable to the Americas.[31] This paradigm, however, coexisted with

---

[31] See Campos-Muñoz 2013: 136–41.

grimmer versions of Caesar. Vargas Tejada, in this sense, found in Caesar a case of ancient ambivalence that lent itself perfectly to the oscillations of Bolívar, whose persona swung between the monikers of Liberator and Tyrant. What started out as an allegory then became an agora—an assembly of past and present tropes gathered in the same place. Bolívar was the tyrannical Julius Caesar; Vargas Tejada, consequently, wanted to be a defender of Liberty. But history can be resilient: he ended up rehearsing the misfortunes of his tragic Cato even though he aspired to perform the conspiracy of a salvationist Brutus (in fact, in an unbearable twist of irony, an *incomplete* version of a poem titled "Brutus" was found in the lodgings of Vargas Tejada after the failure of his conspiracy). Through Olmedo, a poetic version of Bolívar came to be assaulted by history; through Vargas Tejada, poetry struck back. When in 1844, Pietro Tenerani presented his statue of Bolívar appareled as a Roman senator, he was (maybe consciously) condensing in bronze the vertiginous history of Bolívar's Classicalization. In all likelihood, none of those involved in this turbulent chapter of history would have objected to this representation.

4[1]

Mythographers

De repente, Lenita canta a Valsa do Orfeu e vem a estranha sensação da vida que já foi e eu estou novamente no Teatro Municipal com você, e o Leo Peracchi está dirigindo a orquestra, os frisos dourados do Municipal brilham sob a luz.

Suddenly, Lenita sings the Waltz of Orpheus, and the strange feeling of a bygone life dawns on me, and I am back again at the Municipal Theatre with you, and Leo Peracchi is directing the orchestra, while the golden friezes of the Municipal [Theatre] shine under the lights.
  Antônio Carlos Jobim, Letter to Vinicius de Moraes, February 15, 1965

Preliminaries

Greco-Roman myths loom large in the literary practice of modern Latin America. In the closing remarks of her survey on the adoption of Greek tragedies in the region, Pilar Hualde Pascual reminds us that "cada año surj[e]n nuevas versiones de los trágicos griegos en Iberoamérica, hasta el punto que resulta ilusoria cualquier pretensión de exhaustividad al revisar un tema particularmente fecundo" (2012: 215) ("every year new versions of Greek tragedies appear in Latin America, to the point that any aspiration to exhaustiveness in reviewing a matter so particularly prolific must be deemed illusory"). The range of cases studied in José Antonio López Férez's 2009 compilation, *Mitos clásicos en la literatura española e hispanoamericana del siglo XX* ("Classical Myths in Spanish and Spanish American Literatures of the twentieth Century"), appears to

---

[1] A version of the sections of this chapter that deal with Orpheus in Brazil was published in Spanish in *Latin American Research Review* 47, Special Issue (2012): 31–48. I thank LARR for their permission to reuse this material.

corroborate Hualde Pascual's impressions. Considering the convoluted cultural history of Latin American Classicisms, the scale of this phenomenon is unsurprising. The creative and defining relationship between New World intellectuals and the Classical tradition, assessed in the three previous chapters in terms of foundational, chorographic, and political dynamics, has yielded an inexhaustible corpus of literary reformulations of Greco-Roman motifs. And, among the various modes of Classical reception in Latin America, the rewriting of myths may well be the predominant mode.

One of the most important lessons that Marx adopted from Hegel is the notion that, once a phenomenon acquires a certain dimension, what was in principle a quantitative expansion ends up undergoing a qualitative transfiguration—in other words, the proliferation of a phenomenon can transform the nature of the phenomenon itself.[2] If this principle has some bearing in the field of aesthetics, the very magnitude of the Latin American obsession with Greco-Roman myths, particularly in the modern period, raises a series of compelling theoretical questions about the practice of myth-writing in the region. For instance, what are the cultural and philosophical transformations of the category of "Classical myth" in its Latin American versions? What is the discursive surplus of a myth beyond its function as a recognizable narrative and a source of traditional characters? Where are the borders between Classical and modern, Greco-Roman and Latin American, transhistorical and regional, narrative and political, and personal and aesthetic, when the Classical myth has successfully permeated the cultural fabric of a Latin American community?

While this line of inquiry is, within the coordinates of cultural studies, already compelling in and of itself, the examination of modern (and modernist) Classical mythological narratives in South America is especially useful in relation to the overall argument of this book, as it adds a whole new dimension to the larger question of the Classics in Latin America. It may not seem so, since the mythological apparatus of ancient Greece and Rome has already been showed as playing an important role in the cases examined in each of the three preceding chapters—in the Parnassian fantasies of Diego Mexía and Clarinda's *mundus novus*, as seen in Chapter 1; in the relocation of pious Aeneas within the

---

[2] Here is one of multiple examples of Marx's investment in this Hegelian principle. In comparing the medieval guild system of production with the capitalist mode of production of his own time, Marx offers a contrast between the limited number of workers associated with a single master in the former system, and the proliferation of workers and the capitalization of their labor in the latter. The very notion of labor changes in the process, hence Marx concludes, "Here, as in natural science, is shown the correctness of the law discovered by Hegel, in his *Logic*, that at a certain point merely quantitative differences pass over by a dialectical inversion into qualitative distinctions" (1990: 423).

celebratory discourse of colonial Lima, as presented in Chapter 2; and in the repertoire of heroes and monsters used to celebrate or condemn Simón Bolívar, as seen in Chapter 3. And yet, there is a difference between, on the one hand, borrowing images, attributes, and episodes from mythical narratives to then incorporate them into a different aesthetic or political project (a poem in praise of poetry, an illustrated map of city walls, a sculpture of a renowned statesman), and, on the other hand, engaging with the actual diegetic apparatus of a myth; in other words, between appropriating the Classics and appropriating one of the very mechanisms by which the Classics circulate and are transmitted—that of mythography.

This latter process consists perforce of more than a relocation of ancient tropes into different cultural, aesthetic, and historical contexts. Rather, it entails a full-fledged engagement with the old and convoluted narrative mass of stories, characters, and portents codified by prestigious ancient writers who were, in turn, drawing from a myriad of previous versions—crystallized in popular accounts, architecture and sculpture, decoration and ware, religious and social practices, and so on. Inasmuch as the rewriting of a myth constitutes an intervention, not a mere borrowing, the mythological diegesis ceases to operate as an authoritative hypotext to serve instead as a field of perennial negotiation. The ancient myth is thus both resilient and pliable—it demands the preservation of distinct features that render the mythic matter recognizable regardless of its mutations, and yet it also offers unlimited narrative latitude for the incorporation of questions and answers that pertain more to the rewriter's identity than the myth's cultural source. And just as the rewriter intervenes in the myth, the myth can also dramatically affect its rewriter. Given the enthusiasm of Latin American artists for Classical mythologies, especially in the context of the region's many modernisms, it might be expected that the examination of mythological rewriting in the past century will provide especially vivid instances to analyze the transformations that myths and writers can exert on each other. The Classicalist processes of intellectual foundation, New-World vindication, and political tropology explored in the previous chapters give way here to the consideration of a further phenomenon: that of mythological intervention.

The main case study explored in this chapter, the appropriation of the myth of Orpheus in the Brazilian scenic arts of the twentieth century, offers an extraordinary opportunity to consider these matters. The impact of the Orpheus tale in modern Brazil has achieved an importance that could not have been foreseen by those who initially propitiated it. The key to understanding this phenomenon is located in the encounter between myth and identity—a process

I will characterize here as "mythography." Delving into the complexities of this category and its pertinence in the history of the Brazilian Orpheus, however, requires a consideration of the extraordinarily efficient ways in which a myth can infiltrate the discursive dimension of cultural identity. To illustrate this particular point, and by way of a prefatory narrative, let us first examine a case concerning the most paradigmatic modern author of Latin America—Jorge Luis Borges. This preliminary analysis illuminates key parameters through which the larger and more radical instance of Orpheus in Brazil can then be examined.

The Other Asterion

In an interview held in his beloved Geneva, less than two years before passing away, an eighty-five-year-old Jorge Luis Borges (1899–1986) insisted—one more time—that at his age death was a desideratum rather than a source of fear. "Para mí, la muerte es una esperanza ... [Me veo i]mpaciente, deseoso de morir de una buena vez" (Gasparini (1984) 1999) ("For me, death is a kind of hope ... [I find myself] impatient, wishing to die once and for all"). In the course of his readings and writings, Borges had rehearsed this mortuary fascination multiple times.[3] Juan Gasparini, his interviewer, reminded him of a precise example: "Como el Minotauro de uno de sus cuentos" (Gasparini (1984) 1999) ("Like the Minotaur of one of your short stories"). Gasparini's quip alludes to Borges's "La casa de Asterión" ("The House of Asterion"), a brief first-person narrative whose protagonist (revealed to be the Minotaur in the surprising conclusion) suggests that death is a form of redemption. Borges appears to concur with the analogy, but instead of elaborating on the redemptive qualities of death, the philosophical implications of his short story, or the symbolic potential of the Minotaur, he replies with a brief anecdote about the composition of the tale:

> Ah, sí, cierto. Ese cuento yo lo escribí ... Yo trabajé en una revista que se llamaba *Los anales de Buenos Aires*. Ahí publicó por primera vez en su vida un cuento Julio Cortázar. Un cuento que ilustró mi hermana. Un cuento que se llamó "Casa tomada." Cuando teníamos que entrar en prensa, había tres páginas en blanco.

---

[3] For Borges, death tends to be a matter of curiosity, melancholy, or resignation rather than of horror. This is the case in stories as canonical as "La muerte y la brújula" ("Death and the Compass"), "El sur" ("The South"), "El inmortal" ("The Immortal"), "El muerto" ("The Dead Man"), and "El Milagro Secreto" ("The Secret Miracle"), among others.

Entonces a mí se me ocurrió un argumento, "La casa de Asterión." ... Aquella noche no salí. Lo escribí antes y después de cenar y a la mañana siguiente. Y a la tarde llevé el cuento. Tomé los datos de un diccionario. Un lindo cuento.

Gasparini 1984

Why, yes, that's true. I wrote that tale ... I worked at a journal called *The Annals of Buenos Aires*. The first short story that Julio Cortázar ever published was printed there. My sister illustrated that story. A short story called "House Taken Over." We had to start the print run, but there were still three blank pages. And then I came up with an argument, "The House of Asterion." ... That night, I did not go out. I wrote it before and after dinner, and during the next morning. In the afternoon I brought the short story [to the press]. I took the details from a dictionary. A nice short story.

Three elements of this response stand out: the journal where the tale was published, the reference to Julio Cortázar, and the hasty circumstances of the short story's genesis. There is something serendipitous in the fact that this journal, in which seminal fictions by two of the most important writers of modern Argentina appeared, was titled, precisely, "The Annals of Buenos Aires." The category of "annals" (from one of Tacitus' Roman historical treatises, organized in *annual* reports) evokes, especially at this late point in Borges's life, not so much a publication venue, but rather his literary and historical canonization, and Borges could not fail to notice that. Already an octogenarian, he had lived most of his long life under the weight of his own extraordinary reputation. Some of his short stories explicitly address the burdensome nature of that prestige—most famously the brief text "Borges y yo" ("Borges and I"). In retrospect, the presence of his early writing in the "Annals of Buenos Aires" seems to foreshadow the role Borges would go on to have in Argentine literary history.

Borges also reports that the very first place where another titan of Argentine literature, Julio Cortázar, published anything at all was the very same journal—and this contribution was none other than "Casa tomada" ("House Taken Over"), arguably the most famous short story he wrote. Perhaps the word "casa" made Borges think of this connection when Gasparini asked about "La casa de Asterión," or perhaps the topic of death reminded Borges that only seven months had passed since Cortázar had died (on February 12, 1984)—indeed, Gasparini's readers could have hardly missed in Borges's reference to Cortázar a note of tribute or homage to his fellow writer. And so, in the context of a reflection on death, in the Geneva where he had spent his adolescent years (and would spend his last ones), Borges manages to subtly orchestrate the diachronic echoes of his own youth and old age through the intersection of Cortázar's literary life story with his own.

The references to the enduring legacies of these two complex careers are, in turn, contrasted by the account of the swift composition of "La casa de Asterión," written between the late evening and the next morning. Borges describes his hastiness as pragmatic (he had to fill three empty pages for the journal) and atypical: "El cuento del Minotauro lo escribí en dos días, cosa que no me sucede ya que yo trabajo muy lentamente: corrijo mucho los borradores" (Gasparini 1984) ("I wrote the short story of the Minotaur in two days, which is something very unusual for me, since I usually work very slowly: I constantly correct my drafts"). At the end of his answer, Borges resorts to popular *gaucho* jargon to express his satisfaction with how well the tale came out in spite of the short process of composition (something unusual, given his self-deprecating tendencies): "[Ese cuento t]uve que improvisarlo y más o menos me salió bien esa guitarreada. Digamos, esa payada..." (Gasparini 1984) ("I had to improvise [that tale] and I think that the *guitarreada* came out well, more or less. A good *payada*, one could say...").[4]

"Más o menos bien": as usual, Borges's opinion of his own work is an understatement. Considering its thoughtful brevity, its clever plot, its deceptive erudition, its narrative fluency, and its melancholic symbolism, it is astonishing that a fictional masterpiece such as "La casa de Asterión" could have been composed in just a few hours. The tale begins with an erudite epigraph extracted from the ancient compilation of Greek myths known as *Library* and traditionally attributed to Apollodorus of Athens: "Y la reina dio a luz a un hijo que se llamó Asterión" (Borges 2005: 608) ("And the queen gave birth to a son who was called Asterion"). Narrating in the first person, Asterion describes his strange abode—a house unique in the world, empty and solitary, full of halls and passageways, whose few basic items (wellheads, drinking troughs, and mangers) are infinitely reproduced. Asterion reports his quotidian activities—running and sleeping, jumping from great heights, and (his favorite pastime) pretending that there is another Asterion to whom he shows the features of his house. Every nine years, Asterion comments in the section that Gasparini brings up in his interview, "entran en la casa nueve hombres para que yo los libre de todo mal" (Borges

---

[4] *Payada* is the traditional call-and-response contest between Argentine guitar players, who typically improvise as an exhibition of musical (the *guitarreada* or strumming of the guitar) and poetic dexterity.

2005: 609) ("nine men enter the house so that I may free them from all evil"). One of these men predicted to Asterion that one day a redeemer (that is, an executioner) would come for him as well. Asterion (like Borges in his interview) finally declares his hopeful expectation for that arrival and wonders how his redeemer will look. The first-person narrative finishes with that open question, but the short story only concludes a bit later, with a brief section separated from Asterion's speech by two blank lines (the significance of this blank space will be highlighted below). This closing section shifts from the first-person narrative to a dialogue that solves the mystery of the protagonist's identity: "—¿Lo creerás, Ariadna?—dijo Teseo—'El minotauro apenas se defendió'" (Borges 2005: 610) ("'Can you believe it, Ariadne?' said Theseus. 'The Minotaur barely defended himself'").

The novelty of Borges's rendering of the well-known story of the Minotaur is, of course, the shifting in the narrative perspective. Traditionally, the Minotaur has been depicted as a mute monster, an absolute otherness lurking in the galleries of an abominable edifice, kept away from the people of Crete and killing the unfortunate victims he receives, until the heroic Theseus, assisted by Ariadne's proverbial thread, slays him. Borges's story (inspired, he mentions in the epilogue of his collection *El Aleph*, by an 1896 painting by George Frederic Watts) offers instead an account of the world perceived through the eyes of a subject who bears a proper name, Asterion, instead of the descriptor "Minotaur" (i.e., "the bull of [King] Minos"). Every element associated with the Minotaur changes when he ceases to be the monster in a maze and becomes Asterion—the labyrinth is a house, the human victims are recipients of compassion and liberation, and the monster is a solitary individual exhausted by the monotony of his existence. The epigraph of the tale, "And the queen gave birth to a son who was called Asterion," becomes especially relevant for this rewriting. Lost in the myriad of names and characters that fill the laborious catalogues of myths in the *Library*, the obscure proper name of the Minotaur would not be recognized by most readers as that of the creature, so the epigraph becomes meaningful only when the story is over. That explains Borges's convenient redaction of his source. The original reads: "ἡ δὲ Ἀστέριον ἐγέννησε τὸν κληθέντα Μινώταυρον" (*Library* 3.1.4)—literally, "And she [Pasiphae, King Minos's wife] gave birth to Asterion, who was called Minotaur." Borges substitutes the pronoun "ἡ" (she) with "the queen," and suppresses the participial complement "τὸν κληθέντα Μινώταυρον" (who was called Minotaur), which clarifies Asterion's identity. These alterations are, of course, strategic, as their absence is precisely what enables the surprising effect of the Borgesian version of the myth.

"La casa de Asterión" appears to radically reconfigure the perspective of the myth. And yet, in crafting a different angle from which to explore the tale, Borges is also reproducing an ancient Classical gesture, one that had already been rehearsed in the multiple retellings of the history of the Minotaur: the recurrent addition of new elements to the myth's basic plot. A glance at some of the Classical textual history of the tale explains this point better. A fragment of the sixth-century-BCE Hesiodic *Catalogue of Women*, perhaps the oldest textual allusion to this myth, offers (at least in what remains of the papyrus) a clear characterization of the Minotaur: from the belly downward he is a man; from the belly upward, a bull (1967: Frag. 145 MW). Fifth-century-BCE lyric poet Bacchyllides explains his origins, with Pasiphae asking Daedalus how to have intercourse with the bull of Poseidon (2002: Frag. 6 (c. 26)). It seems that fifth-century-BCE playwright Euripides, in his tragedy *The Cretans* (today only accessible in a few fragments), had Pasiphae's nurse describe to the terrified king Minos the monstrosity of the baby Minotaur (2008: 472a, 472b). The second story of Palaephatus's *On Unbelievable Tales* (fourth century BCE), dedicated to Pasiphae, is the first extant text that mentions the word "Minotaur": Palaephatus gets through the basic plot quickly in order to rationalize it—explaining, for example, that the father of the Minotaur was not a bull, but a man whose name was Bull (2.10). The second-century-BCE *Library* (attributed to the mythographer Apollodorus, and, again, the source of Borges's epigraph) provides for the first time the name "Asterion" and summarizes the basic plot: the Minotaur, living in the labyrinth designed by Daedalus, is slain by Theseus, assisted by Ariadne's thread (3.1.3–4). Later, in the Roman period, authors such as Diodorus Siculus (*Library of History* 4.61.4–7), Ovid (*The Art of Love* 1.289–326), Hyginus (*Fabulae* 42), and Plutarch (*Life of Theseus* 15.1–23.2) would give longer poetic or analytic accounts of the rest of the details that have come down to us. Over the course of many centuries, then, different Classical writers somehow claimed authorial rights to the myth, not by negating or simply reformulating previous accounts, but also by adding new elements.

When Borges hastily composed "La casa de Asterión," he was following similar protocols. He did not merely rewrite the myth; instead, he added writing to previous writing, and in doing so he yet again negotiated with the very same narrative structure into which Hesiod, Palaephatus, Apollodorus, and so on had also woven their own accounts. Hence the paramount importance of the two seemingly innocuous blank lines that appear toward the conclusion of the story, between the ending of Asterion's speech and the intervention of Theseus. As the hero's comment to Ariadne closes the story without further elaboration, the ending can fully function as the revelation or anagnorisis of the identity of Asterion so long as the reader knows the conventional Classical myth in advance—that previous knowledge is the necessary context for understanding why Theseus suddenly appears at the end of the tale, why he addresses Ariadne, and how Asterion's account fits within the traditional narrative of the Minotaur. If the reader is unaware of the traditional myth, the story becomes meaningless and the aesthetic pleasure of the story's end is lost. The negotiation between Borges's story and the traditional version—which is, in a way, also a negotiation between writer and reader—occurs, precisely, in that penultimate blank space of the page—in its deceptive silence. Far from empty, the two blank lines preceding the end of the short story encapsulate a monumental tradition: from Hesiod through Plutarch, that space contains the centuries of previous narratives in which Theseus and the Minotaur have been required to fight time and time again.

The blank before the end, simultaneously silent and verbose, ends up highlighting the ancient polyphony that constitutes the very substance of myth. Borges's expansion of former accounts of the Minotaur corroborates the narrative's mythical dimension—the story can be enlarged *precisely* because it is a myth. No wonder that subsequent readers of Borges would later rehearse the same gesture: directly influenced by "La Casa de Asterión," Argentine writers Jorge Cabrera and Guillermo Angelelli would compose, respectively, a book of poems (*Asterión y otros poemas* ("Asterion and Other Poems"), 1984) and a unipersonal performance (*Asterión*, 1991), honoring the Borgesian Minotaur. Likewise, Peruvian poet José Watanabe reserved the final section of his collection *Banderas detrás de la niebla* (2006) ("Flags Behind the Mist") for what might be the longest poem he composed: "El otro Asterión" ("The Other Asterion"). Watanabe's beautiful poem imagines the terms of the conversation between Asterion and the imaginary friend he creates in Borges's version, "the other Asterion"—thus adding another postscript to the endless journeys of the Minotaur through his own textual labyrinth. "The Other Asterion" is certainly an instance of the double, one of the most cherished themes of Borges's tropology. Yet within the tradition discussed here, that alterity is also the symbol of the narrative incompleteness constitutive of every myth. No matter how many versions of the Minotaur are available, there is always room for another Asterion.

In the context of the interview between Gasparini and Borges reported above, the already formidable semantic and textual implications of "La casa de Asterión" become exponential, because the narrative voracity of the myth also benefits from the symbiotic relationship Borges draws between the short story and the history of its creation. In the conversational tone of an interview, Borges intertwines the intricate tradition of the Minotaur (with its mythographic meandering, its perennial additions, and millennia of iterations) with a recapitulation of his own life, anecdotes of his career, his youth, the importance of Julio Cortázar, and the literary history of Buenos Aires. His own brief short story, in turn, becomes the point of departure for new literary renderings of the tale of the Minotaur—who, no longer a simple silent monster, also reappears as the tragic prince with a name rescued from an obscure page of Apollodorus's *Library*. These confluences take on a mythical character through the vertiginous intersections in which tale, telling, and teller are entangled. All of a sudden, the myth of the Minotaur seems perfectly apposite as a *figura* for Borges's famously labyrinthine fictions. After the conversation between Gasparini and Borges, it is not difficult to countenance the Argentine writer himself as another Asterion.

This merging of personal experiences, Classical myth, and aesthetic execution is paradigmatic, for the blending of authorial and narrative myths in Borges's Asterion can also be seen in other literatures of Latin America, with analogous processes and similar consequences. In this example, Borges successfully transforms the myth of the Minotaur into a Latin American topos, inasmuch as his Asterion continues engendering its own new permutations. Likewise, other famous Classical mythic cycles rewritten by Latin American writers have followed the zigzagging behavior of the narrative of the Minotaur—prominent examples are the tale of Atlantis, the story of Iphigenia, and the tragedy of Antigone.[5] In all these cases, the parallelism between Latin American narratives and well-known ancient myths is crafted in such a way that the myths end up claiming a Classical status not only because they derive from Greco-Roman antiquity, but also because they are woven into the social and cultural fabric of the places that adopt them. The process through which a Greco-Roman myth becomes a local narrative as well—a process that could be called "mythological contamination"—is the phenomenon that I seek to trace in this chapter. This transformation depends on the mythographers who successively intervene in the tale, each one becoming an author without refuting or foreclosing the work of others. The Borgesian Minotaur, where different layers of textuality

---

[5] In the twentieth century alone, at least four Latin American authors have rehearsed the misadventures of Iphigenia: Teresa de la Parra's *Ifigenia: diario de una señorita que escribió porque se fastidiaba* (1924), Alfonso Reyes's *Ifigenia cruel* (1924), Sebastián Salazar Bondy's *Ifigenia en el mercado* (1963), and Nataniel Dantas's *Ifigênia está no fundo do corredor* (1969). Likewise, the Platonic myth of Atlantis has had a persistent presence since the colonial period (see Tord 1999). Regarding Antigone, see Moira Fradinger's work in progress, provisionally titled "*Antigonas*: A Latin American Tradition." For a detailed catalogue of these and other cases, see Hualde Pascual 2012.

end up irrevocably entangled in a vast discursive network, serves as a superb introduction to the central case studied here: the powerful role of the myth of Orpheus in the scenic arts in twentieth-century Brazil—one of the most important manifestations of the complex transactions between Greco-Roman mythology and modern Latin American fiction.

Let us say a few words about the myth of Orpheus. Though Classical sources are numerous and diverse, the main lines along which Virgil and Ovid (two of its most famous narrators) coincide are simple: Orpheus, the prodigious Thracian poet whose songs could bend the trees and charm the wildest beasts, decided to descend into Hell to rescue his wife Eurydice, who had just died from a poisonous snakebite. Armed only with his lyre and poetic skills, Orpheus makes his way through Hell, appeasing the monsters of Tartarus and providing fleeting consolation to the eternally punished souls of the wicked. Moved by his music, Hades and Persephone—lords of the Underworld——allow him to leave with the soul of his wife, on the single condition that he not turn back to look at her before having completely left the realm of Hell. Orpheus then retraces his own steps back to earth, followed by the mute shadow of Eurydice. The silent return makes him doubtful about the presence of his wife; when he has almost finished his journey, at the very threshold of Hell, he cannot resist his doubt anymore and looks over his shoulder. Eurydice is there, but she must now depart. Orpheus manages to contemplate the specter of his wife one last time before she is irredeemably lost in the shadows of Hades (Virgil, *Georgics* 4.453–527; Ovid, *Metamorphoses* 10.1–85).

The ill-fortuned *katabasis* of Orpheus (depicted countless times in the last two and a half millennia, in textual and fine arts alike) constitutes the core plot of three key pieces in the history of the scenic arts in Brazil: the play *Orfeu da Conceição* (1953) ("Orpheus of Conceição") by Brazilian musician, lyricist and playwright Vinicius de Moraes; the film *Orfeu negro* (1959) ("Black Orpheus"), directed by Marcel Camus; and *Orfeu* (1999), directed by Carlos Diegues. The invocation of Orpheus in this tradition provides one of the most complex and fascinating integrations of Classical and Latin American motifs in the confection of mythical narratives. Unsurprisingly, this is not the first comparative study of the three Brazilian Orpheuses. Following the release of the most recent filmic version, Diegues's *Orfeu*, a series of authors—in particular Charles A. Perrone (2001), Celso de Oliveira (2002), and Jonathon Grasse (2004)—have explored from multiple angles the presence of the myth of Orpheus at different stages of the history of cultural representation in Brazil, emphasizing the key role of the musical movements associated with the play and films. Perrone, in particular, employs Classical categories ("melopeia" and "mimesis") to draw the connection among these pieces in terms of musical and historical dialogues. All these studies coincide in approaching the three pieces (especially the films) as some of the most important audiovisual exercises in representing and debating Brazilian identity in the twentieth century.

I will posit, however, that the analysis of Orpheus in twentieth-century Brazil demands a critical genealogy—one that foregrounds the intricate relationship between the three versions. The reason, I argue here, is that Orpheus is no less mythical in Brazil than in ancient Greece. In fact, he is even more so: in addition to lending its narrative to the representation of Carioca cultural motifs, the tale of Orpheus renews and actualizes, almost ritualistically, the mythical dimension of its Greek versions in its Brazilian avatars. I thus propose a critical history of its transmission, exploring what could be called Orphic counterpoints—the ambiguous, contradictory, and yet powerful symbolic dynamics of a tale that defined the way in which Brazil has been imagined in the last century. To this end, I pay special attention to the creative processes of each version, as well as the historical threads that connect them. As critics have sometimes overlooked the role of the initial version in this process, I also highlight the fundamental importance of the play *Orfeu da Conceição* and its Carioca crafters in the subsequent trajectory of the myth in Brazil. What follows below, then, is a critical account of the mythologization of Orpheus in Brazil—the story of its mythography.

The Creation of a Carioca Orpheus

If the Orpheus of the Greek tradition traced its mythic origins to the distant Thrace, the Brazilian Orpheus may have its precursors in France, where three Orpheuses were composed during the first half of the twentieth century. Two of them were by Jean Cocteau (1889–1963): the avant-garde tragedy *Orphée* (1926) and, much later, its homonymous adaptation to cinema (1950). The third was penned by Jean-Paul Sartre, who, commissioned by Leopold Senghor, wrote the piece titled "Orphée Noir" ("Black Orpheus") as a prologue to the famous *Anthologie de la Nouvelle Poésie Nègre et Malgache* (1948) ("Anthology of the New Black and Malagasy Poetry"). Cocteau's pieces adapt the myth to the France of his time, rendering his Orpheus the symbol of an existentialist poet trapped in an irrational bourgeois society. Sartre, in accordance with the anti-colonialist and anti-racist *Negritude* movement promoted by Senghor and Aimé Cesaire, devises a more political version of the myth: the Orpheus of his prologue is an allegory of the black poet who explores his own subjectivity (something previously denied to him) through the exercise of poetry. These three French Orpheuses articulate a meaningful intellectual and cultural context for the first scenic Brazilian intervention in this myth: the play *Orfeu da Conceição. Tragédia carioca em três âtos* (definitive version, 1953) ("Orpheus of *Conceição*. Carioca Tragedy in Three Acts") by Vinicius de Moraes.

Moraes—Brazilian poet, musician, playwright, and diplomat, putative father (along with Antônio Carlos Jobim and João Gilberto) of the Carioca bossa nova rhythm and one of the most influential intellectuals in Brazil—does not refer explicitly to the French Orphic tradition until 1959 (when *Orfeu negro* was shot), but likely had previous contact with the ideas and images that Cocteau and Sartre had developed. Moraes traveled to Europe in 1952, commissioned by the Brazilian government to study the organization of European film festivals. In Cannes, where Cocteau's second *Orphée* had premiered only two years earlier, Moraes could easily have been exposed to the popular French Orpheuses. That might explain the similarities between his version and the French version: like Sartre's, Moraes's Orpheus aspires to embody the vindication of black culture in Brazil—a gesture explicitly framed in a note to the play's *dramatis personae*: "Tôdas as personagens da tragédia devem ser normalmente representadas por atores da raça negra" (Moraes 1967: 15) ("All the characters of the tragedy must normally be performed by black actors"). Likewise, while Cocteau had imagined his bard in the streets of Paris, Moraes transferred the Orphic tale to the *favelas* or slums in Rio de Janeiro, where an autochthonous Orpheus performs with his faithful *violão* (guitar) the chords of his enchanting samba. This same instrument eventually became the preferred medium for performing the harmonies of the highly successful bossa nova movement.

But the history of the composition of the Brazilian play is more complex than its interaction with its French antecedents. In an early testimony about the origin of the drama (included in the first prologue to *Orfeu da Conceição*, in 1956), Moraes recalls that one night, sixteen years before the play was staged for the first time, he was at the house of a friend, architect Carlos Leão, in Rio de Janeiro, when, "depois de ler numa velha mitologia o mito grego de Orfeu, dava eu início aos versos do primeiro ato, que terminei com a madrugada raiando sôbre quase tôda a Guanabara, visível de minha janela" (1967: 13) ("after reading the Greek myth of Orpheus in an old book of mythologies, I began the verses of the first act, which I finished when the dawn was breaking over almost the entire Guanabara bay, visible from my window"). But in a second testimony (an interview with José Eduardo Homem de Mello, on September 2, 1967), Moraes adds that, while he was reading the myth—in a French compilation of Greek mythology, he clarifies this time—he perceived the sound of a *batucada* from one of the adjacent Carioca *morros* (hills), which led him "a pensar na vida dos negros de morro e a helenizar a sua vida" (Homem de Mello 1967: 59) ("to think of the lives of the black men in the *morro* and to hellenize their lives").[6] These different accounts of the conception of the play are compatible, but emphasize different phenomena: the first recalls an inspirational rapture from reading a Classical myth, while the second adds to the process the serendipitous sound of a local *batucada*.

The rest of Moraes's story details the play's compositional peripeteia. Having drafted the first act in 1940, Moraes had to wait until 1946 to write the second and third, this time in Los Angeles, where he was sent on his first diplomatic commission as vice-consul. But he lost the third act during his return to Brazil, in 1950, and only three years later could he rewrite it—in 1953, when he departed for a second trip to France, this time as second secretary of the Brazilian Embassy. Later that same year, having completed the play, Moraes participated in and won one of the three first positions in the theatrical contest commemorating the fourth centenary of the city of São Paulo. The play was published the following year, in 1954, in the journal *Anhembi*, and finally staged in September 1956 in the Municipal Theater of Rio de Janeiro.[7]

This intricate story is important not so much because of its precision or lack thereof (which is somehow irrelevant), but because of the foundational importance Moraes gives it. By repeating and detailing—in interviews, presentations, and prologues—the meanderings of his Orpheus, Moraes reveals his investment in the complex compositional process of the drama, and not simply in its thematic contents or scenic virtues. From the beginning, Moraes defines his Orpheus as the confluence of very dissimilar elements: the archetypal vision of Guanabara bay in Rio de Janeiro, a French compilation of Greek myths, and a *batucada*. This polyphonic origin blends with the convoluted composition of the play overall: a first act in 1940, two more in 1946, the loss of the third act in 1950, its rewriting in 1953, and finally, the premiere of the play in 1956;

---

[6] See also Perrone 2001: 50.
[7] These details have been gathered from three different sources, including: a) Moraes's presentation of the play, "A propósito de *Orfeu da Conceição*" ("On *Orfeu da Conceição*"), dated September 19, 1956 (a week before the premiere of the play, says the author) and included at the beginning of the reprint of the drama (1967: 13–14); b) Homem de Mello 1976; and c) the commemorative website *Vinicius de Moraes*.

moreover, all these episodes occur in the course of an incessant diplomatic itinerancy through South America, North America, and Europe. By constantly retelling these events, Moraes demonstrates that the uneven history of the writing of his play is part of the play's meaningfulness, to the point that the compositional narrative finds its way into the original prologue and subsequent reprints. The textual development of *Orfeu da Conceição* is in this way emphatically presented as a phenomenon in which creative or authorial responsibility is not exclusive to the author himself, but is also dependent on the historical and geographical randomness of the writing process. Little by little, *Orfeu da Conceição* starts to acquire its own myth of origins, a myth in which the vatic voice of Orpheus comes not only from Moraes, but also from the circumstances in which the play could and could not have been written, lost, and rewritten. The irregular geographical and chronological confluences associated with the composition of *Orfeu da Conceição* thus correspond to Moraes's "hellenization of the *favela* blacks" not only because of the adaptation of the Greek Orphic *katabasis* to Rio de Janeiro, but also in the heterotopy that characterizes the writing of the play. Symptomatically, and almost as a metatextual commentary on the theatrical genre and the fatalist component of its Classical origins, Moraes declares in his original prologue that "[é] dificil prever o destino de uma peça de teatro" (1967: 13) ("it is difficult to foresee the fate of a dramatic piece").

This genesis might even seem *too* complex for a work that is narratively quite simple. At first sight, *Orfeu da Conceição* appears to simply transpose the basic elements of the Classical plot into the Carioca slums, with black characters substituting for their Greek antecedents. Orpheus is a prodigious samba musician and iconic figure in the *favela* of the "morro da Conceição" ("*Conceição* Hill") in Rio de Janeiro. Eurydice, his beloved, is assaulted by a broken-hearted suitor and stabbed to death (an adaptation of the Classical snakebite). Orpheus, armed only with his guitar, then descends into a seedy joint on the outskirts of the hill where the traditional carnival of Rio de Janeiro is celebrated, and is finally assassinated by a group of frenzied women. The plot recapitulates the conventional tale of Orpheus's idealized love and the obsession that leads him to his own destruction. Moraes's version, however, finds its mechanism of expression not so much in its argument as in what this justifies: the execution of an entire musical concept within the narrative frame of the play. Expressly designed to create a constant interaction between the pieces coming from the pit orchestra and the songs of the individual actor performing Orpheus, the music of the play constitutes its central and permanent dramatic motif.

But this integration of musical compositions into the play is not equivalent to that of a typical Broadway musical—where the lovers, the barber, or the director of a school are all fully capable of singing and dancing. Although intensely melodic, Moraes's play pointedly concentrates the musical force in the figure of Orpheus, who (save for the brief intervention of a chorus that serves as his counterpoint in the third act) appears in the play as the only singer, musician, poet, and composer. Moraes thus identifies the sacred properties of the lyre of the Classical Orpheus with the tremendous cultural importance of the samba movement that originated in the slums, concentrated here in a single figure. Both the Greek and the black Brazilian poets, he comments in the first prologue to the play, are culture heroes:

> Esta peça é uma homenagem ao negro brasileiro, a quem, de resto, a devo; e não apenas pela sua contribuição tão orgânica à cultura deste país, melhor, pelo seu apaixonante estilo de viver que me permitiu, sem esforço, num simples relampejar do pensamento, sentir no divino músico da Trácia a natureza de um dos divinos músicos do morro carioca.
>
> 1967: 14

> This play pays homage to the black Brazilian, to whom, in one way or another, I owe it. And not only for his most organic contribution to the culture of this country, but rather because of his fascinating style of life, which allowed me—without much effort, in a simple lightning bolt of thought—to feel in the divine Thracian musician the nature of one of the divine musicians of the Carioca hills.

By signaling the "most organic contribution" of black Brazilian music to Brazilian culture, Moraes defines, in Gramscian key, the character of the Orphic musician in terms of a cultural function. His Black Orpheus, contrary to Cocteau's individualist hero, embodies here a constitutive cultural dimension of Brazil. His "organicity" explains why Orpheus does not appear detached from his community or surroundings even if most of the creative energy represented in the play is concentrated in him. On the contrary, as the people living in the *morro* recognize when commenting on his delirium after Eurydice's death, Orpheus' ills affect the entire community, because his health, like the music of his *violão*, reflects and sustains social local harmony. In fact, the role of the Orphic singer in the community is defined by Orpheus himself in ontological terms, most clearly when he faces the personification of death, "a dama negra" ("the black lady"). Upon encountering her, Orpheus proclaims:

> No morro manda Orfeu! Orfeu é a vida!
> No morro ninguém morre antes da hora!
> Agora o morro é vida, o morro é Orfeu
> E a música de Orfeu! Nada no morro
> Existe sem Orfeu e a sua viola!
>
> Moraes 1967: 42

> Only Orpheus rules in the *morro*! Orpheus is life!
> In the *morro* no one dies before their time!
> Now the *morro* is life, the *morro* is Orpheus
> and the music of Orpheus! Nothing in the *morro*
> can exist without Orpheus and his guitar!

Orpheus's self-invocation, presented in the third person so as to emphasize his own role as a vital principle, creates an existential correspondence between life in the Carioca slums and its music. From this melic existentialism, Orpheus derives another principle—the conservation of social harmony—predicated on a heteronormative coexistence:

> Cada homem no morro e a sua mulher
> vivem só porque Orfeu os faz viver
> Com sua música! Eu sou a harmonia
> E a paz, e o castigo! Eu sou Orfeu
> o músico!
>
> Moraes 1967: 42

> Each man in the *morro*, and his woman,
> live only because Orpheus makes them live
> through his music! I am harmony,
> peace, punishment! I am Orpheus,
> the musician!

It is in these lines, more than in all the Classical plot which, *mutatis mutandis*, is adapted to the Carioca *morro*, where the reincarnation of Orpheus in Brazil acquires its full sense. The musical harmony that the Carioca Orpheus creates with his *violão* constitutes the physical and aesthetic manifestation of a social and ultimately ontological harmony.[8] Moraes renders his Orpheus a prism through which popular Afro-Brazilian culture is projected onto the community in order to protect its existence.

---

[8] Sixteenth-century Scottish writer Robert Henryson had similarly depicted the poet finding in the structure of the universe the elements of musical notation. A summary of this and three other versions of Orpheus in post-Classical Europe can be found in Browne 1910.

Certainly, the economic and social marginality of the actual Carioca *morros* are not the center of Moraes's attention. His vision of the *morro* is that of a cultural ecosystem that hosts an enormous aesthetic and expressive richness, and that vision would soon radically affect the way in which Brazil represented itself to the world. It is no accident that Moraes chose to associate himself with the young musician who would become one of the most influential Brazilian artists: Antônio "Tom" Carlos Jobim, creator of all the music in *Orfeu da Conceição*. Nor is it accidental that the melodious sambas of the play paved the way for what would soon become the international success known as bossa nova. Through the Thracian bard in the Carioca slums, Moraes was actually forging his own mythology and establishing the foundations of the musical and cultural impact that would be advanced by the next generation of this tradition, the film *Orfeu negro* ("Black Orpheus"), by French director Marcel Camus.

Orpheus in Color

The concept of what would become *Orfeu negro* was a reality even before the premiere of *Orfeu da Conceição*. The racial characterization marking this Orpheus was, of course, anticipated in Sartre's aforementioned preface from 1948, "Orphée Noir" (which likely inspired the title of the film), but already in 1955, one year before the play debuted, Moraes had been in contact with French producer Sacha Gordine to prepare the filmic version of his *Orfeu da Conceição*. The same year, Moraes and Gordine traveled together from France to Brazil, seeking (unsuccessfully) financial backing for the movie (Homem de Mello 1976: 60; *Vinicius de Moraes*, "Vida," "[Year] 1955"). Moraes continued with the project and did not lose sight of it even during the 1956 rehearsals of *Orfeu da Conceição*. A shortly time later, the French filmmaker Marcel Camus would assume the direction of the *Orfeu negro* project. Moraes adapted the play to a film script, though in the international advertising of the movie it would not be attributed to Moraes but to the editors, Jacques Viot and Camus himself. Conscious of the relevance of the musical apparatus of the play, Moraes also decided to employ the recently-created bossa nova musical style to compose, with Tom Jobim, the famous soundtrack of *Orfeu negro*.[9]

---

[9] Bossa nova was a very new genre. Critics suggest that the first instantiation of bossa nova appeared one year before *Orfeu negro* premiered—in the seminal 1958 LP *Canção do amor demais*, with vocals by Elizete Cardozo, lyrics by Vinicius de Moraes and Antônio Carlos Jobim, and musicalized by João Gilberto and Jobim.

The international success that *Orfeu negro* achieved surpassed the expectations of its creators. Immediately after its initial 1959 release, the film received the prestigious Palme D'Or at the Cannes Festival (1959), as well as the Academy Award for Best Foreign Language Film (1960). Its soundtrack sold millions of copies, and the movie was exhibited in countries all over the world. The vast circulation of the film was also the point of departure for the internationalization of Brazilian rhythms—in particular, samba and bossa nova. The movie promptly became a milestone not only in Brazilian filmmaking history, but also—and especially—in Brazil's self-representation, as it came to be the primary source of an image of Brazil for the rest of the world. Peter Rist and Timothy Barnard have estimated that *Orfeu negro* "has almost certainly been seen by more non-Brazilians than any other film shot in that country and is likely to have provided a first introduction to Brazilian culture for more Europeans and North Americans than any other art work" (qtd. by Perrone 2001: 46).

The dilemma of this success is that *Orfeu negro* incubated and spread a lasting stereotype of Brazil, a vision that dissected the country into three elements: soccer, Carnival, and natural beauty. The Orpheus of this film, a streetcar driver (played by Breno Mello, in real life a professional soccer player), falls in love with a provincial Eurydice (played by Marpessa Dawn, a US-born actor whose voice was dubbed for the Portuguese version of the movie), who has just arrived in the cosmopolitan and crowded Rio de Janeiro during the Carnival season. An anonymous man disguised as Death harasses Eurydice. While Cariocas celebrate the traditional Carnival, Orpheus abandons his role as the leader of his particular *escola de samba* (samba troupe) and departs for the ultimately unsuccessful rescue of his beloved, while everyone else carouses and hails the fleeting happiness of the festivity.

Among the many clichés accumulated in this picture, it is worth highlighting two particular motifs, especially because of their differences with respect to the original play. First, while *Orfeu da Conceição* focuses on the Classical myth and uses the Carioca context to rework the story as a vehicle of Afro-Brazilian popular culture, *Orfeu negro* offers, to put it bluntly, an ill-narrated account of Orpheus and Eurydice serving mainly as a pretext for an exoticizing depiction of Brazil. Shot in color at a time when most productions were monochromatic, the Carioca slums are presented as a *locus amoenus* where green hills, white sand, sun, and *fantasias* (or carnival attire) fuse with a collective happiness, naturalized and musical. The film concentrates not on the narrative, but on the rhythms and colors imposed on the plot. With these as his cinematographic priorities, Camus adjusted his lens to project a life in the *favela* tantamount to a constant carnival—one which does not show economic or social contradictions, but solely melodramatic difficulties. The result of this focalization is the inexpensive tragedy of a Eurydice who, running away from her faceless enemy, finally perishes at the touch of a high-voltage wire—a cable whose current Orpheus unsuspectingly activates while looking for her, without ever becoming aware of his involuntary homicide.

The second main difference between the play and the movie is a corollary of the first: while the theatrical scenography of *Orfeu da Conceição* could somehow bear the idealization of the Carioca slums without mortifying local audiences, the exoticizing *Orfeu negro*, shot in the real slums of Rio de Janeiro, could not but feel jarring. For many Brazilian viewers, the direct exhibition of images that Carioca citizens could easily recognize, and the disassociation between those images and the scenic representation, was intolerable. The consequence of this disjunction was that, despite the overwhelming international success of the film, local reception was angry and indignant. Brazilian musician Caetano Veloso, an adolescent when the movie was first screened, has summarized this public reaction in an oft-cited passage from his 1997 autobiography, *Verdade Tropical* ("Tropical Truth"):[10]

> Eu e toda a platéia ríamos e nos envergonhávamos das descaradas inautenticidades que aquele cineasta francês se permitiu para criar um produto de exotismo fascinante. A crítica que os brasileiros fazíamos a esse filme pode ser resumida assim: "Como é possível que os melhores e mais genuínos músicos do Brasil tenham aceitado criar obras-primas para ornar (e dignificar) uma tal enganação?"
>
> 252

> I laughed along with the entire audience and together we were shamed by the shameless lack of authenticity the French filmmaker had permitted himself for the sake of creating a fascinating piece of exoticism. The critique we Brazilians made of the film can be summed up in this way: "How is it possible that the best and most genuine musicians in Brazil could have agreed to create masterpieces to adorn (and dignify) such a deception?"
>
> Sena 2002: 159

Veloso's final question (which he attributes to Brazilians in general) was more valid than he imagined. Camus, "that French filmmaker" who somehow borrowed the Sartrean label of "Orphée Noir" to apply it to "a product of fascinating exoticism," also shortchanged his Brazilian collaborators. As published letters

---

[10] This passage is cited by Perrone (2001: 51), Grasse (2004: 309, n. 4), and Landazuri 2010.

between Moraes and Jobim evince, the relationship between these two and Camus was difficult from the beginning. In a letter dated September 22, 1958, Jobim complained to Moraes about the editorial modifications that Camus intended to make to the lyrics Moraes had composed for *Orfeu negro* (Jobim 1958a). Five days later, on September 27, an infuriated Jobim wrote again to Moraes explaining that, after the modifications imposed by Camus, "[h]á vários versos que não cabem na música, porém deixei-os assim para que examines bem o sentido do Camus. Ficamos fulos de raiva (Tê e eu), porque ele não quer teus lindos versos, que ficaram lindos com a música" (Jobim 1958b) ("there are many verses that don't fit anymore within the music; but I am leaving them as they are now, so that you can examine better the sense Camus seeks. Both Tê and I were absolutely enraged, because he does not want to keep your beautiful lines, which go so nicely with the music").[11] The letter continues criticizing Camus, "Esse francês é bobo!" ("That Frenchman is a fool!"), to finish with an eloquent plea: "me diz quando eu posso dar um chute na bunda desse francês. Ou se aguardo que ele faça o filme com nossa música primeiro" (Jobim 1958b) ("let me know when I can kick the ass of that Frenchman, or if I must first wait until he has finished the film with our music").

Despite such strained relationships, it seems that the project proceeded efficiently, for about half a year later, on June 12, 1959, the film premiered—in France, not in Brazil. The final sentence of Jobim's letter, "let me know ... if I must first wait until he has finished the film with our music [to kick Camus's ass]," also illustrates the pragmatic approach of the Brazilian composers: despite their resentment, they were willing to yield on issues as delicate as Camus's editorial interventions in their original lyrics. If the composition of *Orfeu da Conceição* had reflected the confluences of French, Afro-Brazilian, and Classical motifs, all of them articulated in the course of a long and irregular writing history, the filming of *Orfeu negro* appears, rather, to be the product of many ideological, creative, and economic frictions.

The scale, nevertheless, would end up tipping in favor of Camus, who was more dexterous in commercial affairs than his Brazilian associates. As Moraes's letters to Jobim reveal, Moraes himself had no direct involvement in the production of the film, and the evidence seems to corroborate what Veloso mentions in his autobiography: "E notório que Vinicius de Moraes ... saiu airado da sala de projeção durante uma sessão promovida pelos produtores antes da

---

[11] "Tê" is Thereza Hermanny, Jobim's first wife.

estréia" (Veloso 1997: 252) ("It is well known that Vinicius de Moraes...left the theater irate, during a screening organized by the producers before the premiere"; Sena 2002: 159). Ironically, the aesthetic disgust of Moraes ended up anticipating the minimal profitability that the successful *Orfeu negro* signified for him and Jobim: as Perrone reports, the poet and the musician only received 10 percent of the royalties resulting from the extremely lucrative soundtrack (2001: 53). Of course, neither Moraes nor Jobim was content with such a meager percentage. Four years after the premiere, Moraes was still haunted by this expropriation, describing to his friend—in a letter from Rome on November 8, 1963—the continued international success of the creation from which they were barely getting anything: "Tocam a gente por aí tudo, Tonzinho [Tom]. Eu acho que não vai haver outro jeito senão tomar advogado contra a SBACEM [Sociedade Brasileira de Autores, Compositores e Editores de Música], porque francamente da raiva. Estamos em todos os *jukeboxes*, desses de quiosque de café de rua" (Moraes 1963) ("Our music is played everywhere, Tonzinho. I think we will have no other option but to find a lawyer and sue the SBACEM [Brazilian Association of Authors, Composers, and Editors of Music] because, honestly, this is infuriating. We are played in all those jukeboxes you find in cafe stands on the streets"). In the same letter, Moraes vividly describes his friend Mario Perrone's remonstration on learning of the paltry sum Moraes was earning from the film: "Se você não processar, EU PROCESSO!" (Moraes 1963) ("If you don't sue them, I WILL!").

As these letters reveal, despite the success of the movie and Moraes's and Jobim's international consecration as crafters of a tremendously influential musical movement, they experienced a constant uneasiness regarding the film, one that oscillated between economic disappointment and the cultural anxiety about their participation in what their fellow Brazilians considered an utter deception. The disappointments, in fact, mirror and merge into each other: Camus's exploitation of the image of Brazil to satisfy consumer trends in an international market corresponded to the actual appropriation of copyrights and royalties of the legendary soundtrack created by Moraes and Jobim. Brazil and two Brazilians in particular were thus ironically estranged from the film. Tellingly, the original poster of the movie does not mention Jobim and barely refers to Moraes as the author on whose work the script was based. On top of it all, the movie was described in the same poster as a "co-production franco-italienne" ("a French–Italian co-production"), with no allusion whatsoever to the Brazilian actors, musicians, and technicians who largely made up the cast and crew.

Moraes and Jobim's anxiety regarding *Orfeu negro* was, in sum, a composite of economic, representative, and authorial marginalization. Their consequent reaction is not surprising: alienated from their own music and repelled by the film's exoticism, they rediscovered in their old *Orfeu da Conceição* the genuinely Brazilian Orpheus, opposed to the fraudulent forgery of Camus. On February 15, 1965, Jobim wrote to Moraes from Los Angeles to confess how, while listening to his own "Valsa do Orfeu" ("Waltz of Orpheus") performed by Lenita Bruno, "[veio] a estranha sensação da vida que já foi e eu estou novamente no Teatro Municipal com você, e o Leo Peracchi está dirigindo a orquestra, os frisos dourados do Municipal brilham sob a luz" (Jobim 1965) ("the strange sensation of a bygone life [came over me] and I am once again in the Municipal Theatre with you, and Leo Peracchi is directing the orchestra, while the golden friezes of the theater shine under the lights"). In the intimacy of a letter to his friend and co-creator of the first Orpheus, Jobim transforms the memory of the sparkling friezes of the Municipal Theatre into the sign of an *aetas aurea* or Golden Age lost upon the arrival of the cinematographic Orpheus. This nostalgia is compounded by the fact that Jobim gained an international reputation in part due to the very film he repudiates, and that fame was one reason why he had found a place in the artistic milieu of Los Angeles in 1965. The resultant retrospective ambivalence, a mixture of resentment and *saudade*, emerges in the way Jobim juxtaposes his memories of the first and second Brazilian Orpheuses: "No outro dia passou *Orfeu negro* na TV, e Tê e eu vimos. Tudo doblado em inglês ... A música *também* ... Horrível!!! Mas eu continuo na fossa da orquestra do Municipal e o Leo está regendo ..." (Jobim 1965) ("The other day Tê and I watched a rerun of *Orfeu negro* on TV ... Everything was dubbed into English. *Even* the music ... It was horrible!!! But I still remain in the orchestra pit of the Municipal Theatre, while Leo is directing us ..."). Jobim was particularly upset with the English dubbing of the soundtrack, an operation as illegitimate for him as Camus's infamous editorial interventions. The solution, then, was an imaginary return to the 1956 orchestra pit—a sort of modernist *katabasis* to the space where the "genuine" music of the dramatic Orpheus still dwells.

But while Jobim sighed for the paradise lost, Moraes pondered how to regain it. Throughout this epistolary exchange, Moraes was planning, in collaboration with US composer Ray Gilbert, the creation of a new Orpheus: this time a musical properly speaking, meant for Broadway. In a letter signed in Rio de Janeiro on November 22, 1966, Moraes presented the project to Jobim and explained what kind of participation he sought to negotiate with Gilbert.

Although Moraes does not say it, it is clear that he sees the bad experiences with *Orfeu negro* as a cautionary tale:

> Digo eu [a Gilbert], como condição para dar a autorização ...

> I am telling [Gilbert], as a condition for giving permission: [Moraes's self-citation is provided in English] "Tell the guys in Broadway, also, that I would like to do it on a participation basis, as author of the original play and of the lyrics of the songs in it. Tell them also that more songs should be included, by Jobim, *with original lyrics by me: and that this is a must.*"
>
> Moraes 1966; emphasis in the original

The musical universe of Orpheus, conceived in *Orfeu da Conceição* and consecrated by *Orfeu negro*, is once more the focus of attention. To meet the demands of Broadway, Moraes realized the necessity of expanding the melodic repertoire of the original play, while also insisting that he and Jobim remain involved in any new compositions. His fear of losing control was manifest: "Pedi também um certo 'artistic control in the adaptation, so that the spirit of the original play will not be distorted or betrayed'" (Moraes 1966) ("I also requested a degree of 'artistic control in the adaptation, so that the spirit of the original play will not be distorted or betrayed'"). Betrayal, distortion, a "certain artistic control": Moraes's lexical choices were manifestly haunted by the specters of the two Brazilian *Orfeus*.

There is a crude irony in how Moraes seemed to suppose that the Broadway producers' appropriation of his creations and Jobim's could have possibly been less predatory than Camus's. Instead, the possibility of resurrecting his Orpheus in New York constituted for him a chance for vindication and restitution. In fact, when *Orfeu da Conceição* was reprinted, in 1967, Moraes reserved a line of the new preface to announce that "[a]gora mesmo, fortes produtores da Broadway estão interessados em transfomá-la num grande musical" (1967: n.p) ("right now, important producers on Broadway are interested in transforming [the play] into a great musical"). The gesture was critical, for the announcement of the Orpheus musical in the prologue of the play's second edition intended to render the linkage between the two explicit. The new Orpheus was meant to be a literal re-make of the original drama. Symptomatically, in this prologue the film *Orfeu negro* is barely mentioned.

We know from his letters that Moraes persevered with the idea of staging his *Orfeu* in New York until at least 1970. The project, however, was never finalized (it is mentioned for the last time in a letter to Jobim of October 22, 1970).

Meanwhile, Jobim continued to express from Los Angeles his frustration and nostalgia for the already Classical Brazilian Orpheus. In a letter of December 10, 1966, Jobim recounted an anecdote that not only typifies the peripeteias presented so far, but also anticipates future incarnations of the Thracian in Brazil:

> O nome do Orfeu aqui é enorme e imortal, é estátua de bronze inoxidável, e o filme não podia ser mais ao gosto americano do que é... [Q]uando, em conversa, eu disse que gostava mais da peça original do que do filme, porque este me parecia muito irreal e meio Brasil *Exotique*, a turma ficou puta e me disse: "It's not supposed to be real, it doesn't intend to be real, etc." Claro que uma certa irrealidade existe em qualquer obra de arte (e eu não sou contra ela), mas é uma irrealidade que serve para mostrar a realidade, e não as idéias do sr. Camus, que, para mim, são, às vezes, de gosto duvidoso... [E]u, pessoalmente (*I, personally*), prefiro a Realidade Real, a Realidade Irreal ou a Irrealidade Real. O Camus parece que prefere a Irrealidade Irreal. Mas, que faz sucesso aqui, faz...

> The name of Orpheus is here enormous and immortal, a stainless-bronze statue, and the film could not be more suited to the taste of an American audience... [W]hen I said, in the course of a conversation, that I preferred the play to the film, because the movie seemed to me quite unreal and pretty much an *Exotique* Brazil, people around me got really pissed and told me "It's not supposed to be real, it doesn't intend to be real, etc." Of course, there is a certain degree of unreality in any work of art (and I'm not against it), but such an unreality is meant to show a reality, not simply the ideas of Mr. Camus, which in my opinion are, sometimes, quite dubious. I, personally, prefer the Real Reality, the Unreal Reality, and the Real Unreality. Camus, instead, seems to prefer the Unreal Unreality. But there is no doubt that he was quite the success here...

One can detect a degree of diplomatic moderation in Jobim's criticism here, and yet his position is clear. The film having been produced eight years before, and then exhibited and decorated almost everywhere, the problem is no longer framed in terms of artistic control or economic unfairness. The issue at stake is now the representational quality of the movie, its capacity to show through fiction (the "unreality") a certain reality. Jobim thus improvises a quick literary theory through variations on "reality" and "unreality," which he levies as both a creator and a critic. His opinion, in fact, chimes with the one later expressed by Veloso, which questioned the participation of "genuine" Brazilian musicians in a work of deception.

Confirmations, Rebuttals, and Antitheses

By 1999, when Carlos Diegues was finishing shooting the third scenic version of Orpheus, *Orfeu*, he already had a place in the history of Brazilian cinematography for works such as *Xica da Silva* (1976) and *Bye Bye Brasil* (1979). Like Veloso, he was a teenager when *Orfeu negro* premiered, and his reaction to the film was equally negative: "I detested Camus's film because it depicts the *favela* in an allegorical way, as a perfect society in which only death is bothersome" (qtd. in Perrone 2001: 51). For Diegues and Veloso, Camus had created a superposition of myths: the tale of Orpheus, his musical love for Eurydice, and his forlorn *katabasis* had been only a pretext on which another myth had been imposed, that of "Happy Brazil," so palatable to international audiences. In homage to the original 1956 play, and especially as a refutation of the 1959 film, Diegues returned to the fable of Orpheus, determined to emphasize precisely those aspects that Camus had ignored.

In *Orfeu*, the Carioca slums are a world in which daily life and the poet's music coexist with institutionalized violence. Diegues's Orpheus is a handsome, well-known and highly respected musician (very similar to his avatar in *Orfeu da Conceição*), an eternal bachelor with whom all the ladies are in love. The season is, once again, Carnival, which allows the film to highlight the social prestige of the poet, who has led his samba school to victory for two consecutive years. The reputation of this Orpheus in the *favela* is such that he is capable of negotiating as an equal with both the aggressive Carioca policemen and the mobsters who control the drug traffic in the area. In this way, as Moraes wished it, Orpheus fulfills the delicate role of sustaining harmony in the *morro*, despite the general violence. But the sudden arrival of beautiful Eurydice disrupts the usual self-control of the poet, who abandons his lover of the moment and begins to pursue the new beauty. This new muse also exerts a powerful effect on Orpheus's social position: when she witnesses the public execution of a rapist by the drug boss Lucinho, Eurydice indirectly persuades Orpheus to take a stand against him, so the poet faces Lucinho and orders him to abandon the *favela* immediately. The sudden enmity of Orpheus, formerly a friend of Lucinho, sparks the latter's hatred against Eurydice. Tragedy strikes when Lucinho accidentally shoots Eurydice in the course of an argument, at the very moment that Orpheus achieves his third consecutive victory in the Carnival's samba contest. When Orpheus learns about the crime, he hunts down and assassinates Lucinho, after which he descends down a precipice seeking the corpse of his beloved. Orpheus finally returns to the *favela*, visibly deranged, holding the remains of Eurydice, until his former lover, in a jealous rage, pierces his chest with an improvised spear.

This new storyline clearly intends to challenge its immediate antecedent. The main difference is social: Diegues insists that, as opposed to the anonymous pursuer of Eurydice in *Orfeu negro*, it is not now an abstract and faceless death that unleashes the tragedy, but the violence that rises from the *favela* itself. Nor does this film incorporate a palliative final scene as Camus's had done, with a shot of a group of kids who, playing Orpheus's guitar and dancing at daybreak, symbolically resurrect the poet. In the new version, instead, a little boy shrieks horribly next to the corpses of the lovers, while a bird's-eye shot zooms out from the sinister scene. Fully aware of the historical, cultural, and aesthetic importance of the compositions used in the 1959 film, Diegues also takes special care with the soundtrack, seeking the same excellence that consecrated the original. For this, he sought none other than Caetano Veloso. In the new version, a superb soundtrack performed and edited by Veloso recovers the compositions of the Moraes-Jobim partnership and incorporates new original themes into the classic repertoire.

The evident revisionist intention of this new Orpheus convinced most of its critics. Enrique Desmond Arias and Corinne Davis Rodrigues call it an accurate depiction of the alternative "legalities" of the *favela*—in particular, the vigilante role assumed by drug lords (2006: 53).[12] Oliveira, for his part, suggests that after the frustration of the Broadway project, this version would have satisfied the wishes of Moraes (2002: 454). Grasse, more definitive, pictures the two filmic *Orfeu*s as ideological contenders and concludes that "Diegues wins the war over national representation" (2004: 306). None of them, however, read the sharp review that Brazilian film critic Ruy Gardnier had published in the electronic journal of cinema, *Contracampo*, right after the premiere of Diegues's film. Gardnier summarizes the core of his critique thus:

> O cinema de Carlos Diegues em *Orfeu* é o oposto do trabalho do antropólogo. Enquanto este tenta despir-se de todos os preconceitos e de todos os saberes preexistentes ao seu objeto de estudo, o sr. Diegues sobe ao morro com todas as idéias já feitas e mediatizadas por quem cria a imagem externa das favelas. Longe de dar uma outra cara ao morro, longe de buscar uma outra interpretação, em suma, longe de fazer ficção, *Orfeu* não é um filme capaz de sair do joguete de

---

[12] Although Arias and Rodrigues analyze Diegues's *Orfeu*, they mistakenly refer to the movie as *Orfeu negro*—a confusion which again typifies the complex confluences among the three Brazilian Orpheuses.

cartas marcadas que é essa 1h50min de lugares-comuns sobre os que habitam esse universo tão complexo. O *Orfeu* de Vinícius de Moraes é uma fábula, mas em *Orfeu* não há fabulação. Carlos Diegues não dá nova cara a ninguém, nem essa parece ser sua intenção.

1999

Carlos Diegues's cinematographic work in *Orfeu* is completely opposed to that of an anthropologist. While an anthropologist tries to put aside all his prejudices and previous knowledge of his object of study, Mr. Diegues climbs the hills with all his ideas already set and mediatized by those who create an external image of the slums. Far from giving a new face to the hills, far from looking for an alternative interpretation, in sum, far from doing fiction, *Orfeu* is a film incapable of escaping his game of loaded dice: one hour and fifty minutes of commonplaces about the people who live in such a complex universe. Vinicius de Moraes's *Orfeu* is a fable, but in *Orfeu* there is no fabulation. Carlos Diegues doesn't grant a new face to anyone, nor does that seem to be his intention.

Aware of the tradition of Orpheuses to which Diegues and Veloso are responding, Gardnier implies that the pure exhibition of violence is not enough to justify the film as a representational artifact, given that, without a new angle of interpretation, violence can easily become gratuitous. And his diagnosis is correct: the display of violence in Diegues's *Orfeu* is hyperbolic and pervasive, but it does not offer any analysis of the social processes that create and propagate it. Perhaps in 1959 an exposition of this sort might have functioned as a valid visual denunciation, but by 1999 the mere picture of Carioca violence was rather banal. Little by little, it becomes clear that the movie is only interested in rephrasing, uncritically, the stereotypical dangers of the *favelas*: how violence is everywhere, how common people live in a state of fear, and so on. Diegues portrays violence as an ontological rather than social phenomenon, and as such its presence is rendered both inexorable and inscrutable. This lack of analysis is reflected in the rigid representation of characters who either never change or change from one moment to the next without any process in between. Orpheus's sudden concern for the unrest that Lucinho and his men are creating in the *favela*, for instance, occurs only under the influence of Eurydice, in a narrative so abrupt that it suggests Orpheus is merely trying to (successfully) impress her. His artificial adoption of a socially transformative drive (opposed to his initial role of balancing contending powers) is oddly contradicted by the lovers' decision to abandon the *favela*. The ideal, almost bucolic affair between Orpheus and Eurydice becomes, confusingly, a reason to run away from the social problems that they supposedly sought to challenge.

The central problem of Diegues's film might be the tension between the Classical mythical narrative and the *favela* background that the filmmaker intends to foreground. Clearly, Diegues aspires to negate the myth of a merry Brazil presented in *Orfeu negro* through the exhibition of the social turmoil of the *favelas*. Yet in attempting to meld the conventional lines of the myth—the tragic love story of Orpheus and Eurydice—with a vision of violence in Rio de Janeiro, he refuses to risk an interpretation of such a reality and ends up fabricating a new simplification: the myth of poor Brazil, of the *favelas* as a no-man's land in a constant state of violence. Gardnier concluded that "Carlos Diegues doesn't grant a new face to anyone, nor does that seem to be his intention," but I would suggest that Diegues's predicament is the opposite: aware of the tremendous symbolic importance of Orpheus, the filmmaker attempts to give a new face to everything—a newness, of course, relative to the oldness of *Orfeu negro*—and the result is an uncritical and poor administration of the film's images. Diegues's *Orfeu* jumps from the original myth of the Thracian Orpheus to the dangers in the *favelas*, to the corruption of the police forces, to the tyranny of drug lords, to the celebrations of the Carnival in Rio de Janeiro, to the importance of Brazilian music, to the new Protestantism competing with the traditional Catholicism, to the arrival of foreign rhythms, etcetera. Diegues wants to say it all, and the result is a dysfunctional juxtaposition of themes and scant attention to the formation of social tensions. There is no exploration of the violence—no fabulation, says Gardnier—because there is no time to scrutinize anything.

The scattered nature of the film follows a simple, reductive organizing principle: Orpheus and Eurydice represent love, while Lucinho and his men embody destruction. When Jeff Vordam commends Dieges for "not marginalizing his characters with strict 'hero' and 'villain' tags," mentioning as sole evidence the "deeply conflicted" Lucinho (and adding that "Eurydice is unequivocally good, a picture of unspoiled beauty"), he misses the point. It is true that the conflict is not one of hero vs. villain—but that is because it is something more abstract: a conflict between an erotic force vs. a destructive one. Diegues intends to define the contours of a social problem, and instead ends up characterizing an Eros and a Thanatos that consume each other. He does not succeed in overcoming the archetypal, inexplicable death that haunted Eurydice in the old *Orfeu negro* by Camus. Diegues does not challenge previous myths, but rather regurgitates them by offering up negatives of the images presented in *Orfeu negro*, without managing to overcome the purely figurative dimension of those images.

Thus, despite its contesting impetus, Diegues's Orpheus was unable to overcome the shadow of a motif which, even in the twenty-first century, still constitutes a heavy burden in the cultural history of Brazil. About a decade after the screening of Diegues's *Orfeu*, on September 9, 2010, a restaging of the original *Orfeu da Conceição*, composed by Moraes and musicalized by Jobim, was suddenly announced under the title of *Orfeu: o maior musical brasileiro* ("Orpheus: The Greatest Brazilian Musical"). Directed by Aderbal Freire-Filho, the official website of the project noted that Orpheus has already become a literal Brazilian myth in its own right: "é um marco na dramaturgia brasileira e se tornou um mito entre os espetáculos nacionais. Apresentá-lo agora reafirma a potência da irradiação cultural que ele promove" ("Apresentação" 2010) ("[It] constitutes a touchstone for Brazilian dramaturgy and became a myth among national spectacles. To present it now is to reaffirm the powerful cultural irradiation it promotes").[13] The term "myth," used here in a broad and rhetorical sense, actually corresponds to the Classical sense of the word in terms of its symbolic role: to be the source of a "powerful cultural irradiation" in a national context.

It seems that the abundant material provided on the website was intended to illustrate the "powerful cultural irradiation" of the play. Aside from a calendar of performances and information on actors, director, and staging, the site provides some other items: one link collects numerous reviews of the remake; another, the various logos that were considered for publicizing the project, but were ultimately rejected; other links provide information about Moraes and Jobim; another, a PDF containing correspondence between Moraes and Jobim about both *Orfeu da Conceição* and *Orfeu negro* (the source of citations in this chapter). But perhaps the most peculiar link is one labeled "Barack Obama." This section contains, as an implicit international endorsement, a fragment of Obama's 1995 autobiography, *Dreams From My Father*, translated into Portuguese as *A origem dos meus sonhos* ("The Origin of my Dreams"). In the passage cited, Obama recounts that, when he was sixteen years old, his mother took him to the movies to see a film that she had watched when she was much younger—in fact, "o primeiro filme estrangeiro que ela já tinha visto na vida" ("Barack Obama" 2010) ("the first foreign film she had watched in her life"): Camus's *Orfeu negro*![14] In a

---

[13] Originally, the website was available at www.orfeunegro.net. This URL is now disabled—the current one (http://www.showbras.com.br/orfeu/) is listed in the Bibliography.

[14] Rather than using the original English text by Obama to retro-translate the Portuguese rendering of his memoirs, I have preferred to produce an English translation of the Portuguese translation to preserve its connotations.

fascinating game of shifting mirrors, Obama looks at his mother while she looks at the movie screen, and reads on her face, with painful precision, the very reaction that Moraes and Jobim, and then Diegues and Veloso, so disliked:

> Subitamente percebi que a representação dos jovens negros,[15] que eu via agora na tela, a imagem inversa dos sombrios selvagens de Joseph Conrad, era o que minha mãe havia levado com ela para o Havaí muitos anos antes, uma reflexão das fantasias simples que haviam sido proibidas a uma garota de classe média branca do Kansas, a promessa de uma outra vida: quente, sensual, exótica, diferente.
>
> "Barack Obama" 2010

> Suddenly, I realized that the representation of young blacks that I was now watching on the screen, the opposite image of the somber savages depicted by Joseph Conrad, was the image that my mother had carried with her to Hawaii many years before—a reflection of the simple fantasies that had been forbidden to a middle-class white girl from Kansas—the promise of another life: warm, sensual, exotic, different.

This citation succinctly dramatizes a number of paradoxes. It is not only that the producers are profiting from the success of *Orfeu negro* to publicize the remake of *Orfeu da Conceição*, even though the authors of the latter so despised the former; nor that the same website publicizes the letters in which the authors explain their hostile reaction toward Camus's film. On top of this, the website also cites Obama's reminiscence, contemplating the promise of a "warm, sensual, exotic, different" life, four adjectives that reflect the very stereotypes that Brazilians artists like Diegues and Veloso have been challenging for half a century. The chronological dislocations of the website also seem to contaminate Obama's own narrative, which sketches a younger version of his mother as he contemplates her contemplating a film: "Minha mãe era aquela menina com o filme cheio de belas pessoas negras na cabeça, seduzida pela atenção de meu pai, confusa e sozinha, procurando fugir da clausura da vida de seus pais" ("Barack Obama" 2010) ("My mother was that young girl with the film filled with the images of beautiful black people on her mind; a girl seduced by the attention my dad gave her; a disoriented and lonely girl, trying to escape from the life of seclusion of her parents"). Time and parenthood seem to be fluid when Orpheus is at stake: while the Portuguese title of Obama's memoirs transforms the dreams of his father into the source of

---

[15] While the Portuguese translation reads "jovens negros" or "young blacks," Obama's original wording is actually "childlike blacks" (2004: 124). There is an implicit disapproval in that term that is omitted from the Portuguese translation.

his own dreams, his narrative voice, in the reminiscence of his teenage years, juxtaposes the adult version of his mother with an image of her youth. Even in the imagination of Obama, eerily instrumentalized by Brazilian producers, the Greek and Carioca myth of Orpheus is the convulsive signifier where the most capricious chronologies, geographies, and antitheses converge indistinctly.

Conclusions

In addition to descending into Hell and temporarily redeeming his wife from the realm of death, Orpheus was responsible for another feat: the Greeks that told his tale also imagined him as the prototype of author and writer. M. L. West recapitulates the moment in which Plato, through the voice of Adeimantus, complains about the proliferation of books which, attributed to Orpheus (also to Musaeus), inundated fifth-century-BCE Athens (West 1983: 21; Plato, *Republic* 364e–5a). Plato alludes to the multitude of religious texts whose composition was attributed to the Thracian poet, and whose pages, with greater or lesser poetic fortune, catalogued human and divine genealogies, announced prophecies, dispensed oracles, explained the protocols of rites and mysteries, and even prescribed vegetarian diets. But toward the second half of the fourth century BCE, a certain Androtion of Athens declared that Orpheus could not be considered the author of the plethora of books attributed to him, because his original Thrace, everyone knew, was a country of unsophisticated savages. How could a Thracian, then, be the source of so much wisdom? Devotees of Orpheus, however, would respond to Androtion's reasoning with a formidable answer: although Thracian, Orpheus was capable of writing because he had received the gift of writing directly from the Muses, conferring it in turn on humanity (Detienne 2003: 132–3). Orpheus thus became the source of writing, and by extension, of culture. His story was simultaneously myth and mythography—any piece of writing was a testament to his genius. The manner in which Virgil (*Georgics* 4.523–9) and Ovid (*Metamorphoses* 11.50–4) conclude their narrations of the myth of Orpheus confirm this: even after being brutally murdered by the Bacchantes, the head of Orpheus continues to sing and prophesy as it is swept along in the Ebro river. Orpheus, like language itself, lends its signifiers to any signified.

It is remarkable that the mythic reputation of the Thracian bard appears fully rehearsed in the history of his reformulations in Brazil. In the various versions of Orpheus, as well as in the various participants of the introductory example of

Borges and the Minotaur, a mythical tale recovered from ancient Greece and projected onto Latin America combines its narrative fabric with the details of its weaving. Both Orpheus and Asterion provide the fabric of a grammar that is not only textual, but also compositional, historical, geographical, aesthetic, national, vital, and authorial. In a way, they become mythical precisely through these dimensions.

Detienne suggests that "in mythography, the writing down of myth, there is as much life, invention, and showmanship as there is in the art of weaving together stories to the strains of a lyre" (2003: xii). The cases presented above demonstrate that even in our days, as happened in ancient Greece, the root γράφειν (gráphein), the written component of mytho-graphy, only captures part of the process. Beyond the pages of Hesiod, Palaephatus, and Plutarch, the tale of the Minotaur constantly migrated through the surfaces of vases and craters, paintings and sculptures, and houses and temples, until it arrived in the 1896 oil painting that inspired, through its melancholy gesture, the short story hastily composed by Borges. No less convoluted is the Brazilian Orpheus: the motif of Cocteau and the allegory of Sartre both contaminate the idea that Moraes crafts in Rio de Janeiro while reading a French compilation of Greek myths. The staging of Moraes's tragedy, musicalized by Jobim, seeks to highlight the importance of popular music in Brazil, and is later appropriated by Camus and reproduced in a film that ostracizes its original creators and infuses in them the anxiety of recomposing the original tale in the shape of a Broadway musical, of all things. The effects of this movie, which exoticizes Brazil but at the same time engenders its most characteristic rhythms, haunts Diegues and Veloso to the point that the two of them end up presenting an opposite but equally essentializing version. And finally, the old desire of Moraes and Jobim to recover the first Orpheus is realized in a musical that strangely decides to advertise itself by digitally publishing letters in which Moraes and Jobim lamented their original project, and with a citation from Obama that is mired in stereotypes of which he himself disapproves. It is in this convoluted trajectory, and not in the plot itself, where the incessant and ever-incomplete myth of Orpheus in Brazil dwells.

More than sixty years after the premiere of *Orfeu da Conceição*, and as his ancient Greek acolytes once reckoned, Orpheus is still the author of all the books. No two Orpheuses peacefully coexist, and yet all of them inhabit the same space, because despite innumerable rebuttals, Orpheus is impervious to refutation. His vitality, his constitutive contradiction, renders him now more mythical than ever. Whether placed in Hades or at the summit of a Carioca hill, screened in the halls of the Festival of Cannes or imagined in a Broadway theater, one could argue that Orpheus's decision to look over his shoulder and lose his wife forever was not a misstep or accident. Rather, it was the inevitable gesture of one who cannot be consistent if not in the assimilation of dissonant voices and admission of contradictions; one who exists in the musical flux of his own counterpoints; one who descends into the very last circle of Hell to rescue his beloved, only to lose her again, by his own volition—as Virgil once put it, *iam luce sub ipsa*—on the very verge of light itself (*Georgics* 4.490).

5

Coda: Pedagogues

No basta leer a los clásicos ... Es menester "ser" clásicos
en la acepción más amplia que este término encierra.

It is not enough to read the classics ... We must "be" classical
in the broadest sense of the word.
   Giuseppina Grammatico, "Lo clásico como cimiento de *humanitas*"

Preliminaries

In 2003, the Chilean Society of Classical Studies published the extensive two-volume compilation *América Latina y lo Clásico* (*Latin American and the Classical*, henceforth *ALC*), perhaps the first comprehensive study by Latin American scholars of the relationship between their traditions and those of ancient Greece and Rome.[1] Edited by Giuseppina Grammatico Amari, then president of the Chilean Society of Classical Studies, the project was offered to the public as "el resultado de un esfuerzo colectivo realizado por académicos de varias universidades, miembros de las distintas Asociaciones de Estudios Clásicos Iberolatinoamericanos, interesados en conservar la presencia y vigencia de lo clásico en sus respectivos países" (2003: 7) ("the result of a collective effort by scholars from various universities, members of the different Associations of Iberian–Latin American Classical Studies, all interested in preserving the presence and relevance of the Classical in their respective countries"). The project is truly transnational, including pieces by scholars from Chile, Peru, Brazil, Argentina, Paraguay, Costa Rica, Bolivia, Cuba, Mexico, Uruguay, Spain,

---

[1] Not to be confused with the more recent *América Latina y lo clásico; lo clásico y América Latina* (Cruz and Huidobro 2018). This volume was also published in Chile, so perhaps the title's chiasmus is expressly intended to differentiate this book from its predecessor.

Portugal, Greece, and Italy. The goal: to illustrate, theorize, and analyze the relationship between Latin America and the Classics.

While many of the essays in *ALC* read as standard scholarly pieces, the preliminaries (Section I, described in detail below) adopt a humanist diction and style that might surprise some readers. The project defines itself in terms of a canonical and traditionalist vision of the Greco-Roman legacy, adopting the reverential attitude with respect to the Classics that used to characterize the old model of "masterpieces of world literature." The *ALC* thus makes stylistic and conceptual gestures that current Classical criticism tends to avoid: under the direction of Grammatico, the Classics are expressly presented as the cradle of civilization, as the exceptional site where the essence of what deserves to be called "culture" was conceived. Grammatico posits that, inasmuch as the terminology used to define the "human" derives from Latin, only the knowledge of Classical *humanitas* can ensure the full realization of human capacities. Humanity, in this sense, must be defined in terms of Greco-Roman ideals. With a marked lyrical accent, almost piously, the introductory section of the ALC project offers, to the critical eye of current scholarship, an array of essentialisms that might have gratified Gilbert Highet (see Introduction), but would likely provoke theoretical and political skepticism today.

Ironically, it is because the problematic aspects of *ALC* are easily identifiable that the need to discuss them turns out to be challenging. I describe this as a need because, within the logic of this book, addressing the ideological and conceptual framework of the project edited by Grammatico is an unavoidable task. The *ALC* project represents, as far as I have been able to determine, the first explicit attempt to produce from within Latin America—in fact, from a capacious, collaborative "Iberian–Latin American" perspective—a comprehensive consideration of the relationship between the region and the Classics. Its succinct title, which simply links "América Latina" and "lo Clásico," conveys in its generality the entire conceptual framework into which this study also falls. This merits some self-critical attention, for the transhistorical approach adopted in the course of this book has taken us from the earliest coinage of the category of the New World to very modern forms of Latin American Classicisms, and in this chapter, the distance between critical discourse and object of study becomes rather slender. Because of this, the *ALC* project imposes two unusual difficulties. Firstly, the research produced by the participants in the project often resonates with this book, yet the vestiges of conservative humanism expressed in the *ALC*'s preliminaries must be addressed very critically. However—and this is the second difficulty—those features are so manifest in *ALC* that their identification would merely yield a rather banal catalogue of critical anachronisms. This latter point can be rephrased with a question mark: what would be the point of interrogating the textual phenomenon of a conservative view of the Classics when it is so evident?

This closing chapter offers a narrative strategy to navigate these quandaries. By way of a coda to this book, I read the ideological and editorial apparatus in which the *ALC* project is framed as a synthesis of the negotiations, dramatizations, and appropriations sketched in the previous chapters. Four different modalities have been examined in those chapters: the early colonial creation of Classical avatars at the juncture between Old and the New Worlds, as illustrated by Acosta, Mexía, and Clarinda; the configuration of the New World anxiety in the chorographic works of Limenian artists of the baroque such as Nolasco Mere and Valdés; the fashioning of Classical *dramatis personae* during the Latin American Age of Revolution, epitomized by Bolívar via Olmedo and Vargas Tejada; and the mythographic amalgamation of local, personal, cultural, and Classical identities, as exemplified by Borges's affiliation with the Minotaur and, more extensively, by Orpheus in Brazil. Implicitly and yet systematically gesturing toward the ideological substratum of those four cases, the *ALC* project envisions the history of the Classics in Latin America as a familiar and even genetic phenomenon. I thus view this case as a condensation of the imbricate and often hazardous tradition of Classical Latin America, arguing that the *ALC*'s introductory section, even though it dates to the early twenty-first century, is so emphatic in its histrionic take on that tradition that it verges on a performance of ancient pagan rituals. I begin by examining closely some of the various items included in Section I of *ALC*, highlighting their conceptual and ideological aspirations. Then I relate this analysis to a mythic account already visited in Chapter 2, and repeatedly alluded to in the course of the *ALC* project: the encounter between the Trojan Aeneas and the ghost of his father Anchises in the Elysian Fields, as described in Virgil's *Aeneid* 6.681–899.

Let us start by pointing out a singular characteristic of *ALC*: the heterogeneity of materials and subjects included within the project. This inclusiveness was encouraged from its very genesis. Under the direction of Grammatico, the 2003 publication of *ALC* has its origin in an interdisciplinary seminar held two years earlier in Sicily, an event in which scholars from all Latin America and parts of Europe gathered to discuss what would become the title of the project— the relationship between Latin America and "lo Clásico" (the "Classical"). The 2001 seminar in Sicily thus became the stage to discuss all of the materials associated with that broad theme, so diverse that just providing a summary proves a difficult task.

The two volumes are organized in seven sections. Sections II through VII cover various matters, with articles about periods in Latin American Classicisms, regional adaptations of Classical motifs, Classical philology produced in Latin America, and programmatic proposals for Classical Studies projects, as well as a selection of Classical iconography from the region. The materials in Section I, however, are much more heterogeneous. As this section will be the focus of this analysis, I provide a detailed summary of its contents.

Section I, comprising the activities that took place in Erice, Sicily, in 2001, is divided into two parts. Part 1 is titled "Misión de Estudio: Vestigios del mundo clásico en la Sicilia occidental" ("Research Delegation: Vestiges of the Classical World in Western Sicily"). It contains the minutes of a roundtable; a series of photographs of ancient ruins in Sicily, taken during excursions scheduled as part of the research trip; and a collection of poems in ancient Greek, Latin (with Spanish translations), and Italian, which were read during the excursions. Section I, Part 2, titled "Seminario Ericino 'América Latina y lo Clásico'" ("The Erician Seminar 'Latin America and the Classical'"), is even more variegated. It is presented as the proceedings of the international congress "América Latina y lo Clásico," held in Erice and sponsored by UNESCO, and it contains the following:

1. the seminar's statement of purpose (with the project's justification, its specific goals, a list of sponsors, and two questionnaires to be completed by participants);
2. a reprinting of Grammatico's 1981 paper "El inquietante embrujo de la Potnia Erycina" ("The Disturbing Bewitchment of the Potnia Erycina"),[2] which examines an ancient cult to Venus practiced in Erice, Sicily;[3]
3. the "Acto inaugural del seminario 'América Latina y lo Clásico'" ("Inaugural Ceremony of the Seminar 'Latin America and the Classical'"), with summaries of papers that three European professors read for the inaugural event of the congress;
4. the manifesto *Monumentum Erycinum*—which includes a proposal, written in Latin, for the creation of an Iberian–Latin American Federation of Classical Studies; a facsimile of the attendees' signatures and their

---

[2] This is how the English abstract, included in the volume, translates the title.
[3] This paper was later published in *Semanas de Estudios Romanos* (Valparaíso, 1984).

nationalities; copies of letters from societies of Classical Studies in Chile, Bolivia, Cuba, Mexico, and Uruguay supporting the project; and an open letter to Latin American Ministers of Education insisting on the urgency of Classical Studies and the teaching of ancient Greek and Latin in Latin American schools;

5. the papers "Lo clásico como cimiento de *humanitas*" ("The Classical as the Foundation of *humanitas*"), by Grammatico; and "El legado de Roma" ("The Legacy of Rome"), by Antonio Alvar Ezquerra.

These are the main contents of both the *ALC* project in general, and of its heterogeneous preliminaries in particular. In what follows, I offer an examination of these items, focusing on their Virgilian undertones —particularly with regard to the interview between Aeneas and Anchises in the Underworld. By concentrating on the editorial and institutional framework of *ALC*, I foreground the affinities between academic endeavor and ritualistic performance as dramatized in the project. This analysis also serves as a conclusion to the present study by providing a succinct twenty-first-century instantiation of the fraught history of the Classics in the cultural history of Latin America.

Monuments to the Origin

There is something reminiscent of the avant-garde movements in the multiplicity of documents described above, which, aside from conventional conference papers, include a manifesto composed in Latin, a selection of pictures of old ruins in Sicily, and official letters submitted to ministries of education in Latin America. Yet all these various documents still share as a common denominator a certain prefatory tone. Whether through photographs, poems, manifestoes, official correspondence, or inaugural acts, the reader is constantly invited to witness the imminent arrival of a new movement: a new collective enterprise undertaken by Latin American intellectuals interested in the Classical tradition. The declamatory intonation of the academic manifesto "Monumentum Erycinum" exemplifies the performative dimension of this foundational attitude. To examine its stylistic features properly, it is worth citing the document at length:

Monumentum Erycinum
Hodie, Kalendis Martiis anni duo et millesimi septigesimi quinquagesimi quarti post urbem conditam, in oppido erycino dicato olim Veneri, deae tutelari

montis, et hoc tempore venerandae virgini Assumptae Deiparae, congregantur, ad celebrandum colloquium "De America Latina et Lingua et Humanitate Classica," ut legati gentium novi orbis:

- Ex republica cilensis, Giuseppina Grammatico, praeses Societatis Studiorum Classicorum SCHEC;Miguel Castillo Didier, Otto Dörr, Llalile Llarlluri, Antonio Saldaño, Carlos Salinas, magistri Literarum Humanarum, Artis Medicae, Historiae, Scientiae et Iurisprudentiae. [Here follows a list of members from the *republicae argentina, brasiliana, costarricensi, paraguaiana* and *peruviana*]

etiamque, ut legati gentium veteris orbis:

- Ex republica graeca, Christos Clairis, magister Universitatis Sorbonianae [Here follows the delegates from the *republicae hispanica, italica, and lusitana*].

Testibus legatis Italiae atque Graeciae, legati Societatum Hiberiae, Lusitaniae et Americae Latinae proponunt constitutionem Federationis Ibero-Latino-Americanae Studiorum Classicorum ad incrementum cultus eorumdem. Sunt enim haec studia generationi futurae pignora maximae curae et libertatis et humanitatis, iuxta limina novi aevi.

Grammatico 2003: 93, italics in the original

Ericinian Memorial

Today, on the Calends of March, in the year two thousand seven hundred fifty-four after the foundation of the city [of Rome], in the town of Eryx, formerly consecrated to Venus, tutelary goddess of the mount, and at the present time dedicated to the venerable Virgin of the Assumption, the Mother of God, [the following people] have gathered, to celebrate the Colloquium "On Latin America and the Classical Language and *Humanitas*," as delegates of the peoples from the New World:

- From the Chilean Republic: Giuseppina Grammatico, president of the Society of Classical Studies SCHEC; Miguel Castillo Didier, Otto Dörr, Llalile Llarlluri, Antonio Saldaño, Carlos Salinas, professors of the Humanities, Medicine, History, Science, and Jurisprudence. [Here follows a list of Argentine, Brazilian, Costa Rican, Paraguayan, and Peruvian delegates.]

Likewise, as delegates of the peoples of the Old World:

- From the Greek republic, Christos Claris, professor at the Sorbonne. [Here follows a list of Spanish, Italian, and Portuguese delegates.]

Before the delegates from Italy and Greece as witnesses, the delegates of the Spanish, Portuguese, and Latin American Societies propose the constitution of the Iberian–Latin American Federation of Classical Studies, to promote the development of those studies. For they are, right at the threshold of a new age, pledges to the future generation of the greatest concern for both liberty and *humanitas*.

The *Monumentum Erycinum* is Latinate in a way that goes beyond its language of composition. From the start, Roman time and space explicitly define the series of adverbial complements introducing the subject of the opening sentence. First are the Calends, the first day of each month according to the Roman calendar, selected here as an auspicious date for initiating the project—a convenient choice, since the Calends were the days on which the Roman *pontifex minor* officially announced the Nones of a given month, which would determine the way in which business would then be conducted.[4] The month chosen for the event is March, which some ancient sources claim was the first month of the year in certain archaic Roman calendars—the Calends of March, then, operates as a sort of New Year's Day.[5] The organizers also chose to date the event not *anno Domini*, "in the year of our Lord," but *ab urbe condita*, "the city having been founded"—that is to say, in a year calculated on the basis of a chronology which, according to the tradition initiated by the Roman scholar Varro, started with the founding of the city of Rome (estimated to be 753 BCE).[6] In short, the *Monumentum* is not signed in AD 2001, but rather in 2754 AUC.

The selection of the location for the seminar, and its characterization, follow the same atavistic logic. Located on the western coast of Sicily, Erice (the old town where, according to Virgil, the Trojan Anchises was buried), with its syncretic cult to Venus/Mary, seems the perfect setting for the creation of the Iberian–Latin American Federation of Classical Studies. The cults to Venus and Mary, the most important *generatrices* in the Classical and Christian traditions respectively, lend their generative character to the primordial nature of the dates

---

[4] See Varro, *On the Latin Language* 6.27, and Macrobius, *Saturnalia* 1.15.9–10.
[5] The role of March as the first month of an ancestral year is a deduction from the names of the months between July (formerly *Quintilis*) to December, which etymologically seem to point to a ten-month year starting in March. There has been a long debate on this issue. Allen (1947) surveys the debate and concludes that the tradition of the ten-month year is highly improbable. Hanna reminds us that ancient authors, among them Macrobius and Censorinus, reported the existence of such a ten-month year, but he does not vouch for it (2005: 99). Michels does admit a Roman year originally starting in March (1967: 18), while Brind'Amour emphatically denies its existence (1983: 225).
[6] The main source for the Varronian chronology comes from one of his most devoted readers, Roman grammarian Censorinus (*De die natali* 21.4–6). For more details, see Samuel 1972: 250–1.

chosen for the event. The result is a hypertrophied genesis: the *Monumentum* is surrounded by inaugural acts, introductions, and papers on the foundations of Rome and classical *humanitas*; placed on the Calends of March in the first year of the third millennium in the Christian calendar, while also following an old Roman system of dating; set in the storied Erice; and arranged under the auspices of Pagan and Christian religious figures of maternity and fertility. In short, the proclamation of the *Monumentum* is temporally, spatially, and ritualistically primal, conceptually original and, all in all, wholeheartedly Classical.

The *Monumentum* is also transatlantic, but this does not erase the identity markers of the seminar participants. The document carefully reminds the reader that the first group of signatures belongs to the "delegates of the peoples from the New World," while the other list enumerates the "delegates of the peoples from the Old World." The categories "Old World" and "New World"—which in current scholarship are historiographic and rhetorical, but not properly denotative—are thus used to describe contemporary America and Europe. Furthermore, the two lists of delegations from the New and Old Worlds appear officially endorsed by two distinguished witnesses: the Italian professor Giusto Picone *ex republica italica* ("from the Italian republic"), and the Greek professor Christos Clairis *ex republica graeca* ("from the Greek republic"). It is irrelevant that Dr. Clairis signs the document as a professor from Université La Sorbonne, Paris V, for what really matters in the manifesto is the symbolic dimension of his nationality. The manner in which the scholars *ex republicis graeca italicaque* are presented is thus consistent with the spirit of the *Monumentum*: summoned in the town of Erice—a site mythically Trojan, and historically Hellenistic and Roman—Italian professor Picone and Greek professor Clairis are invited not only as witnesses of the *ALC* project, but also as literal representatives of the Classical world, heirs of ancient Greece and Rome sanctioning, with their presence, the incursion of Latin America into their fiefs.

Yet the most enigmatic of all these elements is the clause that concludes the manifesto: *iuxta limina novi aevi*, "right at the threshold of a new age." The phrase is consistent with the message conveyed not only by the *Monumentum* but by all the documents of Section I—to wit, that the event constitutes the origin and announcement of a new time. In fact, the clause *iuxta limina*, literally "very much close to the threshold," implies two types of proximity: first, proximity to something else (*limina*), and second, closeness to that state of proximity (*iuxta*). In devising this sort of doubled proximity, the final clause reveals the anxiety behind the project: the configuration of a new New World ironically defined by and performed through the Classics. More than a mere point of departure, then, the project defines itself as a sort of hyper-imminence, as a vestibule to the threshold of the promised coming age. Like Hercules's pillars installed at the end of the world to warn travelers of its limits (see the Introduction), the threshold invoked here is "monumental"; but in contrast to those pillars, and in the tradition inaugurated by Charles V, the wardens of this doorway encourage the new travelers to go *plus ultra*.

The prophetic dimension of the manifesto resonates, in turn, with a component of Section I, Part 1: a collection of poems that had been recited during the course of field research in western Sicily. This section is preceded by the following clarification: "Reúne los textos en griego y en latín, con sus respectivas traducciones, y los textos en italiano, que fueron leídos durante la misión de estudio, en los lugares apropiados, y que luego fueron recitados en una sesión especial, al final del Seminario"; an English translation accompanies the brief passage: "This gathers the texts in Greek and Latin, with their due [sic] translations, and the texts in Italian that were read during the study mission, in those places where appropriate, and that were later recited in a special session at the end of the seminar" (2003: 35). While no explanation clarifies the meaning of the phrase "in those places where appropriate," its significance soon becomes apparent when considering the poems themselves. In Greek, Sappho's "To Aphrodite," Aeschylus' "Hymn to Zeus" (extracted from his *Agamemnon*), Euripides' "Prayer to Zeus" (extracted from *The Trojans*), Euripides' "Prayer to all the Gods" and "To Artemis" (both excerpted from his *Hippolytus*), Sophocles' "Hymn to the Lofty Laws of the Gods" (extracted from his *Oedipus Rex*), the Homeric Hymn to Demeter, and a poem by fourth-century Greek poet Palladas entitled "Know Thyself." In Latin, three excerpts from Virgil's *The Aeneid*, labeled here as "The Last Toil," "The Prophecy of Apollo," and "Sacrifice in the Temple of Venus"; an excerpt from Lucretius's *De rerum natura* and labeled here as "Nourishing Venus"; and four poems to the town of Erice by the poet Dino D'Erice—penname of Dino Grammatico, the host of the entire event. Most of these poems are actually extracts from larger works. Together, they form a genuine pagan book of prayers—to Zeus, Artemis, and so on—painstakingly collected by the *ALC* organizers.

The accompanying photographs taken during the trip—mainly images from temples to Zeus, Aphrodite, and Juno, as well as ancient theaters—then become the visual key to deciphering the obscure caption indicating that the poems were read "in those places where appropriate": apparently, the poems to the gods were recited at some of the temples of the divinities addressed by the texts. The excursion in Sicily is thus transformed into a religious pilgrimage, one in which devoted scholars walk through the ruins of ancient temples, piously declaiming ancient Greek and Latin hymns to the gods on their way to the town of Erice. "Performative" seems too mild an adjective to describe this undertaking, unless we think of a very specific type of performance: a religious ritual.

The mimetic and histrionic activities of *ALC*, undertaken in the name of a new academic and institutional project at the beginning of the twenty-first century, gestures toward and even outdoes the principle we encountered in the previous chapters—that one must embody the Classics in order to talk about them. While the authors examined earlier defined their foundational, revolutionary, or aesthetic projects through textual amalgamations of Classical authors and motifs (be it the city of Lima and its Virgilian walls, the heroes of *The Iliad* as models of revolutionary fighters, or the mythic Orpheus in the streets of Rio de Janeiro), the founders of the Iberian–Latin American Federation of Classical Studies take a more radical approach: a physical journey to the Classical world itself, traversing the Atlantic, symbolically recrossing the Pillars of Hercules, and turning the premise of *plus ultra* inside out in order to reach Erice. The directionality of this journey is significant: in their attempt to project Latin America onto the Classical tradition, these scholars undertake a New World quest for the discovery of European antiquity, from west to east, in a search of Classical origins that takes them to the primal shores of Erice in western Sicily.

But this orientation is not completely new. It has its own place in the European literary canon, as illustrated by a passage from Canto VI of Dante's *Paradiso*, in which Emperor Justinian reminds Dante the Pilgrim that:

> Poscia che Constantin l'aquila volse
> contr'al corso del ciel, ch'ella seguio
> dietro a l'antico che Lavina tolse,
> cento e cent'anni e più l'uccel di Dio
> ne lo stremo d'Europa si ritenne,
> vicino a' monti de' quai prima uscìo ...
>
> 6.1–6

> After Constantine turned the eagle back
> against the course of the heaven, which it had
> followed with that ancient one who took Lavinia,
> twice a hundred years and more God's bird
> remained at the edge of Europe, near the
> the mountains from which it first came forth ...
>
> Durling 2011: 123

The Dantean account of the to-and-fro flight of the imperial eagle provides a fitting image for the aspirations of the *ALC* project. In more than one passage of the *Aeneid*, Virgil writes that in a primal age, men from Italy crossed the Mediterranean eastward to found the city of Troy.[7] This is significant because the main purpose of the *Aeneid* is to explain how the Trojans who survived the destruction of their city eventually rebuilt their kingdom on Italian land. The Trojans' westward journey to what would become Rome inadvertently constituted, in this sense, a restoration, a fated return to their origins. Their "eagle"—the royal emblem adopted as the symbol of imperial movement—flew back to Italy under the aegis of the hero whom Justinian calls "l'antico" ("the ancient one," Aeneas), from the ruins of the city of Priam to Rome, the New Troy. But, as Dante's *Paradiso* explains, that was not the end: when, millennia later (in 324 CE), Constantine decided to transfer the seat of the empire from Rome to Byzantium (subsequently called Constantinople), the same imperial eagle flew back yet again, "against the course of heaven" (that is to say, from west to east, since the visible rotation of the sky moves westward), remaining for more than 200 years in the hills of Constantinople where Justinian ruled—very close to the ancient seat of Troy in northwestern Anatolia.

Under the specter of the eagle's imperial flight that moved back and forth from Italy to Troy, from Troy to Rome, and from Rome to Byzantium, the *ALC* project seems to ironically imitate, in transatlantic fashion, the protocols of a new *nostos* or homecoming journey. Inverting the directionality of the Europeans who, crossing the ocean, brought the Classical tradition to the New World, a cohort of Latin American Classicists dramatizes the "return" of Classical America to southern Italy, specifically to Erice, praising the ancient divinities in old tongues and observing sacred rites. With its ritual poems and a scholarly manifesto signed in the year 2754 AUC, the project's re-enactment of the long history of Classical Latin America is almost uncanny. Erice, the Sicilian town chosen as site of the event, thus acquires an extraordinary symbolic importance.

Back to Erice

One of the articles in Section I, "El inquietante embrujo de la Potnia Erycina" ("The Disturbing Bewitchment of the Potnia Erycina") is singular because it

---

[7] The Italian origins of Dardanus, son of Jupiter and progenitor of the Trojan race, is referred to in multiple passages in *The Aeneid*: see, for instance, 3.167–8 and 7.205–8. In fact, the idea that the Trojans' arrival in Italy constitutes a "return," as predicated in the speech by Constantine in *Paradiso*, also appears explicitly in *The Aeneid* (7.240–2).

dates back to 1981—that is, it predates the *ALC* project by two decades. Grammatico, however, justifies the essay's reprint in 2003 by presenting it as a conceptual justification of the selection of Erice as the site for the foundation of the Iberian-Latin American Federation of Classical Studies. Strategically placed between Parts 1 and 2 of Section I (that is, connecting the field work in Sicily with the *ALC* project proper), the paper describes the city of Erice as the site of an ancient cult to the *Potnia Erycina* or Lady of Erice, a local female divinity (later identified with Astarte by the Carthaginians and with Venus by the Romans). The article is filled with details about the features and attributes of the goddess, as well as the characteristics of her cult in the history of her syncretisms. Since the piece makes no reference at all to Latin America, Grammatico adds the following footnote to the reprint: "Nos ha parecido oportuno volver a publicar [este artículo] ahora aquí, a modo de respuesta a la pregunta "¿Por qué Erice?", patente o latente en todos los participantes en el Seminario ericino" (Grammatico 2003: 61) ("We thought it would be convenient to republish [this article] here and now, as an answer to the question 'Why Erice?'—an explicit or implicit query of all the participants of the Erician Seminar"). The reader is thus invited to discover the reasons why Erice was selected for the event by reading Grammatico's erudite examination of the history of this cult. And while Grammatico's study is truly insightful, it is also punctuated by the lyrical gestures that characterize the *ALC* project as a whole. It is in these moments that the rationale for the selection of Erice emerges:

> Hay ciudades que cambian vertiginosamente y otras que parecen eternizarse en el tiempo, que no podrían concebirse distintas de como nacieron, y así permanecen, testimonios de una forma de ser, perfecta, que otrora alcanzaron y de cuya memoria siguen viviendo. Enmarcados en su contexto natural, sus monumentos y documentos nos hablan, con la voz que les es propia, de las grandezas y miserias de los hombres que allí vivieron y murieron, y esa voz se insinúa en el alma despertando vibraciones de una indefinible sugestión.
>
> No son muchas, pero las hay, esparcidas aquí y allá por el mundo: una de ella es Eryx, la Ciudadela del Monte.
>
> 2003: 61

> There are cities that change vertiginously, and there are others that seem to last forever in time, that could not be conceived differently from how they were born, and so remain as evidence of a perfect form of being, which they formerly achieved, and in whose memory they still exist. In their natural context, their monuments and documents speak to us, with a voice of their own, about the feats and miseries of the people who lived and died there—with a voice that

subtly reveals itself to the soul, awakening in us vibrations of an indefinable suggestion.

These cities do not abound, but do exist, scattered here and there all over the world. One such is Eryx, the Citadel of the Mount.

A distinction between transformation and perfection is at play here. Grammatico, trained in Latin and fond of etymology, knows well that "perfecto" derives from the prefix *per* (completely, thoroughly) and the past participle of *facere* (to make, to do), thereby conveying the idea of something fully terminated, completely done, and consequently immutable. The perfect city, more than founded, is "born in its natural context." And while the perfection of the city is natural, it is also exceptional: "These cities do not abound, but do exist." Such an idyllic depiction, when originally written in 1981, functioned as a panegyrical introduction to an ethnographic and philological survey of the *Potnia* cult in Erice. In 2001, however, the same lines serve a wholly different purpose. In the context of a project that seeks to revitalize (almost literally) the Latin American relationship with the Classical tradition, the radical consistency of Erice as a "city that never changes" provides an exceptional fiction to overcome the chronological and geographical distances between the ancient and modern worlds. Eternally set *in illo tempore locoque*, Erice provides the truly perfect site for the self-Classicalization of the founders of the Federation.

But this is not the only motivation behind the selection of the Sicilian Erice. The Citadel of the Mount also occupies a conspicuous place in the Greco-Roman mythological tradition, as it plays a key role in the epic wanderings of Aeneas. A tradition deriving from Classical mythology explains that Erice was named after Eryx, son of Venus and Butes (an Argonaut and beekeeper). Eryx was, therefore, half-brother of Aeneas, though from a different generation.[8] King of the city and a gifted pugilist, Eryx was nevertheless defeated (and killed) during a boxing match with Heracles, who was trying to recover one of the cows he had previously stolen from Geryon during the tenth of his labors. Eryx was buried on the steep mountain where he had built a temple for Venus.[9] The city thereafter bore the name of the fallen boxer.[10]

According to the fifth book of *The Aeneid*, Aeneas and his fleet detoured to Erice to escape dangerous winds after slipping away from Carthage. Coincidentally, the ashes of Aeneas's father, Anchises, had previously been buried in Erice, and so the

---

[8] See *Aeneid* 5.23–4.
[9] See *Aeneid* 5.400–20.
[10] Various Classical sources report the death of Eryx. See, for instance, Apollodorus (*Library* 2.5.10) and Virgil (*Aeneid* 5.391–420).

hero decided to take advantage of his forced stop and commemorate his father's death with athletic contests. While the games are taking place, the Trojan women, tired of the incessant traveling and instigated by the goddess Juno and her servant Iris, burn part of the fleet, causing Aeneas to again despair of his future. Yet amid his lamentations, the ghost of Anchises appears and commands Aeneas to descend into the Underworld, so that he can be granted a genealogical prophecy: "Tum genus omne tuum et quae dentur moenia disces" (*Aeneid* 5.737) ("Then shalt thou learn of all thy race, and what city is given thee"; Fairclough 1950: 495). Aeneas follows his father's instructions. With the aid of the Sybil, he crosses the terrible threshold of the Underworld and eventually reaches the shadow of his father.

As scholars familiar with the context of the composition of *The Aeneid* know, the interview between Aeneas and Anchises in the Elysian Fields, with its succinct survey of Roman history, constitutes a paradigmatic instance of the conflation of political discourse and mythology. As father and son contemplate the countless souls bathing in the subterranean waters of the Lethe, Anchises describes the process the Greeks called metempsychosis, according to which the souls of the dead go through a process of cleansing and forgetfulness in the Underworld in order to return to Earth, incarnated in new bodies. Anchises is thus able to show to his son the souls of those who will become the most important figures in the history of Rome. Among the parade of the souls of mythical and historical figures—Romulus, Remus, Numa, and Cato, for instance—Anchises gestures toward some of the most important figures of Virgil's own time:

> huc geminas nunc flecte acies, hanc aspice gentem
> Romanosque tuos. hic Caesar et omnis Iuli
> progenies, magnum caeli ventura sub axem.
> hic vir, hic est, tibi quem promitti saepius audis,
> Augustus Caesar, Divi genus, aurea condet
> saecula qui rursus Latio regnata per arva
> Saturno quondam, super et Garamantas et Indos
> proferet imperium (iacet extra sidera tellus,
> extra anni solisque vias, ubi caelifer Atlas
> axem umero torquet stellis ardentibus aptum).
>
> *Aeneid* 6.788–97

Hither now turn thy two eyes: behold this people, thine own Romans. Here is Caesar, and all Iülus' seed, destined to pass beneath the sky's mighty vault. This, this is he, whom thou so oft hearest promised to thee, Augustus Caesar, son of a god, who shall again set up the Golden Age in Latium amid the fields where

Saturn once reigned, and shall spread his empire past Garamant and India, to a land that lies beyond the stars, beyond the paths of the year and the sun, where heaven-bearing Atlas turns on his shoulders the sphere, inset with gleaming stars.

Fairclough 1950: 561, 563

The prophetic announcement of the foundation of Rome is thus substantiated by this vision of the psychic (in the Classical sense) existence of its most renowned sons. As such, more than a reflection or a second version of the Troy that Aeneas abandoned in flames, Rome becomes its natural rehabilitation. Like a plant from a seed, Rome is not essentially different from Troy, but rather a regrowing of the ancient city. Augustus is, in this way, a spiritual contemporary of his ancestors Aeneas and Anchises. In fact, in the logic of metempsychosis, the Roman Augustus even becomes an anachronistic precursor of the Trojan Aeneas, because his empire is destined to restore the *Saturnia Regna* or Golden Age that the mythic Saturn, father of Jupiter, had brought about in Latium at the dawn of time.[11] The circular genealogy of *Saturnia Regna*–Troy–Rome is a manifestation of a millenarian revolution that overcomes the linearity of past, present, and future, imposing a radical principle of synchronic identity. The poetic temporality in the verses cited above confirms this. The future tense in the participle *ventura*, "forthcoming" or "about to come," used to characterize "all the seed of Iülus," does not contradict but rather complements the emphatic present tense of the line immediately following, "this man, this is he [*est*] whom you so often hear [*audis*] promised to you." In other words, Anchises does not say "this *will be* the future," but rather "this *is* the future." As the *Aeneid* belongs to the historical moment in which Imperial Rome claimed to have achieved its own apotheosis under the rule of Augustus, the prophecy of Anchises is meant to be, for both Aeneas and the Roman contemporaries of Virgil, not a revelation, but rather a self-evident truth. Through the "Trojanization" of Rome and the subterranean revelation of Anchises, Virgil transforms the Homeric trope of *katabasis*, the descent into the Underworld, into a transcendentalist form of imperial propaganda.

Bound to the vibrations of these Underworld echoes, the metaphor that Grammatico uses to illustrate the relevance of the Classics in our time is also subterranean. As she writes in "Lo clásico como cimiento de *Humanitas*" ("The Classical as Foundation for *Humanitas*"):

---

[11] See the Introduction for more on the *Saturna Regna* trope (p. 21).

> Lo clásico recoge el pasado, tiene en cuenta el presente y anticipa el futuro. Es multidimensional, no descuida ningún punto de vista, todo lo penetra en profundidad, todo lo pondera, lo incorpora a sí y lo asimila. El largo trabajo que desarrolla en nuestro interior no es indoloro. Tiene mucha semejanza con el de los mineros. Solo una excavación profunda asegura el suceso: todo resultará entonces a las mil maravillas. Naturalmente hay un secreto: las verdaderas profundidades no son nunca "profanas." Descuidar el ángulo de lo sacro impide ese descenso a las entrañas de la Verdad que asegura el éxito feliz de la obra. Los clásicos parecen haberse hecho cargo de ese invisible conducto que enlaza lo sagrado y lo profano. Su recorrido le es familiar. Anhelan unir los polos de eje, en nombre de una co-presencia de consanguineidad y otreidad que a la vez los enlaza y los separa: se proponen restaurar la condición primigenia en que las dos esferas parecían coincidir y el *hábitat*, arriba o abajo, era común.
>
> 2003: 106

> The Classical recovers the past, apprehends the present and anticipates the future. It is multidimensional, it disregards no point of view, it deeply penetrates into everything, it ponders everything, it subsumes everything and assimilates it. The vast task it fulfills within us is not painless. It is very similar to the labor of miners. Only a deep excavation ensures its success: everything will then turn out wonderfully. Naturally, there is a secret, for the true depths are never "profane." Neglecting the sacred dimension of this process would prevent one from this descent into the entrails of that Truth which ensures the favorable outcome of the task. The Classics seem to have taken charge of that invisible conduit which links the sacred and the profane. Its path is familiar to them. They want to join the two poles of the axis, in the name of a co-presence of kinship and otherness that connects and separates them simultaneously. They seek to restore the primordial condition in which these two spheres seemed to coincide and where *habitat*, above or below, was something common.

In her definition of the "Classical," Grammatico seems to distil the aim of the ALC project—that is to say, it integrates past, present, and future; it is both multidimensional and multi-perspectival; and it is everywhere and (to use a neologism) *everywhen*. But much more telling is the metaphor of the proper approach to the Classical: mining. Through its allusions to toil and pain, its emphasis on depth, its fatiguing verticality, and its promise of a transcendental truth, Grammatico meticulously rephrases the laborious quest of Aeneas descending into the Underworld to receive the revelation of Anchises. The search for the Classics, like Aeneas's *descensus ad Inferos*, connects the chthonic and the ethereal—the underworld and the upper world. The perpendicular character of the image and the extraordinary value of what is found in the depths complement the comparison with mineral extraction (though the actual economic and social dynamics of historical mining, in particular in the New World, have to be overlooked so as not to compromise the intended gravitas of the analogy).

Ultimately, these metaphors reaffirm the merging of the *ALC* participants with the Classical World, but the principle of identification is rendered explicit and literal:

> No basta leer a los clásicos y soñar con ellos un mundo más justo, más bueno, más bello, si nos desentendemos de la tarea que nos atañe. Es menester "ser" clásicos en la acepción más amplia que ese término encierra, y absolutamente conscientes de la dimensión valórica que el "ser clásicos" comporta. Como seres humanos que somos, debemos ubicarnos en el lugar que nos corresponde y no abdicar a ningunos de nuestros derechos y a ninguno de nuestros deberes. Sabedores de que lo humano y lo divino se corresponden, no hemos de despreciar una religación que nos enaltece, religación a lo divino, en primer lugar, y luego a lo humano en todas sus formas, social, política, familiar, individual, comunitaria. En conformidad con él, tenemos que responder al llamado que nos invita a anteponer la verdad a todas las otras cosas, por apreciables que éstas aparezcan.
>
> ¡Seremos griegos en la medida en que la fantasía, la belleza y la creatividad nos arrebaten; seremos romanos en la medida en que nos seduzca el deseo de escribir nuestro nombre en el libro de la historia! ¡Y, por sobre todo, seremos humanos en la medida en que no dejemos que las semillas de la *humanitas* se vuelvan estériles por nuestra desidia!
>
> Grammatico 2003: 119

It is not enough to read the classics and to imagine, through them, a world that is nobler, more just, more beautiful, if we neglect the task before us. We must "be" classical in the broadest sense of the word, and absolutely conscious of the value implied by "being classical." As the human beings that we are, we must assume our rightful place, abdicating from neither our rights nor our responsibilities. Understanding the correspondence between the human and the divine, we must not reject a reconnection that exalts us; a reconnection, in the first place, with the divine, and in the second place, with the human in all its forms: social, political, familial, individual, and communitarian. Consequently, we must respond to the call that invites us to place truth above all other things, however estimable they may seem.

We will be Greeks insofar as we allow ourselves to be caught up in fantasy, beauty, and creativity! We will be Romans insofar as we are seduced by the desire to inscribe our names in the book of history! And, above all else, we shall be human insofar as we do not allow the seeds of *humanitas* to become sterile through our apathy!

In proclaiming the necessity of becoming Classical "in the broadest sense of the word," Grammatico defines the identification with the Classical world not only as an academic endeavor, but also a matter of necessity, of right, and of humanity. Borrowing from Mircea Eliade's well-known dichotomy of the sacred and the profane, the links between the Classics and the present are equivalent to a "reconnection" between the human and the divine, in the same way that the interview between Aeneas and Anchises relinks the Roman Empire with its mythical origins. And the teleology that justifies this aspiration is, as in the case of the Classicalized version of mining, a search for a capitalized Truth—hidden, precious, and divine. A distinct aura of religiosity pervades Grammatico's conclusion: humanity and *humanitas*, presented as identical, are only reachable through the verticalities of Classical scholarship, which lead both up to the realm of the divine and down to the holy see of Truth. Being Classical is being a person. Hence the sequence of hurrahs that structure Grammatico's closing syllogism: "We will be Greeks!" and "We will be Romans!" are the premises that make possible the conclusion "We will be humans."

* * *

Even as we highlight the Classical essentialisms so vividly illustrated here, a few caveats are in order. First, we should not be too ready to cynically dismiss the devoted fascination of the *ALC* organizers with their subject, which they approached not merely as an object of study but also as a philosophical foundation for their identities. Second, even some of the most peculiar features of the preface—for example, the Latin manifesto and the open letter sent to ministries of education across Latin America demanding the rehabilitation of Greek and Latin instruction in school curricula—have a pragmatic dimension to them. Even today, it can be very challenging for Latin American students to gain access to training in Classical literature, languages, and philology, so the enthusiasm with which the *ALC* project was received by scholars from the region may respond more to the practical promotion of Classical studies than the wholesale adoption of the aspirations and rhetoric of the organizers. Finally, the rich compendium of essays included in the two volumes speaks eloquently to the fecundity that Latin American scholars found in exploring their own histories and identities in terms of the Classics. Regardless of the disagreement we may have regarding the conservative brand of humanism of the preliminaries, the *ALC* project is an indispensable resource for those interested in the complex history of the Classics in Latin America.

But what I have found especially compelling in the examination of this final case study are its remarkable echoes with the transhistorical narrative proposed in the course of this book—through case studies spanning half a millennium. It is almost impossible not to notice that the foundational impetus of the *Monumentum Erycinum* manifesto distinctly evokes the labors of the intellectual figures of the early colonial period who (as seen in Chapter 1) sought to fashion themselves as avatars of Classical founding figures. The palpable desire of the *ALC* organizers to resolve the paucity of Classical training across Latin America, seen as a serious deficit when contrasted to the long-standing tradition of Classical scholarship in Europe, clearly recalls the New World anxiety that (as discussed in Chapter 2) moved writers to compensate for the "brief history" of Lima through narrative, cartographic, and poetic extravagances. The 2001 pilgrimage to ancient ruins and the reading of pagan anthems to the dormant gods of Sicily, which the *ALC* project documents with photographs and bilingual transcriptions of the poems themselves, recalls the uncanny impersonation of Classical motifs that found such fertile ground (considered in Chapter 3) in Simón Bolívar's time. Finally, the highly conscious selection of Erice, point of departure for the katabatic journey of Aeneas, as the site of the conference, offers yet another instantiation of the fascinating confluence of myths and the history of their adaptation, a process which (as seen in Chapter 4) has characterized the presence of the myth of Orpheus in the scenic arts of twentieth-century Brazil. I believe that these resonances provide a superb opportunity for some concluding remarks. But first it must be stated, to assuage any concerns about too deterministic a reading of these five cases, that the goal of this book has been only to propose a narrative, not a rigid logic of stages in a grand history of the Classics in Latin America. None of the cases selected was inevitable, and their historical linkages are a matter of contingency, not necessity. Likewise, the coincidences to be found between the *ALC* project and the cases examined in the previous four chapters are ultimately arbitrary and can only be expounded on by a process of literary narrativization (but then again, this proviso is perhaps redundant, as the writing of history itself is always bound to those narrative terms).

The editorial and rhetorical decisions by which Grammatico defines the significance of the *ALC* project thus provide a neat summary of the transhistorical course of Classical Latin America. The chronicle of the anxiety regarding the New, the Old, and the Classical, inaugurated by Columbus and Vespucci and presented in this book as a parade of avatars, chorographers, personae, and mythographers, culminates in the anticipation of a future when the scholars gathered in Erice will become "Classical." This trajectory provides the elements for one of the many possible genealogies of the Classics Plus Ultra—across the Atlantic in a way that could not have been prefigured by the imperial imagination of Charles V and his inveterate pillars. Hence the relevance of this line of inquiry. Our case studies illustrate how pervasive and recurrent a role Classical narratives have played in the perennial exercises of self-definition that punctuate the cultural histories of Latin America. But the wide scope of this approach may be timely even today, as those histories continue to grapple with the legacy of the label *mundus novus*—that is, with the centuries of tensions, fusions, and contradictions defining the relationships among the local, the national, the colonial, and the transatlantic; the European and the American; the indigenous, the criollo, and the mestizo; the "Western" and "Non-Western;" and the developed, underdeveloped, third-worldly, and global. None of the cases studied in this book could, of course, fully illustrate the complexities of the Classics in South America, nor has that been my purpose. In this book, rather, I have conceived of the Classics as lenses through which to re-evaluate critical moments in the cultural history of South America, hoping (not unlike the scholars involved in the *ALC* project) to entice readers from different areas in Latin American and Classical Studies to probe further the fascinating potential of these conjunctions and to consider the comparative appeal of examining Latin American Classicisms from different periods. Were that to occur, whether the theses presented in these chapters are favored or challenged, I would consider the primary goal of this book accomplished.

Bibliography

Acosta, José de. (1590) 1962. *Historia natural y moral de las Indias. En que se tratan de las cosas notables del cielo/elementos/metales/plantas y animales dellas/y los ritos/y ceremonias/leyes y gobierno de los indios.* Ed. Edmundo O'Gorman. México D.F.: Fondo de Cultura Económica.
Acosta, José de. (1590) 2002. *Natural and Moral History of the Indies.* Trans. Frances M. López-Morillas. Durham, NC: Duke University Press.
"Ad Urbem Limam Americae Meridionalis Regiam." 1687. In Valdés 1687, n.p.
Aelius Donatus. 1959. "Vita Vergilii." *Suetonius.* Vol. 2. Ed. John C. Rolfe. Bilingual ed. Cambridge, MA: Harvard University Press: 464–83.
"Al mesmo padre ..." (sonnet). 1687. In Valdés 1687, n.p.
Alatorre, Antonio. 1997. "De nuevo sobre traducciones de las *Heroidas*." In Marta Elena Venier (ed.), *Varia lingüística y literaria. 50 Años del CELL: 2. Literatura de la Edad Media al siglo XVIII*, 21–51. n.p.p.: Colegio de México.
Alfieri, Vittorio. 1966. *Le tragedie.* Ed. Pietro Cazzani. Verona: Arnoldo Mondadori.
Allen, Bernard Melzar. 1947. "The Early Roman Calendar." *Classical Journal* 43, no. 3: 163–8.
Ambrose, John W., Jr. 1965. "The Ironic Meaning of the Lollius Ode." *Transactions and Proceedings of the American Philological Associations* 96: 1–10.
Andújar, Rosa and Konstantinos P. Nikoloutsos, eds. 2020. *Greeks and Romans on the Latin American Stage.* London: Bloomsbury.
Angelelli, Guillermo. 1991. *Asterión.* Unipersonal performance.
Apollodorus. 1921. *The Library.* 2 vols. Bilingual ed. Trans. Sir James George Frazer. Cambridge, MA: Harvard University Press.
"Apresentação." 2010. In *Orfeu: o maior musical brasileiro* 2010.
Arias, Enrique Desmond and Corinne Davis Rodriguez. 2006. "The Myth of Personal Security: Criminal Gangs, Dispute Resolution, and Identity in Rio de Janeiro's Favelas." *Latin American Politics and Society* 48, no. 4: 53–81.
Aristotle. 1926. *The "Art" of Rhetoric.* Bilingual ed. Trans. John Henry Freese. Cambridge, MA: Harvard University Press.
Aristotle. 1962. *Metaphysics. Books 1–9.* Bilingual ed. Trans. Hugh Tredennick. Cambridge, MA: Harvard University Press.
Aristotle. 1995. *Poetics.* Bilingual ed. Trans. Stephen Halliwell. Cambridge, MA: Harvard University Press.
Aulus Gellius. 1967. *Attic Nights.* Vol. 3. Bilingual ed. Trans. John C. Rolfe. Cambridge, MA: Harvard University Press.

Bacchyllides. 2002. *Dithyrambes. Épinices. Fragments.* Bilingual ed. Trans. Jean Irigoin. Paris: Les Belles Letres.

"Barack Obama." 2010. In *Orfeu: o maior musical brasileiro* 2010.

Barrera, Trinidad. 1990. In Mexía (1608) 1990. *Parnaso antártico*.

Beckjord, Sarah. 2007. *Territories of History: Humanism, Rhetoric, and the Historical Imagination in the Early Chronicles of Spanish America*. University Park: Penn State University Press.

Bennett, C. E. 1952. In Horace 1952.

Bocchetti, Carla. 2010a. "El diario de viaje a Grecia de Francisco de Miranda: Grecia en el contexto de la independencia americana." In Bocchetti 2010b, 53–75.

Bocchetti, Carla. 2010b. *La influencia clásica en América Latina*. Bogotá: Universidad Nacional de Colombia, Facultad de Ciencias Humanas.

Bolívar, Simón. (1822) 1833. "Mi delirio sobre el Chimborazo." *Colección de documentos importantes relativos a la vida pública del Libertador de Colombia y del Perú Simón Bolívar, hasta su muerte. Apéndice al tomo vigésimo primero* (Annex to Vol. 21). Caracas: Imprenta de Danniron y Dupouny, 243–4; https://play.google.com/books/reader?id=ty8CAAAAYAAJ&pg=GBS.PP1.

Bolívar, Simón. 1964. *Escritos del Libertador*. Vol. 3. Ed. Cristóbal L. Mendoza et al. Caracas: Sociedad Bolivariana de Venezuela.

Bolívar, Simón. 1964–9. *Cartas del Libertador*. 7 vols. Caracas: Banco de Venezuela, Fundación Vicente Lecuna.

Bolívar, Simón. 1970. *Itinerario documental de Simón Bolívar. Homenaje al Dr. Vicente Lecuna en el centenario de su nacimiento*. Ed. Pedro Grases and Manuel Pérez Vila. Caracas: Ediciones de la Presidencia de la República de Venezuela.

Bolívar, Simón. 1993. *Simón Bolívar Fundamental*. Vol. 2. Ed. Germán Carrera Damas. Caracas: Monte Ávila Editores Latinoamericana.

Bolívar, Simón. 2003. *El Libertador. Writings of Simón Bolívar*. Trans. Frederick H. Fornoff. New York: Oxford University Press.

Borges, Jorge Luis. 2005. "La casa de Asterión." *Obras completas*. Vol. 1, 608–10. Buenos Aires: Emecé.

Borja, Juan de. 1581. *Empresas morales*. Prague: Iorge Nigrin. *Internet Archive*, https://archive.org/details/empresasmorales00borj/mode/1up.

Braidotti, Erminio and John P. Rosso. 2017. "Latin Translations." In Messer and Williams 2017, 145–52.

Briceño Perozo, Mario. 1971. *Reminiscencias griegas y latinas en la obra del Libertador*. Caracas: Texto.

Briesemeister, Dietrich. 1986. "Rodrigo de Valdés, S.J. (1609–1682) y la tradición poética 'en latín congruo y puro castellano.'" *Ibero-Amerikanisches Archiv* 12: 97–122.

Briesemeister, Dietrich. 2000. "La poesía neolatina en la Nueva España en el siglo XVII." In Kohut and Rose 2000, 13–40.

Brind'Amour, Pierre. 1983. *Le calendrier romain. Recherches chronologiques*. Ontario: Éditions de l'Université d'Ottawa.

Browne, William Hand. 1910. "The Transformations of a Legend." *Sewanee Review* 18, no. 4: 404–13.

Buceta, Erasmo. 1925. "La tendencia a identificar el español con el latín. Un episodio cuatrocentista." *Homenaje ofrecido a Menéndez Pidal*. Vol. 1, 85–108. Madrid: Hernando.

Buceta, Erasmo. 1932. "De algunas composiciones hispano-latinas en el siglo XVII." *Revista de filología española* 19: 388–414.

Burke, Peter. 2016. "Hybrid Philosophies." *Hybrid Renaissance: Culture, Language, Architecture*, 153–72. Budapest: Central European University Press.

Burneo, Reinhard Augustin. 2012. *Las murallas coloniales de Lima y el Callao*. Lima: Universidad Ricardo Palma, Editorial Universitaria.

Busto Duthurburu, José Antonio del. 1963. *El conde de nieva. Virrey del Perú*. Lima: Publicaciones del Instituto Riva-Agüero.

Butzer, Karl. W. 1992. "From Columbus to Acosta: Science, Geography, and the New World." *Annals of the Association of American Geographers* 82, no. 3: 543–5.

Cabrera, Jorge. 1984. *Asterión y otros poemas*. Buenos Aires: Agón.

Camacho Rojo, José María. 2004. *La tradición clásica en las literaturas iberoamericanas del siglo XX: Bibliografía analítica*. Granada: Universidad de Granada.

Campos-Muñoz, Germán. 2012. "Contrapuntos órficos. Mitografía brasileña y el mito de Orfeo." *Latin American Research Review* 47, Special Issue: 31–48.

Campos-Muñoz, Germán. 2013. "Cuzco, *Urbs et Orbis*: Rome and Garcilaso de la Vega's Self-Classicalization." *Hispanic Review* 81, no. 2: 123–44.

Campos-Muñoz, Germán. 2015. "The Elasticity of the Archive: The Case of Pedro de Peralta Barnuevo and his *Lima fundada*." *Dieciocho* 38, no. 1: 49–70; http://faculty.virginia.edu/dieciocho/38.1/4.Campos.38.1.pdf.

Cañizares-Esguerra, Jorge. 2018. "José de Acosta, a Spanish-Jesuit Protestant Author: Print Culture, Contingency, and Deliberate Silence in the Making of the Canon." In Jorge Cañizares-Esguerra, Robert Aleksander Maryks, and Ronnie Po-Chia Hsia (eds.), *Encounters between Jesuits and Protestants in Asia and the Americas*, 185–227. Leiden: Brill.

Cardoso, Elizete. 1958. *Canção do amor demais* (album). Festa, LP.

Carlyle, Thomas. 2014. *The Selected Works of Thomas Carlyle*. Ed. F. Randolph Ludovico. n.p.p.: Bibliotheca Cakravarti Foundation.

Casanova, Eduardo. 2008. "El paraíso burlado (Venezuela desde 1498 hasta 2008): Las nueve Musas." *Analítica.com*. Analítica Consulting; https://www.analitica.com/entretenimiento/el-paraiso-burladode-fiestas-y-de-locuras/.

Castany Prado, Bernat. 2016. "'Ovidio Transformado.' La presencia de Ovidio en las dos primeras partes del 'Parnaso Antártico' de Diego Mexía de Fernangil." In Fernández et al. 2016.

Censorinus. 1889. *De die natali*. Ed. Ivan Cholodniak. St. Petersburg. In Bill Thayer (ed.), *LacusCurtius: Into the Roman World*; https://penelope.uchicago.edu/Thayer/E/Roman/Texts/Censorinus/home.html.

Chang-Rodríguez, Raquel. 1998. "Clarinda's Catalogue of Worthy Women in her *Discurso en loor de la poesía* (1608)." *Calíope: Journal for the Society for Renaissance and Baroque Hispanic Poetry* 4, no. 1–2: 94–106.
Chang-Rodríguez, Raquel. 2003. "Ecos andinos: Clarinda y Diego Mexía en la *Primera parte del Parnaso Antártico* (1608)." *Calíope* 9, no. 1: 67–80.
Chang-Rodríguez, Raquel. 2011. "La lírica en la Lima virreinal: Clarinda y el 'Discurso en loor de la poesía' (1608)." *Guaraguao* 15, no. 36: 91–105.
Chueca Goitia, Fernando and Leopoldo Torres Balbas. 1951. *Planos de ciudades Iberoamericanas y filipinas existentes en el Archivo de Indias*. Vol. 1. Madrid: Instituto de Estudios de Administración Local, Seminario de Urbanismo.
Clarinda [Anon.]. 1608. *Discurso en loor de la Poesía*. In Mexía (1608) 1990: 9r–25v.
Cobo, Bernabé. 1601. "Examen del hermano Bernabé Cobo para escolar." In Cobo (1639) 1882: xix–xx.
Cobo, Bernabé. (1639) 1882. *Historia de la fundación de Lima*. Ed. Manuel González de la Rosa. Lima. *Colección de historiadores del Perú*. Vol. 1. Lima: Imprenta Liberal. *Internet Archive*; https://archive.org/details/historiadelafun00cobogoog.
Cocteau, Jean. *Orphée*. 1926. *Tragedie en un acte et un intervalle*. Paris: Delamain et Boutellau.
Coello, Óscar, ed. 2001. *Los inicios de la poesía castellana en el Perú. Fuentes, estudio crítico y textos*. Lima: Fondo Editorial de la Pontificia Universidad Católica del Perú.
"Constitución política de Bolivia de 1826." *Archivio delle Costituzioni Storiche*. Università di Torino: Dipartimento di Scienze Giuridiche; http://www.dircost.unito.it/cs/docs/Bolivia%201826.htm.
Cornejo Polar, Antonio and José Antonio Mazzotti, eds. 2000. *Discurso en Loor de la Poesía. Estudio y edición*. Lima: Latinoamericana.
Corrales, Manuel Ezequiel. 1889. *Efemérides y anales del Estado de Bolívar*. Vol. 1. Bogotá: Casa editorial de J.J. Pérez.
Courcelles, Dominique de. 2003. "La conquête d'un savoir raisonnable : l'*Histoire naturelle et morale des Indes, tant Orientalles qu'Occidentalles* du P. jésuite José Acosta, 1598." In John Lyons and Cara Welch (eds.), *Le savoir au XVIIe siècle: actes du 34e congrès annuel de la North American Society for Seventeenth-Century French Literature, University of Virginia, Charlottesville, 14–16 mars 2002*, 312–21. Tübingen: Gunter Narr Verlag.
Covarrubias, Sebastián de. 1611. s.v. "historia." *Tesoro de la lengua castellana, o española. Nuevo tesoro lexicográfico de la lengua española. Real academia española*; http://ntlle.rae.es/ntlle/SrvltGUISalirNtlle.
Cruz, Nicolás and M. Gabriela Huidobro, eds. 2018. *América Latina y lo clásico; los clásico y América Latina*. Santiago de Chile: RIL Editores.
Cruzado y Aragón, Esteban. 1687a. "Mvda de abſorta..." (sonnet). In Valdés 1687, n.p.
Cruzado y Aragón, Esteban. 1687b. "A La Fama..." (sonnet). In Valdés 1687, n.p.

Curran, Charles E. 2013. "Thomas Aquinas and the Thomistic Tradition." *The Development of Moral Theology: Five Strands*, 31–72. Washington, DC: Georgetown University Press.

Cussen, Antonio. 1992. *Bello and Bolívar: Poetry and Politics in the Spanish American Revolution*. New York: Cambridge University Press.

Dante. 1991. *Commedia. Paradiso*. Ed. Anna Maria Chiavacci Leonardi. Milan: Armando Mondadori.

Dante. 2011. *The Divine Comedy of Dante Alighieri. Volume 3. Paradiso*. Trans. Robert M. Durling. New York: Oxford University Press.

Detienne, Marcel. 2003. *The Writing of Orpheus: Greek Myth in Cultural Context*. Trans. Janet Lloyd. Baltimore, MD: Johns Hopkins University Press.

Díaz González, José Joaquín. 1958. *El juramento de Simón Bolívar sobre el Monte Sacro*. Rome: Scuola salesiana del libro.

Diodorus Siculus. 1935. *Library of History. Volume 2. Books 2.35–4.58*. Bilingual ed. Trans. C. H. Oldfather. Cambridge, MA: Harvard University Press.

Diodorus Siculus. 2000. *Library of History. Volume 3. Books 4.59 to 8*. Bilingual ed. Trans. C. H. Oldfather. Cambridge, MA: Harvard University Press.

Dionysius of Halicarnassus. 1937. *Roman Antiquities. Books 1–2. Vol. 1*. Bilingual ed. Trans. Earnest Cary. Cambridge, MA: Harvard University Press.

Discurso sobre Virreyes y Gobernadores del Perú. c. 1600–50. In *Yndias de Birreyes y Gouernadores del Pirú c. 1600–50*.

Durán Montero, Maria Antonia. 1990. "La entrada en Lima del virrey D. García Hurtado de Mendoza, Marques de Cañete." *Laboratorio de arte* 3: 57–62; http://institucional.us.es/revistas/arte/03/04%20duran.pdf.

Durán Montero, Maria Antonia. 1994. *Lima en el siglo XVII. Arquitectura, urbanismo y vida cotidiana*. Seville: Diputación Provincial de Sevilla.

Durling, Robert M. 2011. In Dante 2011.

Earle, Rebecca. 2007. *The Return of the Native: Indians and Myth-Making in Spanish America, 1810–1930*. Durham, NC: Duke University Press.

"En el preciso momento en que la *Patria* se hallaba mas creida de su aliento, por un nuevo mal acaba de otorgar su testamento." 1818. *Gaceta Extraordinaria de Caracas*. March 16; http://www.bolivarium.usb.ve/pub/gaceta/1818/03/GacetadeCaracas16-03-1818_E_VII.pdf.

"Eruditissimo Patri Roderico de Valdès Limano . . ." 1687. In Valdés 1687, n.p.

Espinosa Pólit, Aurelio. 1980. *Olmedo en la historia y en las letras*. Quito: Casa de la Cultura Ecuatoriana.

Estabridis Cárdenas, Ricardo. 2002. *El grabado en Lima virreinal. Documento histórico y artístico (siglos XVI al XIX)*. Lima: Fondo Editorial de la Universidad Nacional Mayor de San Marcos.

Euripides. 2008. *Fragments. Aegeus-Meleager*. Bilingual ed. Trans. Christopher Collard and Martin Cropp. Cambridge, MA: Harvard University Press.

Fairclough, H. Rushton. 1950. In Virgil 1950.
Fairclough, H. Rushton. 1970. In Horace 1970.
"Falce minax..." (*epigramma*). 1687. In Valdés 1687, n.p.
Feijóo, Benito Jerónimo. (1726–40) 1924. *Teatro crítico universal*. Vol. 2. Madrid: Ediciones de La Lectura.
Fernández, Cristina Beatriz. 2017. "Un canto sibilino americano (sobre el *Discurso en loor de la poesía*)." *Revista Canadiense de Estudios Hispánicos* 42, no. 1: 25–49.
Fernández, Laura, Bernat Garí, Álex Gómez Romero, and Christian Snoey. 2016. *Clásicos para un nuevo mundo. Estudios sobre la tradición clásica en la América de los siglos XVI y XVII*. Madrid: Centro para la Edición de los Clásicos Españoles.
Firbas, Paul, ed. 2008. *Épica y colonia. Ensayos sobre el género épico en Iberoamérica (siglos XVI y XVII)*. Lima: Fondo Editorial de la UNMSM.
Fomperosa, Pedro de. 1687. "Aprobacion." In Valdés 1687, n.p.
Ford, Thayne. 1998. "Stranger in a Foreign Land: José de Acosta's Scientific Realizations in the Sixteenth Century Peru." *Sixteenth Century Journal* 29, no. 1: 19–33.
Fornoff, Frederick H. 2003. In Bolívar 2003.
Freese, John Henry. 1926. In Aristotle. 1926. *The "Art" of Rhetoric*.
Garabito de Leon y Messia, Francisco. 1687a. "Al Rey Nuestro Señor Don Carlos II. Emperador de las Indias, Rey de las Españas, Monarca Invicto de Ambos Mundos." Dedication. In Valdés 1687, n.p. (pagination from 1 to 6 suggested in citations).
Garabito de Leon y Messia, Francisco. 1687b. "Al Reverendissimo Padre Carlos de Noyelle." In Valdés 1687, n.p. (pagination from 1 to 6 suggested in citations).
Garabito de Leon y Messia, Francisco. 1687c. "Elegia." In Valdés 1687, n.p.
Garabito de Leon y Messia, Francisco. 1687d. "Prologo al lector." In Valdés 1687, n.p (pagination from 1 to 12 suggested in citations).
García, Gregorio. ((1606) 1725) 1981. *Origen de los indios del Nuevo Mundo*. Facsimile of the 2nd. ed. Ed. Franklin Pease. México D.F.: Fondo de Cultura Económica.
Garcilaso de la Vega, Inca. (1609) 2000. *Comentarios reales de los Incas*. Intro. José de la Riva Agüero. México D.F.: Porrúa.
Gardnier, Ruy. 1999. "*Orfeu*, de Carlos Diegues." *Contracampo. Revista de Cinema* 5; http://www.contracampo.com.br/01-10/orfeudecacadiegues.html.
Gasparini, Juan. 1984/1999. "Borges, poeta de todas las ciudades." Interview with Jorge Luis Borges, October 5. *El País*. August 21, 1999; https://elpais.com/diario/1999/08/22/cultura/935272801_850215.html.
Gil, Juan. 2008. "Diego Mexía, un perulero humanista perdido en los confines del mundo." In Jesús Ma. Nieto Ibañez and Raúl Manchón Gómez (eds.), *El humanismo español entre el viejo mundo y el nuevo*, 67–141. Jaén/León: Secretariado de Publicaciones, Universidad de León, and Servicio de Publicaciones, Universidad de Navarra.
Giletti, Ann. 2004. "Aristotle in Medieval Spain: Writers of the Christian Kingdoms Confronting the Eternity." *Journal of the Warburg and Courtauld Institutes* 67: 23–48.

Gobierno de España, Ministerio de Cultura y Deporte. 2010. "Archivo General de Indias." May 18. YouTube video, 15:28; https://www.youtube.com/watch?v=Z3PqkFM2vGY.

González de la Rosa, Manuel. 1882. "El Padre Cobo." In Cobo, *Historia de la fundación de Lima*, ii–xvi.

Gracia, Jorge J. E. 1994. "El escolasticismo: un puente entre la antigüedad clásica y el pensamiento colonial latinoamericano." In Isabel M. Ruscalleda et al. (eds.), *El impacto del humanismo en el Nuevo Mundo*, 14–46. Potomac: Scripta Humanistica.

Grammatico, Giuseppina. 1984. "El inquietante embrujo de la Potnia Erycina." *Semanas de estudios romanos* 2: 37–78.

Grammatico, Giuseppina, ed. 2003. *América Latina y lo Clásico*. 2 vols. Santiago de Chile: Sociedad Chilena de Estudios Clásicos.

Grases, Pedro and Manuel Pérez Vila. 1970. In Bolívar 1970.

Grasse, Jonathon. 2004. "Conflation and Conflict in Brazilian Popular Music: Forty years between 'filming' bossa nova in *Orfeu negro* and rap in *Orfeu*." *Popular Music* 23, no. 3: 291–310.

The Greek Anthology. 1917. Vol. 3. Bilingual ed. Ed. W. R. Paton. Cambridge, MA: Harvard University Press.

Guaman Poma de Ayala, Felipe. 1615/1616. "La villa rica enpereal de Potocchi" (illustration). *The Guaman Poma Website*. Copenhagen: Royal Library; http://www.kb.dk/permalink/2006/poma/1065/en/text/?open=idp594336.

Guibovich Pérez, Pedro. 2007. "Identidad criolla y proyecto político en el *Poema Hispano-Latino* de Rodrigo de Valdés." In M. Marzal and L. Bacigalupo (eds.), *Los jesuitas y la modernidad en Iberoamérica*, 356–67. Lima: Fondo Editorial PUCP / Universidad del Pacífico, IFEA.

Günther Doering, Juan. 1983. Introduction. *Planos de Lima, 1613–1983*. Lima: Municipalidad de Lima Metropolitana, Petróleos del Perú.

Haase, Wolfgang. 1994. "America and the Classical Tradition: Preface and Introduction." In Wolfgang Haase and Meyer Reinhold (eds), *The Classical Tradition and the Americas* (CTA). *Vol. I: European Images of the Americas and the Classical Tradition. Part 1*. Berlin: Walter de Gruyter.

Hampe, Teodoro. 1996. *Bibliotecas privadas en el mundo colonial*. Madrid: Iberoamericana.

Hampe, Teodoro, ed. 1999. *La tradición clásica en el Perú virreinal*. Lima: Fondo Editorial de la Universidad Nacional Mayor de San Marcos.

Hanna, Robert. 2005. *Greek and Roman Calendars: Constructions of Time in the Classical World*. London: Duckworth.

Hardwick, Lorna. 2003. *Reception Studies*. Cambridge: Cambridge University Press.

Hardwick, Lorna and Christopher Stray. 2008. "Introduction: Making Connections." In Lorna Hardwick and Christopher Stray (eds.), *A Companion to Classical Reception*, 1–9. London: Blackwell.

Hasse, Dag. 2014. "Influence of Arabic and Islamic Philosophy on the Latin West." In Edward N. Zalta (ed.), *The Stanford Encyclopedia of Philosophy*. Center for the Study of Language and Information; https://plato.stanford.edu/entries/arabic-islamic-influence/.

Hernández Muñoz, Felipe-G. 1998-9. "Encanto y desencanto griego en la obra de Bolívar." *Praesentia* 2, no. 3: 127-39.

Herodotus. 1926. *The Persian Wars*. Vol. 1. Bilingual ed. Trans. A. D. Godley. London: W. Heineman.

Hesiod. 1967. *Fragmenta Hesiodea*. Ed. R. Merkelbach and M. L. West. London: Oxford University Press.

Hesiod. 1995. *Hesiod. Homeric Hymns. Epic Cycle. Homerica*. Bilingual ed. Trans. Hugh G. Evelyn-White. Cambridge, MA: Harvard University Press.

"Hic vbi . . ." (*epigramma*). 1687. In Valdés 1687, n.p.

Highet, Gilbert. 1949. *The Classical Tradition: Greek and Roman Influences on Western Literature*. New York: Oxford University Press.

Holloway, Anne. 2013. "Sujetos periféricos, diálogos parnasianos: la voz femenina y la epístola en la poesía colonial." In Rodrigo Cacho Casal and Anne Holloway (eds.), *Los géneros poéticos del Siglo de Oro. Centros y periferias*, 233-52. Woodbridge, UK: Boydell and Brewer.

Homem de Mello, José Eduardo. 1976. "Vinicius de Moraes." In *Música popular brasileira*, 58-60. São Paulo: Melhoramentos.

Homer. 1960. *The Odyssey*. Vol. 1. Bilingual ed. Trans. A. T. Murray. Cambridge, MA: Harvard University Press.

Homer. 1999. *The Iliad*. 2 vols. Bilingual ed. Trans. A. T. Murray. Cambridge, MA: Harvard University Press

Horace. 1952. *The Odes and Epodes*. Bilingual ed. Trans. C. E. Bennett. Cambridge, MA: Harvard University Press.

Horace. 1970. *Satires, Epistles, Ars Poetica*. Bilingual ed. Trans. H. Rushton Fairclough. Cambridge, MA: Harvard University Press.

Hualde Pascual, Pilar. 2012. "Mito y tragedia griega en la literatura iberoamericana." *Cuadernos de filología clásica. Estudios griegos e indoeuropeos* 22. *Revistas científicas complutenses*; http://revistas.ucm.es/index.php/CFCG/article/view/39070.

Hubbard, Clyde. 1968. "Monedas coloniales de 1536 a 1732 / Colonial Coinage of Mexico. 1536-1732." *Artes de México* 103: 13-18; https://www.jstor.org/stable/24313038?seq=1.

Hyginus [Mythographus]. 2002. *Fabulae*. Ed. Peter K. Marshall. Berlin: De Gruyter.

Jobim, Antonio Carlos. 1958a. Letter to Vinicius de Moraes, September 22. In *Orfeu: o maior musical brasileiro* 2010, "Cartas Vinicius Tom."

Jobim, Antonio Carlos. 1958b. Letter to Vinicius de Moraes, September 27. In *Orfeu: o maior musical brasileiro* 2010, "Cartas Vinicius Tom."

Jobim, Antonio Carlos. 1965. Letter to Vinicius de Moraes, February 15. In *Orfeu: o maior musical brasileiro* 2010, "Cartas Vinicius Tom."

Jobim, Antonio Carlos. 1966. Letter to Vinicius de Moraes, December 10. In *Orfeu: o maior musical brasileiro* 2010, "Cartas Vinicius Tom."
Johns, Christopher M. S. 1998. *Antonio Canova and the Politics of Patronage in Revolutionary and Napoleonic Europe*. Berkeley: University of California Press.
Jones, Tom B. 1939. "The Classics in Colonial Hispanic America." *Transactions and Proceedings of the American Philological Association* 70: 37–45.
"José Félix Blanco." 2009. *Biografías de Venezuela*. *VenezuelaTuya.com*; https://www.venezuelatuya.com/biografias/blanco_jose_felix.htm.
Kadir, Djelal. 1992. *Columbus and the Ends of the Earth*. Berkeley: University of California Press.
Kadir, Djelal. 1995. "The Post of Coloniality." *Canadian Review of Comparative Literature / Revue Canadienne de Littérature Comparée*, September–December: 431–42.
Kadir, Djelal. 2011. *Memos from the Besieged City: Lifelines for Cultural Sustainability*. Stanford, CA: Stanford University Press.
Kohut, Kart and Sonia V. Rose, eds. 2000. *La formación de la cultura virreinal*, Vol. 1: *La etapa inicial*. Madrid: Iberoamericana–Vervuert.
Kristeller, Paul Oskar. 1961. *Renaissance Thought: The Classic, Scholastic, and Humanist Strains*. New York: Harper.
Laird, Andrew. 2006. *The Epic of America: An Introduction to Rafael Landivar's Rusticatio Mexicana*. London: Bloomsbury.
Laird, Andrew. 2007. "Latin America." In Craig W. Kallendorf (ed.), *A Companion to the Classical Tradition*, 222–36. Hoboken, NJ: Blackwell Publishing.
Laird, Andrew and Nicola Miller. 2018. *Antiquities and Classical Traditions in Latin America*. Chichester: Wiley.
Landazuri, Margarita. 2010. Review of *Black Orpheus*, dir. Marcel Camus. *Turner Classic Movies*; http://www.tcm.com/tcmdb/title/68912/Black-Orpheus/articles.html#03.
Lavalle, Juan Antonio de. 1861. "Un poema y un poeta nacional del siglo XVII." *La revista de Lima*, Vol. 3, 1–7. *Google Books*; https://books.google.com/books?id=t64oAAAAYAAJ&printsec=frontcover&source=gbs_ge_summary_r&cad=0#v=onepage&q&f=false.
Lawrence, Jeremy N. H. 1990. "Humanism in the Iberian Peninsula." In Anthony Goodman and Angus MacKay (eds.), *The Impact of Humanism on Western Europe*, 220–58. London: Longman.
Lecuna, Vicente. 1956. *Catálogo de errores y calumnias en la historia de Bolívar*. 3 vols. New York: Colonia Press.
Lee, Bertram T., ed. 1935. *Libros de Cabildos de Lima. Libro primero. Años 1534–1539*. Lima: Torres Aguirre.
Lewis, Charlton T. and Charles Short. 1879. s.v. "classicus." *A Latin Dictionary*. *Perseus Digital Library*; http://www.perseus.tufts.edu/hopper/text?doc=Perseus:text:1999.04.0059.

Liddell, Henry George, Robert Scott, and Henry Stuart Jones. 1940. *A Greek–English Lexicon, revised and augmented throughout by Sir Henry Stuart Jones, with the assistance of Roderick McKenzie.* Oxford: Clarendon Press.

Livy. 1919. *History of Rome.* Vol. 1. Bilingual ed. Trans. B. O. Foster. Cambridge, MA: Harvard University Press.

Lohmann Villena, Guillermo. 1964. *Las defensas militares de Lima y Callao.* Sevilla: Academia Nacional de la Historia del Perú. Escuela de Estudios Hispanoamericanos.

Lohmann Villena, Guillermo. 1999. "Huellas renacentistas en la literatura peruana del siglo XVI." *La tradición clásica en el Perú virreinal.* Lima: UNMSM, Fondo Editorial, 115–27.

Lopetegui, Leon. 1942. *El padre José de Acosta, S.I., y las misiones.* Madrid: Consejo Superior de Investigaciones Científicas.

López Férez, Juan Antonio, ed. 2009. *Mitos clásicos en la literatura española e hispanoamericana del siglo XX.* 2 vols. Madrid: Ediciones Clásicas.

López-Morillas, Frances M. 2002. In Acosta (1590) 2002.

Lupher, David. 2003. *Romans in a New World: Classical Models in Sixteenth-Century Spanish America.* Ann Arbor: University of Michigan Press.

Lynch, John. 2006. *Simón Bolívar: A Life.* New Haven, CT: Yale University Press.

MacCormack, Sabine. 2007. *On the Wings of Time: Rome, the Incas, Spain, and Peru.* Princeton, NJ: Princeton University Press.

Macrobius. 2011. *Saturnalia.* Vol. 1. Bilingual ed. Trans. Robert A. Kaster. Cambridge, MA: Harvard University Press.

Martindale, Charles. 2006. "Thinking through Reception." In Charles Martindale and Richard F. Thomas (eds.), *Classics and the Uses of Reception*, 1–14. Malden, MA: Blackwell.

Marx, Karl. 1990. *Capital.* Vol. 1. Trans. Ben Fowkes. London: Penguin.

Mazzotti, José Antonio. 1996. "Sólo la proporción es la que canta: Poética de la nación y épica criolla en la Lima del XVIII." *Revista de crítica literaria latinoamericana* 22, no. 43–4: 59–75.

Mazzotti, José Antonio. 2000. *Discurso en Loor de la Poesía.* See Cornejo Polar and Mazzotti 2010.

Mazzotti, José Antonio. 2009. "Épica Barroca y esplendor limeño en el siglo XVII: Rodrigo de Valdés y los límites del nacionalismo criollo." In Guillermo Serés and Mercedes Serna (eds.), *Los límites del océano: estudios filológicos de crónica y épica en el Nuevo Mundo*, 135–73. Barcelona: Universidad Autónoma de Barcelona.

Mazzotti, José Antonio. 2016. *Lima fundida. Épica y nación criolla en el Perú.* Madrid: Iberoamericana-Vervuert.

McGinn, Bernard. 2014. "The Tides of Thomism, 1275–1850." In Bernard McGinn, *Thomas Aquinas's Summa theologiae. A Biography*, 117–62. Princeton, NJ: Princeton University Press.

Medina, José Toribio. 1904. *La imprenta en Lima (1584–1824).* Vol. 1. Santiago de Chile. *Google Books*; https://books.google.com/books?id=tOdBAQAAMAAJ&lpg=PR73&

dq=jos%C3%A9%20medina%20pedro%20nolasco%20mere&pg=PP9#v=onepage&q&f=false.

Menéndez y Pelayo, Marcelino. 1894. *Antología de poetas hispano-americanos publicada por la Real Academia Española. Colombia-Ecuador-Perú-Bolivia*. Vol. 3. Madrid: n.p.

Messer, Neal A. and Jerry Williams, eds. 2017. *Poema Hyspano-Latino panegyrico de la fundación, y grandezas de la muy noble, y leal ciudad de Lima*. By Rodrigo de Valdés. New York: Peter Lang.

Mexía de Fernangil, Diego. (1608) 1990. *Primera parte del Parnaso antártico de obras amatorias*. Facsimile ed. and intro. by Trinidad Barrera. Rome: Bulzoni.

Mexía de Fernangil, Diego. 1617. *La segunda parte del Parnáso antártico de divinos Poemas*. Manuscript. Paris: Bibliothèque national de France, Département des manuscrits, Espagnol 389, *Gallica*; https://archivesetmanuscrits.bnf.fr/ark:/12148/cc350004.

Michels, Agnes Kirsopp. 1967. *The Calendar of the Roman Republic*. Princeton, NJ: Princeton University Press.

Monteagudo, Bernardo de. 1977. "Diálogo entre Atahualpa y Fernando VII en los Campos Elíseos." In José Luis Romero and Luis Alberto Romero (eds.), *Pensamiento político de la Emancipación*, 64–71. Caracas: Biblioteca Ayacucho.

Moraes, Vinicius de. 1963. Letter to Antonio Carlos Jobim, November 8. In *Orfeu: o maior musical brasileiro* 2010, "Cartas Vinicius Tom."

Moraes, Vinicius de. 1966. Letter to Antonio Carlos Jobim, November 22. In *Orfeu: o maior musical brasileiro* 2010, "Cartas Vinicius Tom."

Moraes, Vinicius de. 1967. *Orfeu da Conceição. Tragedia Carioca em três âtos*. 2nd ed. Rio de Janeiro: Dois Amigos.

Moraes, Vinicius de. 1970. Letter to Antonio Carlos Jobim, October 22. In *Orfeu: o maior musical brasileiro* 2010, "Cartas Vinicius Tom."

More, Anna. 2013. *Baroque Sovereignty: Carlos de Sigüenza y Góngora and the Creole Archive of Colonial Mexico*. Philadelphia: University of Pennsylvania Press.

Mugaburu, Josephe de. 1918. *Diario de Lima*. Transcribed by Horacio H. Urteaga and Carlos A. Romero. Part 2: *Colección de libros y documentos referentes a la historia del Perú*. Vol. 2. Lima: Imprenta y Librería Sanmarti y Ca. *Diarios, memorias, epistolarios de reyes, diplomáticos e historiadores*; www.alfredoalvar-estudiosdediariosymemorias.es/resultados-cientificos/2/DiariodeLima(1640-1694)deMugaburuporJouv%C3%A9/.

Murray, A. T. 1960. In Homer 1960.

Murray, A. T. 1999. In Homer 1999.

Navarra y Rocaful, Melchor de, Duke of Palata. 1687. Letter to Charles II, October 14. Manuscript. Archivo General de Indias, Sevilla. Signatura Lima, 299.

Navarra y Rocaful, Melchor de, Duke of Palata. (1689) 1859. "Relación del estado del Perú en los ocho años de su gobierno que hace el duque de la Palata al Excmo. Señor Conde de la Moncloba, su subcessor en los cargos de Virrey, Gobernador y Capitan General de estos Reynos del Peru, Tierrafirme y Chile, de que tomó posession el dia

16 de Agosto del año de 1689." *Memorias de los virreyes que han gobernado el Perú durante el tiempo del coloniaje español*. Vol. 2. Lima. *Internet Archive*, archive.org/details/memoriasdelosvir002peru.

Nolasco Mere, Pedro. 1685. *Plano de la ciudad de Lima*. Lima. Map. Archivo General de Indias, Sevilla. ES.41091.AGI/27.22//MP-PERU_CHILE,13BIS. *Portal de archivos españoles*; http://pares.culturaydeporte.gob.es/inicio.html.

Nolasco Mere, Pedro. 1687. *Plano de la ciudad de Lima*. Lima. Map. Archivo General de Indias, Sevilla. ES.41091.AGI/27.22//MP-PERU_CHILE,13. *Portal de archivos españoles*; http://pares.culturaydeporte.gob.es/inicio.html.

Obama, Barack. 2004. *Dreams From My Father: A Story of Race and Inheritance*. New York: Crown Publishers.

Ocaña, Diego de. 2010. *Viaje por el Nuevo Mundo: de Guadalupe a Potosí, 1599–1605*. Madrid: Iberoamericana.

OED (*Oxford English Dictionary*), 3rd ed., s.v. "annals." OED Online; https://www-oed-com.proxy006.nclive.org/view/Entry/7851?rskey=sHsPHy&result=2&isAdvanced=false.

OED (*Oxford English Dictionary*), 3rd ed., s.v. "classic." OED Online; https://www-oed-com.proxy006.nclive.org/view/Entry/33880?rskey=lh48G7&result=1&isAdvanced=false

OED (*Oxford English Dictionary*), 3rd ed., s.v. "classical." OED Online; https://www-oed-com.proxy006.nclive.org/view/Entry/33881?redirectedFrom=classical&.

O'Gorman, Edmundo. 1962. "Prólogo." In Acosta (1590) 1962: ix–liii.

Ojeda A., Ana Cecilia, G. Serafín Marínez, and M. Idania Ortiz. 2005. "Actualidad del relato bolivariano en la integración continental: *Mi delirio sobre el Chimborazo* o la sugestión prometeica." *Cahiers des Amériques latines* 50: 77–87; DOI: 10.4000/cal.8027.

O'Leary, Daniel Florencio. 1953. *Memorias*. 6 vols. Bogotá: Santafé.

Oliveira, Celso de. 2002. "*Orfeu da Conceição*: Variations on a Classical Myth." *Hispania* 85, no. 3: 449–54.

Olmedo, José Joaquín de. 1945. *Obras completas. Poesías*. Ed. Aurelio Espinosa Pólit. Quito: Casa de la Cultura Ecuatoriana.

Olmedo, José Joaquín de. 1960. *Epistolario*. Ed. Aurelio Espinosa Pólit. Puebla: J. M. Cajica.

Orfeu (feature film). 1999. Dir. Carlos Diegues. New Yorker, 2002. DVD.

Orfeu negro (feature film). 1958. Dir. Marcel Camus. Home Vision, 1990. Videocassette.

Orfeu: o maior musical brasileiro. 2010. VM Empreendimentos; http://www.showbras.com.br/orfeu/.

Orphée (feature film). 1950. Dir. Jean Cocteau. 1950. The Criterion Collection, 2003. DVD.

Ortiz, José Joaquín. 1857. Introduction. In Vargas Tejada 1857, iii–vii.

Osorio, Alejandra. 2008. *Inventing Lima: Baroque Modernity and Peru's South Sea Metropolis*. New York: Palgrave.

Ovid. 1914. *Heroides. Amores.* Trans. Grant Showerman. Cambridge, MA: Harvard University Press.
Ovid. 1992. *Metamorphoses. Books V–VIII.* Trans. D. E. Hill. Warminster: Aris & Phillips Ltd.
Ovid. 1996. *Tristia. Ex Ponto.* Bilingual ed. Trans. Arthur Leslie Wheeler. Cambridge, MA: Harvard University Press.
Ovid. 1999. *The Art of Love and Other Poems.* Bilingual ed. Trans. J. H. Mozley. Revised J. P. Goold. Cambridge, MA: Harvard University Press.
Oviedo y Herrera, Luis Antonio de. 1711. *Vida de Sta. Rosa de Santa Maria, Natvral de Lima, y Patrona del Peru. Poema heroyco.* Madrid, por Juan Garcia Infançon. *Google Books*; https://books.google.es/books?id=1_FFAAAAcAAJ&hl=es&pg=PP3#v=onepage&q&f=false.
Palaephatus. 1996. *On Unbelievable Tales.* Bilingual ed. Trans. Jacob Stern. Wauconda: Bolchazy-Carducci Publishers.
Palata, Duke of. In Navarra y Rocaful, Melchor de, 1687 and (1689) 1859.
Parodi, Claudia. 2008. "El lenguage de las fiestas: arcos triunfales y villancicos." *Destiempos* 3, no. 14; http://www.destiempos.com/n14/parodi.pdf.
Pease, Franklin. 1981. Introduction. In García ((1606) 1725) 1981: i–xli.
Peralta y Barnuevo, Pedro de. 1732. *Lima fundada, o conquista del Perú.* 2 vols. Lima: Imprenta de Francisco Sobrino y Bados. *Internet Archive*; https://archive.org/details/limafundadaoconq00pera.
Pérez Vila, Manuel. 1971. *La formación intelectual del Libertador.* Caracas: Departamento de Publicaciones, Ministerio de Educación.
Perilli, Carmen. 2004–5. "Los enigmas de una dama y la fundación de la crítica latinoamericana: el 'Discurso en loor de la poesía.'" *Etiópicas* 1: 130–43.
Perrone, Charles A. 2001. "Myth, Melopeia, and Mimesis: *Black Orpheus, Orfeu,* and Internationalization in Brazilian Popular Music." In Charles A. Perrone and Christopher Dunn (eds.), *Brazilian Popular Music and Globalization,* 46–71. Gainesville: University Press of Florida.
Peru de Lacroix, Luis. 1924. *Diario de Bucaramanga, o vida pública y privada del Libertador Simón Bolívar.* Madrid: Editorial América. *Banco de la República, Biblioteca Virtual. Colombia,* http://babel.banrepcultural.org/cdm/ref/collection/p17054coll10/id/3172.
Pindar. 1997a. *Nemean Odes. Isthmian Odes. Fragments.* Bilingual ed. Trans. William. H. Race. Cambridge, MA: Harvard University Press.
Pindar. 1997b. *Olympian Odes. Pythian Odes.* Bilingual ed. Trans. William H. Race. Cambridge, MA: Harvard University Press.
Plato. 2003. *The Republic. Books I–V.* Bilingual ed. Trans. Paul Shorey. Cambridge, MA: Harvard University Press.
Pliny. 1938. *Natural History. Volume I: 1–2.* Bilingual ed. Trans. H. Rackham. Cambridge, MA: Harvard University Press.

Pliny. 1942. *Natural History. Volume II: 3–7.* Ed. H. Rackham. Bilingual ed. Cambridge, MA: Harvard University Press.

Plutarch. 1919. *Lives. Vol. VII. Demosthenes and Cicero. Alexander and Caesar.* Bilingual ed. Trans. Bernadotte Perrin. Cambridge, MA: Harvard University Press.

Plutarch. 1998. *Lives. Vol. I. Theseus and Romulus. Lycurgus and Numa. Solon and Publicola.* Bilingual ed. Trans. Bernadotte Perrin. Cambridge, MA: Harvard University Press.

Pomeroy, Sarah B. 2002. *Spartan Women.* Oxford: Oxford University Press.

Quadro, Francisco de. 1687. "Carta de edificación." In Valdés 1687: §1–§XI.

Quintilian. 2001. *The Orator's Education.* Vol. 4. Bilingual ed. Trans. Donald Russell. Cambridge, MA: Harvard University Press.

Race, William H. 1997a. In Pindar 1997a.

Race, William H. 1997b. In Pindar 1997b.

Rackham, H. 1938. In Pliny 1938.

Rackham, H. 1942. In Pliny 1942.

Ramos Sosa, Rafael. 1992. *Arte festivo en Lima virreinal (siglos XVI–XVII).* Sevilla: Junta de Andalucía.

Rivers, Elías L. 1996. "La alabanza de la poesía." *Revista de crítica literaria latinoamericana* 22, no. 43–4: 11–16.

Rodríguez Demorizi, Emilio. 1966. *Poetas contra Bolívar. El Libertador a través de la calumnia.* Madrid: Gráficas Reunidas.

Rodríguez Garrido, José Antonio. 2011. "La égloga *El Dios Pan* de Diego Mexía Fernangil y la evangelización en los Andes a inicios del siglo XVII." In *Manierismo y transición al Barroco. Memoria del III Encuentro Internacional sobre Barroco,* 307–19. Pamplona: Fundación Visión Cultural / Servicio de Publicaciones de la Universidad de Navarra.

Rojas, Arístides. 1891. *Leyendas históricas de Venezuela. Segunda serie.* Caracas: Imprenta y litografía del Gobierno Nacional.

Rojas Otálora, Jorge E. "Bolívar y Olmedo: el epinicio griego y la *Victoria de Junín.*" In Bocchetti 2010b, 77–92.

Rolfe, John C. 1959. See Aelius Donatus 1959.

Rolfe, John C. 1967. See Aulius Gellius 1967.

"Rome Italy Simón Bolívar Statue." 1934. Photograph, May 13. *Tribune Photo Archives* (no longer operational).

Rose, Sonia. 1999. "'Un latinista andaluz indianizado': Diego Mexía de Fernangil y la translación de la cultura humanística al Nuevo Mundo." In *Passar as fronteiras. II Colóquio Internacional sobre Mediadores Culturais. Séculos XV a XVIII,* 395–406. Lagos: Centro de Estudos Gil Eanes.

Rosenthal, Earl E. 1971. "Plus Ultra, Non Plus Ultra, and the Columnar Device of Emperor Charles V. *Journal of the Warburg and Courtauld Institutes* 34: 204–28.

Rosenthal, Earl E. 1973. "The Invention of the Columnar Device of Emperor Charles V at the Court of Burgundy in Flanders in 1516." *Journal of the Warburg and Courtauld Institutes* 36: 198–230.

Ruiza, Miguel, ed. 2010. "Luis Vargas Tejada." *Biografías y vidas*; https://www.biografiasyvidas.com/biografia/v/vargas_tejada.htm.

Ruiz Pérez, Pedro. 1991. "Composiciones hispano-latinas del siglo XVI: los textos de Fernán Pérez de Oliva y Ambrosio de Morales." *Criticón* 52: 111–39. *Centro Virtual Cervantes*; https://cvc.cervantes.es/literatura/criticon/PDF/052/052_113.pdf.

Samuel, Alan E. 1972. *Greek and Roman Chronology: Calendars and Years in Classical Antiquity*. Munich: C.H. Beck.

Sartre, Jean-Paul. 1969. "Orphée Noir." In Léopold Sédar Senghor (ed.), *Anthologie de la nouvelle poésie nègre et malgache de langue française*. 2nd. ed., ix–xliv. Paris: Presses Universitaires de France.

Sena, Isabel de. 2002. See Veloso 2002.

Serrera Contreras, Ramón María and María Salud Elvás Iniesta. 2015. "Grabados y grabadores en la *Relación histórica del viaje a la América meridional* (1748) de Jorge Juan y Antonio de Ulloa." *Antonio de Ulloa. La biblioteca de un ilustrado*. Sevilla: Universidad de Sevilla.

Servius (Maurus Servius Honoratus). 1878. *Servii Grammatici qui fervntvr in Vergilii carmina commentarii. Vol. I. Fasc. I. Aeneidos librorum I–III Commentarii*. Ed. Georgius Thilo and Hermannus Hagen. Leipzig: n.p. *Google Books*; https://books.google.com/books?id=YvQUAAAAQAAJ&lpg=PA1&ots=5JnW3Y30lT&dq=LIBRVM%20PRIMVM%20COMMENTARIVS&pg=PR1#v=onepage&q—oenia&f=false.

Stockdale, James Bond. 1995. "On Public Virtue." In James Bond Stockdale, *Thoughts of a Philosophical Fighter Pilot*, 74–83. Stanford, CA: Hoover Institution Press.

Stok, Fabio. 2007–8. "Sulpicius Apollinaris / Carthaginiensis: un'identità problematica." *Incontri triestini di filologia classica* 7: 201–18. Università degli Studi di Trieste. *Open StarTs*; http://hdl.handle.net/10077/2834.

Strabo. 1923. *Geography. Volume II. Books 3–5*. Bilingual ed. Trans. Horace Leonard Jones. Cambridge, MA: Harvard University Press.

Taboada, Hernán G. H. 2014. "Centauros y eruditos: los clásicos en la Independencia." *Latinoamerica. Revista de Estudios Latinoamericanos* 59: 193–221; https://www.sciencedirect.com/journal/latinoamerica-revista-de-estudios-latinoamericanos/vol/59/suppl/C.

Tauro, Alberto. 1948. *Esquividad y gloria de la Academia Antártica*. Lima: Huascarán.

Thomas, Lucien-Paul. 1909. *Le lyricism et la préciosité cultistes en Espagne. Étude historique et analytique*. Halle: Max Niemeyer. *BnF Gallica*; https://gallica.bnf.fr/ark:/12148/bpt6k24819z/f1.image.

Tord, Luis Enrique. 1999. "La Atlántida, Platón, y los cronistas del Perú." In Hampe 1999, 36–45.

Torres de Mendoza, Luis. 1867. *Colección de documentos inéditos, relativos al descubrimiento, conquista y organización de las antiguas posesiones españolas de America y Oceanía, sacados de los Archivos del Reino, y muy especialmente del de Indias*. Vol. 8. Madrid: Imprenta de Frías y compañía. *Google Books*;

https://ia801409.us.archive.org/11/items/coleccindedocum20ultrgoog/coleccindedocum20ultrgoog.pdf.

Torres Lanzas, Pedro. 1906. *Relación descriptiva de los mapas, planos, etc. del virreinato del Perú (Perú y Chile) existentes en el Archivo General de Indias (Sevilla)*. Barcelona: Imprenta Henrich and Ca. *Google Books*; https://books.google.com/books?id=SroCAAAAYAAJ&printsec=frontcover&source=gbs_ge_summary_r&cad=0#v=onepage&q&f=false.

Tredennick, Hugh. 1962. In Aristotle 1962.

Valdés, Rodrigo de. 1687. *Poema heroyco hispano-latino panegyrico de la fvndacion, y grandezas de la muy Noble, y Leal Ciudad de Lima. Obra postvuma del M.R.P.M Rodrigo de Valdés, de la Compañia de Jesvs, Cathedratico de Prima jubilado, y Prefecto Regente de Estudios en el Colegio Maximo de San Pablo*. Madrid: Imprenta de Antonio Roman.

Vargas Tejada, Luis. 1857. *Poesías de Caro i Vargas Tejada*. Vol. 2. Ed. José Joaquín Ortiz. Bogotá: Imprenta de Ortiz. *Banco de la República, Biblioteca Virtual. Colombia*; http://babel.banrepcultural.org/cdm/ref/collection/p17054coll10/id/3184.

Vargas Ugarte, Rubén. 1968. *Ensayo de un diccionario de artífices de la América meridional. Segunda edición corregida y aumentada*. Burgos: Imprenta de Aldecoa.

Varro. 1999. *On the Latin Language. Books V-VII*. Bilingual ed. Trans. Roland G. Kent. Cambridge, MA: Harvard University Press.

Vélez-Sainz, Julio. 2010. "De traducciones y *translationes*: la fundación de un sistema literario en la Academia Antártica de Diego Mexía y Clarinda." *Neophilologus* 94, no. 1: 55–66.

Veloso, Caetano. 1997. *Verdade tropical*. São Paulo: Schwarcz.

Veloso, Caetano. 2002. *Tropical Truth: A Story of Music and Revolution in Brazil*. Trans. Isabel de Sena. New York: Alfred A. Knopf.

Vinatea, Martina. 2012. "Catalina María Doria y las escritoras del siglo XVII." In Stefano Tedeschi and Sergio Botta (eds.), *Rumbos del hispanismo en el umbral del cincuentenario de la AIH*, 91-7. Rome: Bagatto Libri.

Vinatea, Martina. 2016. "¿Clarinda o Clorinda? El *Discurso en loor de la poesía* y la fortuna de una errata." In Leonardo Funes (ed.), *Hispanismos del mundo. Diálogos y debates en (y desde) el Sur. Anexo digital—sección IV*, 161-9. Buenos Aires: Miño y Dávila.

Vinatea, Martina. 2017. "La dignificación de las lenguas imperiales en el *Poema Hispano-Latino* de Rodrigo de Valdés." In Mariela Insúa and Jesús Menéndez Peláez (eds.), *Viajeros, crónicas de indias y épica colonial*, 195–205. New York: IDEA.

Vinatea, Martina, ed. 2018. *Fundación y grandezas de la muy noble y muy leal Ciudad de los Reyes de Lima*. By Rodrigo de Valdés. New York: IDEA.

Vinicius de Moraes. n.d. V.M. Emprendimentos Artísticos e Culturais LTDA; http://www.viniciusdemoraes.com.br/pt-br.

Virgil. 1950. *Eclogues. Georgics. Aeneid I-VI*. Bilingual ed. Trans. H. Rushton Fairclough. Cambridge, MA: Harvard University Press.

"Vnius ecce . . ." (*epigramma*). 1687. In Valdés 1687, n.p.
Vordam, Jeff. 2000. Review of *Orfeu*, dir. Carlos Diegues. *About Film.com*; https://aboutfilm.com/movies/o/orfeu.htm.
Waldseemüller, Martin. (1507) 1966. *Cosmographiae introductio*. Saint-Dié, 1507. Facsimile ed. Trans. Joseph Fischer and Franz von Wieser. Ann Arbor: University Microfilms.
Watanabe, José. 2006. "El otro Asterión." In *Banderas detrás de la niebla*, 55–9. Lima: Peisa.
West, Delno and August Kling. 1991. "Intellectual and Cultural Background of Christopher Columbus." In Delno West and August Kling (eds.), *The Libro de las Profecías of Christopher Columbus*, 7–40. Gainesville: University of Florida Press.
West, M. L. 1983. *The Orphic Poems*. New York: Oxford University Press.
Wheeler, Arthur Leslie. 1996. See Ovid 1996.
Woolard, Kathryn A. and E. Nicholas Genovese. 2007. "Strategic Bivalency in Latin and Spanish in Early Modern Spain." *Language in Society* 36, no. 4: 487–509.
Yndias de Birreyes y Gouernadores del Pirú [listed as *Discurso sobre Virreyes y Gobernadores del Perú*]. *c*. 1600–50. Madrid: Biblioteca Nacional de España, Manuscript 2585. *Biblioteca Digital Hispánica*; bdh.bne.es/bnesearch/detalle/bdh0000116605.

Index

Academia Antártica 67–68, 70
Acosta, José de 24–25, 35–50, 64, 68–71, 138, 211
Addison, Joseph 161
'Admirable Campaign' 140, 140n.10
'Ad Urbem Limam Americae Meridionalis Regiam' 116–17
'Advertencia al lector' (Acosta) 46
Aeneas
    and his father Anchises 125, 211, 213, 223–24
    and half-brother Eryx 221
    hero of Virgilian epic 74, 80–84
    katabatic journey of 227
    'l'antico' 219
    relocation in Lima 176–77
    story of 93–96
    and the Trojan women 222
Aeneid (Virgil)
    and Aeneas 80–84
    and Anchises 123–24, 211, 221–26
    and comparisons with *Fundación y Grandezas* 102–6
    introduction 26, 28
    and Mexia 59
    Rome and Lima through the eyes of 92–97
    and the Trojans 219
Age of Revolution 133, 135, 151, 153, 169, 171–72, 211
Ajax 135
aletheia 69
Altiplano 59
ALC *América Latina y lo Clásico* (Chilean Society of Classical Studies)
América Latina y lo Clásico (Chilean Society of Classical Studies) 13–14, 209, 209n.1
América Latina y lo clásico (conference) 28, 212

América Latina y lo clásico; lo clásico y América Latina (ed. Cruz/Huidobro) 14, 209n.1
Anchises 74, 81–82, 123–25, 145, 211, 213, 215, 221–23
Androtion of Athens 206
Andújar, Rosa 15
Angelelli, Guillermo 183
Anglo-Spanish War (1595–1604) 60
Angostura Address 159
Anhembi (journal) 188
'The Annals of Buenos Aires' 179
Anne, Saint 51
Antarctic 24–25, 70–72, 117n.63
Anthologie de la Nouvelle Poésie Nègre et Malgache (Sartre) 186
Antigone 184, 184n.5
Antipater of Thessalonica 66
Antiquities and Classical Tradition in Latin America (ed. Laird/Miller) 14–15
antonomasias 8
A origem dos meus sonhos see *Dreams From My Father* (Obama)
Apollo 61, 63, 65–66
Apollodorus 130, 180, 182, 184
'Aprobacion' (Fomperosa) 105
Arabic scholarship 9, 9n.7
Aragua valley 156
Araucos 50
Archivo General de Indias 1, 88n.23
Archytas of Tarentum 35
Argentina 23, 179, 209
Ariadne 182–83
Arias, Enrique Desmond 201
aristeia 136
Aristotle
    commentaries on, written in Mexico 11
    concept of the 'torrid zone' 138
    and Horace 144

introduction 8, 25
  and José de Acosta 34–40, 42, 44–47, 44n.9, 49–50, 70
Armas Antárticas (Zuázola) 70
Ars poetica (Horace) 143–44, 147
Atahualpa 112, 147–48
Athens 34, 133, 180, 206
Atlantis 184
Attic Nights (Aulus Gellius) 17–18, 18n.13
Augustus, Emperor 21, 52, 82, 96, 102–4, 123, 151–53, 156, 222–23
Aulus Gellius 17–18, 18n.13
avatars
  Acosta, the Elder 36–50
  Antarctic Ovid 50–62
  austral muse 62–68
  conclusions 68–72
  introduction 25
  preliminaries 31–36
Ayacucho, Battle of 133–36, 139, 141–46, 148–50, 160, 163, 172
Ayax-cuco 134–35
Aztecs 37
Azuero, Vicente 164, 167–68

Bacchyllides 182
Bakhtin, Mikhail 38
Balboa, Miguel Cabello de 70
Banderas detrás de la niebla (Watanabe) 183
Barnard, Timothy 193
Barrera, Trinidad 51
Battle of Boyacá 159
batucadas 188
Bello, Andrés 140, 151, 156
Blanco, José Félix 153–54, 154n.19
Bocchetti, Carla 14
Boeotia 65, 65n.30
Bogotá 127–29, 155–56, 159, 164–66
Boileau-Despraux, Nicolas 138–39, 146
Bolívar, Fernando 169
Bolívar, María Antonia 157–59, 158n.22
Bolívar, Simón
  and Classical motifs 227
  conclusions 169–73, 170n.28, 171n.29
  conspiracy against 150–69, 155n.21
  determining appearance of 127–29, 127n.1

fashioning of Classical *dramatis personae* 211
heroes and monsters 177
his role in the revolution 130–34, 133n.6
introduction 15, 24, 26–27
and victory in Battle of Ayacucho 135–50, 139nn.8-9, 147n.16
Bolivia 133, 147, 159, 163, 209, 213
Bolivian Constitution (1826) 159
Borges, Jorge Luis 27, 178–85, 178n.3, 207, 211
'Borges y yo' (Borges) 179
Borja, Juan de 59
bossa nova 192, 192n.9
Botero, Giovanni 76
Brazil
  cinematography of 200
  internationalization of rhythms 193
  and myth of Orpheus 27, 177–78, 185–87, 190–91, 199, 204, 206–7, 211, 227
  and *Orfeu negro* 195–96, 203
Briesemeister, Dietrich 99n.38, 104n.42, 108, 120
British Empire 129
Broc, Numa 41
Bruno, Giordano 69
Bruno, Lenita 197
Brutus 166, 168, 173
Buenaventura de Salinas, Fray 102
Buenos Aires 150, 184
Bye Bye Brasil (film) 200
Byzantium *see* Constantinople

Cabrera, Jorge 183
Cadiz 60
Caesar, Julius *see* Julius Caesar
calamus (Ovid) 55
Calends of March 215–16
Calvin, John 63
Camões, Luís de 65
Campbell, Colonel Patrick 171
Camus, Marcel 185, 192–98, 200, 203–5, 207
Cañete, marquis of *see* Don García
Cañizares-Esguerra, Jorge 37
Canova, Antonio 129
'Canto a Bolívar' (Olmedo) 142–43, 148
captatio benevolentiae 57

Caracas 133
Carioca *morros* 188–89, 191–94, 200–201, 207–8
Carlyle, Thomas 169
Caro, Miguel Antonio 14
'Carta de Jamaica' (Bolívar) 133, 170
Carthage 83, 93, 95–96, 221
'Casa tomada' (Cortázar) 179
Castany Prado, Bernat 53, 58, 60
Castillo, Manuel del 153
Catalogue of Women 182
Catholicism 42, 112–13, 117, 120, 203
Catiline 157
Cato, A Tragedy (Addison) 161
'Catón en Útica' (Tejada) 161–65
Cato the Younger 161–69
caudillismo 130
Cesaire, Senghor and Aimé 186–87
Chang-Rodríguez, Raquel 61, 67, 67n.33
Charles II, King of England 112
Charles II, King of Spain 88, 91–92, 96, 98
Charles V, King of Spain 2–3, 55, 217, 228
Château de Valençay 147
Chile 14, 28, 78, 87, 151, 213–14
Chilean Society of Classical Studies 209
Chimborazo mountain 171
chorographers
    conclusions 121–25
    introduction 25
    Pedro Nolasco Mere 85–98
    preliminaries 73–84, 74n.3, 77n.6
    Rodrigo de Valdés 98–121
Christianity 9, 61, 63, 124
Chuquisaca 147
Cicero 11, 118, 122, 132, 157
Ciofano, Ercole 54
civitas 94
Clairis, Christos 216
Clarinda 25, 36, 51–53, 62–63, 66–71, 176–77, 211
Clásicos para un nuevo mundo (ed. Fernández/Garí/Romero/Snoe) 15
The Classical Tradition. Greek and Roman Influences on Western Literature (Highet) 20–21
'The Classical Tradition and The Americas' (Jones) 12–13, 19, 22
'The Classics in Colonial Hispanic America' (Jones) 10

classicum 21
classicus 17–18, 22
Cobo, Bernabé 26, 121–23
Cocteau, Jean 186–87, 207
coda: pedagogues
    back to Erice 219
    monuments to the origin 213–19
    preliminaries 209–13
Cologne 110
Colombia 137, 153, 157–59
Columbus, Christopher 32–33, 42, 227
Comentarios reales (Garcilaso) 35, 44, 105, 145
Commedia (Dante) 62
A Companion to the Classical Tradition (Blackwell) 14
condis 116
Constantine, Emperor 219
Constantinople 219
'Constitución Boliviana' (Bolívar) 133
Contracampo (Gardnier) 201
Córdoba, General José María 137
Cortázar, Julio 179–80, 184
Covarrubias, Sebastián de 43
Creole archive 78
The Cretans 182
Crete 181
criollo identities 99, 120, 131
Cromwell, Oliver 112
Cronos 21
Cruzado y Ferrer, Esteban 118, 120
Cruz, Nicolás 14
CTA *see* 'Classical Tradition and The Americas' (Jones)
Cuba 23
Cussen, Antonio 150–51, 153
Cuzco 78, 95, 105

Daedalus 182
Dante 62, 65, 218–19
Dawn, Marpessa 193
Delia suscitas de Pulvere populum 79, 79n.12
Delius 61
Demorizi, Rodríguez 152–53, 152n.18, 161
De natura Orbi Novis (Acosta) 37, 42–43, 46
De Procuranda Indorum Salute (Acosta) 37, 37n.4

desaevio 59
Detienne, Marcel 233
'Diálogo' (Monteagudo) 147–48
Diario de Lima (Mugaburu) 87
Diego de Ocaña, Fray 77
Diegues, Carlos 27, 185, 200–205, 207
Diodorus Siculus 182
Dionysus 130
'Discurso de Angostura' (Bolívar) 133
Discurso en loor de la poesía (Clarinda) 25, 36, 51, 62–67
'"doctor Figueroa' 65
Don Andrés 78–80, 82
Donatus 104–5
Don García 73–74, 76, 78–80, 82–85, 92, 122
Don Juan de Villela 54
Dreams From My Father (Obama) 204
dubitatio 65
Dupin, Auguste 170

Eclogues (Virgil) 151
Ecuador 133, 159, 171–72
El Aleph (Borges) 181
'El autor a sus amigos' *see* Mexía de Fernangil, Diego
El Conductor (newspaper) 164
El Desengaño (newspaper) 157
El Dios Pan see Mexía de Fernangil, Diego
El divino Narciso (Inés de la Cruz) 131
Eliade, Mircea 226
El Inca Garcilaso de la Vega 35, 38, 78
'El inquietante embrujo de la Potnia Erycina' (Grammatico) 212
El rapto de Proserpina y sueño de Endimión (Medrano) 131
Elysian Fields 147–48, 211, 222
Empresas morales 59
Encyclic Culture 45
Enlightenment 108, 130
Epigramma 115
epinikia 144
Epistula ad Pisones (Horace) 141
Epistulae ex Ponto (Ovid) 56
Ercilla y Zúñiga, Alonso de 50
Erice 215–16, 218–21, 227–28
'Ervditissimo Patri' 118
Eryx 221
Esquilache, Prince of 58–59

ethos 38
Euclid 140
Euripides 182

Fame (goddess) 64
favelas 201–3
Feijóo, Benito Jerónimo 42, 48–49
Ferdinand VII, King of Spain 147–48
Férez, José Antonio López 15, 175
Fernández, Laura 15
Figueroa, Diego de Ávalos y 70
Flavian dynasty 47
Fomperosa, Pedro de 105–6
Ford, Thayne 38, 38n.6
France
    cultural and ideological influence of 129
    and Napoleon 157–58
    and *Orfeu negro* premier 195
    Orphic tradition of 186–87
    parallel of invasion of Spain 147
    war with Spain 88
Freire-Filho, Aderbal 204
Fundación y grandezas de la ciudad de Lima (Mere) 26
Fundación y Grandezas (Valdés) 84, 98–121, 99nn.35-8, 100nn.39-40, 109n.48, 111n.52
fundis 116

Gaceta de Caracas (newspaper) 156
Gaius Plinius Secundus *see* Pliny the Elder
Garabito de Leon, Francisco 101–7, 104n.42, 105n.43, 109nn.47, 49, 111n.51, 112–15, 119–20
García, Gregorio 32–35, 68–71
Garcilaso de la Vega, Inca 44, 95, 105, 145
Gardnier, Ruy 201–3
Garí, Bernat 15
Garrido, Rodríguez 52, 61
Gasparini, Juan 178–81, 183–84
Geats 58
Georgics (Virgil) 151, 208
Gerbi, Antonello 33
Germantown Academy, Pennsylvania 169
Gery on 2, 221
Gilberto, João 187
Gilbert, Ray 197
Gil, Juan 60–61

Gordine, Sacha 192
Goya, Francisco de 147
Grammatico, Amari 14, 211–12, 220–21, 223–27
Gran Colombia 159
Grasse, Jonathon 185, 201
Great Colombia project 133
Greece
  lyric poets in 144
  and mythography 180, 207
  and Orpheus myth 186, 206–7
  Orphic *katabasis* 189
  and Tiresias 145
  tragedies of 175
  and the Underworld 152
Greeks and Romans on the Latin American Stage (ed. Andújar/Nikoloutsos) 15
Guadalquivir river 1
Guaman Poma, Felipe 3–4, 145
Guanabara bay 188
Guanahani 32
Guatemala 23
Guibovich Pérez, Pedro 106–7
Gulf of Papagayo 55
Günther Doering, Juan 91
Guyana 166

Haase, Wolfgang 12–13, 19–22, 22n.16
Halicarnassus 130
Hardwick, Lorna 16
Hegel, Georg Wilhelm Friedrich 176
Heliconian Muses 64
Henry IV, King of France 48
Heracles 2, 3, 5, 9, 221
Herodotus 9, 48
Heroides (Ovid) 25, 51–52, 56, 60–62, 66
Hesiod 21, 182–83, 207
Highet, Gilbert 20–22, 22n.16, 210
Historia de la fundación de Lima (Cobo) 26, 121–22
Historia general y natural de las Indias (Oviedo) 41
Historia naturalis (Pliny) 11
Historia natural y moral de las Indias (Acosta) 25, 35–43, 46–50, 68–69, 138
History of our own Times 48
Holy Roman Empire 98, 110
Homem de Mello, José Edwards 188
Homer 11, 50, 136, 138–40, 149, 223

Horace 130, 141–44, 143n.12, 146, 148–50
Huayna Capac 136, 144, 146, 148, 172
Huidobro, María Gabriela 14
Hurtado de Mendoza, Garciá *see* Don Garciá
Hurtado de Mendoza, Don Andrés *see* Don Andrés
Hyginus 182

Iberian–Latin American Federation of Classical Studies 215
Ibis (Ovid) 51
Ibn Rushd 8–9
Ides of March 153
The Iliad 138, 142, 154, 164, 218
Incas
  and Bolívar 138
  defeat at Vilcabamba 47–48
  execution of Atahualpa 112
  fate of Empire of 38, 147–48, 147n.16
  imposing structures of 78
  introduction 3, 15
  and Mexía de Fernangil 61
  and Olmedo 146–47
  and Pichincha volcano 124
  practices of 37
  and the prophecy motif 125
  and the Spanish conquistadors 124, 145
Indiano poets 2, 65
Inés de la Cruz, Sor Juana 131
Iniesta, María Salud 91
Inquisition 69
Institutio oratoria (Quintilian) 144
Inventing Lima (Osorio) 76
Iphigenia 184, 184n.5
Isabella Jagiellon, Queen 54
Italy 93, 113

Jiménez, Salvador 165
Jobim, Antônio Carlos 24, 27, 187, 192, 195–99, 204–5, 207
Jones, Tom B. 10–12, 14
Julius Caesar 35, 81, 133–34, 153, 158, 161–64, 167–69, 172–73
Junín, Battle of 14–15, 132–33, 136–39, 141–42, 145–46, 148, 150, 172
Juno 93
Jupiter 93–94, 96, 98, 223
Justinian, Emperor 219

Kadir, Djelal 9n.9, 32n.1, 69, 132n.4
Kalevala 32
katabasis 123, 223, 227
Kristeller, Paul Oskar 8

La Araucana (Ercilla y Zúñiga) 50
'La casa de Asterión' (Borges) 27, 178–83, 207
La influencia clásica en América Latina (ed. Bocchetti) 14
Laird, Andrew 14–15
l'antico 219
Latin American Federation of Classical Studies 28
laudatio artium 51
Lavdes 118
'la verdadera Poesia' (Mexía de Fernangil) 67
Leão, Carlos 187
Le cause della grandezza e magnificenza della città (Botero) 76
Le Lutrin 138–39
Leon, Mateo de 74
lethe 69
Lethe 222
Lewis, T. 17–18
Liberator, *see* Bolívar, Simón
Library (Apollodorus) 182
Life of Cato (Plutarch) 161
Lima
    and Aeneas 177
    baroque artists in 211
    and cherubim emblem 92
    'City of the Kings' 110, 117
    Classical imagery in 73–80, 73n.1–2, 78n.9, 82
    Classical self-imagination of 85–87, 96
    and 'doctor Figueroa' 65
    and Don Juan de Villela 54
    emulation of Rome 106
    foundation of by Pizarro 102
    greatness of 98–99
    grief of 114
    introduction 25–26
    and *Lima fundada* 124
    role as New World Elysium 82–84, 112, 116, 121
    role of in transatlantic empire 97, 97n.32
    and Saint Rose 123–24
    and Simon Bolívar 150
    tradition of self-glorifying literature 100, 105–7, 131
    young Jesuit scholars in 122
Lima fundada (Barnuevo) 26, 84, 124–25
Limenian *tapadas* 62
Liñán y Cisneros, Melchor 86–87
Livy 130
'lo Clásico' 211
locus amoenus 65
Lohmann Villena, Guillermo 91
Lonja, the 1–3
López-Morillas, Frances M. 44, 46–47
Low Countries 87–88
Lucan 50
Lupher, David 15
Luther, Martin 63

MacCormack, Sabine 15, 41, 41n.7
macuquinas (coins) 3
'Manifiesto de Carúpano' (Bolívar) 155
Mantua 114
Marc Anthony 163
Margaret of Antioch, Saint 51
Martí, José 14
Marx, Karl 176, 176n.2
Mazzotti, José Antonio 77n.6, 99n.38, 100n.40, 111n.52, 111n.53, 121
Medrano, Juan Espinoza 131
Melchor de Navarra y Rocafull *see* Palata, Duke of
Mello, Breno 193
Mello, José Eduardo Homen de 188
Memorial de las historias del Nuevo Mundo, Piru (Buenaventura) 102
Menéndez y Pelayo, Marcelino 166
Mesoamerica 76
Messer, Neal A. 99–100, 107, 109, 109n.50, 113, 114n.55, 118n.66
mestizaje 61
Metamorphoses (Ovid) 60
Metaphysics (Aristotle) 34, 44–45, 44n.9
metempsychosis 222
Mexía de Fernangil, Diego 24–25, 36, 50–68, 50n.16, 55n.22, 70–71, 101, 176, 211
Mexico 15, 23, 60, 158
Mexico City 78

'Mi delirio sobre el Chimborazo' (Bolívar) 171
Miller, General William 136–37
Miller, Nicola 15
Minos, king 182
Minotaur myth 27, 178, 180–85, 206–7, 211
Miscelánea Antártica (Balboa) 70
Miscelánea Austral (Figueroa) 70
Mitos clásicos en la literatura española e hispanoamericana del siglo XX (Férez) 15, 175–76
Monteagudo, Bernardo de 147
Montero, María Antonia Durán 77
Monte Sacro 133, 139
Monumentum Erycinum 213–17, 227
Moraes, Vinícius de 27, 185–90, 192, 195–98, 201, 204–5, 207
More, Anna 77–78
'morro da Conceição' 189
Mount Parnassus 66
Mugaburu, Josephe de 87
mundus novus 6, 42, 69, 176–77, 228
mundus vetus 31
Municipal Theater, Rio de Janeiro 188
Muñoz, Juan Bautista 1
'The Murders in the Rue Morgue' (Poe) 170
Muses, temple of the 59
Muse, the 65–67, 69
mythographers
 a Carioca Orpheus 186–92
 conclusions 206–9
 confirmations, rebuttals, antitheses 200–206
 introduction 27
 Orpheus in color 192–200
 other Asterion 178–86
 preliminaries 175–78

Napoleon Bonaparte 129, 147, 157–58
Naturalis historia (Pliny) 41–42, 44–45, 48, 105
Navarra y Rocaful, Melchor de *see* Palata Duke of
Necochea, General Mariano de 137
Negritude movement 186–87
Neoclassicism 138–39, 156
Nero, Emperor 47, 152, 155–56, 165

New Granada 133, 156, 159
Nikoloutsos, Konstantinos P. 15
Ninfas d'el Sur 64
Noah 32–33
Nolasco Mere, Pedro 26, 87–88, 88n.21-3, 91–98, 97n.32
novomundista narratives 47
Noyelle, Charles de 113

Obama, Barack 204–7
'occiduas Thiaras' 110
Odysseus 154, 154n.20
The Odyssey (Homer) 146
O'Gorman, Edmundo 37n.4, 43, 45n.10, 48n.11
oikoumenai 26, 33, 121, 131
Oliveira, Celso de 185, 201
Olmedo, José Joaquín de 26, 133–51, 153, 160, 172–73, 211
Oña, Pedro de 65
On Heroes, Hero-Worship and the Heroic in History (Carlyle) 169
On Unbelievable Tales (Palaephatus) 182
On the Wings of Time: Rome, Spain, the Incas, and Peru (MacCormack) 15
Orationes (Cicero) 11
Orfeu da Conceição (Moraes) 185–95, 197–98, 200, 204–5, 207
Orfeu (film) 185, 200–204
Orfeu negro (Camus) 185, 192–98, 200–201, 203–5
Orfeu: o maior musical brasileiro (Moraes/Jobim) 204
Origen de los indios del Nuevo Mundo (García) 32
Orphée 186–87
'Orphée Noir' (Sartre) 186, 192, 194
Orpheus myth 24, 27, 177, 185–93, 197–98, 200–208, 211, 218, 227
Ortiz, José Joaquín 161
Osorio, Alejandra 76–77
Otálora, Jorge E. Rojas 135
Ovid 25, 36, 51–57, 53n.18, 59–62, 66–69, 71, 130, 185
Oviedo, Gonzalo Fernández de 41, 45, 47
Oviedo y Herrera, Luis Antonio de 26, 33, 84, 123–24

Paez, General José Antonio 157–58
Palaephatus 182, 207
Palata, Duke of (Navarra y Rocaful) 85, 87–88, 87n.19-20, 91–92, 96–97
Palatine Hill, Rome 94
Panama 87–88
Panhellenic festivals 144
Paradiso (Dante) 218–19
Parallel Lives (Plutarch) 168
Paredes, Gregorio 140
Parnaso antártico (Clarinda) 63–64, 66–67, 70
Parnaso antártico (Mexía de Fernangil) 63
Pascual, Pilar Hualde 175–76
Pasiphae 182
pasquinades 152
Paulding, Hiram 132
Pausanias 152, 164–65
Pax Romana 21
Pease, Franklin 33, 33n.2
pedagogues 27
Peninsular War 147
Peralta Barnuevo, Pedro de 26, 84, 96, 124–25
Perrone, Charles A. 185–86
Perrone, Mario 196
Persia 165
personae
    conclusions 169–73
    conspiracy of 1828 150–69
    introduction 26
    José Joaquín de Olmedo 134–50
    preliminaries 127–34, 130n.3
Peru
    and 'Alto Perú' 163
    and the British government 140
    end of political subjugation 135
    female poets of 64
    intellectual agents in 70
    introduction 11, 23, 26
    and José de Acosta 35
    and the Marquis of Torre Tagle 157
    and Mexía de Fernangil, Diego 58
    and New World anxiety 73, 75, 78, 121
    and Pedro Peralta 124
    and standard mythical episodes 82
    and Valdés's poem 100, 108, 121–22
Peruleros 58, 61, 70

Piazza Spagna 139
Pichincha volcano 124
Picone, professor Giusto 216
Pillars of Heracles 2–4, 2n.2-3, 6, 9, 218
Pindar 130, 144, 149
Pizarro, Francisco 102, 124–25
Plato 35, 38, 41, 206
Pliny the Elder 11, 25, 37–38, 41–50, 69, 103, 105
Plus Ultra 1–3, 6
Plutarch 130, 161, 168–69, 182–83, 207
Poe, Edgar Allan 170
Poetics (Aristotle) 144
Pólit, Espinosa 142–43
Pompey 161
ponet 94
Portugal 23, 112
Potnia Erycina 220
Potosí, city of 3, 59, 61
Pozo, Mario Briceño 15
Prado, Bernat Castany 53
Priam 219
Primera parte del Parnaso antártico de obras amatorias (Mexía de Fernangil) 25, 36, 50–53, 58–62
'Proemio al lector' 43–44
Protestantism 203
Publio Ovidius Naso 52
Pythagoras 35

Quechua 3
Quintilian 144, 144n.13

Reception Studies 16
'Recuerdos de Boyacá' (Tejada) 160–61
Regnault, Robert 48
Reinhold, Meyer 12
Reminiscencias griegas y latinas en las obras del Libertador (Pozo) 15
Remus 94
Renaissance
    and Acosta 41
    and comparisons with Virgil 102
    Greco-Roman lingo of 83
    introduction 11
    and tradition of *Antichità di Roma* treatises 106
Rhetoric (Aristotle) 38
Ricaurte, José Ignacio París 127

Rimac river valley 65
Rio de Janeiro 189, 193–94, 203, 218
Rist, Peter 193
Riva-Agüero, José de la 157
Rodrigues, Corinne Davis 201
Rodríguez, Simón 132–33, 139
Rojas, Arístides 151–52, 155
Romans in a New World: Classical Models in Sixteenth-Century Spanish America (Lupher) 15
Romanticism 130, 166
romanzones (Menéndez y Pelayo) 166, 166n.27
Rome
   and the *Aeneid* 98, 123
   and Anchises 145
   and Augustus 223
   and Cato 162
   Civil War of 161
   Empire of 226
   fire of 152
   foundation of 93–96, 215, 222–23
   imperial poetry of 151
   Lima comparisons 105–7
   and Monte Sacro 133, 139
   Spain and its language 113, 119–20
   tales and characters of 130, 132
   and Virgil 82
Romero, Álex Gómez 15
Romulus 94–96
Roscio, Germán 165
Rose of Lima, Saint 123–24
Roulin, François Désiré 128

Sáenz, Manuela 166
San Martín, José de 150
Santa Fe de Bogotá 156
Santander, General Francisco de Paula 159, 165
Santiago de Chile 151
São Paulo 188
Sarmatians 58
Sartre, Jean-Paul 186–87, 192, 194, 207
Saturn 223
Saturnia Regna 21, 223
Sea of Atlas 9
Segunda parte del Parnaso antártico de divinos Poemas (Mexía de Fernangil) 25, 51–53, 58–61

Senghor, Leopold 186
Serrera Contreras, Ramón María 91
Servius Honoratus, Maurus 93
Short, Charles 17–18
Sicily 211–12, 215, 217–19, 227
Sinon 152
Snoey, Christian 15
'Sociedad Filológica' 165–66
Socrates 132–33, 165
Sonsonate 55, 59
Sorrows (Ovid) 57
Southern Cross 112
Spain
   army of 137
   and Battle of Boyacá 159
   and cherubim emblem 92
   and Christianity in the New World 124
   conquest of the Incas 47–48
   and the conquistadors 124
   Empire of 1, 112, 119, 129
   introduction 23, 26
   Muslim heritage of 120
   and the Peninsular War 147
   pride in its language 113
   and United Provinces 153, 155
   war with France 88
Sparta 133, 152
Statius 50
Stok, Fabio 104
Strait of Magellan 108, 112
Stray, Christopher 16
Sucre, José Antonio de 135, 142, 163
Sun worship 61
Sybil 222

Tacitus 179
Tartarus 152
Tasso, Torquato 62
Tauro, Alberto 70–71
Teatro crítico universal (Feijóo) 48–49
Tejada, Juan Manuel García 155–56
Tejada, Luis Vargas 159–69, 162n.24, 172–73, 211
Tempe 65
Tenerani, Pietro 127–29, 173
Tenochtitlan, city of 78
Tercera parte (Mexía de Fernangil) 51
terra cognitura 72
terra incognita 72, 74

Tesoro de la lengua castellana o española (Covarrubias) 43
Theophrastus 46–47
Thersites 153–56
Theseus 182–83
Thomist theology 9
Tiresias 145
Titus, Emperor 45, 48
Toledo, Francisco de 47–48
Toro, Fernando del 139
Torre Tagle, Marquis of 157
Torrid Zone 40
Tovar, Juan de 45
The Tragedy of Julius Caesar (Shakespeare) 161
translatio studii et imperii 53, 55
Tres Reyes Magos 110
Tristia and Ex Ponto (Ovid) 52, 56, 58
Troy 82, 95, 106, 152, 219, 223
Tucca 104

Underworld 213, 222–24
UNESCO 212
United Provinces of New Granada 133, 153, 155
United States 169–71
Utica 161

Väinämöinen 32
Valdés, Rodrigo de 26, 98–124, 211
'Valsa do Orfeu' (Jobim) 197
Varius 103–4
Vélez-Sainz, Julio 61, 67
Veloso, Caetano 27, 194, 200–202, 205, 207
Venezuela 133, 140, 152, 159, 165–66
Venus 93–95, 98, 221
Veracruz 86
Verdade Tropical (Veloso) 194
verecundia 103
Vespasian, Emperor 43, 45, 47
Vespucci, Americo 33, 49, 227

Victoria de Junín. Canto a Bolívar (Olmedo) 26, 135–36, 140, 142, 146, 148, 153, 160
Vida de Santa Rosa de Santa María (Oviedo y Herrera) 26, 84, 124
Vila, Manuel Pérez 132
Vinatea, Martina 62, 62n.27, 100n.39, 121
Viot, Jacques 192
Virgil
　adopted citation of 83
　and the *Aeneid see Aenid*, the
　and Andrés Bello 151
　and Bernabé Cobo 122–23
　bucolic taste of 146
　burial of Anchises 215
　and the *Georgics* 151, 208
　home-town of Mantua 114
　introduction 8, 11, 21, 25–26, 28
　and *La Araucana* 50
　and Orpheus 185, 206
　poems of 130
　and Rodrigo de Valdés comparisons 101, 107, 115
Vordam, Jeff 203

Washington, George 161–62
Watanabe, José 183
Watts, George Frederic 181
West, M. L. 206
Williams, Jerry 99–100, 107, 109, 109n.50, 113, 114n.55, 118n.66
Works and Days (Hesiod) 21

Xica da Silva (film) 200

'year of the four Emperors' 47
Yndias de Birreyes y Gouernadores del Pirú (manuscript) 75–77, 75n.4, 79

zeugma 93–94
Zuázola, Juan de Miramontes y 70

www.ingramcontent.com/pod-product-compliance
Lightning Source LLC
Chambersburg PA
CBHW062128300426
44115CB00012BA/1855